ANONYMI MONOPHYSITAE
THEOSOPHIA

SUPPLEMENTS TO

VIGILIAE CHRISTIANAE

Formerly Philosophia Patrum

TEXTS AND STUDIES OF EARLY CHRISTIAN LIFE AND LANGUAGE

EDITORS

J. DEN BOEFT — R. VAN DEN BROEK — W.L. PETERSEN
D.T. RUNIA — J.C.M. VAN WINDEN

VOLUME LVI

ANONYMI MONOPHYSITAE
THEOSOPHIA

AN ATTEMPT AT RECONSTRUCTION

BY

PIER FRANCO BEATRICE

BRILL
LEIDEN · BOSTON · KÖLN
2001

PA
4451
.T49
2001

This book is printed on acid-free paper.

Library of Congress Cataloging-in-Publication Data

Anonymi Monophysitae theosophia : an attempt at reconstruction / [compiled
and edited by] Pier Franco Beatrice.
 p.   cm. — (Supplements to Vigiliae Christianae, ISSN 0920-623X ; v. 56)
English and Greek.
Includes bibliographical references and index.
ISBN 9004117989 (alk. paper)
 1. Christianity and other religions—Early works to 1800. 2.
Paganism—Early works to 1800. 3. Theology—Early works to 1800.
I. Beatrice, Pier Franco, 1948- II. Series.

PA4451 .T49 2001
230'.16—dc21
                                                            2001025788
                                                                  CIP

Die Deutsche Bibliothek – CIP-Einheitsaufnahme

Beatrice, Pier Franco :
Anonymi monophysitae Theosophia : an attempt at reconstruction / by
Pier Franco Beatrice. – Leiden ; Boston ; Köln : Brill, 2001
  (Supplements to Vigiliae Christianae ; Vol. 56)
  ISBN 90–04–11798–9

ISSN 0920-623X
ISBN 90 04 11798 9

PRINTED IN THE NETHERLANDS

Paulae uxori carissimae

CONTENTS

FOREWORD AND ACKNOWLEDGMENTS

I first encountered the *Theosophy* in 1989, during my many years of research into Porphyry's treatise against the Christians.[1] The *Theosophy* is a text that is difficult to interpret, and rarely receives much attention from scholars. It attracted my curiosity right from the start, stimulating me to investigate the philological aspects and contents, in a work that has proven satisfying, though there have been moments of fatigue and discouragement.

A number of indispensable preparatory contributions, to which I refer the reader for further analysis, and the results of which are exploited here, were presented and discussed on the occasion of various international conferences: the 10th Congress of the North American Patristics Society in Chicago in 1994; the 3rd Meeting of the International Society for the Classical Tradition in Boston in 1995; again in 1995 the Congress on the Christian apocryphal literature in Lausanne and Geneva, and the 12th Conference on Patristic Studies in Oxford; in 1996 the Congress on the Christian Apologists and Greek culture at the Institut Catholique of Paris; in 1997 at the Belgian Academy of Rome the Congress on the religious syncretisms of the ancient Mediterranean world; and finally, both in 1999, the 13th Patristic Conference of Oxford and the 11th International Congress of Classical Studies at Kavala (Greece). I have grateful memories of all the people with whom I exchanged opinions on those occasions and from whom I received precious advice and suggestions. To all I express my sincere, unconditioned thanks.

I also wish to express my gratitude to the scientific Institutions which facilitated my research, generously providing me with manuscripts, microfilms and all the necessary bibliographic material: St. Mark's Library in Venice; the Biblioteca Estense in Modena; the Vatican Library; the Pontifical Institute of Oriental Studies in Rome; the Bayerische Staatsbibliothek in Munich; the Universitätsbibliothek in Tübingen; the Bibliothèque Nationale of Paris; the Greek section of the Institut de Recherche et d'Histoire des Textes again in Paris.

---

[1] The complete list of my publications on the subject can be found in P.F. Beatrice, "Porphyrius", in *TRE* XXVII (1997), pp. 54–59.

I have had the opportunity to enlarge and deepen my knowledge of Greek religion and philosophy thanks to the long and fruitful collaboration with the "Mentor" project of the "Centre d'Histoire des Religions" of Liège University. The positive conclusion of my research was made possible thanks to the generous hospitality of the Theology Department of Boston College, where I spent the whole, unforgettable academic year 1998/99 as Joseph Professor of Patristic Theology.

Finally, my warm thanks go to the members of the Editorial Board of the series "Supplements to Vigiliae Christianae", who have done me the honour of accepting this manuscript, and to Mr. Theo Joppe, Ms. Julie Plokker and Mr. Pim Rietbroek of the publishing house Brill, whose kind cooperation and support through the publication process have been very helpful.

Let benevolent readers judge the quality of the work. For the moment I assume full responsibility for any gaps or errors that there might be. I am perfectly aware that, in publishing a critical edition of this text, I am treading new ground, with the inevitable risks that this involves. The reconstruction of the *Theosophy* has been in fact no easier a task than that attempted hitherto for other works of classical Antiquity which have been lost, such as Aristotle's *Protrepticus*[2] or Porphyry's *Philosophy from Oracles*.[3] I hope that other scholars will manage to do a better job in the future, also thanks to this present effort!

Padua, June 29, 2000
feast of the Apostles Peter and Paul

---

[2] One can find a well-informed presentation of the relevant problems in A.-H. Chroust, *Aristotle. New light on his life and on some of his lost works*, vol. II: *Observations on some of Aristotle's lost works*, London, 1973, pp. 86–104 and 332–345: "A Brief Account of the Reconstruction of Aristotle's *Protrepticus*".

[3] See G. Wolff, *Porphyrii de philosophia ex oraculis haurienda librorum reliquiae*, Berlin, 1856. This old and precious book was reprinted at Hildesheim in 1962, but no one has dared so far to publish a new edition. On this question see P.F. Beatrice, "Towards a New Edition of Porphyry's Fragments against the Christians", in ΣΟΦΙΗΣ ΜΑΙΗΤΟΡΕΣ. *"Chercheurs de sagesse"*. *Hommage à Jean Pépin* (Études Augustiniennes—Série Antiquité, 131), Paris, 1992, pp. 347–355.

INTRODUCTION

1. *From Steuchus to Erbse*

The incomplete text of the *Theosophy* has come down to us by utter chance. One fragment after another, it has gradually come to light, taking shape thanks to a series of fortuitous discoveries of individual passages handed down by several manuscripts kept in a number of libraries in Europe.

Certain oracles we now read in the *Theosophy* were quoted as long ago as the sixteenth century by the Italian humanist and bishop, Augustinus Steuchus, in his *De perenni philosophia*.[1] We do not know, however, which manuscripts he used; the variant readings he adopted are in any case of the highest interest. In particular, he quoted the following oracles: I,2 in III,15; I,4+18 in III,16; I,5 (just a few lines) in II,19 and III,17; I,15, 16 and 22 in III,17; I,24+26 in III,14; I,39 in III,16.

However, the modern history of the scientific reconstruction of the *Theosophy* really only begins with the *Supplément à l'Anthologie grecque* by the French scholar N. Piccolos, who was the first to publish twelve oracles Ἐκ τῆς Θεοσοφίας found in the manuscript *Florent. Laurent. plut.* 32,16, fol. 379v–380r, of the thirteenth century.[2] A few years later, in the appendix to his edition of Porphyry's *Philosophy from Oracles*, the German scholar Gustav Wolff published thirteen oracles from two manuscripts, again the *Florent. Laurent. plut.* 32,16 and the *Neapol. Borb.* II F 9 of the fourteenth century.[3]

These oracles, mentioned by Steuchus, Piccolos and Wolff, can also be read in a manuscript belonging to the University Library of Tübingen, identified as *Tub. Mb* 27 in Wilhelm Schmid's catalogue.[4]

---

[1] This work was published for the first time in Lyons in 1540.

[2] N. Piccolos, *Supplément à l'Anthologie grecque*, Paris, 1853, pp. 173–186.

[3] See G. Wolff, *Porphyrii de philosophia ex oraculis haurienda*, pp. 229–240. These oracles were also reprinted by E. Cougny, *Epigrammatum Anthologia Palatina cum Planudeis et Appendice Nova*, t. III, Parisiis, 1890, cap. VI.

[4] W. Schmid, *Systematisch-alphabetischer Hauptkatalog der königlichen Universitätsbibliothek zu Tübingen, M. Handschriften. B. Griechische. Verzeichnis der griechischen Handschriften der königlichen Universitäts-Bibliothek*, Tübingen 1902, pp. 51–53.

It is a miscellaneous paper codex comprising 186 sheets, written by Martin Crusius' pupils for their master. In 1579, one of these, Bernhard Haus, had only partially transcribed the contents of a manuscript belonging to Johannes Reuchlin, the famous codex *Argentoratensis gr.* 9 (thirteenth or fourteenth century) containing the so-called *Epistle to Diognetus*, which was to be destroyed in 1870 during the Prussian bombing of the City Library of Strasbourg.[5] On fol. 67r–87r of the Tübingen copy there is a short collection of oracles and philosophical sayings under the title Χρησμοὶ τῶν Ἑλληνικῶν θεῶν, *Oracles of the Greek gods.*

This transcription is certainly partial and the title is not the original one. In fact, we know from Henri Estienne that this collection of oracles was entitled *Theosophia*. This is exactly the same title also known to Piccolos and Wolff.[6] Despite this, for us the Tübingen apograph is the only source left, and it is all the more precious if we think that another copy of the Strasbourg manuscript, composed between 1586 and 1592 by Johannes J. Beurer, professor at Freiburg im Breisgau, seems to have been completely lost.[7]

It was not until 1881, three centuries later, that Karl J. Neumann announced that he had discovered the Tübingen manuscript, and that he would shortly proceed with the complete publication of the fragments that it contained.[8] But the *editio princeps* of the work, that since then has been commonly referred to as the *Tübingen Theosophy*, was to be the work of another German philologist, Karl Buresch, who brought it to light a few years later as an appendix to his dissertation on the oracle of Claros.[9]

---

[5] For more information see H.I. Marrou, *À Diognète* (SC 33 bis), Paris, 1965, pp. 8 ff.

[6] H. Stephanus, *Iustini philosophi et martyris Epistula ad Diognetum et Oratio ad Graecos nunc primum luce et Latinitate donatae*, Paris, 1592, p. VIII: *Sed quum librum quendam, qui 'Theosophia' vocatur, (is non aliud quam oraculorum synagogen quandam habet) simul cum his Iustini opusculis in lucem venire idem Beurerus cuperet, nec alia ratione niteretur quam quod in eodem illo volumine unde haec Iustini sumpta sunt inveniatur: ego duabus de causis eius assentiri desiderio nolui, ac ne potui quidem. Una est, quod nihil ad Iustini argumentum illa faciant: nec mirum sit tamen istis eius libellis ibi subiungi, quum veteres scripta diversa, et nihil omnino commune inter se habentia, in uno eodemque volumine consuenda curarent. Altera, quod non solum bona pars illorum oraculorum apud varios scriptores exstet, et plerique illius 'Theosophiae' loci emendari inde possint, sed multo etiam plura colligi ex iis queant: ut olim, quum aliquid temporis eidem collectioni tribuissem, cognovi.*

[7] See J.C.T. Otto, *Corpus apologetarum christianorum saeculi secundi*, vol. III, t. II, Jena, 1879, 3rd ed., pp. XXIV ff.

[8] K.J. Neumann, "Über eine den Brief an Diognet enthaltende Tübinger Handschrift Pseudo-Justin's", *ZKG* 4 (1881), pp. 284–287.

[9] K. Buresch, *Klaros. Untersuchungen zum Orakelwesen des späteren Altertums nebst einem*

Nevertheless, it would never have been possible to understand the original structure and meaning of this strange and disorderly collection of oracles of Greek gods, sayings of Greek and Egyptian sages and Sibylline oracles, and therefore its real place in the history of early Christianity if, in 1906, Karl Mras had not published a text he had discovered in Rome in the sixteenth-century codex *Ottobon. gr.* 378, fol. 18r–25v.[10] Mras had no difficulty in demonstrating that the Roman codex contained an original passage from the *Theosophy*, whereas the text transmitted by the Tübingen manuscript was to be considered a late epitome, at times imprecise and unfaithful, the author of which intentionally took his distance from the original, expressing diverging opinions in some points.

Mras' conclusions were rightly accepted by a young German philologist, Hartmut Erbse, who, in the dark years of the Second World War, published a collection of several Greek theosophical texts under the title *Fragmente griechischer Theosophien*.[11]

In his extensive and detailed introduction Erbse dissected, with admirable philological insight, the relationships between the numerous manuscripts belonging to a tradition that is highly complicated and problematic because of the absence of reliable external data of reference. The two main pieces of Erbse's collection are the epitome from the Tübingen manuscript (= T) edited by Buresch, which he designated as θ, and the original passage published by Mras, which he designated as Θ. He then added some other small collections of sayings which reveal more or less close affinities with the *Theosophy*, such as the oracles already disclosed in 1691 by Richard Bentley in his famous *Epistula ad Millium*,[12] the so-called *Symphony* edited by J.B. Pitra[13] and W. Scott – A.S. Ferguson,[14] the *Prophecies of the Seven Sages* published by A. Delatte,[15] and other fragmentary materials.

Anhange, das Anecdoton ΧΡΗΣΜΟΙ ΤΩΝ ΕΛΛΗΝΙΚΩΝ ΘΕΩΝ enthaltend, Leipzig, 1889 (repr. Aalen, 1973), pp. 87–131.

[10] K. Mras, "Eine neuentdeckte Sibyllen-Theosophie", *WSt* 28 (1906), pp. 43–83.

[11] H. Erbse, *Fragmente griechischer Theosophien* (Hamburger Arbeiten zur Altertumswissenschaft, 4), Hamburg, 1941.

[12] R. Bentley, *The Works*, edited by A. Dyce (1836–1838), vol. II, London, 1836, repr. in the series "Anglistica et Americana", 131, Hildesheim-New York, 1971, pp. 249–255.

[13] J.B. Pitra, *Analecta sacra et classica spicilegio Solesmensi parata*, V,2, Parisiis-Romae, 1888, pp. 305–308. In the same work, pp. 302–305, Pitra published another collection of rare oracles under the title *Persica*.

[14] W. Scott – A.S. Ferguson, *Hermetica*, IV: *Testimonia*, Oxford, 1936, pp. 225–227.

[15] A. Delatte, *Anecdota Atheniensia*, I: *Textes grecs inédits relatifs à l'histoire des religions*

Erbse's edition indubitably marked great progress, and is to be considered a fundamental stage in the study of the manuscript transmission of Greek theosophical fragments. But because of the war it did not receive the attention it deserved, and it did not produce a reawakening of interest in these texts. Moreover, in 1943 a fire destroyed the publishing house in Hamburg with all the copies of the dissertation. So, many scholars were unaware of it, and kept on resorting to the old, partial edition by Buresch. Suffice it to think that Robert M. Grant was only able to read Erbse's edition thanks to a loan by his teacher Arthur D. Nock,[16] and Henry Chadwick confessed a few years ago that he had not even been able to consult it in a place like Cambridge.[17] Erbse's edition is totally absent in the article "Theosophia" written by Heinrich Dörrie for the *Kleine Pauly*,[18] and there is no trace of it even in the well-documented booklet by Jean-Louis Siémons entitled *Théosophia*.[19]

This is why scholars should gladly welcome the reprinting, at a distance of 54 years, of this rare edition by Erbse in the Teubner collection.[20] The text is reproduced in a substantially unchanged form; the only important innovation is the collation of the codex *Mutinensis misc. gr.* 126 for the original fragment of the Sibylline prophecies edited by Mras.

2. *The reasons and criteria for this new edition*

Yet one might ask, what need is there to publish a new edition of the *Theosophy* in a collection of patristic texts just a few years after

---

(Bibliothèque de la Faculté de Philosophie et Lettres de l'Université de Liège, fasc. 36), Liège-Paris, 1927, pp. 328–330.

[16] R.M. Grant, "Greek Literature in the Treatise 'De Trinitate' and Cyril 'Contra Julianum'", *JThS* 15 (1964), pp. 265–279, 268, n. 1: "My knowledge of Erbse's book is due to a generous loan (and gift to the Harvard College Library) by my late teacher A.D. Nock".

[17] H. Chadwick, "Oracles of the End in the Conflict of Paganism and Christianity in the Fourth Century", in E. Lucchesi – H.D. Saffrey (eds.), *Mémorial André-Jean Festugière. Antiquité païenne et chrétienne* (Cahiers d'Orientalisme, X), Genève, 1984, pp. 125–129, 125, n. 1: "in a book as rare as the gold of Ophir and not accessible to me".

[18] H. Dörrie, "Theosophia", in *KP* V (1975), 732.

[19] J.-L. Siémons, *Théosophia. Aux sources néoplatoniciennes et chrétiennes (2ᵉ–6ᵉ siècles)*, Paris, 1988.

[20] *Theosophorum Graecorum Fragmenta, iterum recensuit* Hartmut Erbse (BSGRT), Stutgardiae et Lipsiae, 1995.

the reprinting of Erbse's edition? In my opinion there are at least two reasons, both equally valid.

The first reason is that the time seems to be ripe to circulate, among scholars interested in the literature and history of early Christianity, this important text which has been so unjustly ignored up till now.

We have to acknowledge that, as Heinrich Dörrie remarked in 1975, this work has not yet been systematically put to scientific use.[21] It may seem strange, but the undeniable fact is that the *Theosophy* has rarely been exploited, and then almost exclusively by classical philologists, historians of Greek philosophy, and students of ancient religions. Both editors, Buresch and Erbse, were interested in this text only for the "pagan" material, and did not bother to investigate the "Christian" context in which this singular work saw the light. An important article on the *Theosophy* was published by Kurt von Fritz in Pauly's *Real-Encyclopädie*,[22] and its documentary value was rightly appreciated by a historian of Greek religion of the calibre of Martin P. Nilsson.[23] Brief mention is made by Jürgen Hammerstaedt in the recent *Einleitung in die griechische Philologie*.[24]

On the other hand, the *Theosophy* is normally absent from patristic and theological encyclopedias as, for example, the *Dictionnaire de Spiritualité*,[25] the *Encyclopedia of the Early Church*[26] and the *Encyclopedia of Early Christianity*.[27] The *Theosophy* is not mentioned at all in the *Clavis Patrum Graecorum* by Maurits Geerard,[28] and there is equally total silence in the standard manual of Byzantine theological literature by Hans-Georg Beck:[29] a really paradoxical destiny for an ancient Christian work!

---

[21] H. Dörrie, in *KP* V (1975), 732: "Eine wiss. Auswertung dieser Texte hat noch nicht stattgefunden".

[22] K. von Fritz, "Theosophia", in *PRE* 2. Reihe, 10. Halbband (1934), 2248–2253.

[23] M.P. Nilsson, *Geschichte der griechischen Religion*, Munich, 1950, II, pp. 464 f.

[24] J. Hammerstaedt, "Spätantike", in *Einleitung in die griechische Philologie*, ed. by H.-G. Nesselrath, Stuttgart und Leipzig, 1997, pp. 294–315, 312.

[25] See the article by A. Faivre, "Théosophie", in *DSp* XV (1991), 548–562.

[26] *EEChurch*, ed. by A. Di Berardino – W.H.C. Frend, Cambridge, 1992.

[27] *EEChris*, ed. by E. Ferguson, New York, 2nd ed., 1997.

[28] See M. Geerard – F. Glorie, *CPG* (CChr.SG), vol. V: *Indices, Initia, Concordantiae*, Turnhout, 1987, and M. Geerard – J. Noret (adiuvantibus F. Glorie et J. Desnet), *CPG, Supplementum* (CChr.SG), Turnhout 1998.

[29] H.-G. Beck, *Kirche und theologische Literatur im byzantinischen Reich* (HAW, Zwölfte Abteilung, Zweiter Teil, Erster Band), München, 2nd ed., 1977.

The second reason which prompted me to undertake the present research is of a strictly philological and historic-literary nature.

Precious though his edition may be, Erbse limits himself to juxtaposing a series of fragments, trying to untangle the intricate manuscript tradition in a manner that is certainly daring, but with results that are at times frankly debatable. Moreover, he makes no real effort to recover the original text of the *Theosophy* and to interpret it coherently in its own cultural and theological context. In other words, his edition is not without flaws and gaps, and therefore it is to a great extent unsatisfactory and inadequate to our present needs. I felt a profound revision was required for a more reliable critical text of the treatise, as will be clearly seen in the following pages.

Any attempt to reconstruct the *Theosophy*, illustrating its structure, doctrinal contents, sources, purpose and method of composition, cannot disregard the summary to be found in the Tübingen manuscript, which acts as a real guide for the editor. An anonymous Byzantine scribe wrote that introduction after the Council of Constantinople of 692 CE (the so-called Quinisext Council or Council in-Trullo), since he reckoned the *Apostolic Constitutions* among the apocrypha (βιβλίων παρεγγράπτων).[30] The summary provides us with the following information.

The work entitled *Theosophy* (see *Epit.* 1: Ὁ τὸ βιβλίον συγγεγραφώς, ὅπερ ἐπιγέγραπται ΘΕΟΣΟΦΙΑ . . .; *ibid.* 5: ΘΕΟΣΟΦΙΑ δὲ τὸ βιβλίον ἐπέγραψεν . . .), which is the object of the present edition, is the continuation, in a certain sense a justificatory appendix, of a seven-book work, now completely lost, *On the Right Faith* (*Epit.* 1: ἑπτὰ βιβλία ΠΕΡΙ ΤΗΣ ΟΡΘΗΣ ΠΙΣΤΕΩΣ).[31] The *Theosophy* is divided into four books: the first book (the eighth of the whole work) is a collection of oracles of the Greek gods; the second (ninth) deals with the theologies

---

[30] This work was condemned in the second canon of that Council: see J.D. Mansi, *Sacrorum Conciliorum nova et amplissima collectio*, XI, Paris, 1901 (repr. Graz, 1960), 940, and K.J. Neumann *apud* K. Buresch, *Klaros*, pp. 89 f.

[31] See A.D. Nock, "Oracles théologiques", *REA* 30 (1928), pp. 280–290, repr. in Idem, *Essays on Religion and the Ancient World*, Oxford, 1972, I, pp. 160–168, 163: ". . . la *Théosophie* que son premier paragraphe donne comme une suite à sept livres *Sur la vraie Foi*, donc comme une sorte d'appendice justificatif". R. Lane Fox, *Pagans and Christians in the Mediterranean World from the Second Century A.D. to the Conversion of Constantine*, London, 1988², repeatedly writes that the title of this work was Περὶ τῆς ὀρθῆς πίστεως. The title of all the eleven books was instead Θεοσοφία, according to P. Athanassiadi, *Damascius. The Philosophical History. Text with translation and notes*, Athens, 1999, p. 353.

of the Greek and Egyptian sages; the third (tenth) exploits the oracles of the Sibyls; in the fourth (eleventh) extracts from the book of Hystaspes are cited.[32] The book is concluded by a concise, universal chronicle from Adam right up to Emperor Zeno.

As far as possible, it is my intention to fill this index with appropriate materials. To succeed in this aim, I have carried out exhaustive research, over a period of several years, which has enabled me to discover other important portions of the work that have up till now been totally ignored in the discussion. In my opinion, a critical edition of the *Theosophy*, which aims at arranging the material in an order as close to the original text as possible, should be structured as follows.

The anonymous Byzantine *Epitome* (ἐπιτομή) should be followed first of all by the *Preface* (προοίμιον). Here the author explains the general plan of his work, and reveals the main sources of his religious thought, that is, Plato, Aristobulus, Diodorus Siculus and the *Wisdom of Solomon*.

All the oracles reproduced in the Tübingen manuscript should be attributed to the first book. To these we could usefully add the oracle uttered to the Egyptian king Thoulis (I, 49), also recorded in the second book of John Malalas' *Chronography*[33] and in Bentley's collection; the oracular response to the Pharaoh Petissonius (I, 50), quoted in the third book of Malalas' work,[34] and the two inscriptions of the Scamander (I,56 and I,62) transmitted exclusively by the *Symphonia*.

The second book should gather together all the theological sentences currently scattered, with repetitions and variations of different extent, in the Tübingen manuscript and other minor collections of sayings by Greek sages and Hermetic extracts, especially the *Symphonia*.

The third book should contain the Sibylline oracles. The fragment edited by Mras, which forms a large part of it, in this edition has the title *Fragm.* A. Of course, the relevant paragraphs of the Tübingen manuscript cannot be published in the text, as they give only an inaccurate summary of the original passage discovered by Mras. They have been partially recorded in the apparatus, with the exclusive purpose of documenting the method used by the Byzantine epitomizer.

---

[32] H. Erbse, *Theosophorum Graecorum Fragmenta*, p. XI, wrongly states that the book of Hystaspes was quoted *in decimo libro*.
[33] *Ioannis Malalae Chronographia* (CSHB), ed. L. Dindorf, Bonnae, 1831, p. 25.
[34] Dindorf, pp. 65–66.

However, in my opinion, another long fragment of the third book of the *Theosophy* can be recovered, if we are willing to admit that the Greek oracle of the so-called Tiburtine Sibyl must have originally belonged to it. Commonly known as the Baalbek Oracle, this very important text was edited for the first time by Paul J. Alexander.[35] A series of correspondences of various kinds has convinced me that this is most probably a passage of the *Theosophy*,[36] which we have printed below as *Fragm.* B of Book III.

Unfortunately, we do not possess any original fragment of the *Wisdom of Hystaspes*, an apocalyptic work, fruit of Greco-Iranian syncretism, which may with good reason be dated to the beginning of the second century of our era. Extracts of this work were quoted in the fourth and last book of the *Theosophy* (thus *Epit.* 2: ἐν δὲ τῷ τετάρτῳ ἢ ἐνδεκάτῳ παράγει χρήσεις Ὑστάσπου τινὸς κτλ.). Regarding this, we must point out that the word χρήσεις should be translated as "extracts" or "quotations", and that, therefore, Hans Windisch was quite wrong in translating it as "oracles" (*vaticinia*), as if it were the equivalent of χρησμοί.[37] This mistake has given rise to a long series of odd conjectures about the nature of the inexistent "Oracles" of Hystaspes.

Yet, it is still possible to form a certain idea, however vague and approximate, of the content of this work, thanks to some indications passed down by Justin Martyr,[38] Clement of Alexandria[39] and, above all, Lactantius.[40] The author of the *Theosophy* was certainly familiar with a recension of Hystaspes' book that had already been rewritten in the Christian sense. It is from this Christianized version that he most probably took some passages that prophesied the Incarnation of the Lord (see again *Epit.* 2: θείων μυστηρίων ἀποκάλυψιν δεξαμένου περὶ τῆς τοῦ σωτῆρος ἐνανθρωπήσεως). Among these passages there was also the famous prophecy by Zoroaster to Hystaspes concerning the Virgin Birth and the coming of the Great King, which we know of

[35] P.J. Alexander, *The Oracle of Baalbek. The Tiburtine Sibyl in Greek Dress* (DOS 10), Washington D.C., 1967.
[36] See P.F. Beatrice, "Das Orakel von Baalbek und die sogenannte Sibyllentheosophie", *RQ* 92 (1997), pp. 177–189.
[37] H. Windisch, *Die Orakel des Hystaspes* (Verhandelingen der koninklijke Akademie van Wetenschappen te Amsterdam, Afdeeling Letterkunde Nieuwe Reeks, Deel XXVIII, No. 3), Amsterdam, 1929.
[38] Justin, *Apol.* I,20,1 and I,44,12.
[39] Clement, *Strom.* VI,5,43,1.
[40] Lactantius, *Div. Inst.* VII,15,19 and VII,18,1–2.

only from late Syrian sources.[41] This text has been reprinted here as the only surviving and recognizable fragment of Book IV of the *Theosophy*.

The loss of the world chronicle which concluded the *Theosophy* is particularly serious. It can, however, be made up for, at least in part, with the publication of the so-called *Excerpta Latina Barbari*, a Merovingian chronicle of the seventh/eighth century, translated into Latin from a lost Greek chronicle.[42]

There are several reasons for believing that this lost Greek chronicle, if not absolutely identical, was in any case very similar to the final chronicle of the *Theosophy*. In fact, it was based on a previous Alexandrian chronicle dating back to the beginning of the fifth century (Annianus?), but it reached Anastasius' reign (*Chron.* VII,17,2), at precisely the time in which the *Theosophy* was composed. Moreover, the Greek source of the *Excerpta*, referring explicitly to the authority of Julius Africanus, started with Adam and placed the Incarnation of the Lord in the year 5500, exactly as the author of the *Theosophy* does.

The author of the Greek chronicle certainly knew the *Birth of Mary* (the so-called *Protevangelium of James*), the same apocryphal work also mentioned by the Byzantine epitomizer among the texts used by the author of the *Theosophy* (see *Epit.* 4).[43] Even the "telegraphic" style chosen by the Greek chronicler fits the definition of "very concise" (συντομώτατον), employed by the Byzantine epitomizer to characterize the method of the final world chronicle of the *Theosophy* (see *Epit.* 2). As further confirmation of the closeness of that Greek chronicle to the *Theosophy* we must finally point out the revealing fact that in both we meet the same characters and the same authors, for example the patriarch Henoch, the prophets Isaiah and Daniel, the Pharaoh Petissonius, Hermes Trismegistus, Orpheus and Musaeus, the philosophers Heraclitus, Diagoras and Porphyry, the poets Euripides and Menander.

---

[41] For a thorough analysis of this subject see P.F. Beatrice, "Le livre d'Hystaspe aux mains des Chrétiens", in *Les syncrétismes religieux dans le monde méditerranéen antique* (Institut Historique Belge de Rome. Études de Philologie, d'Archéologie et d'Histoire Anciennes, 36), ed. by C. Bonnet – A. Motte, Bruxelles-Rome, 1999, pp. 357–382.

[42] The best introduction to the study of this very difficult and enigmatic work is still the comprehensive article by F. Jacoby, "Excerpta Barbari", in *PRE* VI,2 (1909), 1566–1576.

[43] For more details see P.F. Beatrice, "Traditions apocryphes dans la 'Théosophie de Tübingen'", *Apocrypha* 7 (1996), pp. 109–122.

3. The apologetic project of the 'Theosophy'

The author of the *Theosophy* sets himself the aim of showing that the oracles of the Greek gods, the theologies of the Greek and Egyptian sages, and the oracles of the Sibyls agree with the Sacred Scriptures about God, the cause and beginning of all things, and about the Trinity in the one Godhead (*Epit.* 1). To this is added the revelation of the divine mysteries concerning the Incarnation of the Saviour, received by the Persian king Hystaspes on account of his deep religious fervour (*Epit.* 2).

In the author's intention, the numerous quotations of Biblical texts, taken from the Old Testament and even more from the New Testament, are meant to confirm the truth of the religious message expressed by certain "pagan" texts and to highlight the continuity of the revelation of divine Wisdom in the transition from paganism to Christianity. The organization of the chronographic material in the final chronicle also seems to conform to this plan, if we consider that the presentation of the events of the Biblical history is regularly alternated with information on the pagan nations.

The apologetic project pursued by the author of the *Theosophy* is clear: to provide the proof that there exists a basic harmony, a *symphonia*, between the religious and philosophical wisdom of the pagans—i.e. Greeks, Egyptians and Persians—and the Christian revelation handed down in the divine Scripture. According to him, the gods of paganism, Phoebus, Demeter, Pallas, Bacchus, Aphrodite, are false gods (I,37: ἕκαστος τῶν νόθων θεῶν), but the testimonies of the pagan sages about God come straight from God himself, who gave the wise men the task of educating the pagans. This is why their words are judged as absolutely necessary (*Pref.* 2: οὐ δεῖ ἀποβάλλειν τὰς τῶν σοφῶν ἀνδρῶν Ἑλλήνων περὶ τοῦ θεοῦ μαρτυρίας). If that is the way things are, the stubbornness with which some pagans still resist in their erroneous convictions is no longer justifiable.

Evidently, still in the age of Zeno and Anastasius some people were affected by the disease of paganism (III A, 1,9), but according to the prophecy of the Sibyls, God's judgement was incumbent over the blindness of those who obstinately clung to their absurd beliefs and idolatrous practices (III A, 2,13–14).[44]

---

[44] In the following pages I develop some observations already carried out in P.F.

The *Theosophy* develops these ideas systematically, in a way which was unknown to the previous apologetic literature. However, this project took shape in its general lines from as far back as the second century, both in the syncretistic Gnostic movement, which was most open to the influences of Hellenistic culture, and among orthodox apologists.

Irenaeus of Lyons, for example, accuses the Valentinians of taking their doctrines from their "prophet" Homer,[45] and Hippolytus of Rome attributes the origin of Gnostic speculations at times to the "prophet" Homer,[46] and at times to the first Greek theologians, Musaeus, Linus and Orpheus.[47] But Justin Martyr, who certainly was not a Gnostic, recommends reading the Sibyl and Hystaspes, despite the death sentence pronounced by the Roman legislators against all those who made use of these subversive texts.[48]

After Justin, Clement of Alexandria mentions an apocryphal work, perhaps the *Acts of Paul*, in which the apostle Paul invites his listeners to give serious attention to the pagan prophecies of the Sibyl and of Hystaspes about the uniqueness of God and the future coming of the Son of God: these are the most illustrious of the Greeks that God has established as "prophets" in their own language, distinguishing them from ordinary men, so that they might save the pagans in the same way in which the Old Testament prophets were called for the salvation of the Hebrews.[49] In the *Paedagogus*, Clement states that "Homer is a prophet without being aware of it",[50] and in another passage he does not hesitate to label as "prophets" those same people whom the Greeks called "sages".[51]

Between the end of the third and the beginning of the fourth century, the *Cohortatio ad Graecos* by Pseudo-Justin acknowledges the prophetic authority of Orpheus, the Sibyl and Hermes Trismegistus.[52] In Latin Christianity, around the same time, the pamphlet *Quod idola dii non sint*, gives credit to the monotheistic doctrine of the magician

---

Beatrice, "Pagan Wisdom and Christian Theology according to the 'Tübingen Theosophy'", *JECS* 3(1995), pp. 403–418.

[45] Irenaeus, *Adv. haer.* II,14,2; II,22,6; IV,33,3.
[46] Hippolytus, *Ref. omn. haer.* V,8,1.
[47] Hippolytus, *Ref. omn. haer.* V,20,4.
[48] Justin, *Apol.* I,20,1 and I,44,12.
[49] Clement Al., *Strom.* VI,5,42,3–43,1.
[50] Clement Al., *Paed.* I,6,36,1.
[51] Clement Al., *Strom.* V,4,22,1–24,1.
[52] The Greek text is now available in the edition by M. Marcovich, *Pseudo-Iustinus*.

Ostanes, of Plato and Hermes Trismegistus.[53] Lactantius frequently resorts to the evidence taken from Orpheus, Hermes Trismegistus, the Sibyls and Hystaspes in order to explain the truth of the Christian doctrine to his pagan audience.[54] But on this point Lactantius introduces a considerable innovation. Indeed, he seems to have been the first Christian apologist to quote not only the usual pagan philosophical and religious texts, but also the oracles of the Greek god Apollo.[55]

In the Greek world, at the end of the fourth century, the treatise *On the Trinity*, attributed to Didymus the Blind, aims at corroborating the Christian doctrine with arguments taken from the wisdom of "those outside" (οἱ ἔξω; οἱ ἔξω σοφοί; ἡ ἔξωθεν σοφία), i.e. the pagans.[56] The author appeals to various theological texts which are very similar to those used by the *Theosophy*. One oracle has even been reproduced in both works.[57] This is no surprise, since at that time there must have been various Christian collections of oracles which, unfortunately, have disappeared, such as the Χρησμῳδίαι Ἑλληνικαί.[58]

One of the oracles mentioned in the *Theosophy*, the prophecy of Apollo to the Athenians about the transformation of a temple into a church of the Virgin Mary (I,54–55), is known from another source of the first half of the fifth century, the homily of Theodotus of Ancyra on the Theotokos.[59] In the context of a harsh anti-Jewish

---

Cohortatio ad Graecos, De Monarchia, Oratio ad Graecos (PTS 32), Berlin-New York, 1990. See also the in-depth commentary by C. Riedweg, *Ps.-Justin (Markell von Ankyra?). Ad Graecos de vera religione (bisher "Cohortatio ad Graecos")*. *Einleitung und Kommentar* (SBA 25/1–2), Basel, 1994.

[53] The date of composition of this work and its attribution to Cyprian of Carthage is a moot question. See E. Heck, "Pseudo-Cyprian, 'Quod idola dii non sint' und Lactanz, 'Epitome Divinarum Institutionum'", in *Panchaia. Festschrift für Klaus Thraede* (JAC ErgBd. 22), Münster i.W., 1995, pp. 148–155.

[54] See e.g. Lactantius, *Div. Inst.* I,5–7; IV,27,20; VII,15–21; *Epit.* 68,1.

[55] For this feature of Lactantius' apologetic method see in particular *Div. Inst.* I,7.

[56] See the texts collected in *De Trin.* II,27 ff. (PG 39, 753 A–965 B). Unfortunately, a modern critical edition, with apparatus and commentary, of this section of the work is still lacking.

[57] The oracle quoted in *De Trin.* III,21 (PG 39, 913 B) is the same as in *Theosophy* I,32.

[58] See E. Bratke, *Das sogenannte Religionsgespräch am Hof der Sasaniden* (TU 4,3), Leipzig, 1899, pp. 129–217.

[59] Theodotus of Ancyra, *Oratio in Sanctam Mariam Dei Genitricem*, § 14, in *Homélies mariales byzantines. Textes grecs édités et traduits en latin* par M. Jugie (PO 19, fasc. 3, n° 93), Paris, 1925 (repr. Turnhout, 1974), pp. 333 f. The Greek text comes from

polemic, this famous bishop, who was a strong supporter of the anti-Nestorian party, remarked that the truth of the Christian faith had been preannounced both to Greeks and barbarians, for the damnation of the unbelievers (καὶ κατὰ τὴν Ἑλλάδα καὶ βάρβαρον προκεκηρυγμένην τὴν παρ' ἡμῖν ἀλήθειαν εἰς κρίμα τῶν ταύτην ἀθετούντων).[60] This is exactly the same apologetic perspective of the *Theosophy*.

Among the pagan works in prose used by Christian apologists, the Hermetic writings are a favourite point of reference not only in Didymus' *On the Trinity*,[61] but also in the treatise by Cyril of Alexandria *Against Julian*,[62] certainly one of the main sources from which the author of the *Theosophy* borrowed his ideas.

As is clear, the *Theosophy* fits into a long apologetic tradition that has gradually become more extensive over the centuries. In a certain sense, the *Theosophy* can be seen as the climax, the point of arrival, the ripe fruit of this tradition, which aims at the Christian appropriation of the most authoritative voices of paganism: the Wisdom of the Greek poets and philosophers, the Egyptian wisdom of Hermes Trismegistus, the oracles of the Sibyls, the Iranian prophecies of Zoroaster collected in the *Wisdom of Hystaspes*, and even the oracles of the Greek gods.

The *Theosophy*, heir to this tradition, has in turn contributed to keeping alive this apologetic interest in the pagan prophecies of Christianity and in handing down this missionary programme to later generations.

In the sixth century, an otherwise unknown Timothy was mentioned by the Byzantine chronicler John Malalas as the source of pagan oracular traditions which bear a striking similarity to the material to be found in the *Theosophy*.[63] Perhaps it is not by mere chance

---

the codex *Paris. gr.* 1171, fol. 96v–107v (tenth century). H. Erbse, *Theosophorum Graecorum Fragmenta*, pp. 35 f. does not know this edition and quotes from the Latin translation printed in PG 77, 1430 C–D. This oracle has been variously transmitted in the Byzantine tradition. For example, according to Malalas' Book IV (pp. 77–78 Dindorf), the question was not asked by the Athenians but by the Argonauts at Cyzicus. C. Mango, "The Conversion of the Parthenon into a Church: the Tübingen Theosophy", *DCAH* 18 (1995), pp. 201–203, overlooks Theodotus' homily.

[60] *Ibid*. On Theodotus see R. Caro, *La Homiletica Mariana Griega en el Siglo V* (Marian Library Studies, New Series, vol. 3), Dayton, Ohio, 1971, pp. 156–197.

[61] See PG 39, 756 B ff.

[62] See R.M. Grant, "Greek Literature".

[63] I owe this interesting remark to E. Jeffreys, "Malalas' Sources", in *Studies in Malalas*, ed. by E. Jeffreys with B. Croke and R. Scott (Byzantina Australiensia, 6), Sydney, 1990, pp. 167–216, 194 ff.

that Malalas also proves to be quite close to the *Excerpta Barbari*,[64] the Latin version of that Greek chronicle written during the reign of Anastasius, which largely coincides with the final chronicle of the *Theosophy*. In the seventh century, an anonymous Byzantine compiler put together a huge work of fifteen books to demonstrate that the Christian faith had already been proclaimed by the pagan sages of numerous ancient nations.[65] In the eighth century, the author of the *Passio s. Artemii*, most probably John of Damascus, recalls the evidence of the pagan prophecies and makes the martyr quote the first part of an oracle of Apollo which is also to be found in the *Theosophy*.[66] Other Byzantine hagiographic texts, such as the *Passions* of St. Catherine of Alexandria and St. Lucy, contain quotations from Orpheus, Sophocles, and Plato, which are very similar to the ones collected in the *Theosophy*.[67] What is even more interesting is that various Syriac, Coptic and Arabic sources bear witness to the deep influence the *Theosophy* had even on those Eastern Christian traditions.[68]

But the most striking and significant influence of the *Theosophy* on later literature is certainly to be seen in the anonymous *Prologue* to the Byzantine collection of the *Sibylline Oracles*. This prologue, the date of which is still uncertain, has been handed down only through the family of manuscripts currently indicated with the letter Φ. The author briefly explains that the reason that induced him to collect

---

[64] See again E. Jeffreys, "The Chronicle of John Malalas, Book I: A Commentary", in *The Sixth Century: End or Beginning?*, ed. by P. Allen and E. Jeffreys (Byzantina Australiensia, 10), Brisbane, 1996, pp. 52–74.

[65] See Photius, *Bibl., Cod.* 170 (ed. R. Henry, vol. II, Paris, 1960, pp. 162–165).

[66] *Passio S. Artemii* 27–28 and 46 (ed. B. Kotter, *Die Schriften des Johannes von Damaskos*, V: *Opera homiletica et hagiographica*, in PTS 29, Berlin-New York, 1988, pp. 216–218 and 228).

[67] These textual affinities have been pointed out by J. Bidez, "Sur diverses citations, et notamment sur trois passages de Malalas retrouvés dans un texte hagiographique", *ByZ* 11 (1902), pp. 388–394; E. Klostermann – E. Seeberg, *Die Apologie der Heiligen Katharina* (SKG.G I,2), Berlin, 1924; S. Costanza, "Sull'utilizzazione di alcune citazioni teologiche nella Cronografia di Giovanni Malala e in due testi agiografici", *ByZ* 52 (1959), pp. 247–252.

[68] For the study of these Oriental sources I refer the reader to the following contributions: G. Graf, *Geschichte der christlichen arabischen Literatur*, I: *Die Übersetzungen* (StT 118), Città del Vaticano, 1944, pp. 483–486; A. van Lantschoot, "Trois pseudo-prophéties messianiques inédites", *Muséon* 73 (1960), pp. 27–32; R. van den Broek, "Four Coptic Fragments of a Greek Theosophy", *VigChr* 32 (1978), pp. 118–142; S. Brock, "A Syriac Collection of Prophecies of the Pagan Philosophers", *OLoP* 14 (1983), pp. 203–246; Idem, "Some Syriac Excerpts from Greek Collections of Pagan Prophecies", *VigChr* 38 (1984), pp. 77–90.

these oracles, up till then scattered and of difficult access, into a single continuous work, was to make it easier to interpret them and, therefore, to facilitate the diffusion of the spiritual advantages that may be drawn from these texts, advantages which are certainly greater than those, however important, obtained from the laborious study of Greek literature.

As has already been correctly observed for some time now, the section of the prologue including the etymology of the name "Sibyl", the catalogue of the ten Sibyls, the legend of the arrival of the Sibylline books in Rome and the quotation from Firmianus Lactantius, is entirely borrowed from the third book of the *Theosophy* (III A, 1,2–12). This shows that whoever wrote this introduction to the collection of the Sibylline oracles knew the *Theosophy* very well and highly appreciated both its documentary value and its apologetic teaching.[69]

4. *The presence of Porphyry in the 'Theosophy'*

Among the numerous pagan authors mentioned in the *Theosophy*, the Neoplatonist Porphyry of Tyre (233–305 A.D. ca.) deserves closer consideration in this introduction, due to his particularly important role.

Porphyry is mentioned by name several times in the *Theosophy*. Two oracles are quoted from his *Philosophy from Oracles*. The first oracle comes from the second book (I,24–26: Πορφύριος ἐν τῷ δευτέρῳ βιβλίῳ τῆς ΕΚ ΛΟΓΙΩΝ ΦΙΛΟΣΟΦΙΑΣ),[70] while the second (I,27) is completely new. A fragment on the unknowability of God (II,13) derives very probably, as Henri Dominique Saffrey has noted in a perceptive study, from Porphyry's *Commentary on the Parmenides*.[71] Moreover,

---

[69] See J.J. Collins, "Sibylline Oracles (Second Century B.C.–Seventh Century A.D.). A New Translation and Introduction", in *The Old Testament Pseudepigrapha*, vol. I: *Apocalyptic Literature and Testaments*, ed. by J.H. Charlesworth, London, 1983, pp. 327–329.

[70] It is worth noting, however, that Steuchus, *De perenni philosophia* III,14 (Lugduni, 1540, pp. 155–157), writes: *Adducitur hoc oraculum non a Christianis, sed a Porphyrio Christianorum hoste, decimo libro* εὐλογίων (sic!) φιλοσοφίας. A similar reading ἐκ τοῦ δεκάτου τῶν Πορφυρίου εὐλογιῶν (sic!) φιλοσοφίας is to be found in the codex *Ambrosianus* 569 (N 234 sup.) of the sixteenth century. See A. Mai, *Philonis Iudaei, Porphyrii philosophi, Eusebii Pamphili opera inedita*, Mediolani, 1816, pp. 59–64.

[71] H.D. Saffrey, "Connaissance et inconnaissance de Dieu: Porphyre et la 'Théosophie de Tübingen'", in J. Duffy and J. Peradotto (eds.), *Gonimos. Neoplatonic*

the author of the *Theosophy* is aware of certain biographical details of Porphyry's life. For example, he knows that Iamblichus was a disciple of Porphyry's (II,14) and that Porphyry was a Christian in his youth (II,25). However, he indignantly rejects the slanderous statement according to which Porphyry apostatized after being beaten by some Christians at Caesarea in Palestine.[72] Porphyry's greed for money then led him to marry a rich, old Jewess, the mother of five children.[73]

A passage from Porphyry's *History of Philosophy* is also mentioned (II, 38). The same work is quoted again in the final chronicle (VII,4,4). Porphyry's *History of Philosophy* was already very well known and appreciated by Christian apologists such as Eusebius of Caesarea, Theodoret of Cyrrhus and Cyril of Alexandria.[74] It may be legitimately supposed that it supplied the author of the *Theosophy* with doxographical material on the history of Greek philosophy from the origins right up to Plato, especially for the second book which deals with the sentences of the sages.

The undeniable knowledge of Porphyry shown by these quotations makes it highly probable that Porphyry's *Philosophy from Oracles* was, if not the unique, certainly the main source of the first book of the *Theosophy*, devoted to the interpretation of the pagan oracles. Indeed, it may reasonably be believed that even the very idea of collecting the oracles of the gods came from Porphyry's work. We must, therefore, ask ourselves what relationship existed between Porphyry's collection of oracles and the analogous Christian collection of the *Theosophy*.[75]

---

and Byzantine Studies presented to Leendert G. Westerink at 75, Buffalo N.Y., 1988, pp. 1–20, repr. in Idem, *Recherches sur le Néoplatonisme après Plotin* (Histoire des doctrines de l'Antiquité Classique, 14), Paris, 1990, pp. 11–30.

[72] The story is reported by Socrates, *Hist. eccl.* III,23,38.

[73] Porphyry's *avaritia* had already been criticized by Lactantius, *Div. Inst.* V,2,3. See P.F. Beatrice, "Antistes philosophiae. Ein christenfeindlicher Propagandist am Hofe Diokletians nach dem Zeugnis des Laktanz", in *Ricerche patristiche in onore di Dom Basil Studer* (= *Augustinianum* 33), Rome, 1993, pp. 31–47. However, the author of the *Theosophy* wrongly claims, probably following Eunapius, *Vitae soph.* IV,2,5, that Porphyry's wife Marcella had five children. As Porphyry himself states in *Ad Marcellam* 1, she had seven children, five daughters and two sons.

[74] See the excellent presentation by A. Ph. Segonds, "Les fragments de l'*Histoire de la Philosophie*", published in appendix to É. des Places, *Porphyre. Vie de Pythagore. Lettre à Marcella*, Paris, 1982, pp. 163–197.

[75] R.M. Ogilvie, *The Library of Lactantius*, Oxford, 1978, pp. 24 and 55, unnecessarily postulates that Arnobius, Lactantius and the author of the *Theosophy* used a Christianized version of Porphyry's collection of oracles.

Clearly, it cannot but be a relationship of challenge or rivalry. In his work Porphyry had collected various oracles of Greek gods such as Apollo, Hecate and Sarapis, in order to offer a philosophical reinterpretation of them in the light of the doctrines that had developed in the Neoplatonic school, thanks to the teachings of his master Plotinus. This programme is clearly stated in the prologue to the *Philosophy from Oracles* quoted by Eusebius of Caesarea in his *Preparation for the Gospel.*[76] Moreover, for Porphyry, recourse to the oracles, that is, to the most genuine and authoritative expressions of the pagan religious tradition, had the basic function of supporting a radical attack on the provocative Christian claim to own the truth. This means that the *Philosophy from Oracles* is the only real anti-Christian treatise that was ever written by Porphyry, as I have tried to demonstrate in a series of previous articles.[77]

Before the *Theosophy*, numerous Christian writers had already undertaken the difficult task of confuting Porphyry, starting with Methodius of Olympus, Arnobius of Sicca and Eusebius of Caesarea at the beginning of the fourth century, up to Theodoret of Cyrrhus in the middle of the fifth century. They had developed a whole series of arguments both of a strictly philosophical nature and of Biblical exegesis to defend the Christian doctrine threatened by Porphyry's acute and upsetting criticism. But none of them had until then thought of writing a work which might replace Porphyry's anti-Christian treatise by making use of the same technique of composition, that is, by presenting the texts of the oracles followed by a doctrinal comment. Now, the *Theosophy* adopts this procedure, which is an innovation in the apologetic tradition. While in Porphyry's work the gods were invoked as witnesses of the truth of the old pagan traditions, in contrast to the falsehood of Christianity, in the *Theosophy* their oracles are quoted with the opposite intention of upholding the truth of the Christian doctrines of the Trinity and the Incarnation.

It should be stressed that the oracles quoted in the *Theosophy* cannot be labelled "Chaldaean" oracles in the technical sense of the term, since there is no evidence to support this claim.[78] In fact, these

---

[76] Eusebius, *Praep. Evang.* IV,7,1–2.
[77] See P.F. Beatrice, "Porphyrius", and the bibliography cited there.
[78] A critical discussion of the traditional thesis developed by H. Lewy, *Chaldaean Oracles and Theurgy. Mysticism, Magic, and Neoplatonism in the Later Roman Empire*, nouv. éd. par M. Tardieu, Paris, 1978, can be found in R. Majercik, *The Chaldaean Oracles. Text, Translation and Commentary* (Studies in Greek and Roman Religion, 5), Leiden, 1989.

oracles sound strikingly similar to those uttered and collected in the temples of Didyma and Claros.[79] A few lines of one of these oracles (I, 2) were carved on a stone wall of the city of Oenoanda.[80] The author of the *Theosophy*, however, does not limit himself to reinterpreting authentic pagan oracles in a manner which is favourable to Christian doctrine; he does not hesitate to resort to bogus oracles when in need.

Pierre Batiffol was the first to point out the existence of fictitious theological oracles in the *Theosophy*.[81] However, it is not always easy to discover the Christian forgeries, since those which seem to be oracles fabricated by the Christians might, on closer investigation, prove to be pure and simple pagan texts. For example, I think that the oracle from Coptos on the Virgin Birth of the Son-Logos (I,42) is to be connected with an old pagan Egyptian ritual described only by Epiphanius of Salamis;[82] in the same way, the oracle on the "consubstantiality" (ὁμοούσιος) of the Son-Logos with the Father-Nous, found in the burial vaults (σύριγγες) of the Valley of the Kings near Thebes (I,45), has nothing to do, in my opinion, with the Christian doctrine of the Trinity formulated in the Nicene creed, but is an original document of Egyptian theology to be rather paralleled with the *Poimandres*, the first treatise of the *Corpus Hermeticum*.[83]

This is a highly questionable issue, and in this field there is still a lot of work to be done. At any rate, there can be no doubt concerning the impressive case provided by the Delphian oracle of the god Apollo (I,5) who complains of being defeated by Christ. Christ is the celestial man who expels Apollo with violence from his temple, but whom Apollo now recognizes as his one true God. This oracle, a purely Christian invention, was conceived to contradict a

---

[79] See the in-depth examination by Th.L. Robinson, *Theological Oracles and the Sanctuaries of Claros and Didyma*, Harvard diss., 1981, esp. I, pp. 183–266, and II, pp. 323–466.

[80] See A.S. Hall, "The Klarian Oracle of Oenoanda", *ZPE* 32 (1978), pp. 263–268.

[81] P. Batiffol, "Oracula Hellenica", *RB* 13 (1916), pp. 177–199. The standard work on the problem of literary fraud in the ancient world is that by W. Speyer, *Die literarische Fälschung im heidnischen und christlichen Altertum. Ein Versuch ihrer Deutung* (HAW I/2), München, 1971.

[82] Epiphanius, *Pan.* 51,22,9–11.

[83] See *CH* I, 10. The word ὁμοούσιος, on the contrary, is placed in a clearly Christian context in *Theosophy* I, 62. Much more on this subject in the forthcoming article by P.F. Beatrice, "The Word 'Homoousios' from Hellenism to Christianity" (Master Theme of the Thirteenth International Conference on Patristic Studies held in Oxford in August 1999).

famous pagan oracle of Apollo, quoted and commented on by Porphyry in the *Philosophy from Oracles*. In that oracle the god maintained the exclusively human nature of Christ and claimed that he had been justly condemned to death by the Chaldaean judges, that is, by the Jews.[84]

The polemical attitude of the *Theosophy* with respect to the *Philosophy from Oracles* seems to be confirmed by the adoption of the title itself. As Eusebius pointed out, Porphyry had set himself the dual aim of demonstrating the value of the pagan theological oracles in contrast with the Christian doctrines and, at the same time, of exhorting his followers to attain that intellectual wisdom which he, with a word particularly dear to him, liked to call "theosophy" (εἴς τε προτροπὴν ἧς αὐτῷ φίλον ὀνομάζειν θεοσοφίας).[85] John Philoponus confirms Eusebius' information when he says that Porphyry called theurgy "practical theosophy" (τήν τε πρακτικὴν θεοσοφίαν, οὕτω τὴν μαγείαν καλῶν), by which he meant that also recourse to theurgical techniques guarantees some form of religious wisdom, albeit inferior to philosophical theosophy.[86] The word *theosophy* was introduced by Porphyry in the philosophical vocabulary of Neoplatonism,[87] while Eusebius seems to be the first Christian apologist to have taken this word as a new definition of the Christian religion.[88]

The author of the *Theosophy* chose this polemical title for his anthology of oracles and philosophical sayings in order to demonstrate that also the pagans had received their wisdom from God (*Epit.* 5: διὰ τὸ ὑπὸ τοῦ θεοῦ καὶ τοὺς Ἕλληνας σοφισθῆναι). Theosophy, that is, religious wisdom of things divine, can only be achieved through the Christian revelation transmitted in the Scripture, but the truth of Christianity is also confirmed by the very authorities of paganism, educated by God. The content of theosophy, in particular, is the Christian doctrine of the Trinity and the Incarnation.

---

[84] We know the content of this pagan oracle thanks to three Christian writers: Lactantius, *Div. Inst.* IV,13,11; Eusebius, *Dem. Evang.* III,7; Augustine, *De Civ. Dei* XIX,23. For a full analysis see P.F. Beatrice, "Monophysite Christology in an Oracle of Apollo", *IJCT* 4 (1997/98), pp. 3–22.

[85] Eusebius, *Praep. Evang.* IV,6,3.

[86] Philoponus, *De opif. mundi* 200, 20–26 (= fr. 340 a Smith, p. 388).

[87] See e.g. Porphyry, *De abst.* II,35; II, 45,2–4; IV,9. 17; *De Styge* fr. 378 Smith, p. 459, and H. Lewy, *Chaldaean Oracles*, p. 444. On the contrary, according to R. Lane Fox, *Pagans and Christians*, p. 680, the word θεοσοφία seems to be a Christian coinage.

[88] Eusebius, *Praep. Evang.* I,5,12.

For the material used, the method followed and the polemical aims pursued, the *Theosophy* appears to be the work capable of refuting and replacing Porphyry's *Philosophy from Oracles* in the religious and philosophical culture of that time.

5. *Paganism and Judaism in the 'Theosophy'*

The fact that the *Theosophy* is an "apologetic" work in the most obvious sense is a statement which, at this point, needs no further proof. This means that the *Theosophy* is a work aimed first of all at fighting against the disease of Greco-Oriental idolatry (III A, 1,9: τοῖς νοσοῦσι τὰ τῶν Ἑλλήνων), using the well-tested method of recourse to the religious traditions of the pagans. However, another aspect of the religious controversy carried out in the *Theosophy* also deserves our attention.

An oracle placed in the mouth of Apollo contains serious insults against the Jews. They are defined as being rather impudent, foolish and ungodly, since their life does not proceed righteously; they have even repudiated the Law handed down by their fathers (I,53). This oracle does not come from any pagan collection, certainly not from Porphyry's *Philosophy from Oracles* in which, as Eusebius and Augustine report, the Jews were greatly praised at least for their monotheistic faith and for having crucified Christ.[89] It is therefore a forgery produced by the Christian author of the *Theosophy*.

Controversy against the Jews is an important feature of the Christian apologetic tradition right from the earliest centuries. It finds its justification above all in the accusation of "deicide" brought against the Jews by the Christians from the very beginnings. This polemical theme is also present in the Sibylline prophecies. In this section of the third book of the *Theosophy*, the author says that the Jews refused to recognize the Emmanuel prophesied by Isaiah (III A, 1,19), and did not hesitate to strike God by nailing him to the cross (III A, 1,26–29).

A saying attributed to the Greek legislator Solon explicitly holds the treacherous people of the Jews responsible for having condemned the incarnate Word to death on the cross (II,50). The strength of this anti-Jewish attitude is highlighted by another late Byzantine col-

---

[89] See Eusebius, *Dem. Evang.* III,7; Augustine, *De Civ. Dei* XIX,23.

lection of prophecies of the Greek sages (Δ = Διήγησίς τινος φιλοσόφου περὶ τῶν ἑπτὰ Ἑλλήνων τῶν φιλοσόφων διὰ τὴν ἄνω πρόνοιαν), also derived in some way from the *Theosophy*. Here the poet Homer denounces the crucifixion of the Lord as the work of the perfidious race of the Jews.[90]

In another oracle of the *Theosophy* (I,40), Apollo exalts the Hebrew Moses along with the Egyptian Hermes and Apollonius of Tyana, since those three men were the only ones to have had the privilege of contemplating the divine nature. This is an authentically pagan oracle which is not in contrast with the openly anti-Jewish orientation of the *Theosophy*. Indeed, the author of the *Theosophy* draws a clear distinction between Moses, whose exceptional religious personality is recognized even by a pagan oracle, and the Jews who betrayed the Law and crucified the Saviour.

It is interesting to note that for the Christian author of the *Theosophy* this Egyptian Hermes, i.e. Hermes Trismegistus, is not the same as the god Hermes, elsewhere called "Logios" (I,28–29).[91] Hermes Trismegistus was only a man, the author of pagan religious texts which the author of the *Theosophy* reused in support of Christian theology. Most probably following Diodorus Siculus[92] and Julius Africanus,[93] he actually introduces Hermes Trismegistus as Faunus, son of Picus (Zeus), an expert in eloquence and in the arts of magic and divination (*Chron.* IV,3,3: *Hermem terbeatissimum*).

At any rate, the figure of Moses is not involved in the anti-Jewish controversy. In the Pseudo-Orphic poem currently known as *Testament of Orpheus* (II,3), Moses is celebrated as the descendant of the ancient race of the Chaldaeans (φύλου ἄνωθεν Χαλδαίων), and an expert in astrology (ἴδρις . . . ἄστρων τε πορείης καὶ σφαίρης). He is the man born from the waters (ὑδογενής) who received the Ten Commandments (δίπλακα θεσμόν) from God.

There has been much debate as to the origin, structure and textual

---

[90] See the text in Erbse, *Theosophorum Graecorum Fragmenta*, p. 134.

[91] On the distinction between the god Hermes Logios and Hermes Trismegistus see G. Fowden, *The Egyptian Hermes. A Historical Approach to the Late Pagan Mind*, Cambridge, 1986, repr. Princeton NJ, 1993, pp. 201 f.

[92] See Diodorus, *Bibl.* VI,5,1–3. Diodorus' work is an important source of religio-historical information for the author of the *Theosophy*. See P.F. Beatrice, "Diodore de Sicile chez les Apologistes", in *Les apologistes chrétiens et la culture grecque* (ThH 105), ed. by B. Pouderon – J. Doré, Paris, 1998, pp. 219–235.

[93] See Julius Africanus, *Chron.* fr. 12 in M.J. Routh, *Reliquiae sacrae*, II, Oxford, 1846², repr. Hildesheim-New York, 1974, p. 264.

history of this poem, and many hypotheses have been proposed. Today, it is generally admitted that it is a Judeo-Hellenistic forgery composed as an imitation of an Orphic *hieros logos*. The original text was then variously expanded and manipulated by Christian apologists, Clement of Alexandria, Pseudo-Justin, Eusebius of Caesarea, Cyril of Alexandria, Theodoret of Cyrrhus. The *Theosophy* contains the last and the fullest known version, which at times preserves good ancient variant readings. I do not intend to go further into the discussion, for which I refer the reader to the specific bibliography.[94] Here I only wish to stress the following point.

According to the Tübingen manuscript, the wisdom of the ancient Chaldaeans praised by Orpheus in the ll. 27–28 was that of Abraham (II,2: τὴν τῶν πάλαι Χαλδαίων σοφίαν, δηλαδὴ τὴν τοῦ Ἀβραάμ). Clement of Alexandria, referring to the same poem, had already written that here the allusion was to Abraham or to his son (τὸ γένος Χαλδαίῳ, εἴτε τὸν Ἀβραὰμ λέγων τοῦτον εἴτε καὶ τὸν υἱὸν τὸν αὐτοῦ).[95] Based only on these two pieces of evidence, the idea of the existence of an "Abrahamic" version of the poem, as distinct from a later "Mosaic" version, has found wide acceptance in the bibliography.

In reality, a marginal gloss of the Tübingen manuscript identifies the anonymous Chaldaean as Moses (ὁ γὰρ τὴν δεκάπτυχον γράψας Μωσῆς τῶν Χαλδαίων ἔμπειρος ἦν καὶ τῆς ἀστρονομίας). Philo of Alexandria confirms that Moses was a Chaldaean who possessed knowledge of the celestial bodies (see Philo, *Vita Mos.* I,5: Μωυσῆς γένος μέν ἐστι Χαλδαῖος; see also *ibid.* I,23: τὴν τῶν οὐρανίων Χαλδαϊκὴν ἐπιστήμην). He bore an Egyptian name meaning "saved from the waters" (*ibid.* I,17: εἶτα δίδωσιν ὄνομα θεμένη Μωυσῆν ἐτύμως διὰ τὸ ἐκ τοῦ ὕδατος αὐτὸν ἀνελέσθαι· τὸ γὰρ ὕδωρ μῶυ ὀνομάζουσιν Αἰγύπτιοι).

This means that the "Abrahamic" version of the Pseudo-Orphic poem never existed, or that at least there seems to be no need for

---

[94] Among the most important contributions, see N. Walter, *Der Thoraausleger Aristobulos. Untersuchungen zu seinen Fragmenten und zu pseudepigraphischen Resten der jüdisch-hellenistischen Literatur* (TU 86), Berlin, 1964; N. Zeegers – Vander Vorst, *Les citations des poètes grecs chez les apologistes chrétiens du IIe siècle* (Université de Louvain, Recueil de travaux d'histoire et de philologie, 4e série, fasc. 47), Louvain, 1972, pp. 192–197; C. Riedweg, *Jüdisch-hellenistische Imitation eines orphischen Hieros Logos. Beobachtungen zu OF 245 und 247 (sog. Testament des Orpheus)* (Classica Monacensia, 7), Tübingen, 1993. The best available introduction to the long scholarly debate is that by C.R. Holladay, *Fragments from Hellenistic Jewish Authors*, vol. IV: *Orphica* (SBL Texts and Translations 40; Pseudepigrapha Series, 14), Atlanta, 1996.

[95] Clement Al., *Strom.* V,14,123,2.

this superfluous hypothesis. The words δηλαδὴ τὴν τοῦ Ἀβραάμ could simply be an interpolation of the Byzantine compiler recalling the rather doubtful explanation (Abraham or Isaac?) of Clement of Alexandria. If so, they are to be deleted. Interpolations of this kind should be no surprise, if one considers the extent of the interventions of the anonymous epitomizer. These interventions were revealed by the discovery of the original text of the *Theosophy* by Mras in the codex *Ottobonianus*, and then confirmed by the codex of Modena used by Erbse.

6. The 'Theosophy' and Manicheism

In the *Theosophy* traditional, anti-Jewish motifs accompanied the controversy with the pagans. Paganism and Judaism clearly appear as two enemies to be fought, not to be integrated by means of more or less elaborate syncretistic speculations. There is no margin of compromise with either of the two. This irrefutable fact leads me to reject as totally unfounded the opinion according to which the *Theosophy* was a Manichean work written by an otherwise unknown Aristocritus. This hypothesis was brought forward by A. Brinkmann,[96] and was later shared, among many others, by P. Alfaric,[97] H. Windisch,[98] and J. Bidez – F. Cumont.[99]

The *Theosophy* of the Manichean Aristocritus is mentioned exclusively in a formula of anti-Manichean abjuration used by the Byzantine Church from the sixth century on.[100] According to this rare and precious source, the purpose of this work was to demonstrate, from the typically Manichean syncretistic point of view, that Judaism, Greek paganism, Christianity and Manicheism professed a single, identical doctrine (τὴν ἀθεοτάτην βίβλον Ἀριστοκρίτου, ἣν ἐκεῖνος ΘΕΟΣΟΦΙΑΝ ἐπέγραψεν, δι᾽ ἧς πειρᾶται δεικνύναι τὸν Ἰουδαισμὸν καὶ τὸν Ἑλληνισμὸν

---

[96] A. Brinkmann, "Die Theosophie des Aristokritos", *RMP* 51 (1896), pp. 273–280.

[97] P. Alfaric, *Les Écritures manichéennes*, t.II: *Étude analytique*, Paris, 1918, pp. 107–112; 169–172; 181–182; 199–205.

[98] H. Windisch, *Die Orakel des Hystaspes*, pp. 42 and 97.

[99] J. Bidez – F. Cumont, *Les Mages hellénisés. Zoroastre, Ostanès et Hystaspe d'après la tradition grecque*, Paris, 1938, vol. II, pp. 363 f.

[100] Greek text and English translation by S.N.C. Lieu, "An Early Byzantine Formula for the Renunciation of Manichaeism: the 'Capita VII contra Manichaeos' of Zacharias of Mytilene", *JAC* 26 (1983), pp. 152–218, esp. 188 f., and commentary at p. 213, with further bibliography.

καὶ τὸν Χριστιανισμὸν καὶ τὸν Μανιχαισμὸν ἓν εἶναι καὶ τὸ αὐτὸ δόγμα).

It is to be noted, first of all, that there is never any mention of Manicheism in the extant fragments of the *Theosophy*, though this textual fact might simply be due to an accident of the manuscript tradition. What is more important is that the harsh judgments both on pagans and Jews do not fit in well with the syncretistic content of the Manichean work. This is a decisive argument which opposes all attempts to identify the two works as one.

The conclusion seems inevitable, and is today widely accepted:[101] the Manichean *Theosophy* of Aristocritus, if it ever existed, and the *Theosophy* I have tried to reconstruct in this edition are two works with the same title, but totally different as regards both their origin and their religious message.

In the text of the *Theosophy*, at least in its present condition, along with the controversy against pagans and Jews, there are no traces of a parallel controversy against heretics. It may be easily imagined that theological controversy was not lacking in the previous seven-book treatise *On the Right Faith*. The absence of a clearly recognizable polemical context makes it particularly difficult to define the author's theological position. To do this, only the few internal problematic indications offered by the text are available.

7. *A monophysite work*

A theological work which ended its world chronicle with the Emperors Zeno and Anastasius, both involved in the Christological debates that followed the Council of Chalcedon, could not avoid taking a stand in this controversy. So, it is reasonable to expect its author to have left some signs which, on an attentive and unbiased reading of the text, would reveal his authentic religious allegiance.

Indeed, a number of elements, albeit slight, would lead us to believe that the *Theosophy* had a monophysite origin. First of all, the "fortune" of the work, that is, the influence that it undoubtedly exerted in certain Syriac, Coptic and Arabic ecclesiastical documents, as well as in the Byzantine world, would be difficult to explain unless

---

[101] See M. Goodman in E. Schürer, *The History of the Jewish People in the Age of Jesus Christ (175 B.C.–A.D. 135)*. A New English Version Revised and Edited by G. Vermes – F. Millar – M. Goodman, Edinburgh, 1986, vol. III, part I, pp. 628 f.

we admit that the theology of the treatise was fundamentally oriented towards Monophysitism.[102]

The mention of the *Testament of the Lord and the Commandments of the Apostles* (*Epit.* 4: ΔΙΑΘΗΚΗ ΤΟΥ ΚΥΡΙΟΥ ΚΑΙ ΔΙΑΤΑΞΕΙΣ ΤΩΝ ΑΓΙΩΝ ΑΠΟΣΤΟΛΩΝ), an apocryphal work which was currently in use exclusively in the monophysite church of Syria, can only confirm the vital connections of the *Theosophy* with that theological trend. Also the *Birth and Assumption of the Virgin Mary* (*ibid.*: ΓΕΝΝΗΣΙΣ ΚΑΙ ΑΝΑΛΗΨΙΣ ΤΗΣ ΑΧΡΑΝΤΟΥ ΔΕΣΠΟΙΝΗΣ ΗΜΩΝ ΘΕΟΤΟΚΟΥ) points towards Monophysitism.[103] This apocryphal Marian work is the main source for the section of the final chronicle that deals with the narration of the events referring to the birth of John the Baptist and of Jesus Christ (*Chron.* VIII, 3,6–17).

It is true that, considering the widespread diffusion of the theme of Isaiah's martyrdom throughout ancient Christian literature, its brief mention in *Chron.* V,4,3 does not reveal anything specific about the doctrinal affinities of the *Theosophy.* However, the Pseudo-Dionysian echoes in the sentences attributed to Plato (II,53) and to Menander (II,56) again indicate the existence of special contacts between the *Theosophy* and monophysite circles. Plato's spurious sentence, which I have managed to reconstruct for the first time from fragments scattered in various manuscripts, recalls the contents of the Areopagite's treatise *On the Divine Names.*[104] In this chapter Plato is credited with the famous Hermetic sentence on the difficulty of knowing God and the impossibility of speaking about God (Θεὸν νοῆσαι μὲν χαλεπόν, φράσαι δὲ ἀδύνατον).[105] As is known, the basic identity of views between Hermes and Plato's *Timaeus* 28c (τὸν γὰρ πατέρα καὶ ποιητὴν τοῦδε τοῦ παντὸς εὑρεῖν τε ἔργον, καὶ εὑρόντα εἰς πάντας ἐξειπεῖν ἀδύνατον) had already been remarked by Lactantius.[106] The sentences attrib-

---

[102] See the studies quoted above in n. 68.

[103] I have dealt with the apocryphal material of the *Theosophy* in the article "Traditions apocryphes".

[104] See L. Bréhier, "La légende des Sages païens à Byzance", in *Mélanges d'histoire du Moyen-Age Louis Halphen*, Paris, 1951, pp. 61–69, 66 ff., commenting upon the text of the codex *Matrit. gr.* 115, fol. 127 r, of the fifteenth century, edited by S. Lambros in *Neos Hellenomnemon* 21 (1927), pp. 376–377.

[105] See *Exc.* I,1 (ed. Festugière, t. III, p. 2). This Hermetic quotation is also to be found in Ps. Justin, *Coh.* 38,2; Greg. Naz., *Orat.* 28,4; Cyril, *C. Iul.* I,43; *Passio s. Artemii*, 28 (ed. Kotter, V, p. 217). On the diffusion of this sentence see Scott-Ferguson, *Hermetica* IV, p. 238, n. 4, and the comprehensive articles by A.D. Nock, "The exegesis of Timaeus 28 C", *VigChr* 16 (1962), pp. 79–86, and J. Pépin, "Grégoire de Nazianze, lecteur de la littérature hermétique", *VigChr* 36 (1982), pp. 251–260.

[106] Lactantius, *De ira* 11,11: *Unus est igitur princeps et origo rerum deus, sicut Plato in*

uted to Plato and Menander should be assessed, along with the quotation from Porphyry's *Commentary on the Parmenides* (II,13), as an eloquent testimony to the author's strong inclination toward that kind of apophatic theology developed a few years earlier in its most complete form by Pseudo-Dionysius.

In this context we must certainly not underestimate the fact that the very term "theosophy" had been significantly accepted in the theological terminology of the Areopagite. This technical term is used as many as three times in the Pseudo-Dionysian *corpus*: once with the precise meaning of "divine wisdom transmitted by the Scriptures" (τῆς ἐκ λογίων ... θεοσοφίας),[107] and twice with the meaning of "divine doctrine belonging to the Christians" (τῆς καθ᾽ ἡμᾶς θεοσοφίας;[108] τῆς Χριστιανῶν ... θεοσοφίας).[109] In this sense, it may be said that, if it is true that the title *Theosophy* expresses the polemical intent of the author with regard to Porphyry, at the same time it also reveals his loyalty to a precise orientation of mystical theology rooted in the Pseudo-Dionysian tradition.

At this point, the allusion to the Book of Revelation 4,6.8 (I,62), which has up till now remained completely unnoticed, may prove important. This meaningful discovery also leads us toward that monophysite milieu where there was a particularly keen interest in the last, controversial book of the Bible. The Pseudo-Dionysian writings teem with references to the Apocalypse,[110] and Ecumenius, the author of the earliest commentary on the Apocalypse written in Greek, corresponded with Severus, the monophysite Patriarch of Antioch.[111]

Finally, if the Alexandrian connection of the *Theosophy*, endorsed by various authors, were to be irrefutably demonstrated, it too might be an argument of notable weight in this direction, since in the second half of the fifth century Alexandria was the acknowledged capital of monophysite resistance to the Council of Chalcedon.[112]

Timaeo et sensit et docuit; cuius maiestatem tantam esse declarat, ut nec mente conprehendi nec lingua exprimi possit. Idem testatur Hermes; see also the explicit citation in *Epit.* 4,4–5.

[107] Ps. Dionys., *De div. nom.* 2,2 (ed. B.R. Suchla, in PTS 33, Berlin-New York, 1990, p. 125).

[108] *De div. nom.* 7,4 (p. 199).

[109] *De Myst. Theol.* I,1 (ed. A.M. Ritter, in PTS 36, Berlin-New York, 1991, p. 141).

[110] See John of Scythopolis, *Scholia in librum de divinis nominibus* II,1 (PG 4, 212 C), and the Biblical index in PTS 36, p. 244.

[111] On this enigmatic writer and his obscure work see J.C. Lamoreaux, "The Provenance of Ecumenius' Commentary on the Apocalypse", *VigChr* 52 (1998), pp. 88–108.

[112] See B.E. Daley, "Apollo as a Chalcedonian: A New Fragment of a Controversial

These arguments are indirect, external and, on the whole, fairly peripheral. Luckily, there are in the *Theosophy* some explicit doctrinal declarations which strongly support the thesis of its monophysite origin.

The short treatise of Christology, placed in Apollo's mouth in the famous bogus oracle mentioned above (I,5),[113] presents all the features of moderate monophysite Christology as known through the documents of the second half of the fifth century, that is, the works of the monophysite Patriarch of Alexandria, Timothy Aelurus, and the *Henotikon* of Emperor Zeno. Moreover, in the fragment of the theosophy of the Sibyls discovered by Mras, it is clearly stated that in the mystery of the hypostatic union the human nature was "absorbed" or "annihilated" by the divine Logos (III A, 2,11: Ἐν τούτῳ γάρ ἐστι τὸ μυστήριον ἐν τῷ νενικῆσθαι τὴν ἀνθρωπείαν φύσιν κτλ.). The use of this verb reveals the typically monophysite point of view with regard to the Incarnation. Even the theopaschite formula "One of the Trinity" (τοῦ ἑνὸς τῆς αὐτῆς . . . τριάδος), at the beginning of Book II, can be explained for that time only as an expression of the monophysite orientation of the author.[114]

An interesting and, in my opinion, decisive confirmation of these statements of a purely doctrinal character may be found in the *Kaiserkritik* of the Tiburtine Sibyl. This oracle represents the author's judgment on the religious policies of the Byzantine emperors of the eighth generation, that is, of the emperors involved in the theological disputes that followed the Council of Chalcedon (III B, 16–20). Leo I, who openly favoured the dogma of Chalcedon, blaspheming against the monophysite truth, was struck by the divine curse which deprived him of his kingdom and of his life. Basiliscus, too, suffered the same fate for having betrayed, with the issue of the pro-Chalcedonian *Antenkyklion*, the monophysite cause which he had previously embraced with the publication of the *Enkyklion*. Apart from the lukewarm and substantially dissatisfied judgment of the ambiguity of Zeno, the author's whole unconditioned approval goes to Anastasius. The latter, in fact, did not hesitate to depose those who, like the

---

Work from Early-Sixth Century Constantinople", *Traditio* 50 (1995), pp. 31–54, 33, n. 13.

[113] See p. xxviii.

[114] More details can be found in P.F. Beatrice, "Monophysite Christology in an Oracle of Apollo", pp. 11 ff.

pro-Chalcedonian Patriarch Euphemius of Constantinople (495/96), wounded and damaged monophysite orthodoxy.[115]

8. *A millenarian work*

The author of the *Theosophy* is a monophysite theologian. His position appears to be close to that of the radical Syro-Egyptian *akephaloi* who were active at the end of the fifth century.[116] But he is also a convinced millenarian. The insistent reproposal of this perspective throughout the work proves that millennialism mattered to him very much.

The author of the *Theosophy* quotes Psalm 89,4 (2 Peter 3,8), Gen. 2,2 and I John 2,18, to maintain that the world is to last six thousand years. This means that the incarnation of Christ is to be placed in the year 5500 after Adam (*Epit.* 3; cf. *Chron.* VIII,3,8). In this he is the heir of a long and deep-rooted chiliastic tradition that goes back to Julius Africanus and Hippolytus of Rome (first half of the third century). He must certainly have known of the *Chronography* of Julius Africanus, whose name is quoted three times in the final chronicle (*Chron.* VI,2,13; VI,2,18; VII,5,2).

Consequently, the end of the world was expected to take place in the year 6000, and should have coincided with the year 500 A.D. or, rather, with the year 507/8. The author of the *Theosophy* was a follower of the Alexandrian chronology, as is shown by the fact that he adopts the theory of the cosmic cycles having a duration of 532 years (*Chron.* IX,3,3). This computation was introduced by Annianus in the early years of the fifth century, forecasting the end of the world for the year 508.[117]

---

[115] I have explained the reasons for this new interpretation of the Tiburtine Sibyl in my essay "Das Orakel von Baalbek". There, I have expressed my criticism of the generally held opinion about the Chalcedonian origin of this oracle.

[116] The best general treatment of the post-Chalcedonian controversies is to be found in the monumental work by A. Grillmeier, *Christ in Christian Tradition*, vol. II: *From the Council of Chalcedon (451) to Gregory the Great (590–604)*, part 1: *Reception and contradiction. The development of the discussion about Chalcedon from 451 to the beginning of the reign of Justinian*, Engl. tr., London-Oxford, 1987. However, neither the *Theosophy* nor the Baalbek Oracle are ever mentioned here.

[117] Along with the standard work by V. Grumel, *Traité d'études byzantines*, I. *La chronologie*, Paris, 1958, it is also very useful to see W. Adler, *Time immemorial. Archaic history and its sources in Christian chronography from Julius Africanus to George Syncellus* (DOS 26), Washington D.C., 1989.

The prophecy of the Tiburtine Sibyl strongly supports this millenarian chronology. Constantinople, founded in 330 A.D.—she says—, will not reach its 180th year of life, and its domain will end with the world before 510 (III B, 11); the labour pains of the cosmos, that is, the final period of history, will begin with the reign of Leo I (III B, 16); Ariadne's power will cease 32 years after the death of Leo I (474 A.D.), that is, by 506 (III B, 17), and the reign of Anastasius will last at most eleven years, that is, until 503 (III B,20).

Various other Byzantine and Oriental sources of monophysite inspiration state that the year 6000 of the world fell during the reign of Anastasius.

At the beginning of the sixth century, Ecumenius, to whom we owe the first Greek commentary on the Book of Revelation, places the end of the world at five hundred years after the first coming of Christ on the basis of the traditional chiliastic chronology found in Psalm 89,4 and 2 Peter 3,8.[118] John Malalas says that the Lord appeared on earth on the sixth millennium day, at the end of time.[119] According to the *Chronicon pseudo-dionysianum* the year 6000 coincides with the sixteenth year of Anastasius,[120] while in the *Chronicon ad annum Domini 846 pertinens* the year 6000 of the world is the first year of Anastasius.[121] Peter of Alexandria, in his universal chronicle which goes up to 912 A.D., claims that the sixth millennium was completed in the fifteenth year of Anastasius, that is, in the year 505 A.D.[122] For Michael the Syrian, the monophysite Patriarch of Antioch, the sixth millennium ended in the second (or, according to other people, in the fourteenth) year of the reign of Anastasius, which coincided with the year 814 of the Seleucid era, that is, the year 504 A.D.[123]

Despite slight differences in the identification of the exact year,

---

[118] See the Greek text recently edited by M. de Groote, *Oecumenii Commentarius in Apocalypsin* (TEG 8), Leuven, 1999, pp. 67–68 and 248.

[119] Malalas, X, pp. 228–229 Dindorf.

[120] *Incerti auctoris Chronicon pseudo-dionysianum vulgo dictum*, ed. J.-B. Chabot in CSCO 121, Script. Syri 66, Lovanii, 1949, p. 12.

[121] See *Chronica Minora* II, ed. E.-W. Brooks, interpr. J.-B. Chabot in CSCO 4, Script. Syri 4, Louvain, 1960, p. 166. According to a marginal gloss other people said that it was the nineteenth year of Anastasius.

[122] This text is quoted by W. Brandes, "Anastasios ὁ δίκορος: Endzeiterwartung und Kaiserkritik in Byzanz um 500 n. Chr.", *ByZ* 90 (1997), pp. 24–63, 55, n. 217.

[123] *Chronique de Michel le Syrien patriarche jacobite d' Antioche (1166–1199)*, trad. par J.-B. Chabot, t. II, Paris, 1901, pp. 167 ff.

the tradition seems to be unanimous. It is worth pointing out that this chiliastic calculation was preserved exclusively in sources of monophysite provenance. This "coincidence", too, could be a further signal of the monophysite origin of the *Theosophy*.[124]

However, all the forecasts found in the oracle of the Tiburtine Sibyl proved to be equally mistaken, since in 510 Constantinople was in excellent condition, Ariadne died in 515 and Anastasius in 518. This means that the author of the prophecy was writing before these events, and certainly not after 503, the presumed year of the end of the reign of Anastasius.

As we might expect, the author of the *Theosophy* did not know the archaic Judeo-Christian doctrine of the thousand-year reign of Christ with His saints. Yet, he believed that Henoch and Elijah had been assumed into heaven in a form of provisional immortality (III A, 2,7; the assumption of Henoch is also recalled in *Chron.* I,1,8) and that, at their return, they would be killed by the Antichrist, but would then be revived by the Lord (III B, 28). In any case, he still defends the idea that the world history unfolds in six thousand years, basing his argument on the traditional typological exegesis of the Hexameron. In this case, too, he appears to be a representative of monophysite theology, where millennialism continued to circulate for several centuries.[125]

9. *The date and place of composition*

The problem of the dating of the *Theosophy* is extremely complex because the text does not offer any clear and decisive clues. For this reason we can only express more or less probable hypotheses.

The fact that the world chronicle placed at the end of the work goes from Adam up to Zeno (†491), according to the information supplied by the Byzantine epitomizer (*Epit.* 2), would seem to indicate that the text was written during the reign of Anastasius (491–518),

---

[124] Research on the Byzantine apocalyptic literature is still in its early stages. For a first contact with this intricate tradition one can consult W. Brandes, "Die apokalyptische Literatur", in *Quellen zur Geschichte des frühen Byzanz (4.–9. Jahrhundert). Bestand und Probleme*, ed. by F. Winkelmann and W. Brandes, Amsterdam, 1990, pp. 305–322.

[125] See W. Witakowski, "The Idea of Septimana Mundi and the Millenarian Typology of the Creation in Syriac Tradition", in R. Lavenant (ed.), *V Symposium Syriacum 1988* (OrChrA 236), Roma, 1990, pp. 305–322.

as it was normal practice to end the chronographic narration imme-
diately prior to the time of the living emperor. Besides, we have
noted that the author of the *Theosophy* expected the end of Constantinople to take place before 510 and the end of the world no later
than the year 507/8, while he expected the end of Anastasius and
of Ariadne between 503 and 506. The work must, therefore, have
been composed between 491 and 503. Perhaps it is possible to reduce
this interval of time even more.

The manuscripts *Athen. B.N. gr.* 1070 and *Paris. gr. suppl.* 690 report
that Apollo's oracle on Christ (I,5) was engraved on a plate found
in the 21st year of Anastasius, that is, in 511/12. Instead, the codex
Marcian. gr. 573 states that the discovery was probably made in the
first year of Anastasius (491/2). Unfortunately, the indications that
follow as to the month and the day do not fit in with the year. It
must be concluded that we are facing a textual corruption. Amongst
so much confusion, only the fourth indiction of Anastasius can be
taken as the most reliable element. During the reign of Anastasius,
the fourth indiction fell twice, in 496 and in 511. Now, the year
511 is to be excluded because it falls after the end of the world,
which was expected to take place not later than 507/8. So, only the
year 496, the fifth year of Anastasius' reign, can be taken into consideration as the year of the discovery of the oracle, and as the *terminus post quem* for the composition of the *Theosophy*.[126]

An important argument, in a certain sense a decisive one for a
more precise dating, is now provided by the Baalbek Oracle which,
in my opinion, belongs to the third book of the *Theosophy*. On the
basis of various historical observations, all equally valid, its first editor Alexander had no difficulty in placing the prophecy of the
Tiburtine Sibyl in the years between 502 and 504, in coincidence
with the start and the first phase of the Persian war. This dating is
amply confirmed by other internal elements of the text. So the year
502/3 would be the most appropriate dating both for the *Theosophy*
and for the previous treatise *On the Right Faith*. Alexander also suggested that the Baalbek Oracle might have been written in Heliopolis
of Phoenicia (Baalbek), or in the neighbouring region, due to the
author's evident admiration for the temples of that important religious centre (see III B, 9).[127]

---

[126] See the discussion in P.F. Beatrice, "Monophysite Christology", pp. 15 f.
[127] J.P. Alexander, *The Oracle of Baalbek*, pp. 41–47.

One might add that the first of the twelve famous mountains listed in *Chron.* II,7,5 is Mount Lebanon, which is in Phoenicia between Byblos and Berytus. However, the fact that the *Theosophy* may have been composed at Baalbek, or in the neighbouring region, does not necessarily mean that the author was a Phoenician. Indeed, he shows a keen interest in Egyptian wisdom in general (*Epit.* 1 and *Pref.* 3). Certain oracles (I,41–45) betray a considerable, very probably direct, knowledge of Egyptian places such as Ombos, Coptos, Elephantine, and the so-called σύριγγες, the burial vaults of the Valley of the Kings.[128] It has also been rightly pointed out that the author of the *Theosophy* is familiar with the Alexandrian recension of the Biblical text (*Pref.* 1 and II,5). On the whole, all this reveals his close contacts with Egypt and its cultural and ecclesiastical traditions.[129] Nor should his evident interest in Constantinople and its providential mission be overlooked (I,17).

The discussion on the place of composition of the *Theosophy* thus inevitably involves the investigation of the cultural background of its author. This man seems to have travelled extensively, acquiring a variety of cultural experiences, and to have possessed an open-mindedness that for that time was quite out of the ordinary.[130]

10. *The author and his cultural background*

It is a well-known fact that trying to discover the authors of anonymous early Christian works is always a risky business, the results of which are often uncertain. We could mention numerous examples of attempts at restitution that have been discussed at length, but have not yet been definitively and satisfactorily concluded. Some

---

[128] The correct meaning of the rare word σύριγγες is given by Pausanias, *Perieg.* I,42,3, and Aelianus, *De nat. anim.* VI,43 and XVI,15. See also two Egyptian inscriptions in W. Dittenberger, *OGIS*, vol. II, Lipsiae, 1905, pp. 432 f., n. 694, and p. 462, nos. 720–721. For the first editor Buresch, *Klaros*, p. 109, this word meant the Libyan tribe of the Σηράγγαι or Σιράγγαι mentioned by Ptolemaeus, *Geogr. enarr.* IV,6,17; consequently he printed the wrong text: κατὰ τοὺς λεγομένους Σηράγγας. Unfortunately, he was followed by W. Scott – A.S. Ferguson, *Hermetica* IV, Oxford, 1936, p. 226, and Erbse (in both editions).

[129] This remark by Buresch, *Klaros*, p. 91, was accepted by Erbse, *Fragmente griechischer Theosophien*, p. 3; *Theosophorum Graecorum Fragmenta*, pp. XIII f. See most recently P. Athanassiadi, *Damascius. The Philosophical History*, pp. 353 f. Of course, familiarity with Egypt does not entail the Egyptian origin of the author and his work.

[130] See the perceptive note 129 by G. Fowden, *The Egyptian Hermes*, p. 181.

years ago I myself dealt with the so-called *Epistle to Diognetus*, indi-
cating Polycarp of Smyrna as the possible writer of that mysterious
document.[131] Elsewhere, I suggested that Apollos of Alexandria, the
great rival of Paul at Corinth, could be the most probable author
of the encratite *Gospel according to the Egyptians*.[132] I am well aware of
the difficulties involved in undertakings of this kind. However, the
data that have emerged so far are clear enough to sketch a fairly
precise portrait of the author of the *Theosophy*, and make it legitimate to attempt to propose, just as a working hypothesis, the name
of the person who might have written such an unusual work.

The author of the *Theosophy* is a man who has read a vast amount
of literary, historiographic and philosophical works of classical antiquity. He also possesses a profound knowledge of Greco-Roman and
Oriental religious traditions. The impressive number of quotations
demonstrates the obviousness of this statement. It is difficult to establish how much of this material is due to first-hand reading. It cannot be excluded that he resorted to those manuals and anthologies
which formed the usual tools for the encyclopedism of his time (suffice
it to think of the anthology of Stobaeus or the sentences of Menander).

As regards his knowledge of the Patristic tradition, the following
remarks are to be made.

With the exception of Cyril of Alexandria's treatise *Against Julian*,
of which he seems to be the oldest witness (II,45–49), the *Divine
Institutes* by Firmianus (Lactantius) (III A, 1,7–8), and the *Chronography*
by Julius Africanus (*Chron.* VI,2,13; VI,2,18; VII,5,2), he does not
quote any other Christian writer.[133] Nonetheless, it is difficult to deny
that he drew useful information and solid teaching also from other
apologetic works such as the *Cohortatio* by Pseudo-Justin, the *Preparation
for the Gospel* and the *Proof of the Gospel* by Eusebius of Caesarea, and
the treatise *On the Trinity* attributed to Didymus the Blind. Perhaps
Clement of Alexandria should be included in this list. The fundamental idea that the source (πηγή) of Wisdom wished to benefit all

---

[131] P.F. Beatrice, "Der Presbyter des Irenäus, Polykarp von Smyrna und der Brief
an Diognet", in *Pléroma. Salus carnis. Miscelánea en homenaje al P. Antonio Orbe*,
Santiago de Compostela, 1990, pp. 179–202.

[132] P.F. Beatrice, "Apollos of Alexandria and the Origins of the Jewish-Christian
Baptist Encratism", in W. Haase (ed.), *ANRW* II.26.2, Berlin-New York, 1995, pp.
1232–1275.

[133] R.M. Ogilvie, *The Library of Lactantius*, p. 53, completely overlooks the quotation of Lactantius in the *Theosophy* because he only uses the Tübingen excerpt which
lacks any reference to Lactantius.

men indifferently, Greeks and barbarians (*Pref.* 1), had already been put forward by Theodoret of Cyrrhus in his treatise *The cure of pagan maladies* VIII,2–3. Also the identification of paganism with a disease (III A, 1,9: τοῖς νοσοῦσι τὰ τῶν Ἑλλήνων) refers back to the title and apologetic programme of this famous treatise by the bishop of Cyrrhus (Ἑλληνικῶν θεραπευτικὴ παθημάτων).

The literal quotation from Lactantius reveals another very interesting aspect of the culture of the author of the *Theosophy*, namely, his knowledge of Latin, something which had become very rare among the Byzantine writers of that period.[134] This makes it very likely that he was also able to read the Latin text of Virgil's *Aeneid*, which he used in the catalogue of the Sibyls.[135] The quotation of Lactantius' text in the *Theosophy* is also important for another reason. The editor of Lactantius' work in the *Corpus Scriptorum Ecclesiasticorum Latinorum*, Samuel Brandt, published the entire Greek text of the *Theosophy* III A, 1,9–12 (from Ἐπεὶ οὖν τὰ παρ᾽ ἡμῖν εὑρισκόμενα τὰ Σιβυλλιακὰ to τὸν ἄνθρωπον ἐδημιούργησεν) as Lactantius' *Fragm. VIII* (*spurium*).[136] This Greek fragment is again mentioned in the fifth volume of the recent, authoritative *Handbuch der lateinischen Literatur der Antike*.[137] Now, the publication of the Latin quotation from Lactantius gives definitive evidence that the Greek text of the alleged fragment 8 has nothing to do with Lactantius, but is an integral part of the *Theosophy*, which is clearly inspired by Pseudo-Justin's *Cohortatio* 37,2–3.

That the author of the *Theosophy* had a fair knowledge of Lactantius' apologetic work is also proven by the sequence of the Sibylline fragments in the third book. At times, he seems to be translating Lactantius' text, so close is the adherence to the Latin model. For instance, the title of Chrysippus' work ΠΕΡΙ ΘΕΟΤΗΤΟΣ (III A, 1,3) can only derive from a misinterpretation of the Latin *De divinatione* found in Lactantius, *Div. Inst.* I,6,9. This evident dependence on Lactantius has convinced me to consider with special attention, for the Greek text of the Sibylline oracles, the readings found in Lactantius, rather than those handed down in the remaining manuscript tradition.

---

[134] Lactantius, *Div. Inst.* I,6,13, is quoted in III A, 1,8.
[135] Virgil, *Aen.* VI, 35 f. is mentioned in III A, 1,3.
[136] See CSEL 19, p. CX and CXII; CSEL 27, pp. 158–160.
[137] See A. Wlosok," L. Caecilius Firmianus Lactantius", in *Restauration und Erneuerung. Die lateinische Literatur von 284 bis 374 n. Chr.* (HLL 5), ed. by R. Herzog, München, 1989, § 570, pp. 375–404, 404: "Lact. frg. 8, aus der sogenannten Sibyllen-Theosophie".

I have already presented the monophysite and millenarian ideas of the author of the *Theosophy*. Now, I may add that his use of the Biblical text is that of a writer who generally follows the Septuagint for the Old Testament and the Alexandrian recension of the New Testament. However, he does this not in a servile way, taking some liberties which reveal that he was a strong and original character.

What may legitimately be deduced from these observations? Which writer of that period possessed the necessary features for us to credit him with the authorship of a work thus conceived? I believe that the name of the monk Severus of Sozopolis, who became the mono-physite Patriarch of Antioch from 512 to 518 A.D., could be pro-posed not without grounds. The name of Severus has always struck me as the only one able to give a satisfactory answer to the numer-ous queries that emerged during the preparatory studies, the prin-cipal conclusions of which are given below.

11. *Severus of Antioch?*

Severus of Antioch's familiarity with the classical tradition, with the religious philosophy of paganism and ecclesiastical literature was decidedly outstanding, as is confirmed by his biographer, Zacharias Scholasticus.[138]

He reports that Severus, born in Sozopolis in Asia Minor, stud-ied both Greek and Latin grammar and rhetoric at Alexandria,[139] and that he then went to Berytus to take a course in Roman civil law.[140] There, he devoted himself to the systematic study of the writ-ings of the Christian apologists against paganism.[141] These biographical data shed light on the numerous references to Egyptian and Phoenician paganism that are so important in the *Theosophy*.

Zacharias tried, rather awkwardly, to conceal the well-known fact that, before his conversion, Severus had really been a convinced fol-lower of pagan religious practices.[142] Severus was reproached for

---

[138] The Syriac text of the *Life of Severus* by Zacharias Scholasticus is edited with a French translation by M.-A. Kugener, *Vie de Sévère par Zacharie le Scholastique*, in PO 2, fasc. 1, n° 6, Paris, 1903 (repr. Turnhout, 1971), pp. 7–115.

[139] PO 2, p. 11.

[140] PO 2, p. 47.

[141] PO 2, p. 53.

[142] The apologetic tendency of Zacharias' biography was keenly highlighted by

these pagan contaminations not only in an anonymous defamatory booklet, to which Zacharias wished to reply by means of his edifying biography, but also in official ecclesiastical documents.[143] Severus himself admitted his pagan religious past in a homily in honour of St. Leontius of Tripolis, the martyr in whose sanctuary he made the decision to convert to Christianity.[144] The extent to which he remained faithful to the classical culture of his youth after his conversion is shown by the fact that he did not think it unfitting to quote sayings of pagan sages and lines of pagan poets even in his cathedral homilies preached to the people of Antioch.[145]

So, it is not surprising that a man with such a past, steeped in profane culture and idolatrous beliefs, composed an apologetic work like the *Theosophy*. Its author carries out a kind of self-purifying ritual, which consists in reducing the great pagan literary, philosophical and religious tradition, by which he had been dominated for so long, to a prophecy of the truth of Christianity. He succeeds in freeing himself of his pagan past by transforming it into a preparatory stage of his conversion. Never, as in this case, have the personal, indeed, autobiographical implications of the apologetic procedure been so clear.

This operation is all the more valuable and becomes particularly significant when we think that the apologetic anthology entitled *Theosophy* acts as the justificatory appendix of a treatise on the orthodox Christian faith. Severus embraced this faith without reserves, and fought long to defend it, paying a very high personal price. This faith was basically the moderate monophysite theology of Cyril of Alexandria, which was transmitted to him principally by Peter the Iberian. Severus developed his own thought in a polemical confrontation on the one hand against the dyophysite Christology of Chalcedon, of Pope Leo, John of Caesarea and Nephalius, and on

---

W. Bauer, "Die Severus-Vita des Zacharias Rhetor", in *Aufsätze und kleine Schriften*, ed. by G. Strecker, Tübingen, 1967, pp. 210–228.

[143] See, e.g., the *Libellus monachorum ad Menam* (ed. E. Schwartz in ACO III, p. 40) and the *Epistola episcoporum orientalium ad Agapetum* (*ibid.*, p. 148).

[144] The Coptic translation of this exceptionally important document was first discovered and edited by G. Garitte, "Textes hagiographiques orientaux relatifs à Saint Léonce de Tripoli. II. L'homélie copte de Sévère d'Antioche", *Muséon* 79 (1966), pp. 335–386.

[145] See the *Laudatio S. Leontii* 5,10 (Garitte, p. 375); 8,11 (Garitte, p. 377); *Hom. cath.* XXVII (PO 36, p. 571). On the classical formation of Severus see in general P.F. Beatrice, "Monophysite Christology", esp. pp. 18 ff.

the other hand against the radical Monophysites such as Eutyches, Sergius the Grammarian and Julian of Halicarnassus.[146]

Now, the spiritual affinity of the author of the *Theosophy* with the apologetic and theological method of the Alexandrian Patriarch is clearly documented not only by the explicit quotations (II,45–49) from Book I of the treatise *Against Julian* (ΥΠΕΡ ΤΗΣ ΧΡΙΣΤΙΑΝΩΝ ΘΡΗΣΚΕΙΑΣ ΚΑΙ ΚΑΤΑ ΙΟΥΛΙΑΝΟΥ ΤΟΥ ΠΑΡΑΒΑΤΟΥ). It would not seem completely unfounded to detect Cyril's influence even in the title of the lost seven-book treatise *On the Right Faith*. This title in fact recalls the three famous speeches by Cyril Περὶ τῆς ὀρθῆς πίστεως.[147] At any rate, the presence of the quotations from Cyril's work is to be assessed as an important argument in favour of the attribution of the *Theosophy* to Severus of Antioch, who chose to fight under the flag of loyalty to the teachings of Cyril of Alexandria.

The *Theosophy* also uses the *Testament of the Lord and the Commandments of the Apostles*, an apocryphal monophysite work which Severus is the first to mention in a letter to a certain Thecla *comitissa*. This is certainly another observation which strongly supports the attribution of the *Theosophy* to the monophysite theologian Severus.[148]

From this point of view, also the striking similarities of Plato's and Menander's sentences (II,53 and 56) with Pseudo-Dionysius' treatise *On the Divine Names*, have considerable weight. Severus is the first author to give literary evidence of the existence of the Pseudo-Dionysian writings. He quotes the Areopagite's famous fourth epistle to the monk Gaius in a letter to a certain John the Hegoumenos.[149] Moreover, certainly not by chance, he twice quotes the treatise *On the Divine Names* II, 9, respectively in *Adversus Apologiam Juliani*, 25,

---

[146] The best available exposition of Severus' theology is that by A. Grillmeier (in collaboration with Th. Hainthaler), *Christ in Christian Tradition*, vol. II: *From the Council of Chalcedon (451) to Gregory the Great (590–604)*, part 2: *The Church of Constantinople in the sixth century*, Engl. tr., London-Louisville, 1995, pp. 17–175.

[147] See the Greek text in ACO I/1,1, pp. 42–72; I/1,5, pp. 26–61; I/1,5, pp. 62–118.

[148] On Severus' mention of this apocryphal work, currently known by the modern title *Octateuch of Clement*, see F. Nau, *La version syriaque de l'Octateuque de Clément* (Ancienne littérature canonique syriaque, fasc. IV), Paris, 1913, pp. 8–11, and B. Steimer, *Vertex Traditionis. Die Gattung der altchristlichen Kirchenordnungen* (BZNW 63), Berlin-New York, 1992, pp. 141–148.

[149] A fragment of this letter is reproduced in the *Doctrina Patrum*, ch. 41, xxiv–xxv (ed. F. Diekamp – B. Phanourgakis – E. Chrysos, *Doctrina Patrum de Incarnatione Verbi. Ein griechisches Florilegium aus der Wende des 7. und 8. Jahrhunderts*, Münster, 1981², pp. 309 f.).

and in *Contra additiones Juliani*, 41.[150] According to Pseudo-Zacharias, Severus had seriously studied the works by Hierotheus, Dionysius, Titus and Timothy.[151]

As well as a monophysite theologian, Severus is also an adherent of chiliasm, just like the author of the *Theosophy*. He is still fully convinced of the validity of the hexaemeral typology according to which world history would be consumed in six thousand years.[152] Concerning this, it is worth mentioning that, in his *Epist.* 81, Severus makes use of the same two New Testament quotations found in the *Theosophy* (see *Epit.* 3), that is, 2 Peter 3,8 and 1 John 2,18. He also claims that Henoch and Elijah enjoy provisional immortality, but he harshly criticises all those who claim that the same fate is also shared by John the Evangelist.[153] For this reason, if Severus is really the author of the *Theosophy*, it seems advisable to delete the sentence on the provisional immortality of John (III A, 2,7: καὶ διὰ τοῦ ἀγαπῆσαι τὸν τοῦ θεοῦ λόγον Ἰωάννης ὁ εὐαγγελιστὴς μένει ὡς οἱ προλεχθέντες ἕως τῆς δευτέρας τοῦ Κυρίου παρουσίας θανάτου ἄμοιρος) which should rather be considered a later gloss interpolated for theological motives.[154]

It is extremely difficult to establish the Biblical text used by Severus, since it can only be reconstructed through the Syriac translations of his cathedral homilies. Notwithstanding this, the impression is that it was substantially independent and equidistant from both the "Lucianic" recension and the Alexandrian recension.[155] Thus it presents the same relative liberty found in the Scriptural quotations of the *Theosophy*. Unfortunately, the study of Severus' Biblical text is still in its early stages. This situation prevents us from carrying out an in-depth comparison.

The last question concerns the books of magic and demonology. Porphyry's speculations on demons and his polemics against Christianity

---

[150] For the interpretation of these citations I refer the reader to J. Lebon, "Le Pseudo-Denys l'Aréopagite et Sévère d'Antioche", *RHE* 26 (1930), pp. 880–915.

[151] Ps.-Zacharias, *Hist. eccl.* VII,12. I quote the edition by M.-A. Kugener, in PO 2, fasc. 3, n° 8, Paris, 1904 (repr. Turnhout, 1971), p. 272.

[152] See esp. Severus, *Epist.* 79 (PO 14, p. 125); *Epist.* 81 (PO 14, pp. 128–131); *Hom. cath.* II,26 (PO 38, p. 285).

[153] See Severus, *Epist.* 93 (PO 14, pp. 170–177).

[154] See P.F. Beatrice, "Traditions apocryphes", pp. 115 ff.

[155] See the partial analysis by C.J.A. Lash, "The Scriptural Citations in the 'Homiliae Cathedrales' of Severus of Antioch and the Textual Criticism of the Greek Old Testament", in E.A. Livingstone (ed.), *Studia Patristica* 12 (TU 115), Berlin, 1975, pp. 321–327.

were well known to Severus' circle.[156] Zacharias writes that Severus was able to give Christian students his precious advise against paganism and sorcery because he was well acquainted with the books of Zoroaster, Ostanes, and Manetho, which were widely read among the pagan students of Berytus.[157] Severus, then, must have been particularly interested in the use of the Christianized version of the book of Hystaspes in order to show that even Zoroaster, as well as many other pagan sages of the past, had prophesied the Incarnation of the Lord. Not by chance, in the *Theosophy* (II,55) also the name of Ostanes is mentioned in connection with the mystery of the Virgin Birth.

In conclusion, though we must admit that none of these clues alone is enough to prove that Severus was the author of the *Theosophy*, it seems undeniable that their combined strength has a special attractive power and compels us at least to take this possibility into serious consideration. One might even quite legitimately wonder whether the mysterious Timothy, mentioned only by Malalas as an authoritative source for his oracular and chronographic material,[158] is not in actual fact a mere pseudonym intended to designate, in a veiled manner and with all due caution, after the condemnation on the part of Justinian, the author of the *Theosophy*, the great and venerated Patriarch Severus, the guardian of monophysite orthodoxy and therefore the "honour of God".[159]

At any rate, it may be easily understood why the seven-book treatise *On the Right Faith* was lost. Its fate in the Byzantine world was marked by its outspoken monophysite content. Most probably this work is to be identified with Severus' dogmatic treatise *On Faith* which has left traces only in the Coptic-Arabic florilegium *The Precious Pearl*.[160] The *Theosophy*, on the contrary, was amply reused and therefore survived, albeit only in fragments and through extensive contamination, for several centuries more, as it offered abundant material

---

[156] See Zacharias in PO 2, p. 42.
[157] Zacharias' long digression on this subject is found in PO 2, pp. 57–76, and 90 f.
[158] See E. Jeffreys, "Malalas' Sources", pp. 194 ff.
[159] Timothy was also the pseudonym used by Salvian of Marseille in his work *Ad ecclesiam*: see A.E. Haefner, "A Unique Source for the Study of Ancient Pseudonymity", *AThR* 16 (1934), pp. 8–15.
[160] See G. Graf, "Zwei dogmatischen Florilegien der Kopten. A. Die kostbare Perle", *OrChrP* 3 (1937), pp. 49–77, 75; Idem, *Geschichte der christlichen arabischen Literatur*, I, pp. 418 f.

for the apologetic controversy against pagans and Jews, and for
chronographic speculation.

12. *Manuscripts and editions*

Since this edition of the *Theosophy* was conceived and structured rather
differently from Erbse's edition of the Greek theosophical fragments,
it can only be based on a manuscript documentation that largely
differs from the one used by the illustrious German scholar. A list
is given below of the manuscripts and editions which were used for
the preparation of the present edition, following the order of the
individual sections of which the work is composed.

Part 1

For the Byzantine summary, the Preface and the collection of oracles
in Book I, *testis unicus* is nearly always the codex Mb 27 (sixteenth
T   century), fol. 67r–87r, of the University Library at Tübingen (= T).
After Buresch's *editio princeps* and the two editions by Erbse (1941
and 1995), the manuscript's deciphering no longer presents any problem. However, in the absence of other sources, it is now no longer
possible to measure its exact distance from the original, and to check
its degree of reliability. Only for the oracle of Apollo about Christ
(I,5) do we possess a longer version which has every probability of
being the authentic one.
      Buresch had already discovered the long text of this oracle in the
F   codex *Athen. B.N. gr.* 1070 (thirteenth century), fol. 186v (= F), but
he only published it in the appendix of his dissertation, without dis-
cussing it in depth.[161] The complete text of the oracle, with the
prophecies of the seven sages, was later published by A. Delatte.[162]
Erbse reproduced it in both his editions, but, falling prey to an evo-
lutionistic prejudice of a positivistic kind, he assessed it, in my opinion erroneously, as a later amplification of the short text of the
Tübingen manuscript, which he considered to be the original one.
Now, the same long version of the oracle is also found in the older
Venice manuscript, the *Marcian. gr.* 573 (ninth/tenth century), fol.

---

[161] K. Buresch, *Klaros*, pp. 130 f.
[162] A. Delatte, *Anecdota Atheniensia*, pp. 328–330.

26–30 (= M).[163] The oracle of Apollo is quoted in full in a frag-   **M**
ment taken from the final part of a lost work of uncertain date, entitled *Symphony* (πρὸς τὰ τέλη τῆς συμφωνίας ἐπεγέγραπτο οὗτος ὁ λόγος,
according to a marginal note), in which the author wished to show
the harmony of the statements of Cyril of Alexandria and of the
divine Scripture with the dogma defined at Chalcedon (Συμφωνία
τῶν παρὰ τοῦ μακαρίου Κυρίλλου τοῦ Ἀλεξανδρείας ἐπισκόπου εἰρημένων
καὶ τῶν παρὰ τῆς θείας γραφῆς πρὸς τὰ παρὰ τῆς ἐν Χαλκηδόνι ἁγίας
συνόδου δογματισθέντα περὶ τῆς πίστεως). It was evidently a typical
dyophysite florilegium, which should not be confused with the *Symphony*
found in the Vatican codex, which will be discussed below in *Part 2*
as a direct witness of the text of the *Theosophy*. It is certainly curious
to see how this oracle was removed from its original monophysite
context to be transformed into a tool for Chalcedonian controversy.
This was only possible thanks to its recognized strength as a polemical anti-pagan document, which guaranteed its survival and allowed
it to be reused in a totally different ecclesiastical milieu.

Thus, the version of the oracle found in the Tübingen manuscript
is to be seen as a later abbreviation, drafted according to the normal practice of the Byzantine epitomizer. Other manuscripts contain only the second part of the oracle. This is, again, the result of
a later mutilation of the same oracle. In this edition, I have printed
the long text of the oracle, with a few slight variations with respect
to the *editio princeps* of the Venice manuscript published recently by
Brian E. Daley.[164]

For some oracles, as may be seen in the apparatus, it was useful
to collate the Tübingen manuscript with Steuchus' work and the
manuscripts already known to Piccolos and Wolff. However, I feel
that in order to arrive at the definition of a text which is presumably closer to the lost original of the oracles contained in I,45 and
I,54–55, as well as of the oracle of Apollo in I,5, we have to resort
to the collation of the Tübingen manuscript with the minor collections listed below, in point 2, first of all with the *Symphony*.

I also believe it is legitimate to incorporate into Book I two other
oracles that are not recorded in the Tübingen manuscript, namely:
a) the oracular response to the Egyptian king Thoulis (I,49), which

---

[163] This manuscript is listed by E. Mioni, *Bibliotheca Divi Marci Venetiarum codices
graeci manuscripti*, vol. II: *Thesaurus antiquus codices 300–625*, Rome, 1985, p. 478.
[164] See B.E. Daley, "Apollo as a Chalcedonian".

was also quoted by Malalas,[165] and is mentioned in the collection of the Oxford codex *Baroccianus* edited by R. Bentley; b) the oracle received by the Pharaoh Petissonius (I,50), which was quoted again by Malalas,[166] and was later transformed into a saying of Solon's, the Athenian sage and legislator. Also the two oracular inscriptions from the Scamander (I,56 and 62), to be found exclusively in the *Symphony*, most likely belonged to the *Theosophy*. However, the edition of Book I would be incomplete without the New Testament quotations which illustrate the thesis of the fundamental agreement between the pagan oracles and the Biblical revelation. These quotations are not to be found in the Tübingen manuscript. Like the oracles from the Scamander, they are recorded only in the *Symphony* of the Vatican codex.

Part 2

The edition of Book II, including the theological sentences of the Greek and Egyptian sages, seems to be even more complex. Only a small part of the material comes from the Tübingen manuscript which must, consequently, be integrated with the data offered by three other minor collections.

Σ
  a) In the first place there is the Συμφωνία ἐκ τῶν παλαιῶν φιλοσόφων τῶν Ἑλλήνων πρὸς τὴν ἁγίαν καὶ θεόπνευστον νέαν γραφὴν κτλ. (= Σ), transmitted by the codex *Vaticanus gr.* 2200 (eighth/ninth century, the famous manuscript of the *Doctrina Patrum de Incarnatione Verbi*), fol. 444–454:[167] partial *editio princeps* by J.B. Pitra,[168] reproduced by W. Scott – A.S. Ferguson[169] and by H. Erbse.[170]

This is certainly the oldest and most authoritative collection. The sayings of the Greek and Egyptian sages have been mixed with certain oracles and distributed by the anonymous compiler in three sections, respectively concerning the Trinity (Περὶ τῆς ἁγίας καὶ πανσέπτου τριάδος), the Incarnation (Περὶ τῆς ἐνσάρκου οἰκονομίας Χριστοῦ τοῦ θεοῦ ἡμῶν), and the Crucifixion (Περὶ τῆς τιμίας καὶ σωτηριώδους αὐτοῦ σταυρώσεως). This late organization of the collection does not, how-

---

[165] Dindorf, p. 25.
[166] Dindorf, pp. 65–66.
[167] See F. Diekamp – B. Phanourgakis – E. Chrysos, *Doctrina Patrum*, p. XIII.
[168] J.B. Pitra, *Analecta*, pp. 305–308.
[169] W. Scott – A.S. Ferguson, *Hermetica*, pp. 225–227.
[170] H. Erbse, *Theosophorum Graecorum Fragmenta*, pp. 91–104. He adds some *fragmenta addubitata* taken from other sources (pp. 105–108).

ever, conceal the very old, probably original, character of the material that is derived, more or less directly, from the *Theosophy*.

The twenty-one New Testament quotations are of particular importance. These quotations, as I have said, are recorded exclusively in this manuscript. However paradoxical it may appear, they have never been published before, not even by the editors, Pitra, Scott-Ferguson, and Erbse, who at different times provided an edition of the rest of the *Symphony*. Erbse, in particular, is of the opinion that they are simply paraphrastic, marginal notes introduced in a disorderly manner by the scribe of the Vatican codex.[171] On the contrary, I think that these quotations belonged to the original text of the *Theosophy*, in the structure of which they played the precise and irreplaceable role of providing the Biblical support for the main thesis of the basic harmony between pagan wisdom and Christian revelation. What I plan to give here is the *editio princeps* of the Vatican *Symphony*. However, the reader should note that the New Testament quotations of the *Symphony* also refer to some oracles belonging to Book I of the *Theosophy*. This is why they have been redistributed in this edition between Books I and II, in the extremely problematic attempt of finding the least-arbitrary placing for each of them.

No less interesting are the Hermetic *excerpta* and the quotations from Cyril's treatise *Against Julian* which the compiler of the *Symphony* evidently took from the *Theosophy* (see II,32–34; 42; 45–49). If one considers that the oldest known manuscript of Cyril's *Against Julian*, i.e. the *Scorialensis* Ψ.III.12, dates back to the thirteenth century, the great value of the *Symphony* becomes clear. This is why the *Symphony* should be held in due consideration also in the preparation of a new critical edition of Cyril's apologetic treatise. The title, structure and content of the *Symphony* reveal its great antiquity. This collection is very close to the *Theosophy* and certainly older than the Vatican codex. For this reason, I believe it is necessary to systematically collate the Tübingen manuscript with the *Symphony* in order to recover, as far as possible, at least some of the authentic readings of the *Theosophy*. The use of the *Symphony* concerns not only the three common oracles of Book I (5, 45 and 54–55), but also certain philosophic and Hermetic sayings of Book II, and above all the precious

---

[171] H. Erbse, *Fragmente griechischer Theosophien*, pp. 143–145. The list of these New Testament citations is not without inaccuracies, which I have tacitly rectified.

quotations from the New Testament and from Cyril which I have tried to put back into place.

The other two minor collections are:

χ   b) Χρησμοὶ καὶ θεολογίαι Ἑλλήνων φιλοσόφων (= χ). Its principal witness is the codex *Oxon. Barocc. gr.* 50 (eleventh century), fol. 375–376 (= B'), used by R. Bentley in his letter *ad Millium*;[172]

π   c) Προφητεῖαι τῶν ἑπτὰ σοφῶν (= π). Its principal witnesses are the codices *Paris. gr. suppl.* 690 (twelfth century), fol. 248v–249r (= P), and *Athen. B.N. gr.* 1070 (thirteenth century), fol. 186r–186v (= F); *editio princeps* by Delatte.[173]

These two collections, of which the considerable distance from the lost original is evident, underwent the same numerous manipulations which produced other even more complicated and fantastic collections of sayings of Greek sages. Erbse designated them with the Greek letters μ, τ, and Δ. These Medieval collections are particularly interesting for the study of the Christian reinterpretation of the sayings of the seven sages, whose prophetic figures were widely represented in Byzantine church paintings from the twelfth to the eighteenth century.[174]

The sayings of π, except that of Menander, are all found in both Σ and χ, while ten oracles and sayings of Σ also appear in χ. So, there is no denying that there is a certain relationship between these three collections, even though greater precision becomes problematic. According to A. von Premerstein, all three derive from an archetype, a lost *Grundsammlung*, which he identified as X. This archetype was later than the *Theosophy*, and was exploited in Malalas' *Chronography* around the year 560.[175] This critical perspective is shared by Erbse.

---

[172] See above, n. 12. The text is reprinted by H. Erbse, *Theosophorum Graecorum Fragmenta*, pp. 109–116.

[173] A. Delatte, *Anecdota Atheniensia*, pp. 328–330. The text is reprinted by H. Erbse, *Theosophorum Graecorum Fragmenta*, pp. 117–122.

[174] Bibliography on this fascinating subject includes V.G. Grécu, "Darstellungen heidnischer Denker und Schriftsteller in der Kirchenmalerei des Morgenlandes", in *Académie Roumaine. Bulletin de la section historique* 10 (1924), pp. 1–68; A. von Premerstein, "Griechisch-heidnische Weise als Verkünder christlicher Lehre in Handschiften und Kirchenmalereien", in *Festschrift der Nationalbibliothek in Wien*, hrsg. zur Feier des 200jährigen Bestehens des Gebäudes, Wien, 1926, pp. 647–666; K. Spetsieris, "Eikones hellenon philosophon eis ekklesias", *EEPS*, II series, 14 (1963/64), pp. 386–458 (in Greek); I.D. Dujčev, *Heidnische Philosophen und Schriftsteller in der bulgarischen Wandmalerei* (Vorträge Rhein. Akad. der Wissenschaften G. 214), Opladen, 1976.

[175] A. von Premerstein, "Griechisch-heidnische Weise", pp. 664 f.

He adds that the *terminus post quem* for dating this common collection, which he designates with the Greek letter ω, may be indicated as the 21st year of Anastasius, that is, 512 A.D., because this is the year of the alleged finding of the oracle of Apollo on Christ (I,5) according to π.

Two main objections may be raised against this ingenious reconstruction. The first is that the date of the finding of Apollo's oracle is not at all certain and that, as I have already remarked in chapter IX, the most probable year seems instead to be 496 (the fourth indiction of Anastasius' prior to the end of the world). Secondly, these three minor collections have three oracles in common with the Tübingen manuscript (I,5; 45; 54–55). This means that there must have been a precise relationship between these four collections. But what kind of relationship was it?

I have felt obliged to reject the chronological argument used by Erbse to sustain that the archetype ω of the three minor collections was written after the *Theosophy*. Besides, there is no reason to think that the author of this alleged common source also used materials other than those transmitted by the *Theosophy*. It seems much simpler to suppose that the oracles and the sayings included in the three collections all originally belonged to the *Theosophy*, and that only the whimsical, now undecipherable, vicissitudes of the manuscript tradition separated, modified and reunited them during the Middle Ages, until they assumed their present form. So, I am compelled to think either that the hypothetical archetype ω, which according to Erbse was different from, and later than, the *Theosophy*, never existed, or that, if it really did exist, it was only an intermediate collection, itself entirely derived from the *Theosophy*. In this latter case, it would be completely superfluous and useless for the purpose of recovering the original text.

In this new edition of the *Theosophy*, the sayings of the Greek philosophers and the Hermetic texts, which respectively carry the Greek and Egyptian theologies, are gathered together in Book II. Nevertheless, as it is impossible to determine the original position of the single sayings and their mutual interdependence, I have had to limit myself to listing them in the order in which they appear in the Tübingen manuscript and in the three minor collections mentioned above. Particular preference is to be given to the *Symphony* on account of the antiquity and authoritative nature of the Vatican codex.

In establishing the presumably original text for each saying, I have taken care to avoid reproducing all the numerous repetitions and the secondary variant readings. This process of gradual elimination of the derived material produces considerable simplification, which is certainly useful for a deeper understanding of the history of the text. So, for example, on the basis of this selective criterion, the collection π (the sayings of the seven sages), of its own offers only Menander's saying, as all the other sayings are already more correctly recorded in the other collections. Clearly, this has not been a simple operation, nor are the results absolutely guaranteed. However, it was worth trying, even though a margin of uncertainty inevitably remains.

Part 3

Book III, the *Theosophy of the Sibyls*, consists of two long fragments.

a) The first fragment is taken from the codex *Ottobon. gr.* 378 (six-teenth century), fol. 18r–25v (= λ), discovered and published by K. Mras in 1906.[176] For his new 1995 edition, Erbse was able to personally collate the codex *Mutinensis misc. gr.* 126 (= D; olim III.D.7).[177] Fol. 288v–292v (tenth or eleventh century), were probably written by the same scribe of the codex *Laur. pl.* 5, 3, the only witness of Clement of Alexandria's *Stromateis*, while fol. 293r–294v are in a later hand (fourteenth century).[178] My edition of this fragment is also generally based on these two manuscripts, but in some places I was able to provide better readings.

The relevant paragraphs of the Tübingen manuscript (θ 75–83 in Erbse's edition) cannot be used to reconstruct the authentic text of Book III of the *Theosophy*, because they contain only a summary which sometimes opposes the original content of the section. Never, as in this case, has it been so evident that the Byzantine text transcribed in the Tübingen manuscript is just a late and not completely reliable compilation.

b) The second fragment reports the prophecy of the Tiburtine Sybil. The Byzantine version of this oracle, also known as the Baalbek Oracle, is transmitted by only three manuscripts: the codex *Athos*

λ (margin)

D (margin)

---

[176] K. Mras, "Eine neuentdeckte Sibyllen-Theosophie".

[177] H. Erbse, *Theosophorum Graecorum Fragmenta*, pp. 57–90: 'Textus genuinus Theosophiae Sibyllarum'.

[178] See P.M. Barnard, *Clement of Alexandria. Quis dives salvetur* (TaS V,2), Cambridge, 1897, pp. IX–XII; O. Stählin, *Clemens Alexandrinus*, Erster Band: *Protrepticus und Paedagogus*, 3. durchges. Auf. von U. Treu (GCS 12), Berlin, 1972, pp. XXV–XXVII.

1527 or *Karakallou* 14 (twelfth century), fol. 280v–286v (= K): the **K**
codex *Vatican. gr.* 1120 (fourteenth century), fol. 417–423 (= Q); the **Q**
codex *Athen. B.N. gr.* 2725 (= *suppl.* 725) (sixteenth century), fol.
210v–219v (= A). We owe the *editio princeps* of this text to P.J. **A**
Alexander.[179] He found support in certain Latin manuscripts, already
used by Ernst Sackur, which sometimes help us understand a strongly
contaminated and confused text.[180]

Part 4

It is impossible to know the content of the book of Hystaspes. As I
have already said, some general, indirect pieces of information about
its apocalyptic content are provided exclusively by a few passages in
Justin Martyr, Clement of Alexandria and, above all, Lactantius.[181]
In this desperate situation, I made the decision to reproduce, as the
sole surviving fragment, Zoroaster's famous prophecy to Hystaspes
on the coming of the Messiah.[182]

This text, based on authentic Iranian traditions, was rewritten in
the second century A.D. by Christians living in Mesopotamia, and
was very probably reused by the author of the *Theosophy* as an integral part of his apologetic project aimed at making good use of all
the "pagan" prophecies of Christianity. Zoroaster's Christianized
prophecy is first found in the *Mimrā* VII,21 of the Syriac *Liber
Scholiorum* by Theodore Bar-Koni (eighth century).[183] This text was
translated into French for the first time by the Bollandist Paul Peeters
for the *Mages hellénisés* by Bidez and Cumont,[184] and is now available in the French translation by Robert Hespel and René Draguet.[185]

Part 5

Finally, the universal chronicle which concludes the *Theosophy*. This
is to be identified, in my opinion, with a Greek chronography, no

---

[179] P.J. Alexander, *The Oracle of Baalbek*, Washington D.C., 1967.

[180] See E. Sackur, *Sibyllinische Texte und Forschungen. Pseudomethodius, Adso und die Tiburtinische Sibylle*, Halle, 1898 (repr. Turin, 1963), pp. 115–187.

[181] See above, p. xviii.

[182] See P.F. Beatrice, "Le livre d'Hystaspe aux mains des Chrétiens", pp. 378 f.

[183] *Liber Scholiorum* II (ed. by Addai Scher in CSCO 66, Parisiis-Lipsiae, 1912, pp. 74 ff.; repr. in CSCO 69, Louvain, 1960).

[184] J. Bidez – F. Cumont, *Les Mages hellénisés*, II, fr. S 15, pp. 126–129.

[185] R. Hespel et R. Draguet, *Théodore bar Koni. Livre des Scolies (recension de Séert)*, II. *Mimrè VI–XI* (CSCO 432, Syri 188), Lovanii, 1982, pp. 52 f.

longer in existence, which was translated into Latin in Merovingian Gaul. This version has been preserved only in the very old codex **E'** *Paris. lat. B.N.* 4884 of the seventh/eighth century (= E'). In 1606 Joseph Justus Scaliger published the *editio princeps*,[186] and for this reason the work is currently known as *Barbarus Scaligeri*.[187] Subsequently, the text was republished with the title *Excerpta Latina Barbari* by Alfred Schoene in the *Appendix* VI of his edition of Eusebius' *Chronica*,[188] and by Karl Frick for the Teubner collection.[189]

Some years later, Adolf Bauer demonstrated that the initial pages of the *Excerpta Barbari*, from the creation of Adam until the Διαμερισμὸς τῆς γῆς, that is, the division of the earth among the three sons of Noah and their descendants after the flood (*Chron.* I,1,1–II,7,7), are the almost literal translation of an anonymous Greek fragment of the **H'** codex *Matrit. gr.* 4701 (olim N-121; tenth/eleventh century) (= H'), fol. 51r–63v, entitled Συναγωγὴ χρόνων καὶ ἐτῶν ἀπὸ κτίσεως κόσμου ἕως τῆς ἐνεστώσης ἡμέρας. Bauer thought that this fragment was an integral part of the *Chronicle* of Hippolytus.[190] This means that the author of the *Theosophy* included, in the final world chronicle, a long section of Hippolytus' *Chronicle* without mentioning his name. Whatever the value of this attribution, which is not the object of this investigation, Bauer's important discovery justifies the publication of the Greek fragment of the codex *Matritensis* in the corresponding place of the Latin text of the *Excerpta Barbari*.

Another section of this new edition of the *Excerpta Barbari* is printed in Greek. In fact, besides the long fragment of the *Chronicle* of Hippolytus, the author of the *Theosophy* also incorporated some sentences taken directly from the *Birth of Mary*, the so-called *Protevangelium of James* (*Chron.* VIII,3,6–17). These sentences can now be read in their original Greek wording in the critical edition by Émile de Strycker.[191]

---

[186] See J.J. Scaliger, *Thesaurus temporum*, Leiden, 1606 (repr. Osnabrück 1968), t. I, pars II, pp. 44–70.

[187] See *CPG*, III, n. 5539.

[188] A. Schoene, *Eusebii Chronicorum libri duo*, I, Berolini, 1875, *App.* VI (pp. 173–239).

[189] C. Frick, *Chronica Minora*, vol. I, Lipsiae, 1892, pp. 184–371 (with a Greek retranslation).

[190] A. Bauer, *Die Chronik des Hippolytos im Matritensis Graecus 121* (TU, N.F. XIV,1), Leipzig, 1905. I have used the edition by A. Bauer – R. Helm, *Hippolytus Werke*, IV: *Die Chronik* (GCS 36), Leipzig, 1929; 2nd ed. in GCS 46, Berlin, 1955.

[191] É. de Strycker, *La forme la plus ancienne du Protévangile de Jacques. Recherches sur le papyrus Bodmer 5 avec une édition critique du texte grec et une traduction annotée* (SHG 33), Bruxelles, 1961, pp. 10–13; 39 f.; 363 f.

13. *This edition*

This is all the material available today, on which it is possible to base an edition of the *Theosophy* that sufficiently respects the indications of the manuscript tradition. One can legitimately hope, and it is certainly to be wished, that new discoveries or new attributions, which are always possible, will enrich the picture I have sketched, giving it more precision. At this point though, its essential features ought not to undergo radical alterations.

After what I have said, I must inform the reader that this edition of the *Theosophy* cannot avoid resorting to a totally new numbering of the chapters and paragraphs with respect to the previous editions. Moreover, in the attempt to get as close as possible to the hypothetical original text, this edition avoids following up every slight detail of the destiny of the individual fragments, the manuscript transmission of which is extremely complex and widely contaminated.

Consequently, I have chosen not to follow Erbse's example in composing an all-inclusive *stemma codicum* for every oracle or paragraph of the text, because I believe that it would inevitably be too conjectural, and therefore of little use. For a work like the *Theosophy*, of which we possess only a few *membra disiecta*, fragments of various length, sometimes of dubious attribution and, furthermore, often *incertae sedis*, I have only at most been able to sketch out a rough history of its gradual "disintegration", in the following stages.

1) The *Theosophy* was composed in the years 502/503 A.D., as an appendix to the seven-book monophysite treatise *On the Right Faith*.

2) Its overall use in the Byzantine world was exclusively for purposes related to the *Heidenapologetik*, still very much alive from the sixth to the tenth century. These are the witnesses of the "apologetic" use of the *Theosophy*:

a) the prologue of the *Sibylline Oracles*;

b) the *Passio s. Artemii*;

c) the *Passio s. Catharinae*;

d) the *Symphony* of the Vatican codex (eighth/ninth century);

e) the codex 170 of Photius' *Bibliotheca* (ninth century);

f) the *Symphony* of the tenth-century codex of St. Mark's Library.

3) The final world chronicle was translated into Latin in the Merovingian period (seventh/eighth century).

4) A number of passages had wide diffusion in Syriac (but also in Coptic and Arabic), in the eastern Christian communities, between

the eighth and the fourteenth centuries. Among these translations, besides certain sayings of pagan sages, there are also traces of the prophecy of the Tiburtine Sibyl and of the messianic prophecy of Zoroaster to Hystaspes.

5) Some sections underwent gradual reworking, of a more or less fanciful nature, from the eleventh to the fifteenth century, especially in Byzantine monasteries, with the consequent formation of the various collections of sayings of the seven sages.

6) The work was definitively dismembered between the eleventh and the fifteenth century, with the transformation of some fragments into texts with a life of their own. In this last phase of the manuscript tradition I place:

a) the Modena codex (tenth or eleventh/fourteenth century), the most important witness of the initial part of the theosophy of the Sibyls in Book III;

b) the three codices (the oldest of which, K, is of the twelfth century) containing the oracle of the so-called Tiburtine Sibyl;

c) the Strasbourg codex, dating back to the thirteenth/fourteenth century, which was destroyed in 1870. The contents of this manuscript are today partly accessible thanks to the transcription of the Tübingen codex: the anonymous Byzantine summary, the Preface and a few short passages from the first three books, at times rewritten and in open disagreement with the original text.

In the critical apparatus I have refrained from reproducing the numerous spelling variants which I believe are insignificant, or at any rate negligible, for the purpose of a plausible reconstruction of the text. I have recorded only the elements, the knowledge of which is really necessary for that purpose, and have indicated above all the places in which, after the most accurate checking, I feel that different readings should be adopted from those proposed by the previous editors. During this operation, several imperfections and inaccuracies found in their works have been tacitly corrected.

The same criterion of clarity and simplicity has also been adopted in compiling the apparatus of the sources and Biblical quotations. This is all to the advantage of the legibility and comprehension of the information thus placed at the reader's disposal.

SELECT BIBLIOGRAPHY

List of abbreviations

ACO	=	Acta Conciliorum Oecumenicorum
ANRW	=	Aufstieg und Niedergang der Römischen Welt
AThR	=	Anglican Theological Review
BNGJ	=	Byzantinisch-neugriechische Jahrbücher
BSGRT	=	Bibliotheca Scriptorum Graecorum et Romanorum Teubneriana
ByZ	=	Byzantinische Zeitschrift
BZNW	=	Beihefte zur Zeitschrift für die neutestamentliche Wissenschaft
CChr.SG	=	Corpus Christianorum. Series Graeca
CH	=	Corpus Hermeticum
CPG	=	Clavis Patrum Graecorum
CRAI	=	Comptes rendus des séances de l'Académie des Inscriptions et Belles Lettres
CSCO	=	Corpus Scriptorum Christianorum Orientalium
CSEL	=	Corpus Scriptorum Ecclesiasticorum Latinorum
CSHB	=	Corpus Scriptorum Historiae Byzantinae
DCAH	=	Deltion tēs christianikēs archaiologikēs hetaireias
DOS	=	Dumbarton Oaks Studies
DÖAW. PH	=	Denkschriften. Österreichische Akademie der Wissenschaften. Philosophisch-historische Klasse
DSp	=	Dictionnaire de Spiritualité
EEChris	=	Encyclopedia of Early Christianity
EEChurch	=	Encyclopedia of the Early Church
EEPS	=	Epistēmonikē epetēris tēs philosophikēs scholēs tou panepistēmiou Athēnōn
GCS	=	Die griechischen christlichen Schriftsteller der ersten drei Jahrhunderte
HAW	=	Handbuch der Altertumswissenschaft
HLL	=	Handbuch der lateinischen Literatur
HThR	=	Harvard Theological Review
IJCT	=	International Journal of the Classical Tradition
JAC	=	Jahrbuch für Antike und Christentum
JAC ErgBd.	=	Jahrbuch für Antike und Christentum-Ergänzungsband
JECS	=	Journal of Early Christian Studies
JHS	=	Journal of Hellenic Studies
JThS	=	Journal of Theological Studies
KP	=	Der kleine Pauly
MB	=	Musée belge
OGIS	=	Orientis Graeci Inscriptiones Selectae
OLoP	=	Orientalia Lovaniensia Periodica
OrChrA	=	Orientalia Christiana Analecta
OrChrP	=	Orientalia Christiana Periodica
PG	=	Patrologia Graeca
PO	=	Patrologia Orientalis
PRE	=	Paulys Real-Encyclopädie der classischen Alterthumswissenschaft
PTS	=	Patristische Texte und Studien
RAC	=	Reallexikon für Antike und Christentum

RB   = Revue biblique
REA   = Revue des études anciennes
RHE   = Revue d'histoire ecclésiastique
RMP   = Rheinisches Museum für Philologie
RQ   = Römische Quartalschrift
SBA   = Schweizerische Beiträge zur Altertumswissenschaft
SBL   = Society of Biblical Literature
SC   = Sources chrétiennes
SHG   = Subsidia Hagiographica
SKG.G   = Schriften der Königsberger Gelehrten Gesellschaft. Geisteswissen-
           schaftliche Klasse
StT   = Studi e testi
TaS   = Texts and Studies
TEG   = Traditio Exegetica Graeca
ThH   = Théologie historique
TRE   = Theologische Realenzyklopädie
TU   = Texte und Untersuchungen zur Geschichte der altchristlichen Literatur
VigChr = Vigiliae Christianae
VigChrS = Supplements to Vigiliae Christianae
WSt   = Wiener Studien
WUNT   = Wissenschaftliche Untersuchungen zum Neuen Testament
ZKG   = Zeitschrift für Kirchengeschichte
ZNW   = Zeitschrift für die neutestamentliche Wissenschaft
ZPE   = Zeitschrift für Papyrologie und Epigraphik

Sources

Alexander P.J., *The Oracle of Baalbek. The Tiburtine Sibyl in Greek Dress* (DOS 10), Washington D.C., 1967.
Arnim I. ab, *Stoicorum Veterum Fragmenta*, vol. II: *Chrysippi Fragmenta Logica et Physica*, Lipsiae, 1903.

Bauer A. – Helm R., *Hippolytus Werke*, IV: *Die Chronik* (GCS 46), Berlin, 1955².
Bentley R., *Epistula ad Millium*, in *The Works* II (Anglistica et Americana, 131), Hildesheim-New York, 1971.
Bidez J. – Cumont F., *Les Mages hellénisés. Zoroastre, Ostanès et Hystaspe d'après la tradition grecque*, Paris, 1938.
Brandt S., *L. Caeli Firmiani Lactanti Opera Omnia*, pars I (CSEL 19), Pragae-Vindobonae-Lipsiae, 1890; pars II/1 (CSEL 27), Pragae-Vindobonae-Lipsiae, 1893.
Bratke E., *Das sogenannte Religionsgespräch am Hof der Sasaniden* (TU, N.F. 4,3), Leipzig, 1899.
Buresch K., *Klaros. Untersuchungen zum Orakelwesen des späteren Altertums nebst einem Anhange, das Anecdoton ΧΡΗΣΜΟΙ ΤΩΝ ΕΛΛΗΝΙΚΩΝ ΘΕΩΝ enthaltend*, Leipzig, 1889, repr. Aalen, 1973.
Burguière P. – Évieux P., *Cyrille d'Alexandrie. Contre Julien*, Livres I–II (SC 322), Paris, 1985.

Cougny E., *Epigrammatum Anthologia Palatina cum Planudeis et Appendice Nova*, t. III, Parisiis, 1890.

Delatte A., *Anecdota Atheniensia*, t. I: *Textes grecs inédits relatifs à l'histoire des religions* (Bibliothèque de la Faculté de Philosophie et Lettres de l'Université de Liège, fasc. 36), Liège-Paris, 1927.

Diekamp F. – Phanourgakis B. – Chrysos E., *Doctrina Patrum de Incarnatione Verbi. Ein griechisches Florilegium aus der Wende des 7. und 8. Jahrhunderts*, Münster, 1981².
Dindorf L., *Ioannis Malalae Chronographia* (CSHB), Bonnae, 1831.
Dittenberger W., *Orientis Graeci Inscriptiones Selectae*, vol. I–II, Lipsiae, 1903–1905.

Erbse H., *Fragmente griechischer Theosophien* (Hamburger Arbeiten zur Altertumswissenschaft, 4), Hamburg, 1941.
——, *Theosophorum Graecorum Fragmenta* (BSGRT), Stutgardiae et Lipsiae, 1995.

Frick C., *Chronica Minora*, vol. I, Lipsiae, 1892.

Geffcken J., *Die Oracula Sibyllina*, Leipzig, 1902.
Greene W.C., *Scholia Platonica*, Chico CA, 1981.
Groote M. de, *Oecumenii Commentarius in Apocalypsin* (TEG 8), Leuven, 1999.

Hadot P., *Porphyre et Victorinus* (Études Augustiniennes-Série Antiquité, 32–33), Paris, 1968.
Heil G. – Ritter A.M., *Corpus Dionysiacum*, II (PTS 36), Berlin-New York, 1991.
Hespel R. – Draguet R., *Théodore bar Koni. Livre des Scolies (recension de Séert)*, II. *Mimrè VI–XI* (CSCO 432-Syri 188), Lovanii, 1982.
Holladay C.R., *Fragments from Hellenistic Jewish Authors*, vol. IV: *Orphica* (SBL Texts and Translations 40; Pseudepigrapha Series, 14), Atlanta, 1996.

Jacoby F., *Die Fragmente der griechischen Historiker* (FGrHist), Berlin, 1923 ff.
Jaekel S., *Menandri Sententiae-Comparatio Menandri et Philistionis* (BSGRT), Leipzig, 1964.
Jugie M., *Homélies mariales byzantines. Textes grecs édités et traduits en latin* (PO 19, fasc. 3, n° 93), Paris, 1925, repr. Turnhout, 1974.

Kannicht R. – Snell B., *Tragicorum Graecorum Fragmenta*, vol. 2: *Fragmenta Adespota*, Göttingen, 1981.
Kassel R. – Austin C., *Poetae Comici Graeci*, vol. VII, Berolini et Novi Eboraci, 1989.
Kern O., *Orphicorum Fragmenta*, Berolini, 1922.
Koerte A. – Thierfelder A., *Menandri quae supersunt* (BSGRT), Leipzig, 1953.
Kotter B., *Die Schriften des Johannes von Damaskos*, V: *Opera homiletica et hagiographica* (PTS 29), Berlin-New York, 1988.
Kroll W., *Procli Diadochi in Platonis Rem publicam Commentarii*, I–II, Lipsiae 1899–1901.
Kugener M.-A., *Vie de Sévère par Zacharie le Scholastique* (PO 2, fasc. 1, n° 6), Paris, 1903, repr. Turnhout, 1971.
Kurfess A., *Sibyllinische Weissagungen*, Berlin, 1951.

Lambros S., in *Neos Hellenomnemon* 21 (1927), pp. 376–377.
Lloyd-Jones H. – Parsons P., *Supplementum Hellenisticum* (Texte und Kommentare, 11), Berolini et Novi Eboraci, 1983.

Maass E.M., *De Sibyllarum indicibus*, Gryphiswaldiae, 1879.
Maehler H., *Pindari Carmina cum Fragmentis*, II: *Fragmenta et Indices* (BSGRT), Leipzig, 1989.
Mai A., *Philonis Iudaei, Porphyrii philosophi, Eusebii Pamphili opera inedita*, Mediolani, 1816.
Majercik R., *The Chaldean Oracles. Text, Translation and Commentary* (Studies in Greek and Roman Religion, 5), Leiden, 1989.
Marcovich M., *Heraclitus. Greek Text with a Short Commentary. Editio Maior*, Merida, Venezuela, 1967.
——, *Pseudo-Iustinus. Cohortatio ad Graecos, De Monarchia, Oratio ad Graecos* (PTS 32), Berlin-New York, 1990.
——, *Clementis Alexandrini Protrepticus* (VigChrS 34), Leiden, 1995.

Mitteis L., *Griechische Urkunden der Papyrussammlung zu Leipzig*, Leipzig, 1906.
Monat P., *Lactance. Institutions divines*, Livre I (SC 326), Paris, 1986.
Moraux P., *Aristote. Du ciel*, Paris, 1965.
Mosshammer A.A., *Georgii Syncelli Ecloga Chronographica* (BSGRT), Leipzig, 1984.
Mras K., "Eine neuentdeckte Sibyllen-Theosophie", *WSt* 28 (1906), pp. 43–83.
——, *Eusebius. Die Praeparatio Evangelica* (GCS, Eusebius Werke Achter Band; 2., bearbeitete Auflage herausgegeben von É. des Places), Berlin, 1982–1983.

Nauck A. – Snell B., *Tragicorum Graecorum Fragmenta*, Hildesheim, 1964³.
Nock A.D. – Festugière A.J., *Corpus Hermeticum*, Paris, 1946–1954.

Pease A.S., *M. Tulli Ciceronis De natura deorum*, I, Cambridge Mass., 1955.
Piccolos N., *Supplément à l'Anthologie grecque*, Paris, 1853.
Pitra J. B., *Analecta sacra et classica spicilegio Solesmensi parata*, t.V, Parisiis-Romae, 1888.
Preger Th., *Scriptores Originum Constantinopolitanarum* (BSGRT), I–II, Lipsiae, 1901–1907, repr. 1989.

Radt S., *Tragicorum Graecorum Fragmenta*, vol. 3: *Aeschylus*, Göttingen, 1985.
Routh M.J., *Reliquiae Sacrae*, vol. II, editio altera, Oxonii, 1846, repr. Hildesheim-New York, 1974.
Rzach A., *Oracula Sibyllina*, Leipzig, 1891.

Sackur E., *Sibyllinische Texte und Forschungen. Pseudomethodius, Adso und die Tiburtinische Sibylle*, Halle, 1898, repr. Turin, 1963.
Scaliger J.J., *Thesaurus temporum*, Leiden, 1606, repr. Osnabrück, 1968.
Scher A., *Theodorus bar Koni. Liber Scholiorum II* (CSCO 66), Parisiis-Lipsiae, 1912, repr. in CSCO 69, Louvain, 1960.
Schoene A., *Eusebii Chronicorum libri duo*, Berolini, 1866–1875.
Scott W., *Hermetica. The ancient Greek and Latin writings which contain religious or philo-sophic teachings ascribed to Hermes Trismegistus*, vol. IV: *Testimonia with introduction, addenda and indices* by A.S. Ferguson, Oxford, 1936.
Smith A., *Porphyrii Philosophi Fragmenta* (BSGRT), Stutgardiae et Lipsiae, 1993.
Steuchus A., *De perenni philosophia*, Lugduni, 1540.
Strycker É. de, *La forme la plus ancienne du Protévangile de Jacques. Recherches sur le papyrus Bodmer 5 avec une édition critique du texte grec et une traduction annotée* (SHG 33), Bruxelles, 1961.
Suchla B.R., *Corpus Dionysiacum*, I (PTS 33), Berlin-New York, 1990.

Viteau M.J., *Passions des Saints Écaterine et Pierre d'Alexandrie*, Paris, 1897.

Wachsmuth C. – Hense O., *Ioannis Stobaei Anthologium*, I–IV, Berolini, 1884 ff., repr. 1958.
Waddell W.G., *Manetho*, London-Cambridge Mass., 1940.
Wehrli F., *Die Schule des Aristoteles. Texte und Kommentar*, Heft VII: *Herakleides Pontikos*, Basel-Stuttgart, 1969².
Winiarczyk M., *Diagorae Melii et Theodori Cyrenaei reliquiae* (BSGRT), Leipzig, 1981.
Wolff G., *Porphyrii de philosophia ex oraculis haurienda librorum reliquiae*, Berlin 1856, repr. Hildesheim, 1962.

Literature

Alfaric P., *Les Écritures manichéennes*, 2 vols., Paris, 1918.
Athanassiadi P., *Damascius. The Philosophical History. Text with translation and notes*, Athens, 1999.

Baldus H.R., "Die Gesandtschaftsreise des Poplas. Zu einem ungewöhnlichen Münztyp Milets unter Commodus", *Chiron* 15 (1985), pp. 187–197.

Batiffol P., "Oracula hellenica", *RB* 13 (1916), pp. 177–199.

Bauer A., *Die Chronik des Hippolytos im Matritensis Graecus 121 nebst einer Abhandlung über den Stadiasmus Maris Magni von Otto Cuntz* (TU, N.F. XIV,1), Leipzig, 1905.

Bauer J.B., "Oracula Sibyllina I 323 ab", *ZNW* 47 (1956), pp. 284–285.

Bean G.E., *Journeys in Northern Lycia 1965–1967* (DÖAW.PH 104), Wien, 1971.

Beatrice P.F., "Antistes philosophiae. Ein christenfeindlicher Propagandist am Hofe Diokletians nach dem Zeugnis des Laktanz", in *Ricerche patristiche in onore di Dom Basil Studer* (= *Augustinianum* 33), Rome, 1993, pp. 31–47.

——, "Pagan Wisdom and Christian Theology according to the 'Tübingen Theosophy'", *JECS* 3 (1995), pp. 403–418.

——, "Traditions apocryphes dans la 'Théosophie de Tübingen'", *Apocrypha* 7 (1996), pp. 109–122.

——, "Porphyrius", in *TRE* XXVII (1997), pp. 54–59.

——, "Hellénisme et Christianisme aux premiers siècles de notre ère. Parcours méthodologiques et bibliographiques", *Kernos* 10 (1997), pp. 39–56.

——, "Das Orakel von Baalbek und die sogenannte Sibyllentheosophie", *RQ* 92 (1997), pp. 177–189.

——, "Monophysite Christology in an Oracle of Apollo", *IJCT* 4 (1997/98), pp. 3–22.

——, "Diodore de Sicile chez les Apologistes", in B. Pouderon – J. Doré (eds.), *Les Apologistes chrétiens et la culture grecque* (ThH 105), Paris, 1998, pp. 219–235.

——, "Le livre d'Hystaspe aux mains des Chrétiens", in C. Bonnet – A. Motte (eds.), *Les syncrétismes religieux dans le monde méditerranéen antique* (Institut Historique Belge de Rome. Études de Philologie, d'Archéologie et d'Histoire Anciennes, 36), Bruxelles-Rome, 1999, pp. 357–382.

Brandes W., "Die apokalyptische Literatur", in F. Winkelmann – W. Brandes (Hg.), *Quellen zur Geschichte des frühen Byzanz (4.–9. Jahrhundert). Bestand und Probleme*, Amsterdam, 1990, pp. 305–322.

——, "Anastasios ὁ δίκορος: Endzeiterwartung und Kaiserkritik in Byzanz um 500 n.Chr.", *ByZ* 90 (1997), pp. 24–63.

Bréhier L., "La légende des Sages païens à Byzance", in *Mélanges d'histoire du Moyen-Age Louis Halphen*, Paris, 1951, pp. 61–69.

Brinkmann A., "Die Theosophie des Aristokritos", *RMP* 51 (1896), pp. 273–280.

Brock S., "A Syriac Collection of Prophecies of the Pagan Philosophers", *OLoP* 14 (1983), pp. 203–246, repr. in Idem, *Studies in Syriac Christianity. History, Literature and Theology*, London, 1992, VII.

——, "Some Syriac Excerpts from Greek Collections of Pagan Prophecies", *VigChr* 38 (1984), pp. 77–90.

Broek R. van den, "Four Coptic Fragments of a Greek Theosophy", *Vig Chr* 32 (1978), pp. 118–142.

Cohen S.J.D., "Sosates the Jewish Homer", *HThR* 74 (1981), pp. 391–396.

Collins J.J., *The Sibylline Oracles of Egyptian Judaism* (SBL Diss. Series, 13), Missoula, Montana, 1972.

Colpe C., "Hystaspes", in *RAC* XVI (1994), 1056–1082.

Costanza S., "Sull'utilizzazione di alcune citazioni teologiche nella Cronografia di Giovanni Malala e in due testi agiografici", *ByZ* 52 (1959), pp. 247–252.

Daley B.E., "Apollo as a Chalcedonian: A New Fragment of a Controversial Work from Early Sixth-Century Constantinople", *Traditio* 50 (1995), pp. 31–54.

Delatte A., "Le déclin de la Légende des VII Sages et les Prophéties théosophiques", *MB* 27(1923), pp. 97–111.

Dörrie H., "Theosophia", in *KP* V (1975), 732.

Fowden G., *The Egyptian Hermes. A Historical Approach to the Late Pagan Mind*, Cambridge, 1986, repr. Princeton N.J., 1993.
Fritz K. von, "Theosophia", in *PRE* V,2 (1934), 2248–2253.

Gelzer H., *Sextus Julius Africanus und die byzantinische Chronographie*, Leipzig 1880–1898 (repr. New York, 1967).
Graf G., "Zwei dogmatischen Florilegien der Kopten. A. Die kostbare Perle", *OrChrP* 3 (1937), pp. 49–77.
——, *Geschichte der christlichen arabischen Literatur*, I. Band: *Die Übersetzungen* (StT 118), Città del Vaticano, 1944.
Grant R.M., "Greek Literature in the Treatise 'De Trinitate' and Cyril 'Contra Julianum'", *JThS* 15 (1964), pp. 265–279.
Grillmeier A., *Christ in Christian Tradition*, vol. II: *From the Council of Chalcedon (451) to Gregory the Great (590–604)*, part 1: *Reception and contradiction. The development of the discussion about Chalcedon from 451 to the beginning of the reign of Justinian*, Engl. tr., London-Oxford, 1987.
—— (in collaboration with Th. Hainthaler), *Christ in Christian Tradition*, vol. II: *From the Council of Chalcedon (451) to Gregory the Great (590–604)*, part 2: *The Church of Constantinople in the sixth century*, Engl. tr., London-Louisville, 1995.

Hall A.S., "The Klarian Oracle at Oenoanda", *ZPE* 32 (1978), pp. 263–268.
Hinnells J.R., "The Zoroastrian Doctrine of Salvation in the Roman World. A Study of the Oracle of Hystaspes", in E.J. Sharpe – J.R. Hinnells (eds.), *Man and his Salvation. Studies in Memory of S.G.F. Brandon*, Manchester, 1973, pp. 125–148.

Jacoby F., "Excerpta Barbari", in *PRE* VI,2 (1909), 1566–1576.
Jeffreys E. – Croke B. – Scott R. (eds.), *Studies in Malalas* (Byzantina Australiensia, 6), Sydney, 1990.
Jeffreys E., "The Chronicle of John Malalas, Book I: A Commentary", in P. Allen – E. Jeffreys (eds.), *The Sixth Century. End or Beginning?* (Byzantina Australiensia, 10), Brisbane, 1996, pp. 52–74.
Jones C.P., "An Epigram on Apollonius of Tyana", *JHS* 100 (1980), pp. 190–194.

Klostermann E. – Seeberg E., *Die Apologie der Heiligen Katharina* (SKG.G I,2), Berlin, 1924.

Lamoreaux J.C., "The Provenance of Ecumenius' Commentary on the Apocalypse", *VigChr* 52 (1998), pp. 88–108.
Lane Fox R., *Pagans and Christians in the Mediterranean World from the Second Century A.D. to the Conversion of Constantine*, London, 1988².
Lantschoot A. van, "Trois pseudo-prophéties messianiques inédites", *Muséon* 73 (1960), pp. 27–32.
Levin S., "The Old Greek Oracles in Decline", in W. Haase (ed.), *ANRW* II.18.2, Berlin-New York, 1989, pp. 1599–1649.
Lewy H., *Chaldaean Oracles and Theurgy. Mysticism, Magic, and Neoplatonism in the Later Roman Empire*, nouv. éd. par M. Tardieu (Études Augustiniennes), Paris, 1978.
Lieu S.N.C., "An Early Byzantine Formula for the Renunciation of Manichaeism: the 'Capita VII contra Manichaeos' of Zacharias of Mytilene", *JAC* 26 (1983), pp. 152–218.

Mango C., "The Conversion of the Parthenon into a Church: the Tübingen Theosophy", *DCAH* 18 (1995), pp. 201–203.
Moraux P., "Notes sur la tradition indirecte du 'De caelo' d'Aristote", *Hermes* 82 (1954), pp. 145–182.
Neumann K.J., "Heraclitea", *Hermes* 15 (1880), pp. 605–608.

Neuman, K.J., "Über eine den Brief an Diognet enthaltende Tübinger Handschrift Pseudo-Justin's", *ZKG* 4 (1881), pp. 284–287.
Nock A.D., "Oracles théologiques", *REA* 30 (1928), pp. 280–290, repr. in Idem, *Essays on Religion and the Ancient World*, ed. by Z. Stewart, Oxford, 1972, vol. I, pp. 160–168.
——, "The exegesis of Timaeus 28 C", *VigChr* 16 (1962), pp. 79–86.

Ogilvie R.M., *The Library of Lactantius*, Oxford, 1978.

Parke H.W., *The Oracles of Apollo in Asia Minor*, London-Sydney, 1985.
——, *Sibyls and Sibylline Prophecy in Classical Antiquity*, London-New York, 1988.
Pépin J., "Grégoire de Nazianze, lecteur de la littérature hermétique", *VigChr* 36 (1982), pp. 251–260.
Premerstein A. von, "Griechisch-heidnische Weise als Verkünder christlicher Lehre in Handschriften und Kirchenmalereien", in *Festschrift der Nationalbibliothek in Wien*, hrsg. zur Feier des 200 jährigen Bestehens des Gabäudes, Wien, 1926, pp. 647–666.
——, "Neues zu den apokryphen Heilsprophezeiungen heidnischer Philosophen in Literatur und Kirchenkunst", *BNGJ* 9 (1930/1–1931/2), pp. 338–374.

Riedweg C., *Jüdisch-hellenistische Imitation eines orphischen Hieros Logos. Beobachtungen zu OF 245 und 247 (sog. Testament des Orpheus)* (Classica Monacensia, 7), Tübingen, 1993.
——, *Ps.-Justin (Markell von Ankyra?). Ad Graecos de vera religione (bisher 'Cohortatio ad Graecos')*. *Einleitung und Kommentar* (SBA 25/1–2), Basel, 1994.
Robert L., "Trois oracles de la Théosophie et un prophète d'Apollon", *CRAI* 1968, pp. 568–599.
——, "Un oracle gravé à Oinoanda", *CRAI* 1971, pp. 597–619 (both articles are reprinted in Idem, *Opera Minora Selecta*, V, Amsterdam, 1989, pp. 584–639).
Robinson Th. L., *Theological Oracles and the Sanctuaries of Claros and Didyma*, Harvard diss., 1981.

Saffrey H.D., "Connaissance et inconnaissance de Dieu: Porphyre et la 'Théosophie de Tübingen'", in J. Duffy and J. Peradotto (eds.), *Gonimos. Neoplatonic and Byzantine Studies presented to Leendert G. Westerink at 75*, Buffalo N.Y., 1988, pp. 1–20, repr. in Idem, *Recherches sur le néoplatonisme après Plotin* (Histoire des doctrines de l'Antiquité Classique, 14), Paris, 1990, pp. 11–30.
Siémons J.L., *Théosophia. Aux sources néoplatoniciennes et chrétiennes (2ᵉ–6ᵉ siècles)*, Paris, 1988.
Spetsieris K., "Eikones hellenon philosophon eis ekklesias", *EEPS*, II series, 14 (1963/64), pp. 386–458.
Speyer W., "Zum Bild des Apollonios von Tyana bei Heiden und Christen", *JAC* 17 (1974), pp. 47–63, repr. in Idem, *Frühes Christentum im antiken Strahlungsfeld. Ausgewählte Aufsätze* (WUNT 50), Tübingen, 1989, pp. 176–192.

Walter N., *Der Thoraausleger Aristobulos. Untersuchungen zu seinen Fragmenten und zu pseudepigraphischen Resten der jüdisch-hellenistischen Literatur* (TU 86), Berlin, 1964.
West M.L., *The Orphic Poems*, Oxford, 1983.
Windisch H., *Die Orakel des Hystaspes* (Verhandelingen der koninklijke Akademie van Wetenschappen te Amsterdam Afdeeling Letterkunde Nieuwe Reeks, deel XXVIII, No. 3), Amsterdam, 1929.

Zeegers-Vander Vorst N., *Les citations des poètes grecs chez les apologistes chrétiens du IIᵉ siècle* (Université de Louvain, Recueil de travaux d' histoire et de philologie, 4ᵉ série, fasc. 47), Louvain, 1972.

NOMINA PHILOLOGORUM IN
APPARATU LAUDATORUM

Alexander
Alexandre
Bauer (A. Bauer)
J.B. Bauer
Beatrice
Bentley
Bidez
Brandt
Bratke
Buresch
Burguière
Burkert
Castalio
Cumont
Daley
Delatte
Diels
Dindorf
Dübner
Elter
Erbse (1995)
Erbse diss. (1941)
Ferguson
Festugière
Frick
Geffcken
Gelzer
Hadot
Hall
Hartel
Helm

Holladay
Jacoby
Jaekel
Jones
Jugie
Kannicht
Kaufmann
Kern
Koerte
Kroll
Kurfess
Lewy
Maass
Maehler
Mai
Marcovich
Mendelssohn
Mitteis
Monat
Moraux
Mosshammer
Mras
Mullach
Nauck
Neumann
Nock
Pease
Piccolos
Pitra
Preger
Radt

Riedweg
Robert
Robinson
Routh
Rzach
Sackur
Scaliger
Schenkl
Scher
Schoene
Scott
Sedulius
Smith
Snell
Stadtmüller
Stephanus
Steuchus
Struve
Strycker de
Sylburg
Thierfelder
Youtie
Wachsmuth
Waddell
Wehrli
Wesseling
Wilamowitz
Windisch
Winiarczyk
Wolff

CONSPECTUS SIGLORUM CODICUM ADHIBITORUM

A	=	Athen. B.N. gr. 2725 (suppl. 725), saec. XV/XVI
A'	=	Ambros. 569, saec. XVI (ed. Mai)
A"	=	Paris. gr. 451, saec. X
B	=	Neapol. Borb. II F 9, saec. XIV
B'	=	Oxon. Barocc. gr. 50, saec. XI
B"	=	Monac. 351, saec. XV
C	=	Cremon. 160, saec. XV
D	=	Mutinensis misc. gr. 126, saec. XI–XIV (olim III.D.7)
D'	=	Paris. gr. 467, saec. XVI
E	=	Matritensis gr. 115, saec. XV
E'	=	Paris. lat. B.N. 4884, saec. VIII (Excerpta Barbari)
F	=	Athen. B.N. gr. 1070 (olim 32), saec. XIII
F'	=	Laurent. pl. 55, 7, saec. XV
F"	=	Laurent. pl. 11, 17, saec. XV
H	=	Ambros. E 64 sup., saec. XV
H'	=	Matritensis gr. 4701 (olim N–121), saec. X–XI
K	=	Athous gr. 1527 (Karakallou 14), saec. XII
L	=	Laurent. pl. 32,16, saec. XIII
L'	=	Lips. Univ. 70, saec. XVI
L"	=	Paris. gr. 2850, saec. XV (a.D.1475)
M	=	Marcian. gr. 573, saec. IX–X
M'	=	Paris. gr. 2665, saec. XIV/V
M"	=	Marcian. class. XI cod.1, saec. XIV/XV
m	=	consensus codd. MF
N	=	Paris. gr. 400, saec. XIV
O	=	Paris. gr. 854, saec. XIII
O'	=	Ottobon. gr. 411, saec. XIV/XV
Ox	=	Barocc. gr. 182, saec. XI/XII (Ioannis Malalae Chronographia)
P	=	Paris. gr. suppl. 690, saec. XII
P'	=	Paris. gr. 1409, saec. XV
P"	=	Paris. gr. 1630, saec. XIV
Pers.	=	codices vaticani a Pitra usurpati
Ps. Iust., Mon. q	=	Paris. gr. 450, saec. XIV
Ps. Iust., Mon. s	=	Argent. gr. 9, saec. XIII/XIV (nunc deperditus)
Q	=	Vatican. gr. 1120, saec. XIV
Q'	=	Paris. gr. 1168, saec. XIII/XIV
Q"	=	Paris. gr. 396, saec. XIII
R	=	Paris. gr. 2851, saec. XV
S	=	Sinait. 327, saec. XV
S'	=	Scorialensis II Σ 7, saec. XV
T	=	Tubingensis Mb 27, saec. XVI
Th	=	Paris. gr. 1171, saec. X, ed. M. Jugie in PO 19, pp. 318–335
U	=	Paris. gr. 2315, saec. XV
V	=	Vat. Pal. gr. 141, saec. XIV
V'	=	Vindob. ph. gr. 110, vol. I, saec. XVI

V"	=	Vindob. th. gr. 153, saec. XIII/XIV
v	=	consensus codicum BLV
W	=	Vindob. gr. 178, saec. XV
W'	=	Vindob. hist. gr. 96, 6, saec. XV
w¹	=	Explanatio somnii, ed. Sackur, pp. 177 ssq.
w²	=	versio Latina eiusdem operis ed. G. Waitz in MGH, Script. XXII, Hannoverae 1872, pp. 375 sq.
w³	=	versio Latina eiusdem operis in cod. Monac. lat. 17742, saec. XII
w⁴	=	versio Latina in cod. Chicago, Newberry Library, Ry. 6, ff. 198–202, saec. XII (olim Lambac. membr. LXXVII)
w⁵	=	versio Latina in eodem codice, ff. 220–224
x	=	consensus codd. B et V
Y	=	Paris. gr. 1336, saec. XI
Z	=	Sinait. 383, saec. X/XI
α	=	Angel. 43, saec. XIV
β	=	Angel. 22, saec. XI
λ	=	Ottobon. gr. 378, saec. XVI
λ₁	=	Vallicell. 137, fasc. 3, saec. XVII
μ	=	Προφητεῖαι ἑπτὰ Ἑλλήνων σοφῶν περὶ τῆς ἐνανθρωπήσεως τοῦ Κυρίου ἡμῶν Ἰησοῦ Χριστοῦ
π	=	Προφητεῖαι τῶν ἑπτὰ σοφῶν
Σ	=	Συμφωνία, Vatican. gr. 2200, saec. VIII/IX, fol. 444–454
Φ	=	redactio Orac. Sib. (consensus codd. S' W')
χ	=	Χρησμοὶ καὶ θεολογίαι Ἑλλήνων φιλοσόφων
Ψ	=	redactio tertia Orac. Sib.
Ω	=	redactio altera Orac. Sib.

COMPENDIA

AP III	=	E. Cougny, Epigrammatum Anthologia Palatina
Art.	=	Kotter, Passio S. Artemii
Cath.	=	Viteau, Passio S. Catharinae
Cedr.	=	Cedrenus, Historiarum Compendium
CH	=	Corpus Hermeticum
Chron.	=	Chronicon Paschale
CSEL	=	Corpus Scriptorum Ecclesiasticorum Latinorum
FGrHist	=	Jacoby, Die Fragmente der griechischen Historiker
MGH	=	Monumenta Germaniae Historica
OGIS	=	Dittenberger, Orientis Graeci Inscriptiones Selectae
Orph. fr.	=	Kern, Orphicorum Fragmenta
PCG	=	Kassel et Austin, Poetae Comici Graeci
schol.	=	Greene, Schol. Plat. Phaedr.
Su.	=	Suda
Suppl. Hell.	=	Lloyd-Jones et Parsons, Supplementum Hellenisticum
SVF	=	ab Arnim, Stoicorum Veterum Fragmenta
TrGF	=	Tragicorum Graecorum Fragmenta

add.	=	addidit	inf.	=	inferior
ampl.	=	amplificavit	ins.	=	inseruit
ap.	=	apud	iter.	=	iteravit
appr.	=	approbavit	lac.	=	lacuna
attr.	=	attribuit	lin.	=	linea
cett.	=	ceteri	mg.	=	in margine
codd.	=	codices	om.	=	omisit
coll.	=	collocavit	prop.	=	proposuit
conf.	=	confirmavit	rec.	=	recipit
coni.	=	coniecit	ref.	=	refert
cont.	=	contendit	rest.	=	restituit
corr.	=	correxit	sec.	=	secundum
def.	=	defendit	secl.	=	seclusit
del.	=	delevit	sign.	=	signavit
dem.	=	demonstravit	sim.	=	similiter
edd.	=	editores	stat.	=	statuit
em.	=	emendavit	sup.	=	superior
exist.	=	existimavit	suppl.	=	supplevit
exp.	=	expunxit	susp.	=	suspicatus est
expl.	=	explevit	tempt.	=	temptavit
incl.	=	inclusit	transp.	=	transposuit

[ ] quadratis uncis inclusi quae dubia aut interpolata videntur
< > obliquis uncis inclusi quae addenda videntur
†† crucibus inclusi quae corrupta sunt necdum sanari potuerunt
<***> lacuna in contextu verborum

TEXT

<EΠITOMH>

1. Ὁ τὸ βιβλίον συγγεγραφώς, ὅπερ ἐπιγέγραπται ΘΕΟΣΟΦΙΑ, διαλαμ-
βάνει κατ᾿ αὐτὸ τὸ προοίμιον, ὅτι συνέγραψε μὲν πρότερον ἑπτὰ βιβλία
ΠΕΡΙ ΤΗΣ ΟΡΘΗΣ ΠΙΣΤΕΩΣ· ἄρτι δὲ τὸ ὄγδοον καὶ τὰ ἐφεξῆς συγγράφει,
δεικνὺς τούς τε χρησμοὺς τῶν Ἑλληνικῶν θεῶν καὶ τὰς λεγομένας θεολογίας   5
τῶν παρ᾿ Ἕλλησι καὶ Αἰγυπτίοις σοφῶν, ἔτι δὲ καὶ τῶν Σιβυλλῶν ἐκείνων
<τοὺς χρησμοὺς> τῷ σκοπῷ τῆς θείας γραφῆς συνάδοντας καὶ ποτὲ μὲν
τὸ πάντων αἴτιον καὶ πρωτοστατοῦν, ποτὲ δὲ τὴν ἐν μιᾷ θεότητι παναγίαν
τριάδα δηλοῦντας.

2. Ἐν μὲν οὖν τῷ πρώτῳ βιβλίῳ, ὅπερ ἐστὶ πρὸς <τὰ ΠΕΡΙ ΤΗΣ ΟΡΘΗΣ   10
ΠΙΣΤΕΩΣ> προσάγον τὸ ὄγδοον, καὶ τοῖς ἐφεξῆς δυσὶ χρησμῶν τοιούτων
μέμνηται καὶ θεολογιῶν. Ἐν δὲ τῷ τετάρτῳ ἢ ἑνδεκάτῳ παράγει χρήσεις
Ὑστάσπου τινὸς βασιλέως Περσῶν ἢ Χαλδαίων, εὐλαβεστάτου, φησί,
γεγονότος καὶ διὰ τοῦτο θείων μυστηρίων ἀποκάλυψιν δεξαμένου περὶ τῆς
τοῦ σωτῆρος ἐνανθρωπήσεως· ἐπὶ τέλει δὲ τοῦ τεύχους χρονικὸν συν-   15
τομώτατον τέθεικεν ἀπὸ Ἀδὰμ ἕως τῶν Ζήνωνος χρόνων, ἐν ᾧ καὶ δι-
ισχυρίζεται μετὰ τὴν συμπλήρωσιν τοῦ ἑξακισχιλιαστοῦ ἔτους γενήσεσθαι
τὴν συντέλειαν.

3. Ἐπεὶ γὰρ γέγραπται, φησί, ὅτι χίλια ἔτη παρὰ <τῷ> κυρίῳ ὡς ἡμέρα
μία (a), ἐν ἓξ δὲ ἡμέραις ὁ θεὸς τὸν κόσμον ποιήσας τῇ ἑβδόμῃ κατέπαυσε   20
(b), πάντως <χρὴ> μετὰ τὴν παρέλευσιν τῶν ἑξακισχιλίων ἐτῶν, ἅπερ ἀντὶ
ἓξ ἡμερῶν λογίζεται, τὰ πάντα καταπαῦσαι. Διὸ καὶ ὁ Χριστὸς ἐν τῷ πεντα-
κισχιλιοστῷ πεντακοσιοστῷ ἔτει ἐνανθρωπήσας, εἴτ᾿ οὖν ἐν τῷ μέσῳ τῆς
ἡμέρας, ἔλεγεν ὅτι ἐσχάτη ὥρα ἐστίν (c).

1–5. cod. T

a) Ps. 89,4; II Pt. 3,8   b) Gen. 2,2   c) I Io. 2,18.

---

1. ΕΠΙΤΟΜΗ *planitatis causa inserui*: Χρησμοὶ τῶν Ἑλληνικῶν θεῶν T Buresch
1. 7 τοὺς χρησμοὺς *ins.* Buresch   **2.** 10–11 πρὸς [lac.1,5 cm] προάγοντα
ὄγδοον T: πρὸς ὀρθὴν πίστιν προάγον τὸ ὄγδοον *em. et suppl.* Buresch, πρὸς
τὰ περὶ τῆς ὀρθῆς πίστεως προσάγον τὸ ὄγδοον *fortasse olim fuisse coni.* Erbse
|| 12 ἑνδεκάτῳ *em.* Buresch: ἑνδεκάτῳ T || χρήσεις: *hoc verbum, quod* Windisch
in libello qui inscribitur 'Die Orakel des Hystaspes' (1929) 'oracula' *seu* 'vaticinia'
barbare vertit, 'excerpta' *significare probavit* Beatrice, 'Le livre d'Hystaspe' (1999),
pp. 361 sqq.   **3.** 19 τῷ *ins.* Erbse || 21 χρὴ *ins.* Buresch

4. Μέμνηται δὲ καθεξῆς καὶ βιβλίων τινῶν παρεγγράπτων ἤτοι ΔΙΑΘΗΚΗΣ   25
τινὸς ΤΟΥ ΚΥΡΙΟΥ ΚΑΙ ΔΙΑΤΑΞΕΩΝ ΤΩΝ ΑΓΙΩΝ ΑΠΟΣΤΟΛΩΝ καὶ ΓΕΝΝΗ-
ΣΕΩΣ ΚΑΙ ΑΝΑΛΗΨΕΩΣ ΤΗΣ ΑΧΡΑΝΤΟΥ ΔΕΣΠΟΙΝΗΣ ΗΜΩΝ ΘΕΟΤΟΚΟΥ.

5. ΘΕΟΣΟΦΙΑ δὲ τὸ βιβλίον ἐπέγραψεν, ἢ ὅτι παρὰ θεοῦ σοφισθεὶς ἠδυνήθη
τὴν πραγματείαν ἐκθεῖναι ταύτην, ἢ ὅτι αὐτὰ τὰ γεγραμμένα περὶ τῆς τοῦ
θεοῦ σοφίας διδάσκει, ἢ μᾶλλον διὰ τὸ ὑπὸ τοῦ θεοῦ καὶ τοὺς Ἕλληνας   30
σοφισθῆναι ὡς αὐτὸς ἐν <τῷ> προοιμίῳ λέγει.

---

4. 26 διατάξεων *corr.* Neumann: διατάξεως Τ διαταγῶν *fortasse olim fuisse coni.*
Erbse ‖ 26–27 γεννήσεως κτλ.: *opere vulgo* 'Protevangelium Iacobi' *dicto auctor
usus est; vide infra* Chron. VIII, 3,6–17   **5.** 31 τῷ *addidi*

ΘΕΟΣΟΦΙΑ

<ΠΡΟΟΙΜΙΟΝ>

1. Ἐν ἐμαυτῷ γάρ, φησί, γενόμενος πολλάκις τῆς θεοσοφίας τὸ ἄφθονον ἐνενόησα, ὅτι ὡς ἐκ πηγῆς διαρκοῦς ὀχετεύουσα τὴν γνῶσιν καὶ εἰς Ἕλληνας ἤδη καὶ βαρβάρους προῆλθεν, οὐδενί γε τῶν ἐθνῶν τῆς σωτηρίας βασκαίνουσα. 'θεὸς γὰρ οὐδεὶς δύσνους ἀνθρώποις', φησὶν ὁ Πλάτων· καὶ   5
ἡ Σοφία· 'φείδῃ δὲ πάντων, ὅτι πάντα σά ἐστι, δέσποτα φιλόψυχε, καὶ τὸ ἄφθαρτόν σου πνεῦμά ἐστιν ἐν πᾶσιν' (a).

2. Ὅτι οὐ δεῖ ἀποβάλλειν τὰς τῶν σοφῶν ἀνδρῶν Ἑλλήνων περὶ τοῦ θεοῦ μαρτυρίας. Ἐπεὶ γὰρ οὐκ ἔστι τὸν θεὸν τοῖς ἀνθρώποις φαινόμενον δια-λέγεσθαι, τὰς τῶν ἀγαθῶν ἀνδρῶν ἐννοίας ἀνακινῶν ἐκείνους διδασκάλους   10
τῷ πολλῷ ὄχλῳ παρέχεται. Ὥστε ὅστις ἀθετεῖ τὰς τοιαύτας μαρτυρίας, ἀθετεῖ καὶ τὸν θεὸν τὸν [ἐπὶ] ταύτας κινήσαντα.

3. Ὅτι τινὲς ἐδόξασαν τὸν Ἀπόλλωνα εἶναι καὶ Ἥλιον· Αἰγύπτιοι δὲ τὸν Ἥλιον Ὄσιριν ὠνόμασαν· μεθερμηνεύεται δὲ Ἑλληνικῇ διαλέκτῳ Ὄσιρις

1–6. cod. T

---

1. 5 Plat., Theaet. 151 d 1   **3.** 13–19 Diod., Bibl. I,11,1–3 (cf. Eus., P.E. I,9,1–3): Τοὺς δ' οὖν κατ' Αἴγυπτον ἀνθρώπους . . . ὑπολαβεῖν δύο θεοὺς ἀϊδίους τε καὶ πρώτους, τόν τε ἥλιον καὶ τὴν σηλήνην, ὧν τὸν μὲν Ὄσιριν, τὴν δὲ Ἶσιν ὀνομάσαι . . . Μεθερμηνευομένων γὰρ τούτων εἰς τὸν Ἑλληνικὸν τῆς διαλέκτου τρόπον εἶναι τὸν μὲν Ὄσιριν πολυόφθαλμον, εἰκότως· πάντη γὰρ ἐπιβάλλοντα τὰς ἀκτῖνας ὥσπερ ὀφθαλμοῖς πολλοῖς βλέπειν ἅπασαν γῆν καὶ θάλατταν . . . Τῶν δὲ παρ' Ἕλλησι παλαιῶν μυθολόγων τινὲς τὸν Ὄσιριν Διόνυσον προσονομάζουσιν καὶ Σείριον παρωνύμως. Ὧν Εὔμολπος μὲν ἐν τοῖς Βακχικοῖς ἔπεσί φησιν·

ἀστροφαῆ Διόνυσον ἐν ἀκτίνεσσι πυρωπόν,
Ὀρφεὺς δὲ
τοὔνεκά μιν καλέουσι Φάνητά τε καὶ Διόνυσον (fr. 237,3 Kern).

---

a) Sap. Sal., 11,26–12,1

---

1. ΠΡΟΟΙΜΙΟΝ *planitatis causa inserui*
1. 2 τὸ ἄφθονον *cf.* Plat., Tim. 29 e 1 ‖ 3 ἐκ πηγῆς κτλ. *cf.* Thdrt., Graec. aff. cur. VIII,2–3: Εὐπετὲς μὲν γὰρ ἦν καὶ μάλα ῥάδιον τῇ τῆς σοφίας πηγῇ κτλ. Ἀλλ' οὐκ ἐβουλήθη πέντε ἢ δέκα ἢ πεντεκαίδεκα ἢ ἑκατὸν ἢ δὶς τοσούτους τῶν σωτηρίων ἀπολαῦσαι ναμάτων, ἀλλὰ πάντας ἀνθρώπους, καὶ Ἕλληνας καὶ βαρβάρους κτλ. ‖ 5 θεὸς γὰρ οὐδεὶς T: οὐδεὶς θεὸς Plat. ‖ 6 πάντα *om.* Sap. Sal. ‖ καὶ τὸ T: τὸ γὰρ Sap. Sal.   **2.** 8 ἀνδρῶν T: ἀνδρῶν *em.* Buresch ‖ 10 ἐκείνους *malit* Erbse: ἐκείνας T **3.** 13 Ὅτι τινὲς ἐδόξασαν τὸν Ἀπόλλωνα εἶναι καὶ Ἥλιον: *cf.* Eus., P.E. III,15,3 ‖ 13–14 τὸν ἥλιον ὄσιριν *recte transp.* Erbse: τὸν ὄσιριν ἥλιον T Buresch

ὁ πολυ<ό>φθαλμος ἀπὸ τοῦ πάντῃ ἐπιβάλλοντα τὸν ἥλιον τὰς ἀκτῖνας   15
ὥσπερ ὀφθαλμοῖς πολλοῖς πᾶσαν βλέπειν τὴν γῆν. Τινὲς δὲ τῶν Ἑλλήνων
καὶ Σ<ε>ίριον αὐτὸν παρωνύμως ὠνόμασαν, ἕτεροι δὲ Διόνυσον ὡς καὶ
Ὀρφεύς·

  Τοὔνεκά μιν καλέουσι Φάνητά τε καὶ Διόνυσον.

4. Ὅτι οἱ παλαιοὶ τὸ ὑγρὸν Ὠκεάνην προσηγόρευσαν. Δηλοῖ δὲ τὸ ὄνομα   20
τροφὴν [ἢ] μητέρα.

5. Ὅτι Ἀριστόβουλος, ὁ ἐξ Ἑβραίων περιπατητικὸς φιλόσοφος, ἐπιστέλλων
Π<τ>ολεμαίῳ συνωμολόγησεν ἐκ τῆς Ἑβραϊκῆς θεοσοφίας τὴν Ἑλληνικὴν
ὡρμῆσθαι· ʻφανερὸν γάρ ἐστιν, ὅτι κατηκολούθησεν ὁ Πλάτων τῇ καθ᾽
ἡμᾶς νομοθεσίᾳ καὶ δῆλός ἐστι περιειργασμένος ἕκαστα τῶν ἐν αὐτῇʼ.   25

6. Ὅτι Διόδωρος ὁ Σικελιώτης ἐν τριάκοντα, ὥς φησιν, ἔτεσι δι᾽ ἀκρίβειαν
μαθήσεως τὰς Εὐρώπης καὶ Ἀσίας βιβλιοθήκας περιελθὼν καὶ τοὺς
ἀρχαίους ἀναγνοὺς μ᾽ βιβλία συντέταχεν.

---

4. 20–21 Diod., Bibl. I,12,5 (cf. Eus., P.E. III,3,5): Τὸ δ᾽ ὑγρὸν ὀνομάσαι
λέγουσι τοὺς παλαιοὺς Ὠκεάνην, ὃ μεθερμηνευόμενον μὲν εἶναι τροφὴν μητέρα.
5. 24–25 Aristobulus fr. 3 ap. Eus., P.E. XIII,12,1   **6.** 26–28 Ps.Iust.,
Coh. 9,3: Καὶ ὁ ἐνδοξότατος δὲ παρ᾽ ὑμῖν τῶν ἱστοριογράφων, Διόδωρος ὁ
τὰς βιβλιοθήκας ἐπιτεμών, ἐν τριάκοντα ὅλοις ἔτεσιν Ἀσίαν τε καὶ Εὐρώπην,
ὡς αὐτὸς γέγραφεν (cf. Diod., Bibl. I,4,1), διὰ πολλὴν ἀκρίβειαν περιελθὼν
καὶ αὐτόπτης τῶν πλείστων γεγονώς, τεσσαράκοντα ὅλα τῆς ἑαυτοῦ ἱστορίας
βιβλία γέγραφεν.

---

3. 15 πολύφθαλμος T: *em.* Buresch *cf.* Plut., De Is. Os. 10 ‖ 17 σίριον T:
em. Erbse **4.** 20 ὠκεάνην *scripsi duce* Wesseling: ὠκεανόν *cett.* ‖ 21 τροφὴν
μητέρα *scripsi*: τροφὴν ἢ μητέρα T Buresch Erbse τροφῆς μητέρα Mras ‖ *de
utraque coniectura vide* Beatrice, 'Diodore de Sicile' (1998), pp. 233 sqq. **5.** 23
πολεμαίῳ T: *suppl.* Buresch ‖ θεοσοφίας T: φιλοσοφίας Eus. ‖ 24 γάρ ἐστιν
om. Eus. ‖ 25 δῆλος T: φανερός Eus. **6.** 28 συντέταχεν: συνέταγεν T:
συντέταγεν Buresch Erbse

⟨ΒΙΒΛΙΟΝ Α΄

ΧΡΗΣΜΟΙ ΤΩΝ ΕΛΛΗΝΙΚΩΝ ΘΕΩΝ⟩

1. Ὅτι αἰτήσαντός τινος διδαχθῆναι παρὰ τοῦ Ἀπόλλωνος, ὁποῖος ἄν τις
εἴη ὁ πάντων ποιητής, ὁ Ἀπόλλων ἔχρησεν οὕτως·

    Βαβαί, οὐ περὶ μικρῶν ἥκεις <λόγων.>   5
    Τὸν οὐρανοῦ τύραννον ἐκμαθεῖν θέλεις,
    ὃν οὐδ᾽ ἐγὼ κάτοιδα, πλὴν σέβω νόμῳ.
    Λόγος γάρ ἐστι καὶ λόγου πατὴρ γεγὼς
    τὸν οὐρανὸν διέταξε καὶ τὴν γῆν ὅλην.

Ὅτι μὲν γὰρ ἔστι, φησί, καὶ ὅτι υἱὸν ἔχει λόγον, οἶδα καὶ εἰδὼς σέβω·   10
πηλίκος δὲ καὶ οἷος, ἀγνοῶ.

2. Ὅτι Θεοφίλου τινὸς τοὔνομα τὸν Ἀπόλλωνα ἐρωτήσαντος· ᾽σὺ εἶ θεὸς
ἢ ἄλλος;᾽, ἔχρησεν οὕτως·

    Ἔσθ᾽, ὑπερουρανίου κύτεος καθύπερθε λελογχώς,
    φλογμὸς ἀπειρέσιος, κινούμενος, ἄπλετος αἰών·   15
    ἔστι δ᾽ ἐνὶ μακάρεσσιν ἀμήχανος, εἰ μὴ ἑαυτὸν
    βουλὰς βουλεύσῃσι πατὴρ μέγας, ὡς ἐσιδέσθαι.
5   Ἔνθα μὲν οὔτ᾽ αἰθὴρ φέρει ἀστέρας ἀγλαοφεγγεῖς
    οὔτε σεληναίη λιγυφεγγέτις αἰωρεῖται,
    οὐ θεὸς ἀντιάει κατ᾽ ἀταρπιτόν, οὐδ᾽ ἐγὼ αὐτὸς   20
    ἀκτῖσιν συνέχων ἐπικίδναμαι αἰθεροδινής.
    Ἀλλὰ πέλει πυρσοῖο θεὸς περιμήκετος αὐλῶν,
10   ἕρπων εἰλίγδην, ῥοιζούμενος, οὔ κεν ἐκείνου

---

1. cod. T
2. codd. Tv; cf. AP III 6, 140. αὐτοφυής—ἡμεῖς laudat Lact., Div. Inst.
I,7,1

1–2. ΒΙΒΛΙΟΝ Α΄ ΧΡΗΣΜΟΙ ΤΩΝ ΕΛΛΗΝΙΚΩΝ ΘΕΩΝ *planitatis causa inserui*
1. 5 *lac. verbo* λόγων *expl.* Snell Erbse; *verbo* βροτέ Buresch   **2.** 12 ὅτι *om.*
v || τοὔνομα *om.* LP᾽ || 14 ὑπερουρανίου T Buresch Robinson: ὑπὲρ οὐρανίου
Steuchus Piccolos Wolff Erbse || 16 ἔστι v: εἰσὶ T ᾽malim legere ἔστι᾽ T
mg. εἶσι Buresch Lewy || δ᾽ v δὲ T || 17 ἐσιδέσθαι: ἐσιδ[᾽] T || 18 ἔνθα
μὲν: ἔνθα κεν L Piccolos ἔνθακεν B ἐνθάκε Steuchus ἔνθαπερ Wolff || οὔτ᾽
coni. Piccolos: οὐδ᾽ Tv || φέροι Piccolos || ἀγλαοφανεῖς T || 19 σεληναία
Steuchus || 20 αὐτοῖς T || 21 συνέχων: συνεὼν *coni.* Wolff || 22 θεὸς
T: θεοῦ v Piccolos Wolff Lewy || 23 οὔ κεν Buresch Erbse Robinson:
οὐ μὲν Tv Piccolos Wolff

ἁψάμενος πυρὸς αἰθερίου δαίσειέ τις ἦτορ·
οὐ γὰρ ἔχει δαίην, ἀζηχεῖ δ᾽ ἐν μελεδηθμῷ   25
αἰὼν αἰώνεσσ᾽ ἐπιμίγνυται ἐκ θεοῦ αὐτοῦ.
Αὐτοφυής, ἀδίδακτος, ἀμήτωρ, ἀστυφέλικτος,
15 οὔνομα μηδὲ λόγῳ χωρούμενος, ἐν πυρὶ ναίων,
τοῦτο θεός· μικρὰ δὲ θεοῦ μερὶς ἄγγελοι ἡμεῖς.

3. Ἔστι, φησί, πῦρ ὑπεράνω τῆς κοιλότητος τοῦ οὐρανοῦ διηνεκῶς   30
κινούμενον, ἄπειρον ὑπάρχον καὶ μηδὲ ταῖς οὐρανίαις δυνάμεσι θεωρητόν,
εἰ μὴ ἑαυτὸν ὁ πατὴρ παρασκευάσει ὀφθῆναι. Καὶ τῷ αἰθέρι δὲ καὶ τοῖς
ἄστράσι καὶ τῇ σελήνῃ καὶ τοῖς λεγομένοις θεοῖς ἄγνωστός ἐστι ἡ ὁδὸς
τοῦ νοητοῦ πυρὸς καὶ ἐμοί, φησί, αὐτῷ τῷ Ἡλίῳ. Διὰ τοῦτο δὲ, φησί, πᾶσι
φοβερόν ἐστι ἐκεῖνο τὸ πῦρ, διότι ὁ μακρότατος αὐτοῦ αὐλών, εἴτ᾽ οὖν ἡ   35
κατ᾽ εὐθεῖαν ὀξεῖα ὁρμή, μετὰ συστροφῆς καὶ ἤχου γίνεται. Οὗτινος πυρὸς
ὁ ἁψάμενος οὐκέτι μερίσειε τὴν ἑαυτοῦ ψυχὴν πρὸς τὰ αἰσθητά· οὐ γὰρ
ἔχει μερισμὸν ἐκεῖνο τὸ πῦρ, ἀλλ᾽ ἀεὶ ἀϊδίως τοῖς ἀϊδίοις ἐπιμίγνυται. Τὸ
δὲ ὄνομα αὐτοῦ οὐδὲ εἰπεῖν τις δύναται. Τοῦτο οὖν, φησί, τὸ πῦρ ἀληθῶς
θεός, ἡμεῖς δὲ ἐλαχίστη δύναμις ἀγγελικὴ ὑπάρχομεν.   40

4. Τὰ δὲ ἀκόλουθα καὶ ἐν ἑτέρῳ χρησμῷ διεξῆλθεν, εἰπὼν οὕτως·

Ἔσθ᾽ ὑπερουρανίου πυρὸς ἄφθιτος αἰθομένη φλόξ,
ζωογόνος, πάντων πηγή, πάντων δὲ καὶ ἀρχή,
ἥτε φύει μάλα πάντα φύουσά τε πάντ᾽ ἀναλύει.

Πάντα μὲν φύει τὰ καλὰ δημιουργικῶς, πάντα δὲ τὰ φαῦλα προνοητικῶς   45
ἀναλίσκει.

5. Ὅτι ἐρωτήσαντός ποτε τοῦ ἱερέως τὸν Ἀπόλλωνα περὶ τῆς μελλούσης
κρατεῖν θρησκείας, παράδοξον εἶπε χρησμὸν τοιοῦτον ὅστις εὕρηται ἐν

---

3. cod. T
4. codd. Tv; cf. AP III 6, 148
5. Totum oraculum codd. MF (= m) continent; excerpta oraculi accedunt
in variis aliis codicibus quorum praecipui sunt Σ χ Cath. P E Tv Art.; cf.
AP III 6, 149

---

2. 24 δαίσειέ τις Piccolos δείσειέ τις Steuchus Wolff ‖ 25 δαίειν Piccolos
Wolff ‖ μελεδηθμῷ B μελεθμῷ C F᾽ ‖ 26 αἰώνεσσ᾽ T αἰῶσιν v Piccolos
Wolff ‖ 28 χωρούμενος: χωρούμενον Sedulius Steuchus Wolff ‖ μηδὲ λόγῳ
χωρούμενος: μὴ χωρῶν, πολυώνυμος *Oenoandae inscriptio* (*cf.* Hall) ‖ 29 μικρὰ
δὲ θεοῦ μερὶς T: μικρὴ δὲ μερὶς θεοῦ v Piccolos μικρὰ δὲ θεοῦ μερὶς Wolff
3. 32 παρασκευάσῃ Buresch ‖ 37 οὐκέτι T: οὔ κεν *vel* οὐκ ἂν Buresch
4. 41 δὲ *om.* T ‖ 42 ὑπερουρανίου TLP᾽ Piccolos Buresch Robinson: ὑπὲρ
οὐρανίου Wolff Erbse ‖ ἄφθιτος T: ἀφθίτου v Piccolos Wolff ‖ 44 ἥ τε
Piccolos ‖ πάντ᾽ ἀναλύει Buresch Erbse: πάντ᾽ ἀναλίσκει Tv *praeter* x (πάντ᾽
ἀνάσῃ B πάντ᾽ ἀνάσσῃ V) πάντ᾽ ἀναλύσει Wolff   **5.** 47–48 Ὅτι ἐρωτήσαντός
ποτε- χρησμὸν τοιοῦτον T; *introductionem aliam oraculi praebent* PF: Ὅτι ὁ
ψευδώνυμος τῶν Ἑλλήνων θεὸς Ἀπόλλων ἐρωτηθεὶς ὑπὸ (πυνθανομένου αὐτοῦ
P) τινος τῶν αὐτοῦ (αὐτοῦ P) ἱερέων (ἱερείων F) περὶ τοῦ Χριστοῦ χρησμὸν
ἔφησε τόνδε (ἔφησεν· ἔχει δὲ ὧδε P). *Refert* M: τὸν χρησμὸν ... ὃν λέγεται
πεποιηκέναι πρός τινα τῶν αὐτοῦ ἱερέων (μιαιρέων M), πυνθανόμενον αὐτοῦ
(ποιθμένον αὐτὸν M) περὶ τοῦ Χριστοῦ, ὁ ψευδώνυμος τῶν Ἑλλήνων θεὸς
Ἀπόλλων ‖ 48 ὅστις εὕρηται M: ὃς καὶ εὕρηται F εὕρηται δὲ P

Δελφοῖς εἰκὸς τῷ πέμπτῳ ἔτει τῆς βασιλείας Ἀναστασίου, μηνὶ αὐγούστῳ
ιη΄, ἰνδικτιῶνος δ΄, ἡμέρᾳ α΄, γενομένης ἐπομβρίας μεγάλης κατακλυσμοῦ 50
δύναμιν ἐχούσης, ἐγγεγραμμένος ἐν πλακὶ καὶ ἀποκείμενος εἰς τὰ θειμέλια
τοῦ ναοῦ τοῦ αὐτοῦ εἰδωλείου·

    Μὴ ὄφελες πύματόν με καὶ ὕστατον ἐξερέεσθαι,
    δύσμορ᾽ ἐμῶν προπόλων, περὶ θεσπεσίοιο θεοῖο
    ἀμφί τε τηλυγέτοιο πανομφαίου βασιλῆος   55
    καὶ πνοιῆς τῆς πάντα πέριξ βοτρυδὸν ἐχούσης,
  5 τείρεα φῶς ποταμοὺς χθόνα Τάρταρον ἠέρα καὶ πῦρ,
    ἥ με καὶ οὐκ ἐθέλοντα δόμων ἀπὸ τῶνδε διώκει·
    αὐτίκ᾽, ἐρημαῖος δὲ λελείψεται οὐδὸς ἀφήτωρ.
    Ἥδε <τ᾽> ἐμοὶ τριπόδων ἐπιλείπεται ἠριγένεια.   60

Εἶτα ἐμπαθῶς ἀνοιμώξας ἐπήγαγεν·

    Αἲ αἴ ἐμοί, τρίποδες, στοναχήσατε· ἐμπεπύρισμαι
  10 καὶ τοῦδ᾽ οὐκ ἐθέλων ἐλήλαμαι δόμου, οἴχετ᾽ Ἀπόλλων,
    οἴχετ᾽, ἐπεὶ βροτὸς εἷς με βιάζεται, οὐράνιος φώς.

---

49 *post* Δελφοῖς *add.* M: τῆς Θεσσαλονίκης *et* PF: τῆς Ἰταλίας || 49–50 εἰκὸς
τῷ πέμπτῳ ἔτει τῆς βασιλείας Ἀναστασίου, μηνὶ Αὐγούστῳ ιη΄, ἰνδικτιῶνος
δ΄, ἡμέρᾳ α΄ *scripsi*: εἰκὸς τῷ πρώτῳ ἔτει M κα΄ ετ F εἰκαστὸν πρῶτον ἔτος
P || *post* Ἀναστασίου *add.* M: μηνὶ Αὐγούστῳ ιη΄, ἰνδικτιῶνος δ΄, ἡμέρᾳ β΄
|| 51 ἐν πλακὶ καὶ ἀποκείμενος *om.* F || τὰ θεμέλια MP: τὸ θεμέλιον F ||
52 ναοῦ τοῦ M: *om. cett.* || εἰδωλείου Erbse: εἰδωλίου M εἰδώλου FP || ἔχει
δὲ ὁ χρησμὸς οὕτως *in codicibus* MF *ante initium oraculi posita sunt* || 53 μ᾽ *ante*
ὄφελες *om.* MT || με MT: τε FP || ἐξερέεσθαι m Dübner: αὐτὸς ἐρέεσθαι
Tv Piccolos || 54 δύσμορ᾽ ἐμῶν m Dübner: δύστηνε Tv Piccolos Wolff
Buresch Erbse || θεσπεσίοιο θεοῖο m Dübner: θεσπεσίου γενετῆρος Tv ||
55 ἀμφί τε τηλυγέτοιο πανομφαίου βασιλῆος Tv: *om.* m Art. τηλυγέτου Piccolos
|| 56 τῆς – ἐχούσης m Dübner Wolff: ἢ – εἴσχει Tv Piccolos Buresch Erbse
|| βοτρυηδόν M || 57 *versum om.* V τείρεα φῶς m Dübner: οὔρεα γῆν Tv
Piccolos Buresch Erbse τείρεα γῆν Wolff || *post* φῶς: καὶ νάματα, ἠέρα καὶ
φλογόεν πῦρ Dübner || χθόνα M: καὶ FP Art. ἅλα T Piccolos Wolff Buresch
Erbse || 58 διώκει MFP Dübner: διώξει T Steuchus Piccolos Wolff Buresch
Erbse || 59 αὐτίκ᾽, ἐρημαῖος δὲ λελείψεται (λελήψεται T) οὐδὸς ἀφήτωρ T
Piccolos Wolff Buresch Erbse: *om.* m || *versus post* ἀφήτωρ *om.* Steuchus ||
60 ἥδε–ἠριγένεια *om.* T: ἥδε ἐμοὶ Daley οἱ δὲ ἐμοὶ M ἢ δὲ <τ᾽ *add.* Erbse>
ἐμὴ FP δὲ *om.* Art. || ἐπιλείπεται Buresch Erbse: ἔτι λείπεται Daley λείπετε
M λείπετο FP Art. Delatte || 61 εἶτα ἐμπαθῶς ἀνοιμώξας ἐπήγαγεν T Buresch
Erbse περιπαθῶς v Piccolos Wolff || 62 αἲ αἴ ἐμοὶ M Daley: αἲ αἴ με FP
Art. Delatte οἴμοι ἐγώ T Buresch οἴμοι ἐμοὶ Piccolos Erbse οἴ μοί μοι Wolff
|| στοναχήσατε T Buresch Erbse: στοναχήσετε v Dübner Piccolos Wolff ||
62–63 ἐμπεπύρισμαι καὶ τόνδ᾽ οὐκ ἐθέλων ἐλήλαμαι δόμον Σ: *om. cett.* || 64
οἴχεται ἐπι ερωτος Σ || βροτὸς εἷς με Σ: βροτόεις M Daley με βροτός FP
βροτός με Art. γε βροτός με *susp.* Erbse με *om.* F᾽ T φλογόεις Tv Piccolos
Buresch Erbse φλογόεν Wolff || οὐράνιον φῶς Wolff φῶς τριλαμπές E

Καὶ ὁ παθὼν θεός ἐστιν ἀλλ' οὐ θεότης πάθεν αὐτή.   65
"Αμφω γὰρ βροτὸς ἦεν ὁμῶς καὶ ἄμβροτος αὐτός,
ἀθάνατος θνητός τε, θεοῦ λόγος, ἀνδρομέη σάρξ,
15 οὐ μεταμειβομένων οὔτ' ἐς χύσιν ἄμφω ἰόντων
οὔθ' ἑκὰς ἀλλήλων· αὐτὸς θεὸς ἠδὲ καὶ ἀνήρ,
πάντα φέρων παρὰ πατρός, ἔχων δέ τε μητρὸς ἅπαντα,   70
ἀθανάτου παρὰ πατρὸς ἔχων φυσίζοον ἀλκήν,
μητρὸς δ' ἐκ θνητῆς σταυρὸν τάφον ὕβριν ἀνίην,
20 πάντα θ' ἅμ' εἰσορόων τε καὶ ἀμφιθέων καὶ ἀκούων.
Τοῦ καὶ ἀπὸ βλεφάρων ποτ' ἐχεύατο δάκρυα θερμά,
εὖτέ μιν ἀγγελίη λυγρὴ μόλεν οἷο φίλοιο.   75
Αὐτὸς καὶ θρήνων πρόφασιν λῦσεν, ἐκ τοῦ Ἅιδου
ἀνέρα τὸν θρήνησε παλίσσυτον ἐς φάος ἕλκων·
25 ὡς βροτὸς ἐθρήνησε καὶ ὡς θεὸς ἐξεσάωσεν.
πέντε τε χιλιάδας πυρῶν ἐκ πέντ' ἐκόρεσσεν
οὔρεσιν ἐν ταναοῖσι· τὸ γὰρ θέλεν ἄμβροτος ἀλκή.   80
Χριστὸς ἐμὸς θεός ἐστιν, ὃς ἐν ξύλῳ ἐξετανύσθη,
ὃς θάνεν, ὃς τάφον ἦλθεν, ὃς ἐκ τάφου ἐς πόλον ὦρτο.

6. Οὐκ ὤφειλές με, φησί, ὦ ἀθλιώτατε τῶν νεοκόρων, τὴν ἐσχάτην ταύτην

---

6. cod. T

---

5. 65 καὶ ὁ: ὁ δὲ Cath. ‖ ἀλλ' οὐ θεότης Σ: καὶ οὐ θεότης cett. ‖ αὐτή om.
PQ' ‖ 66 ἄμφω—αὐτός om. F ‖ βροτὸς ἦεν ὁμῶς MP Erbse Daley: βροτόσωμος
Cath. Β'ΖΕ ἐρωτος αμα Σ ‖ ἄμβροτος P Erbse Daley: ἄββροτος Μ ἀέρωτος
Σ ‖ 66–67 αὐτός, ἀθάνατος—λόγος om. Σ, χ, Cath. ‖ 67 ἀνδρομέη m Delatte
Erbse Daley: ἀνδρομένη P ‖ 68 οὐ μεταμειβομένων Σ: οὔτε ἀμειβομένων mP
‖ χύσιν m Delatte Erbse Daley: σχίσιν Cath. Buresch ‖ ἄμφω ἰόντων:
ἰώντων ἄμφω Σ ‖ 69 οὔθ' ἑκὰς: τουτι καδδ' Σ ‖ ἠδὲ καὶ m: ἠὲ καὶ P ἤδη
καὶ Σχ Cath. ‖ 70 ἔχων om. Σ ‖ 71 ἀθανάτου Μ Daley: ἀθάνατος FP
Buresch Delatte Erbse om. Σχ Cath. ‖ ἔχων: μὲν ἔχει Σ Cath. ‖ φυσίζοον
Σ ‖ versus post ἀλκήν om. P ‖ 72 δ' ἐκ Σ Cath. Μ: δὲ Fχ ‖ θνητῆς: χθονίης
PQ' ‖ σταυρὸν- ἀνίην: ὕβριν πόνον ἀνίην Σ ‖ 73 πάντα θ' ἅμ' coni. Erbse:
versum om. Σχ Cath. ἅμα Μ Daley: ἅμ' P ‖ 74 τοῦ: ὅς Cath. ‖ 75–78 εὖτέ
μιν—ἐξεσάωσεν: ηνικα αγγελλε φιλοιο θλιψιν μετ εκ δημιαν εσεσθαι σφας
αυτους Σ ‖ 76–78 αὐτὸς—ἐξεσάωσε om. P; olim in diss. del., nunc recte rec.
Erbse ‖ 76 λῦσεν ἐκ τοῦ ἅδου F Buresch Delatte Daley: τἅδου Μ λῦσ' ἐξ
Ἀΐδαο Erbse ‖ 77 ἐς F Buresch Delatte Erbse: εἰς Μ Daley ‖ ἕλκων
Buresch Erbse: ἕλκει F Delatte Daley: ‖ 78 ἐξεσάωσεν Μ: ἐξεσάωσε F ‖
79 πέντε τε F: ὃς πέντε χ Cath. τε om. Μ πέντε καὶ Erbse προσαν και Σ ‖
ἐκ πέντ' om. Cath. ‖ ἐκόρεσσεν F: ἐκόρεσεν Μ κόρεσεν Cath. κορέσατο PQ'
κορέσαι Β'ΖS ‖ 80 οὔρεσιν om. Σ ‖ ἐν ταναοῖσι: ἐναναλωσεν Σ ‖ ἄμβροτος: ἄμφωτος Σ ‖ ἀλκήν PQ' ἄλκει Β' ἔλκει S ‖ 81 Χριστὸς—ἐστιν om. Σ
ἐμὸς θεὸς χΜ: θεὸς ἐμὸς FCath. ‖ ἐν ξύλῳ Cath. Erbse: ἐς ξύλον m ‖
τανύσθη Σ χ ‖ 82 ὃς τάφον ἦλθεν om. χCath. ὃς τάφη Σ ‖ τάφου m: ταφῆς
Σ Β'ΖS Cath. ‖ ὦρτο: ἆλτο Σ πολλῶν ὄλβον χ

ἐρώτησιν ἐρωτῆσαι περὶ τοῦ θεοῦ πατρὸς καὶ τοῦ μονογενοῦς καὶ ἀγαπητοῦ
υἱοῦ αὐτοῦ τοῦ πάσης θείας φήμης καὶ κληδόνος αἰτίου (ὀμφὴ γὰρ ἡ θεία 85
κληδὼν καὶ προαγόρευσις, ἡ τὸ ὂν φαίνουσα) καὶ περὶ τοῦ παναγίου
πνεύματος τοῦ πάντα κύκλοθεν δίκην βότρυος περιέχοντος· τοῦτο γὰρ τὸ
πνεῦμα καὶ μὴ βουλόμενόν με πόρρω τῶν οἴκων τούτων διώξει. Καὶ
παραυτίκα ἔρημος καταλειφθήσεται ἡ φλιὰ τοῦ μαντείου ἡ ἀφιεῖσα καὶ
πέμπουσα πρὸς τὰ ἐντὸς τοὺς μαντεύεσθαι βουλομένους. Φεῦ φεῦ, ἐμοὶ 90
τρίποδες μαντικοί, στενάξατε· ἀπόλλυμαι γὰρ ὁ Ἀπόλλων, ἀπόλλυμαι,
ἐπειδὴ ὁ ἐξ οὐρανοῦ κατελθὼν καὶ γενόμενος ἄνθρωπος, νοητὸν πῦρ
ὑπάρχων, βιάζεται καὶ διώκει με.

7. Ἐκ τοῦ κατὰ Λουκᾶν ἁγίου εὐαγγελίου.

Καὶ οἱ ἐνοχλούμενοι ἀπὸ πνευμάτων ἀκαθάρτων ἐθεραπεύοντο, καὶ πᾶς ὁ 95
ὄχλος ἐζήτουν ἅπτεσθαι αὐτοῦ, ὅτι δύναμις παρ᾽ αὐτοῦ ἐξήρχετο καὶ ἰᾶτο
πάντας (a).

8. Ἐκ τοῦ κατὰ Μάρκον ἁγίου εὐαγγελίου.

Καὶ λαβὼν τοὺς πέντε ἄρτους καὶ τοὺς δύο ἰχθύας ἀναβλέψας εἰς τὸν
οὐρανὸν εὐλόγησεν καὶ κατέκλασεν τοὺς ἄρτους καὶ ἐδίδου τοῖς μαθηταῖς 100
ἵνα παρατιθῶσιν αὐτοῖς, καὶ τοὺς δύο ἰχθύας ἐμέρισεν πᾶσιν. Καὶ ἔφαγον
πάντες καὶ ἐχορτάσθησαν, καὶ ἦραν κλάσματα δώδεκα κοφίνων πληρώματα
καὶ ἀπὸ τῶν ἰχθύων. Καὶ ἦσαν οἱ φαγόντες τοὺς ἄρτους πεντακισχίλιοι
ἄνδρες (b).

9. Ἐκ τοῦ κατὰ Ἰωάννην ἁγίου εὐαγγελίου. 105

Καὶ μετὰ τοῦτο λέγει αὐτοῖς, Λάζαρος ὁ φίλος ἡμῶν κεκοίμηται· ἀλλὰ
πορεύομαι ἵνα ἐξυπνίσω αὐτόν (c).

      Καὶ μετὰ βραχέα·

Ἰησοῦς οὖν ὡς εἶδεν αὐτὴν κλαίουσαν καὶ τοὺς συνελθόντας αὐτῇ
Ἰουδαίους κλαίοντας, ἐταράχθη τῷ πνεύματι ὡς ἐμβριμώμενος, καὶ εἶπεν· 110
Ποῦ τεθείκατε αὐτόν; Λέγουσιν αὐτῷ· Κύριε, ἔρχου καὶ ἴδε. Ἐδάκρυσεν
ὁ Ἰησοῦς (d).

7–14. cod. Σ

---

a) Lc. 6,18–19   b) Mc. 6,41–44   c) Io. 11,11   d) Io. 11,33–35

---

6. 89 καταληφθήσεται Τ *em.* Buresch ‖ φλιὰ Buresch Erbse: φιλιὰ Τ ‖
90 ἐμοὶ Buresch Erbse: ἐμαὶ Τ

10. Ἐκ τοῦ κατὰ Λουκᾶν ἁγίου εὐαγγελίου.

Καὶ ὅτε ἦλθεν ἐπὶ τὸν τόπον τὸν καλούμενον Κρανίον, ἐκεῖ ἐσταύρωσαν
αὐτόν (e).   115

  Καὶ μετ' ὀλίγα·

Ὁ δὲ Ἰησοῦς ἔλεγεν· Πάτερ, ἄφες αὐτοῖς, οὐ γὰρ οἴδασιν τί ποιοῦσιν (f).

11. Ἐκ τῆς α' καθολικῆς ἐπιστολῆς Πέτρου τοῦ ἁγίου ἀποστόλου.

Ποῖον γὰρ κλέος εἰ ἁμαρτάνοντες καὶ κολαφιζόμενοι ὑπομενεῖτε; ἀλλ'
εἰ ἀγαθοποιοῦντες καὶ πάσχοντες ὑπομενεῖτε, τοῦτο χάρις παρὰ θεῷ.   120
Εἰς τοῦτο γὰρ ἐκλήθητε, ὅτι καὶ Χριστὸς ἔπαθεν ὑπὲρ ἡμῶν, ὑμῖν
ὑπολιμπάνων ὑπογραμμὸν ἵνα ἐπακολουθήσητε τοῖς ἴχνεσιν αὐτοῦ, ὃς
ἁμαρτίαν οὐκ ἐποίησεν οὐδὲ εὑρέθη δόλος ἐν τῷ στόματι αὐτοῦ, ὃς
λοιδορούμενος οὐκ ἀντελοιδόρει πάσχων οὐκ ἠπείλει, παρεδίδου δὲ τῷ
κρίνοντι δικαίως· ὃς τὰς ἁμαρτίας ἡμῶν αὐτὸς ἀνήνεγκεν ἐν τῷ σώματι   125
αὐτοῦ ἐπὶ τὸ ξύλον, ἵνα ταῖς ἁμαρτίαις ἀπογενόμενοι τῇ δικαιοσύνῃ
ζήσωμεν, οὗ τῷ μώλωπι ἰάθημεν (g).

12. Ἐκ τοῦ κατὰ Λουκᾶν εὐαγγελίου.

Τότε διήνοιξεν αὐτῶν τὸν νοῦν τοῦ συνιέναι τὰς γραφὰς· καὶ εἶπεν αὐτοῖς
ὅτι οὕτως γέγραπται καὶ οὕτως ἔδει παθεῖν τὸν Χριστὸν καὶ ἀναστῆναι ἐκ   130
νεκρῶν τῇ τρίτῃ ἡμέρᾳ, καὶ κηρυχθῆναι ἐπὶ τῷ ὀνόματι αὐτοῦ μετάνοιαν
εἰς ἄφεσιν ἁμαρτιῶν εἰς πάντα τὰ ἔθνη (h).

13. Ἐκ τῶν πράξεων τῶν ἁγίων ἀποστόλων.

Ὡς δὲ ἐτέλεσαν πάντα τὰ περὶ αὐτοῦ γεγραμμένα, καθελόντες ἀπὸ τοῦ
ξύλου ἔθηκαν εἰς μνημεῖον. Ὁ δὲ θεὸς ἤγειρεν αὐτὸν ἐκ νεκρῶν, ὃς ὤφθη   135
ἐπὶ ἡμέρας πλείους τοῖς συναναβᾶσιν αὐτῷ ἀπὸ τῆς Γαλιλαίας εἰς
Ἰερουσαλήμ (i).

14. Ἐκ τοῦ κατὰ Μάρκον ἁγίου εὐαγγελίου.

Ὁ μὲν οὖν κύριος Ἰησοῦς μετὰ τὸ λαλῆσαι αὐτοῖς ἀνελήμφθη εἰς τὸν
οὐρανὸν καὶ ἐκάθισεν ἐκ δεξιῶν τοῦ θεοῦ (j).   140

15. Καὶ ἐν ἑτέρῳ χρησμῷ περὶ τοῦ ἀεὶ ὄντος θεοῦ λέγων καὶ τὴν ἑαυτοῦ
συνομολογῶν ἀπώλειάν φησιν·

15–23. codd. Tv

---

e) Lc. 23,33   f) Lc. 23,34   g) I Pt. 2,20–24   h) Lc. 24,45–47
i) Act. 13,29–31   j) Mc. 16,19

15. Cf. AP III 6, 150 ‖ 142 ὁμολογῶν v Wolff

῏Ην Ζεὺς ἔστι τε νῦν Ζεὺς κ̣έσσεται· ὦ μεγάλε Ζεῦ,
οἳ οἵ μοι χρησμῶν ὑπολείπεται ἠριγένεια.

16. ῞Οτι ὅτε τὸ Βυζάντιον ᾤκισεν ὁ Βύζας, ζηλοτυπήσας ὁ Αἶμος (Αἰμιμόντου   145
δὲ ἦν ἄρχων, οὗ καὶ ὄρος ἐπώνυμόν ἐστι) καὶ νομίσας, εἰ προκαταλάβοι
ἀνθρώπους ἔτι νεοκαταστάτους, νικήσειν τοὺς Βυζαντίους πέμπει τῶν
οἰκείων τινὰ πρὸς τὸν Ἀπόλλωνα ἐρωτῶν, εἰ περιγενήσεται Βύζαντος.
῎Εχρησεν οὖν ὁ Ἀπόλλων οὕτως·

῎Αγρεο καὶ παλίνορσος ἐπείγεο καὶ λέγε ταῦτα·   150
'οὐ σέ γε Φοῖβος ἄνωγεν ἀμείνονι φωτὶ μάχεσθαι·
κείνου γὰρ θεὸς αὐτὸς ἐὴν ὑπερέσχεθε χεῖρα,
ὃν καὶ γῆ τρομέει καὶ οὐρανὸς εὐρὺς ὕπερθεν
πόντος τ᾽ ἠέλιός τ᾽ ἠδ᾽ ἠέριον χάος αὐτό.'

17. Καὶ ταῦτα μὲν ὁ Ἀπόλλων. Ἐγὼ δὲ τοῦ θεοῦ θαυμάζω τὴν ἄνωθεν   155
περὶ τὸ Βυζάντιον πρόνοιαν, καὶ ὅπως ἀεὶ σύνηθες αὐτῷ, διὰ τὴν πρόγνωσιν,
ἣν ἔχει, προλαμβάνειν ταῖς εὐεργεσίαις τοὺς περὶ αὐτὸν εὐσεβεῖν μέλλον-
τας· ἐπεὶ γὰρ εὔδηλον ἦν αὐτῷ τὸ μέλλον καὶ ὡς ἤδη παρὸν ἠπίσ-
τατο τοῦτο καὶ ἀκριβῶς ἐγίνωσκεν, ὅτι οἱ τὴν πόλιν ταύτην οἰκήσαντες
ἐπιμελῶς αὐτὸν θρησκεύσουσιν, οὐδὲν ἐξ ἐκείνου παθεῖν αὐτοὺς κακὸν   160
συνεχώρησεν.

18. ῞Οτι ἐρωτηθεὶς ὁ Ἀπόλλων, τί θεός, ἐξεῖπεν οὕτως·

Αὐτοφανής, ἀλόχευτος, ἀσώματος ἠδέ τ᾽ ἄϋλος.
Κεῖθεν δ᾽ ἐκ σέλα εἶσι πέριξ σφαιρηδὸν Ὀλύμπου.
῎Ενθεν δ᾽ αὖ τυτθὴ διαείδεται αἰθέρος αὐγή,   165

15. 143 κέσσεται v (*praeter* L Steuchus) Erbse: κ᾽ ἔσσεται L Steuchus Piccolos
Wolff Buresch καὶ ἔσσεται Τ || 144 οἳ οἵ μοι Steuchus Buresch Erbse: οἴη
μοι v Piccolos Wolff οἴη μοι Τ   **16.** Cf. AP III 6, 144 et Hesych., Orig.
Constant. 17, pp. 7–8 Preger || 145 ᾤκησεν BV || 145–146 αἰμίμου τοῦ
δρυμοῦ ἄρχων L Piccolos αἰμιμόντου τοῦ δρυμοῦ Wolff || 148 ἐρωτᾶν L
Piccolos || εἰ περιγενήσεται: περὶ γενησίων L γενεσίων Piccolos || θεοῦ (pro
τοῦ) Βύζαντος Β || 150 ἄγρεο PQ᾽ Τ Buresch Erbse ἔγρεο v Steuchus Piccolos
Wolff || 152 κείνου: κείνῳ Steuchus || ὑπερέσχεθε: ὑπερέσχετο Steuchus ||
153 ὃν καὶ γῆ: ὃν πᾶσα γῆ β || 154 πόντος—αὐτό *om.* β   **17.** 155–161
ἐγὼ δὲ—συνεχώρησεν Τ; *brevius* v: τοῦτο δὲ τῆς προνοίας ἦν τοῦ θεοῦ, τὸ
μέλλον ὡς παρὸν γινωσκούσης· ᾔδει γὰρ ὡς οἱ τὴν πόλιν ταύτην οἰκήσοντες
ἐπιμελῶς αὐτὸν θρησκεύσουσι (θρησκεύουσι BLM”)· διὸ καὶ οὐδὲν αὐτοὺς
κακὸν παθεῖν συνεχώρησεν || *textum dissimilem praebet* β: Καὶ ταῦτα μὲν τῷ
Αἵμῳ ὁ χρησμὸς προηγόρευσεν· ἐγὼ δὲ τὴν ἄνωθεν περὶ τὸ Βυζάντιον τοῦ θεοῦ
θαυμάζω πρόνοιαν, ὅπως ἀεὶ σύνηθες τῷ φιλανθρώπῳ θεῷ, διὰ τὴν πρόγνωσιν
ἣν ἔχει προλαμβάνειν ἀεὶ ταῖς εὐεργεσίαις τοὺς περὶ αὐτὸν εὐσεβεῖν μέλλοντας,
ὡς καὶ τοὺς χρησμοὺς εἰ καὶ ἐκ τῶν ἐναντίων, ἀλλ᾽ ὅμως τῷ Βυζαντίῳ
λυσιτελήσειν μέλλοντας ἀναδίδοσθαι.   **18.** Cf. AP III 6, 151 || 162 ὅτι
ἐρωτηθεὶς ὁ Ἀπόλλων Τ: ὁ (*om.* P᾽) αὐτὸς ἐρωθητεὶς v || τί Τ: τίς v ||
ἐξεῖπεν: εἶπεν Β || 164 ἐκ σέλα κτλ.: ἐξελάων σὲ πέριξ σφαιρηδόν, ὄλυμπον
Steuchus

ἥέλιον, μήνην καὶ τείρεα φωτίζουσα.

5 Ταῦτ᾽ ἐδάην ἔμαθόν τε νόῳ, τὰ δὲ λοιπὰ σιωπῶ
Φοῖβος ἐών· σὺ δὲ παῦε τὰ μὴ θέμις ἐξερεείνων
χεῖνεκα σῆς φυσικῆς σοφίης τάδ᾽ ὑπέρτερα νωμῶν.

19. Ὅτι Ποπλᾷ τινι τοὔνομα ἐρωτήσαντι, εἰ συμφέρει περὶ χρημάτων εἰς   17(
φιλοτιμίας πέμψαι πρὸς βασιλέα, ἀπεκρίνατο οὕτως·

Καὶ τόδε σοι δρᾶσαι πολὺ συμφέρον εὐμενίῃσι
λισσομένῳ Ζηνὸς πανδερκέος ἄφθιτον ὄμμα,
ἐκ δὲ πάτρης στεῖλαι γαίης βασιληίδος ἄστυ
ἐξεσίην σπέρχοντα κλυτὴν πρεσβηίδα πίστιν.   17⌐

20. Ὅτι ἄλλοτε λυπουμένῳ τῷ Ποπλᾷ ὡς καὶ τῶν πραγμάτων ἐναντιου-
μένων αὐτῷ καὶ οὐσίας μειουμένης καὶ τοῦ σώματος οὐκ εὖ ἔχοντος καὶ
μαθεῖν ζητοῦντι, παρ᾽ οὗ ἂν δυνηθείη βοηθείας τυχεῖν, ἔχρησεν οὕτως·

Ἱλάσκου Ζηνὸς βιοδώτορος ἀγλαὸν ὄμμα.

21. Ὅτι Στρατονίκῳ τινὶ ὄναρ ἰδόντι περὶ τῶν τῆς ἰδίας ζωῆς ἐτῶν καὶ   18(
πυθομένῳ, εἰ χρὴ πιστεῦσαι, οὕτως ἀνεῖλεν·

Εἰσέτι σοι δολιχὸς νέμεται χρόνος, ἀλλὰ σεβάζου
ζωοδότου Διὸς ὄμμα θυηπολίῃς ἀγανῆσιν.

22. Ὅτι ὁ Σάραπις τῷ περὶ σοφίας ἐρωτήσαντι οὕτως ἀπεκρίνατο·

Ὅσσον ἐέλδονται χρυσοῦ πολυτιμέος ἄνδρες,   18⌐
τόσσον μαντοσύνης ποθέεις τέλος. Ἀλλὰ τόδ᾽ ἴσθι·
θᾶττόν τοι θνητοῖσι κόρος χρυσοῖο παρέσται,
ἢ σοφίης τέλος εὐρὺ καταζητῶν ἐσαθρήσεις.

5 Τόσση ἀπειρεσίη τέταται βασιλῆος ἐπ᾽ οὐδῷ
ἀθανάτου· κεῖνος δὲ διδοῖ καὶ δῶρον ὀπάζει.   19(

---

18. 168 τὰ μὴ θέμις: οὓς μὴ θέμις Steuchus ‖ 169 χεῖνεκα Erbse: χ᾽ εἵνεκα
Tv Steuchus Piccolos (*praeter* χᾶνεκα B Wolff) ‖ φυσικῆς *om.* L Piccolos ‖
νωμᾶν Steuchus   **19.** Cf. AP III 6, 152 ‖ 170 Ποπλᾷ Wolff Buresch
Erbse Πόπλα LT Piccolos Πόπλα B ‖ 171 φιλοτιμίας LT Piccolos Robert
Robinson: φιλοτιμίαν BV Wolff Buresch Erbse ‖ οὕτως *om.* T ‖ 173 λισ-
σομένεω *et* ἄφιτον T ‖ πανδορκέος BV ‖ 175 σπέρχοντα Tv (*sed* παρέχοντα
B Wolff) Buresch: σπεύδοντα Erbse   **20.** Cf. AP III 6, 153 ‖ 176 Πέπλαι
B ‖ 177 τοῦ σώματος *om.* B ‖ 178 ζητοῦντι LB Wolff Buresch Erbse:
ζητοῦντος T ‖ ἂν *om.* L Piccolos περὶ ὧν ἂν B ‖ βοήθειαν L ‖ 179 ἀγλαὸν
L Buresch Erbse: ἄγλαον T ἱερὸν B   **21.** Cf. AP III 6, 154 ‖ 180 ὄναρ
LT Buresch Erbse: ὄνειρα B ‖ τῶν *et* ἐτῶν *om.* BV ‖ 182 εἰσέτι *coni.*
Piccolos Wolff Robert Robinson: εἰς ἔτι T Buresch Erbse ‖ 183 θυηπολίῃς
em. Erbse: θυηπολίαις Tv Piccolos Wolff Buresch Robinson ‖ ἀγανῆσιν v
Piccolos Wolff Erbse: ἀγαναῖσιν T Buresch Robinson   **22.** Cf. AP III
6, 184 ‖ 184 Σέραπις Piccolos ‖ 185 ἄνδρες v ἀ[T *fort.* ἄνδρες᾽ Tmg.
‖ 186 μανθοσύνης B ‖ 187 τοι *coni.* Nauck *conf.* T: τοῖς LB Piccolos Wolff
‖ 189 ἀπειρεσίη Erbse: ἀπείρητος Tv Steuchus Piccolos Wolff ἀπειρέσιος
coni. Nauck ‖ τέταται: σοφίη Steuchus ‖ 190 καὶ δῶρον: κῦδος BV

23. Ὅτι τῶν καθαρῶς αἰτούντων ἀκούει θεός· ὡς καὶ Ἀπόλλων ἔχρησεν
οὕτως·

Εἴ γέ τις ἱλάσσαιτο θεὸν μέγαν ἠδὲ παράσχοι
σῶμ' ἁγνόν, τοῦδ' ἔκλυε καὶ οἱ κάρτ' ἐπένευσεν.

24. Ὅτι Πορφύριος ἐν τῷ δευτέρῳ βιβλίῳ τῆς ΕΚ ΛΟΓΙΩΝ ΦΙΛΟΣΟΦΙΑΣ   195
αὐτοῦ παρατίθεται χρησμὸν περὶ τοῦ θεοῦ τοῦ ἀθανάτου ἔχοντα οὕτως·

   Ἀθανάτων ἄρρητε πατήρ, αἰώνιε, μύστα,
   κόσμων ἀμφιδρόμων ἐποχούμενε, δέσποτα, νώτοις
   αἰθερίοις, ἀλκῆς ἵνα σοι μένος ἐστήρικται
   πάντ' ἐπιδερκομένῳ καὶ ἀκούοντ' οὔασι καλοῖς,   200
5 κλῦθι τεῶν παίδων, οὓς ἤροσας αὐτὸς ἐν ὥραις·
   σὴ γὰρ ὑπὲρ κόσμον τε καὶ οὐρανὸν ἀστερόεντα
   χρυσῇ ὑπέρκειται πολλὴ αἰώνιος ἀλκή·
   ἧς ὕπερ ἠώρησαι, ὀρίνων φωτὶ σεαυτόν,
   ἀενάοις ὀχετοῖσι τιθηνῶν νοῦν ἀτάλαντον,   205
10 ὅς ῥα κύει τόδε πᾶν τεχνώμενος ἄφθιτον ὕλην,
   ἧς γένεσις δεδόκηται, ὅτι σφε τύποισιν ἔδησας.
   Ἔνθεν ἐπεισρείουσι γοναὶ ἁγίων μὲν ἀνάκτων
   ἀμφὶ σέ, παντόκρατορ βασιλεύτατε καὶ μόνε θνητῶν
   ἀθανάτων τε πάτερ μακάρων. Αἱ δ' εἰσὶν ἄτερθεν   210
15 ἐκ σέο μὲν γεγαῶσαι, ὑπ' ἀγγελίῃσι δ' ἕκαστα
   πρεσβυγενεῖ διάγουσι νόῳ καὶ κάρτεϊ τῷ σῷ.

---

24. 197–215 Porph., De phil. ex orac. haur., fr. 325, pp. 373–374 Smith;
cf. pp. 144–145 Wolff

23. Cf. AP III 6, 185 ‖ 191 ὅτι T: ἐρωτηθεὶς εἰ LB Piccolos Wolff ‖
καθαρῶν v Wolff ‖ ὡς καὶ Ἀπόλλων om. v ‖ 193 ἱλάσοιτο L ‖ 194 ἁγνὸν
Dübner Erbse: ἀγαθὸν cett. ‖ ἐπένευσεν em. Buresch: ἐπένεσεν T ἐπένευσα
C F' M"   **24.** 195 ἐν τῷ δευτέρῳ: ἐκ τοῦ δεκάτου A' Mai; sim. Steuchus:
decimo libro εὐλογίων φιλοσοφίας ‖ 197 ἀθανάτέ τε A' ἀθάνατε Steuchus
‖ 198 κόσμον M" ‖ 199 αἰθέριος CF' αἰθερίης V ‖ μένος Buresch Erbse
Smith: μέρος T ‖ 201 ἤροσας Buresch Erbse Smith: ἤροας T ‖ 202 σὴ:
σοὶ A' ‖ 204 ἧς ὕπερ T Buresch Erbse Smith: ἢ ὕπερ v ὕπερ A' Steuchus
‖ ἠώρησαι Buresch Erbse Smith: ἠαόρησαι T αἰώρησας A' ἠώρησας Steuchus
ὑπερηώρησαι Wolff Mullach ‖ 205 τιθηνῶν Tv A' Mai Wolff Lewy Erbse:
τιταίνων Buresch (hanc coniecturam olim Erbse in diss. probavit) Smith ‖ 206
τεχνώμενος T Steuchus Buresch Erbse Smith: τεχνούμενος B τεκνούμενος L
Wolff τεκνώμενος A' Mai ‖ 207 ἧς Wolff Buresch Erbse Smith: ἣν Tv A'
ἢ Mai ‖ γένεσιν BV ‖ δεδόκηται om. B (ἧς γενέτης vel γενετὴρ δεδόκησαι
coni. Buresch) ‖ 208 ἐπεισρείουσι M" L Buresch Erbse Smith: ἐπεισρέουσι
BP'TV ἐπειωρείουσι CF' ἐπιστροφόωσι A' ἐπειστρεέουσι Steuchus ‖ ἀνάκτων: ἀγγέλων B ‖ 209 παντόκρατορ A'LT Buresch Erbse Smith: παντοπά-
τορ cett. et T mg. ‖ βασιλεύτατε v Steuchus: βασιλεῦ τε A' Mai βασιλέστατε
T Buresch Erbse Smith ‖ μόνον V ‖ 211 γεγαῶσαι A' Steuchus T Buresch
Erbse Smith: γεγαυῖαι cett. ‖ ἀγγελίῃσι Erbse: ἀγγελίαισι T Buresch Smith

Πρὸς δ᾽ ἔτι καὶ τρίτον ἄλλο γένος ποίησας ἀνάκτων
οἵ σε κατ᾽ ἦμαρ ἄγουσιν ἀνυμνείοντες ἀοιδαῖς
βουλόμενόν ῥ᾽ ἐθέλοντες, ἀοιδιάουσι δ᾽ ἐσῶδε.   21

25. Ὅτι τρεῖς τάξεις ἀγγέλων ὁ χρησμὸς οὗτος δηλοῖ· τῶν ἀεὶ τῷ θεῷ
παρεστώτων, τῶν χωριζομένων αὐτοῦ καὶ εἰς ἀγγελίας καὶ διακονίας τινὰς
ἀποστελλομένων, καὶ τῶν φερόντων ἀεὶ τὸν αὐτοῦ θρόνον. Τοῦτο ᾽οἵ σε
κατ᾽ ἦμαρ ἄγουσι᾽ τουτέστι διηνεκῶς φέρουσι· τὸ δὲ ᾽ἀοιδιάουσιν δ᾽ ἐσῶδε᾽
ἀντὶ τοῦ ᾄδουσιν ἕως νῦν.   22

26. Εἶτα ἐπάγει ὁ χρησμὸς τάδε·

Τύνη δ᾽ ἐσσὶ πατὴρ καὶ μητέρος ἀγλαὸν εἶδος
καὶ τεκέων τέρεν ἄνθος, ἐν εἴδεσιν εἶδος ὑπάρχων
καὶ ψυχὴ καὶ πνεῦμα καὶ ἁρμονίη καὶ ἀριθμός.

Δηλοῖ δὲ διὰ τούτων, ὅτι καὶ πατρὸς καὶ μητρὸς φιλοστοργίαν ἐνδείκνυ-   22
ται περὶ ἡμᾶς ὁ θεὸς καὶ ὅτι συγκαταβαίνει διὰ φιλανθρωπίαν· καὶ γίνεται
καὶ αὐτὸς ἄνθρωπος καὶ ὡσεὶ θεοῦ τέκνον ἤτοι δημιούργημα.

27. Ὅτι <***> κατὰ τὸν Πορφύριον τοιόνδε χρησμὸν ἐξήνεγκε·

Νοῦν τεὸν εἰς βασιλῆα θεὸν τρέπε, μηδ᾽ ἐπὶ γαίης
πνεύμασι μικροτέροισιν ὁμίλει· τοῦτό σοι εἶπον.   23

28. Ὅτι ὁ Ἑρμῆς, οὐχ ὁ τρισμέγιστος, ἀλλ᾽ ὁ λόγιος καλούμενος θεὸς
χρησμὸν εἶπε τοιοῦτον·

Εἷς θεὸς οὐράνιος γενέτης, γαῖαν διατάσσων,
οὐράνιόν τε πόλον κατέχων δίνας τε θαλάσσης·
κείνῳ πάντα τέλει τε καὶ ἱλάσκου φρένα κείνου.   23

27–38. cod. T

26. 222–224 Porph., De phil. ex orac. haur., fr. 325, p. 374 Smith; cf. pp.
146–147 Wolff et AP III 6, 216   **27.** 229–230 Porph., De phil. ex orac.
haur., fr. 325 a, p. 375 Smith

24. 214 κατ᾽ ἦμαρ v A᾽ Mai: καθ᾽ ἦμαρ T Steuchus Buresch Erbse Smith
|| σε κατ᾽: ῥ᾽ ἑκὰς coni. Wolff || ἄγουσιν ἀνυμνείοντες: ᾄδουσιν κἀνθυμνείοντες
A᾽ Mai || 215 ἀοιδιάουσι: ἀοιδιάσουσι B ἀεὶ διάγουσι A᾽ Mai || ἐσῶδε: ἐς
ὦπα A᾽ Mai ἐς ὧδε Steuchus   **25.** 216 ἀγγέλων—δηλοῖ: ὁ χρησμὸς ἀγγέλων
δηλοῖ BV || τῶν: καὶ L Wolff || 217 καὶ ante εἰς ἀγγελίας om. V || τινὰς
T Buresch Erbse: om. v Smith || 218–219 τοῦτο—φέρουσι om. v || 219 δ᾽
ante ἐσῶδε om. TV   **26.** 221 τάδε v (om. B) Erbse Smith: ταῦτα T Buresch
|| 222 Τύνη Buresch: ὑνη T γυνὴ C F᾽ || 227 ὡσεὶ T: ὡσανεὶ v Smith ||
τέκνον: τόκον L   **27.** 228 lac. in cod. T [1 cm] (᾽deest nomen proprium
dativi casus᾽ T mg.) verbis τῷ δεῖνα expl. Buresch   **28.** 234 δίνας T: em.
Buresch || 235 φρένα κείνου Buresch Erbse: φρενὶ κεῖνον T

29. Ὅτι <ὁ> αὐτὸς Ἑρμῆς ἐξομνύμενος περί τινος πράγματος ἔφη οὕτως·

Νὴ θεόν, ὃς κρατέει, τόν γ᾽ οὐ προφέρειν ἐνὶ θνητοῖς
δεῖ μάκαρας, ἢν μή τι θεὸν κατὰ σῶμα βιῆται.

Ὁ δὲ λέγει, τοιοῦτόν ἐστι· ὅτι ἡμᾶς τοὺς δοκοῦντας εἶναι μακαρίους ἤτοι
τοὺς δαίμονας, οὐ δεῖ κηρύττειν τὸν ἀληθῆ θεὸν ἐν τοῖς ἀνθρώποις, εἰ μὴ   240
ἄρα <αὐτὸς> σωματωθεὶς βιάσεται ἡμᾶς θεὸν αὐτὸν ὁμολογῆσαι.

30. Ὅτι πυθομένῳ τινί, ποῦ τὸν ἄρρητον θεραπεύσει θεόν, ὁ Ἀπόλλων
δεικνύς, ὡς πᾶς τόπος τῆς αὐτοῦ δεσποτείας ἐστὶ καὶ πανταχοῦ τοὺς
εὐσεβοῦντας ἀποδέχεται, ἔχρησεν οὕτως·

Ζηνὸς πᾶσα πόλις, πάντ᾽ οὔρεα, πᾶσα θάλασσα,   245
πάντη δ᾽ ἀνθρώποις νεύει <πάντη> τε γέγαθεν
εὐσεβέων θνητῶν ὁσίαις τιμαῖσι καὶ ἔργοις.

31. Ὅτι οἱ λεγόμενοι θεοὶ τιμὴν ἑαυτοῖς μνώμενοι καὶ τοῖς ἀγγέλοις
παρενείροντες ἑαυτοὺς ὑπηρετεῖσθαι ὁμολογοῦσι ταῖς βουλαῖς τοῦ ἀορά-
του θεοῦ καὶ τοῖς περὶ ἐκεῖνον εὐσεβοῦσιν ἀκολουθεῖν· διὸ καὶ ὁ Ἀπόλλων   250
ἔχρησεν οὕτως·

Εὐσεβέσιν μερόπεσσιν ὀτρήμονές ἐσμεν ἀρωγοί,
οἳ λάχομεν περὶ κόσμον ἀλήμονα ναιέμεν αἰεί·
ῥίμφα δ᾽ ἐπ᾽ ἀνθρώποισι πονειομένοισι περῶμεν
πειθόμενοι πατρὸς ἡμετέρου πολυαρκέσι βουλαῖς.   255

32. Ὅτι ὁ Ἀπόλλων δηλῶν, ὡς πάντα τοῦ ἀθανάτου θεοῦ ἐξήρτηται καὶ
αὐτῷ μόνῳ δεῖ προσανέχειν, ἔχρησεν οὕτως·

Πάντα θεοῦ μεγάλοιο νόου ὑπὸ νεύμασι κεῖται·
ἀρχὴ πηγή τε ζωῆς καὶ ὑπείροχον εὖχος
καὶ κράτος ἠδὲ βίη καὶ ἰσχύος ἄφθιτος ἀλκὴ   260
καὶ δύναμις κρατερὴ καὶ ἀμφιελικτὸς ἀνάγκη·
εὔχεο τοιγάρτοι μακάρων βασιλῆι μεγίστῳ.

33. Ὅτι ὁ Ἀπόλλων παρενείρων ἑαυτὸν τοῖς ἀγγέλοις ἔχρησε ταῦτα·

Ἄρτι μὲν ἀστερόεντα κατ᾽ οὐρανὸν ἱππότις Ἠὼς
ἕλκει νύκτα μέλαιναν· ἐπειγόμενος δὲ κελαινῆς   265
μητρὸς ὑπ᾽ ἀγκοίνῃσι θέει μεροπήιος Ὕπνος.
Καὶ μακάρων σύμπας στρατὸς ἄπλετος ἀμφὶ μέγιστον

---

29. 236 ὁ *ins.* Buresch ‖ 237 ἐνὶ Buresch: ἐν T ‖ 238 βίηται T: *em.*
Buresch ‖ 241 αὐτὸς *ins.* Buresch   **30.** 242 'Lege ποῦ' T *mg.*: πῶς T
‖ 246 *post* νεύει *lac.* T [2 cm]: 'fort. deest ἀγαθοῖς aut aliud tale' T *mg.*
πάντη *coni.* Buresch Robinson   **32.** Cf. Didym., De Trin. III,21 ‖ 260–261
ἰσχύος *et* ἀμφιελικτὸς *em.* Erbse: ἴσχυος et ἀμφιέλικτος T Buresch Robinson
‖ 262 εὔχεο—μεγίστῳ *om.* Did.   **33.** 264 ἱππότις *em.* Buresch: ἱππότης T

5 πρῶτον ὁμοῦ μάλα πάντες ἀολλέες ἑστηῶτες
διζόμεθ᾿, ὡς κόσμοιο θεμείλιον αὐξήσωμεν.

34. Ὅτι πυθομένου τινὸς τοῦ Ἀπόλλωνος, πότερον μένει ἡ ψυχὴ μετὰ   27ᵛ
θάνατον ἢ διαλύεται, ἐπεκρίθη οὕτως·

Ψυχή, μέχρι μὲν οὗ δεσμοῖς πρὸς σῶμα κρατεῖται
φθαρτόν, ἑοῦσ᾿ ἀπαθὴς ταῖς τοῦδ᾿ ἀλγηδόσιν εἴκει·
ἡνίκα δ᾿ αὖτε λύσιν βροτέην μετὰ σῶμα μαρανθὲν
ὠκίστην εὕρητ᾿, εἰς αἰθέρα πᾶσα φορεῖται   27ᵛ
5 αἰὲν ἀγήραος οὖσα, μένει δ᾿ ἐς πάμπαν ἀτειρής.
Τοῦτο δὲ πρωτογόνος θεία διέταξε πρόνοια.

35. Ὅτι πυθομένου τινός, εἴ γε εἷς ὁ ἄρρητος θεός, ἀπεκρίθη ὁ Ἀπόλλων
οὕτως·

Εἷς ἐν παντὶ πέλει κόσμῳ θεὸς, ὃς κύκλα δίνης   28ᵛ
οὐρανίης θεσμοῖσιν ὁρίσσατο καὶ διέκρινεν
ὥραις καὶ καιροῖς ἰσοζυγέοντα τάλαντα,
νείμας ἀλληλοῦχα τροπαῖς φιλοτήσια δεσμά·
5 ὃν Δία κικλήσκουσι, δι᾿ ὃν βιοτήσιος αἰών,
Ζῆνα δὲ παγγενέτην, ταμίην ζωαρκέα πνοιῆς,   28
αὐτὸν ἐν αὐτῷ ἐόντα καὶ ἐξ ἑνὸς εἰς ἓν ἰόντα.

36. Ὅτι ἐρωτήσαντός τινος τὸν Ἀπόλλωνα, εἰ ἔστιν ἕτερος θεὸς μείζονα
παρ᾿ αὐτὸν ἔχων ἐξουσίαν, ἀπεκρίνατο οὕτως·

Ἔστι θεῶν μακάρων ὕπατος θεός, ὃς χθόνα πᾶσαν
ἀμφὶς ἔχει καὶ κῦμα θ᾿ ἁλὸς καὶ ἀπείριτον οἶδμα   29
ὠκεανοῦ· πάντη δὲ κικλήσκεται εὐρύοπα Ζεύς.
Τῷ γὰρ ὑπείκουσιν μάκαρες, τὸν χρὴ λιτανεύειν.

37. Ὅτι ὁ Ἀπόλλων ἐρωτήσαντός τινος, ποῖον ἕκαστος τῶν νόθων θεῶν
ἔλαχεν ἔργον, ἀπεκρίνατο οὕτως·

Ἀθανάτοισιν ἅπασιν ἔχειν διενείματο τιμὰς   29
ὑψιμέδων γενέτης· Φοίβῳ μαντηγόρον ὀμφὴν
καὶ Δηοῖ καρποὺς καὶ Παλλάδι πῖαρ ἐλαίης
καὶ Βάκχῳ γλευκηρὸν ἀναζέον ἄνθος ὀπώρης

---

34. Cf. Lact., Div. Inst. VII,13,5 ‖ 270 τοῦ Ἀπόλλωνος *em.* Robinson: τὸν Ἀπόλλωνα *cett.* ‖ 272 μέχρι μὲν T Erbse: μὲν μέχρις Lact. ‖ 273 φθαρτὸν— τοῦδ᾿ T: φθαρτὰ νοοῦσα πάθη θνηταῖς Lact. ‖ 274 αὖτε λύσιν T: ἀνάλυσιν *edd. Lactantii* ‖ βροτέην T Lact. Sedulius Wolff: βρότεον Buresch Erbse Robinson ‖ 275 εὕρητ᾿ εἰς: εὕρηται ἐς Lact. ‖ 277 τοῦτο δὲ πρωτογόνος T: πρωτογόνος γὰρ τοῦτο Lact. ‖ θεία T: θεοῦ *coni.* Wolff   **35.** 286 ἐν αὐτῷ Buresch Erbse: εἰς αὐτὸν T   **36.** 292 ὑπείκουσιν *corr.* Buresch: ὑπήκουσι T   **37.** 296 μαντηγόρον *em.* Buresch: μαντήγορι T ‖ 297 Δηοῖ *em.* Neumann: Διΐ T

5   παρθενίου τε γάμοιο νεοζυγέων θ᾽ ὑμεναίων
κοιρανέειν φιλότητος ἀμωμήτῃ γ᾽ Ἀφροδίτῃ.   300

38. Ὅτι ἐρωτήσαντός τινος τὸν Ἀπόλλωνα, εἰ μόνος ὁ ὕψιστός ἐστιν ἄναρχος καὶ ἀτελεύτητος, ἀπεκρίνατο οὕτως·

Αὐτὸς ἄναξ πάντων, αὐτόσπορος, αὐτογένεθλος,
ἰθύνων τὰ ἄπαντα σὺν ἀφράστῳ τινὶ τέχνῃ,
οὐρανὸν ἀμφιβαλών, πετάσας χθόνα, πόντον ἐλάσας,   305
μίξας ὕδατι πῦρ χθόνα τ᾽ ἠέρι καὶ πυρὶ γαῖαν,
5   χεῖμα, θέρος, φθινόπωρον, ἔαρ κατὰ καιρὸν ἀμείβων
εἰς φάος ἦγεν ἄπαντα καὶ ἁρμονίοις πόρε μέτροις.

39. Ὅτι πρὸς τὸν ἐρωτήσαντα, εἰ ἁμαρτάνων τις λανθάνει θεόν, εἶπεν ὁ Ἀπόλλων·   310

Οὐδεὶς ἂν λήθοι τοῖος θεόν, οὐδὲ σοφοῖσι
κέρδεσιν οὐδὲ λόγοισιν ὑπεκφύγοι ἄλκιμον ὄμμα.
Πάντα θεοῦ πλήρη, πάντῃ θεὸς ἐστεφάνωται,
πάντα ζωογονῶν, ὁπόσα πνείει τε καὶ ἕρπει.

40. Ὅτι πρὸς τὸν ἐρωτήσαντα, εἰ δι᾽ ἐπιμελείας βίου δύναται γενέσθαι   315
θεοῦ ἐγγύς, εἶπεν ὁ Ἀπόλλων·

Ἰσόθεον δίζῃ γέρας εὑρέμεν· οὔ σοι ἐφικτόν.
Αἰγύπτου τόδε μοῦνος ἕλεν γέρας αἰνετὸς Ἑρμῆς,
Ἑβραίων Μωσῆς καὶ Μαζακέων σοφὸς ἀνήρ,
ὅν ποτε δὴ χθὼν θρέψεν ἀριγνώτοιο Τυήνης·   320
5   θνητοῖς γὰρ χαλεπὸν φύσιν ἄμβροτον ὀφθαλμοῖσιν
εἰσιδέειν, ἢν μή τις ἔχῃ σύνθημα θέειον.

41. Ὅτι ἐν Ὄμβοις, τῷ φρουρίῳ τῆς Αἰγύπτου Θηβαΐδος, ἦν χρησμὸς γεγραμμένος τοιοῦτος·

---

39. codd. Tv; cf. AP III 6, 155
40–44. cod. T

38. 304 ἄπαντα T: ʻleg. ἕκαστα᾽ T mg. ‖ 305 ἐλάσας: ἐλάσσας T Erbse ‖ 308 ἦγεν T: ʻin antigr. εἶχεν᾽ T mg. ‖ μέτροις T: ʻex coniectura ponitur᾽ T mg.   **39.** 309 τις *om.* T ‖ λανθάνει: ʻin antigr. lectio certa non ponitur᾽ T mg. ‖ τὸν θεὸν BL Wolff ‖ ὁ (*ante* Ἀπόλλων) TBV: *om.* L Piccolos ‖ 311 τοῖος v Steuchus Piccolos Wolff Buresch Erbse: μερόπων T (ʻet hoc ex coniectura᾽ T mg.) ‖ 314 ζωογονέων T   **40.** 319 Μαζακέων *em.* Erbse: μαζακίων T Buresch τῶν καππαδοκῶν T mg. ‖ ἀνήρ T Ἀπολλώνιος mg. ‖ 320 Τυήνης *em.* Scott-Ferguson Erbse Jones: Τυήνας T Buresch Τυάνης Robinson   **41.** 323 Ὄμβοις *scripsi*: ὄμβραις T ὄμβροις Buresch Scott-Ferguson Erbse ‖ τῆς Αἰγύπτου Θηβαΐδος *scripsi*: τῆς ἐν Αἰγύπτου Θημαΐδος T Θηβαΐδος *em.* Buresch τῆς ἐν Αἰγύπτῳ Θηβαΐδος Scott-Ferguson Erbse

Τὸν λόγον υἷα θεοῖο θεόν τε λόγον καλέουσι,　　325
καὶ θεότης κοινή τις ἐν υἱῷ καὶ γενετῆρι.

42. Ὅτι ἐν <Κοπ> τῷ, τῇ πόλει Αἰγύπτου, ὁ χρησμὸς οὗτος ἦν γεγραμμένος καὶ ἀποκρίσεως καὶ ἐρωτήσεως·

    Οὐρανὸς αὐτολόχευτος; ἐμ' <ἤλ> ιε τοῦτο δίδαξον.'
    '<Οὐκ>, ἀλλ' αὐτὸν ἔτευξε λόγος, λόγον υἷα φυτεύσας·　　330
    οἱ δύο δ' αὖ εἷς εἰσι, πατὴρ καὶ κύδιμος υἱός.'
    ''Αλλά μοι ἔννεπε τοῦτο· τίς ἐς χθόνα δῖαν ἱκάνων
5   ἄρρητον σοφίην βροτέην ἐδίδαξε γενέθλην;'
    ''Εκ προθύρων γενετῆρος, ἀπ' οὐρανίων κορυφάων,
    υἱὸς ὅλην κόσμησε βροτῶν πολυτειρέα φύτλην,　　335
    καί μιν ἑοῦσ' ἄχραντος ἀπειρήτη θ' ὑμεναίων
    παρθενικὴ ἐλόχευσε πόνων ἄτερ Εἰλειθυίης.'

43. Ὅτι ἐν Ἐλεφαντίνῃ, τῇ πόλει Αἰγύπτου, χρησμὸς ἐγέγραπτο τοιοῦτος·

    Πνεῦμα θεόρρητον φυσίζοον εἰκόνα πατρὸς　　340
    ἀμφὶς ἔχει· γενετὴρ δ' ἔλαχ' υἱέα, παῖς δὲ τοκῆα·
    οἱ τρεῖς, οἱ δ' αὖ εἰσι μία φύσις, αὐτοὶ ἐν αὐτοῖς.

44. Καὶ ἕτερος χρησμὸς τοιοῦτος·

    Τὸν θεὸν αὐτογένεθλον ἀείναον αὐδάξαντο
    ἄνθρωποι, λόγον ἁγνόν, ὅσοι σοφίην ἐδάησαν,　　345
    καὶ λόγον ἀγλαὸν υἷα πανομφαίοιο θεοῖο.
    Πνεῦμα δ' ἐν ἀμφοτέροισιν ἀκηράσιον ζαθέειον·
    εἰσὶ δέ τις τριὰς ἁγνὴ ἐν ἀλλήλοισιν ἐόντες.

45. Ὅτι ἐν Αἰγύπτῳ κατὰ τὰς λεγομένας σύριγγας ἐγέγραπτο χρησμὸς τοιοῦτος Ἀντιόχου ἱερέως Ἡλιουπόλ<εως>·　　350

---

42. 327 ἐν [lac. 8 mm] τῷ T *suppl.* Buresch 'deest 1 syllaba proprii nominis' T mg. || 328 καὶ ἐρωτήσεις καὶ ἀποκρίσεις ἔχων *coni.* Scott-Ferguson || *oraculi versus* Buresch *inaniter transp. hoc ordine edens:* 1.4–7.2.3.8.9. || 329 ἐμ' ἤλιε *dubitanter scripsi:* ἐμὲ [lac. 8 mm] γε (*vel* νε) T Erbse ἐμ' οὐρανέ Buresch σύ με κοίρανε *coni.* Scott-Ferguson || 330 οὐκ *add.* Erbse: μὲν *post* αὐτὸν *ins.* Buresch || λόγος T Buresch Erbse: λόγῳ Scott-Ferguson || 333 ἄρρητον Scott-Ferguson Erbse: ἄρρητος T Buresch || 336 μιν ἑοῦσ' Buresch Erbse: μιν ἔτ' οὖσ' T ('ἔτι antigr. omittit et scribit καὶ μὴν. Quid si legam καί μιν ἑοῦσ' ἀχρ.' T mg.) || 336–337 καί μιν ἑοῦσ' ἄχραντος κτλ. *cf.* Epiph., Pan. 51,22,9–11: ταύτῃ τῇ ὥρᾳ σήμερον ἡ Κόρη (τουτέστιν ἡ παρθένος) ἐγέννησε τὸν Αἰῶνα || 337 Εἰλειθυίης *scripsi:* Εἰληθυίης T Buresch Erbse　　**44.** 345 λόγον ἁγνόν: λόγου ἁγνοῦ ὅσοι σοφίην *tempt.* Scott-Ferguson || 347 ζαθέειον *conieci:* ζάθειον T Buresch Erbse　　**45.** 349 τὰς λεγομένας σύριγγας *emendavi: cf.* Paus., Descr. I,42,3; Aelian., De nat. anim. VI,43 et XVI,15; OGIS II, nn. 694, 720, 721; ὃ ηὑρέθη ἐν ταῖς σύριγξι ταῖς αἰγυπτίαις *optime* Σ σήραγγας T τοὺς λεγομένους Σηράγγας Buresch Scott-Ferguson Erbse *testimonio* Ptolemaei, Geogr. enarr. IV,6,17 *confisi* || 350 Ἀντιόχου ἱερέως ἡλιουπολ Σ: *suppl.* Pitra Scott-Ferguson Erbse Ἀντιόχου κολοφῶνος B'L'PQ'SZ Ἀντιμάχου κολοφωνίου (*vel* ἐκ κολοφῶνος) Bentley

Ἦν νοῦς εἷς πάντων νοερώτερος, ἄφθιτος ἀρχή,
τοῦδ᾿ ἄπο παγγενέτης νοερὸς λόγος, ἄφθιτος αἰεὶ
υἱός, ἀπαύγασμα νοεροῦ πατρός, εἷς ἅμα πατρί.
Ἐν μὲν ἐπωνυμίη γε διεστηκὼς ἀπὸ πατρός,
εἷς δὲ πέλων σὺν πατρὶ καὶ ἐξ ἑνὸς εἷς, μία τάξις,   355
5   πατρὸς ἐὼν αἴγλης, ὁμοούσιος, ἄφθιτος αἰεὶ
πνεύματι σὺν πρώτῳ ἁγίῳ καὶ σπέρματος ἀρχή.

46. Ἐκ τοῦ κατὰ Ἰωάννην εὐαγγελίου.

Ἐν ἀρχῇ ἦν ὁ λόγος, καὶ ὁ λόγος ἦν πρὸς τόν θεόν, καὶ θεὸς ἦν ὁ λόγος.
Οὗτος ἦν ἐν ἀρχῇ πρὸς τὸν θεόν. Πάντα δι᾿ αὐτοῦ ἐγένετο, καὶ χωρὶς αὐτοῦ   360
ἐγένετο οὐδέν (k).

47. Καὶ μετ᾿ ὀλίγα·

Ὁ ἑωρακὼς ἐμὲ ἑώρακεν τὸν πατέρα (l).

Καὶ πάλιν·

Ἐγὼ καὶ ὁ πατὴρ ἕν ἐσμεν (m).   365

Καὶ αὖθις·

Κἀγὼ ἐν τῷ πατρὶ καὶ ὁ πατὴρ ἐν ἐμοί (n).

48. Ἐκ τῆς πρὸς Ἑβραίους ἐπιστολῆς.

Ὃς ὢν ἀπαύγασμα τῆς δόξης καὶ χαρακτὴρ τῆς ὑποστάσεως αὐτοῦ, φέρων
τε τὰ πάντα τῷ ῥήματι τῆς δυνάμεως αὐτοῦ (o).   370

46–48. cod. Σ

---

45. 351–357 Antiochus Heliopolitanus, auctor aliunde ignotus

---

k) Io. 1,1–3   l) Io. 14,9   m) Io. 10,30   n) Io. 14,10.11
o) Hebr. 1,3

---

45. 351 ἦν νοῦς Σχ:]ννοῦς T *em.* Buresch *qui dubitanter prop.* εἷς νοῦς ‖
ἄφθιτος ἀρχή *om.* Σ: εἰ δέ γε ἔστιν χ ‖ 352 νοερὸς ΣT Buresch Erbse:
νοερώτερος χ ‖ αἰεὶ *om.* Σχ ‖ 353 ἀπαύγασμα Σχ: ἀπαυγὴ τοῦ T Buresch
Erbse ἀπαυγασμὸς Bentley ‖ 354 διεστηκὼς ἀπὸ πατρός Σ Buresch Erbse:
εἰ δέ γε ἔστιν ὡς ἀπὸ πατρός χ διεστὼς ἀπὸ πατέρος T ‖ 355 τάξις Σχ: δόξα
T Buresch Erbse ‖ 356–357 ἐὼν—ἀρχή Σ Erbse (ἐὼν αἴγλης *om.* χ): υἱοῦ
καὶ πνεύματος ἄφθιτος αἰὲν ἐοῦσα T Buresch ‖ 356 ὁμοούσιος *cf.* CH I,10:
καὶ ἡνώθη τῷ δημιουργῷ Νῷ—ὁμοούσιος γὰρ ἦν. *De huius vocis origine, historia et theologica significatione fusius ago in commentatione 'The Word Homoousios from
Hellenism to Christianity', quae typis nondum est mandata*

49. Θοῦλις ὁ Αἰγυπτίων βασιλεὺς ἐπαρθεὶς τοῖς κατορθώμασιν ἠρώτησεν εἰς τὸ μαντεῖον τοῦ Σαράπιδος περὶ ἑαυτοῦ οὕτως· 'Φράσον μοι, πυρισθενές, ἀψευδές, μάκαρ, ὁ τὸν αἰθέριον μετεγκλίνων δρόμον, τίς πρὸ τῆς ἐμῆς βασιλείας ἠδυνήθη ὑποτάξαι τὰ πάντα ἢ τίς μετ' ἐμέ;' Καὶ ἐδόθη αὐτῷ χρησμὸς οὗτος· 375

Πρῶτα θεός, μετέπειτα λόγος καὶ πνεῦμα σὺν αὐτοῖς·
ταῦτα δὲ σύμφυτα πάντα καὶ ἕν τε καὶ εἰς ἓν ἰόντα,
οὗ κράτος αἰώνιον·
ὠκέσι ποσὶ βάδιζε, θνητέ, ἄδηλον διανύων βίον.

50. <Ὁ δὲ Πετισσώνιος Φαραὼ βασιλεὺς εὐθέως ἀπῆλθεν ἐν τῇ Μέμφει 380 εἰς τὸ μαντεῖον τὸ περιβόητον· καὶ ποιήσας θυσίαν ἐπηρώτα τὴν Πυθίαν λέγων· 'Σαφήνισόν μοι, τίς ἐστιν πρῶτος ὑμῶν καὶ μέγας θεὸς τοῦ Ἰσραήλ;' Καὶ ἐδόθη αὐτῷ χρησμὸς οὗτος·>

Ἔστι κατ' οὐρανοῖο μεγάλοιο βεβηκὸς φλογὸς ὑπερβάλλον αἴθριον ἀέναον ἀθάνατον πῦρ, ὃ τρέμει πᾶν, οὐρανὸς γαῖά τε καὶ θάλασσα, 385 ταρτάριοί τε βύθιοι δαίμονες ἐρρίγησαν. Οὗτος ὁ θεὸς αὐτοπάτωρ, ἀπάτωρ, πατὴρ υἱὸς αὐτὸς ἑαυτοῦ, τρισόλβιος. Εἰς μικρὸν δὲ μέρος ἀγγέλων ἡμεῖς. Μαθὼν ἄπιθι σιγῶν.

51. Ὅτι ὁ Συριανὸς ἐν τοῖς ἑαυτοῦ πονήμασιν ἀναφέρει χρησμὸν τοιοῦτον·

Ἓν κράτος, εἷς δαίμων, γενέτης μέγας, ἀρχὸς ἁπάντων, 390
ἓν δὲ δέμας βασίλειον, ἐν ᾧ τάδε πάντα κυκλοῦται,

51–53. cod. T

51. 390–401 Syriani fragmentum aut ex Συμφωνία Ὀρφέως Πυθαγόρου καὶ Πλάτωνος περὶ τὰ λόγια aut ex Εἰς τὴν Ὀρφέως θεολογίαν βιβλία β΄ desumptum; cf. Orph. fr. 169 Kern

49. Fragmentum addubitatum: cf. Malalas II, p. 25 Dindorf ‖ 372 Σαράπιδος *em.* Bentley: Εὐριπίδου Β΄ Εὐριπία S *sed post* τὸ μαντεῖον *nullum divinitatis nomen ref.* Ox, Chron., Cedr., Su. ‖ περὶ αὐτοῦ Β΄ ‖ πρᾶσόν μοι S ‖ 372–373 πυρισθενές ἀψευδές Β΄ Chron Dindorf Erbse: πυρισθένη Ox πυρισθενῆ ἀψευδῆ Q΄ ‖ 374 *post* ἠδυνήθη: τὸ ταῦτα Β΄ τοσαῦτα Erbse ‖ 376 μετέπειτα: ἔπειτα χ ‖ 377 ταῦτα δὲ σύμφυτα πάντα Chron.: σύμφυτα δὲ πάντα Ox Cedr. Su. χ Ρ΄΄ σύμφυτα δὲ ταῦτα πάντα Υ ‖ ἕν τε καὶ *dubitanter scripsit* Erbse ἓν καὶ Υ ἔντομον Chron. *om. cett.* ‖ 379 ὠκέσι: ὠκύσι Β΄ S ὀρθοῖς Chron. ‖ βάδιζε: βαδίζει Β΄ βαδίζειν S ‖ θνητέ *om.* S ‖ διανοιῶν S ‖ βίον Ox Chron.: δρόμον χ **50.** Fragmentum addubitatum: cf. Malalas III, pp. 65–66 Dindorf ‖ 380–383 ὁ δὲ Πετισσώνιος—οὗτος: *haec verba vel similia e codice* Ox *addenda esse suspicatus sum; auctorem oraculi Solonem Atheniensem cont.* χ *et* π, *Chilonem* μ ‖ 380 Μέμφει Chron. Cedr.: Μέμφη Ox Dindorf ‖ 384 ἔστι Cedr. Dindorf: ἔσται Ox Erbse ‖ βεβηκὸς Cedr. Dindorf: βεβηκὼς Ox Erbse ‖ αἴθριον Ox Cedr. Dindorf: αἰθέριον Υ Erbse *om.* πχ ‖ 385 ὃ Ox Dindorf: ὃν Erbse ‖ πᾶν Ox Cedr. Dindorf Erbse: πᾶς Υ *om.* πχ ‖ 386 ταρτάριοί τε βύθιοι Ox Dindorf: ταρτάριοι βύθιοί τε Chron. Cedr. καὶ τάρταροι π Erbse *om.* χ ‖ ἐρρίγησαν Chron. Cedr. Dindorf: ἐρίγησαν Ox ἐρράγησαν Υ *om.* Erbse ‖ 388 ἄπιθι Chron. Cedr. Dindorf: ἄπειθι Ox Υ **51.** 390 γενέτης Τ: γένετο Clem. Eus. Procl. ‖ 391 δέμας βασίλειον: τὰ πάντα τέτυκται Clem. ‖ κυκλοῦται Τ: κυκλεῖται Clem. Eus. Procl.

πῦρ καὶ ὕδωρ καὶ γαῖα καὶ αἰθήρ, νύξ τε καὶ ἦμαρ
καὶ Μῆτις, πρώτη γενέτις, καὶ Ἔρως πολυτερπής·
5 πάντα γὰρ ἐν Ζηνὸς μεγάλῳ τάδε σώματι κεῖται,
πάντα μόνος δὲ νοεῖ, πάντων προνοεῖ τε θεουδῶς·   395
πάντῃ δὲ Ζηνὸς καὶ ἐν ὄμμασι πατρὸς ἄνακτος
ναίουσ᾽ ἀθάνατοί τε θεοὶ θνητοί τ᾽ ἄνθρωποι
θῆρές τ᾽ οἰωνοί θ᾽, ὁπόσα πνείει τε καὶ ἕρπει.
10 Οὐδέ ἕ που λήθουσιν ἐφήμερα φῦλ᾽ ἀνθρώπων,
ὅσσ᾽ ἀδίκως ῥέζουσί περ, οὐδ᾽ εἰν οὔρεσι θῆρες   400
ἄγριοι, τετράποδες, λασιότριχες, ὀμβριμόθυμοι.

52. Ὅτι ἡ Ἄρτεμις ὀλοφυρομένη πρὸς τὸν ἑαυτῆς εἶπε τεμενίτην χρησμὸν
τοιοῦτον·

Παῖς Ἑβραῖος κέλεταί με θεὸς μακάρεσσιν ἀνάσσων,
οὐρανόθεν καταβάς, βρότεον δέμας ἀμφιπολεύων,   405
δύμεναι εἰς Ἀΐδαο καὶ ἐς Χάος νῦν ἀφικέσθαι.
Κείνου δ᾽ οὐκ ἔστιν τὸ δεδογμένον ἐξαλέασθαι.
Χάζομαι ὡς ἐθέλει· τί νυ μήσομαι, δαίμονες ἄλλοι;

53. Ὅτι Ἰουδαίοις χρησμὸν περὶ τῆς συντελείας αἰτήσασιν ὁ Ἀπόλλων
ἔχρησεν οὕτως·   410

Ὦ μέγ᾽ ἀναιδέες, ὦ κακοφράσμονες <ἄνδρες> ἀλιτροί·
τίπτε πρὸς ἡμέτερον δόμον ἤλθετε; πῶς κ᾽ ἐμὸν οὖδας
ἀνθρώποις φθέγξαιθ᾽, οἷς μὴ βίος ὀρθὸς ὁδεύει,
οἳ νόμον ἐκ προγόνων γεννήτορος ἠρνήσαντο;
τοῖσι δ᾽ ἀπ᾽ ἀντολίης κακὸν ἔρχεται ἀπροφάσιστον.   415

Vv. 1–5: cf. Eus., P.E. III,9,2; Stob., Ecl. I,1,23 = Orph. fr. 168, 6–10
Kern; vv.1–4: cf. Clem., Strom. V,14,128,3; Procl., In Plat. Tim. 28c; v.1:
cf. Procl., In Plat. Tim. 31 a; v.4: cf. Procl., In Plat. Tim. 24d, 32c, 29a
= Orph. fr. 170 Kern; v.5: cf. Procl., In Plat. Tim. 28c; vv. 7–8: cf. Procl.,
In Plat. Parm. IV, 959, 21 = Orph. fr. 169 Kern

---

51. 393 πρώτη γενέτις T (γένετις Kern): πρῶτος γενέτωρ Eus. Procl. ‖ 394
Ζηνὸς μεγάλῳ T ('fort. μεγέθει aut tale substantivum in dativo' T mg.): Ζηνὸς
μεγάλου Procl. μεγάλῳ Ζηνὸς Eus. ‖ σώματι Eus. Stob.: σώματα T ‖ 395
πάντα T: 'in antigr. πάντα δὲ μόνος' Tmg. ‖ προνοεῖ τε em. Buresch: προ-
νοεῖται T ‖ θεουδῶς T: 'in antigr. θεοδῶς' Tmg. ‖ 396 πάντῃ δὲ T: οὕτως
δὲ Procl. ‖ καὶ Procl.: κεν T ‖ 399 οὐδὲ ἐπουλήθουσιν T: em. Buresch;
'puto legendum οὐδ᾽ αὐτὸν' Tmg. ‖ 401 ὀμβριμόθυμοι T pro ὀβρ- def. Buresch
Erbse   **52.** Vide Pythiae oraculum Augusto editum: cf. Malalas X, pp.
231–232 Dindorf ‖ 405 ἀμφιπολεύων em. Buresch: ἀμφιπολιτεύων T ‖ 406
νῦν: ἂψ dubitanter Scott-Ferguson ‖ 407 κείνου em. Erbse: κείνῳ T Buresch
53. 411 ἄνδρες ins. Buresch: 'videtur esse mutilus versus' et ad ἀλιτροί 'sup-
ple ἄνδρες' T mg. ‖ 412 κ᾽ Erbse: δ᾽ T Buresch ‖ 413 φθέγξαιθ᾽ em.
Buresch: φθέγξαιτ᾽ T

Ὄμνυμι τὸν κατέχοντα θρόνους ἐπὶ γαῖαν ἄπασαν
καὶ τῶν οὐρανίων μακάρων γεννήτορα κεῖνον,
ὃς κατέχει πόντον πολιὸν γλαυκήν τε θάλασσαν·
πάντα χαμαὶ πεσέει καὶ πάνθ᾽ ἕνα θρῆνον ἀείσει.

54. Ὅτι ἐν τοῖς χρόνοις τοῦ βασιλέως Λέοντος ναὸς εἰδώλου, ὁμῆλιξ τῆς   420
Κυζικηνῶν πόλεως, ἔμελλε παρὰ τῶν πολιτῶν εἰς εὐκτήριον μετασκευ-
ασθῆναι οἶκον τῆς ὑπερενδόξου δεσποίνης ἡμῶν θεοτόκου, καὶ εὑρέθη ἐν
λίθῳ μεγάλῳ κατὰ τὸ πλευρὸν τοῦ νεὼ χρησμὸς ἐγκεκολαμμένος. Ὁ δὲ
αὐτὸς εὑρέθη καὶ ἐν Ἀθήναις ἐν τῷ ἀριστερῷ μέρει τοῦ νεὼ κατὰ τὴν
πύλην, ἀπαραλλάκτως ὅμοιος ὢν ἐκείνῳ· ἐρωτησάντων γὰρ τῶν πολιτῶν   425
τὸν Ἀπόλλωνα οὕτως· ‘προφήτευσον ἡμῖν προφῆτα, Τιτὰν Φοῖβ᾽ Ἄπολλον,
τίνος ἔσται δόμος οὗτος;’ ἔχρησε τάδε·

55. Ὅσα μὲν πρὸς ἀρετὴν καὶ κόσμον ὄρωρε, ποιεῖτε· ἐγὼ γὰρ ἐφετμεύω
τρὶς ἕνα μοῦνον ὑψιμέδοντα θεόν, οὗ λόγος ἄφθιτος ἐν ἀδαεῖ κόρη ἐγκύμων
ἔσται· ὅστις ὥσπερ τόξον πυρφόρον μέσον διαδραμὼν κόσμον ἄπαντα   430

---

53. 416 ἐπὶ Buresch (*in app.*) Erbse: ὑπὸ T Buresch (*in textu*) ‖ 419 πάνθ᾽
ἕνα Erbse: πᾶς ἕνα *olim coni.* Erbse *in diss.* πᾶς θ᾽ ἕνα T Buresch   **54–55.**
Testimonium antiquissimum huius oraculi praebet Theodotus ep. Ancyrae,
Or. in S. Mariam Dei Genitricem (ed. Jugie in PO 19, 333–334). Responsum
Apollinis Sophocli adsignat cod. Paris. gr. 2598, saec. XV, fol. 268v: προφητεία
Σοφοκλέους περὶ τοῦ Χριστοῦ. Σοφοκλῆς ἔφη.   **54.** 421 πόλεως *em.* Buresch:
πόλεων T 'fort. πολιτῶν' T mg. ‖ 424 ἐν Ἀθήναις Erbse: ἐν Ἀθήναισιν T
Ἀθήνησιν Buresch Ἐπίγραμμα εὑρεθὲν ἐν λίθῳ κεκολλαμένον εἰς τὸν λεγόμενον
ναὸν τῶν θεῶν Ἀθηναίων, νυνὶ δὲ τῆς ἁγίας θεοτόκου Σ ‖ *titulus* Ἐρώτησις
Ἰάσωνος βασιλέως τῶν Ἀργοναυτῶν, ὅτε ἐκτίζετο ὁ ναός, εἰς τὸ Πύθιον τοῦ
Ἀπόλλωνος *legitur in* χ: *cf.* Malalas IV, pp. 77–78 Dindorf: καὶ ἀπελθόντες
οἱ Ἀργοναῦται εἰς τὸ μαντεῖον, ἔνθα λέγεται τὰ Πύθια θερμά, καὶ ποιήσαντες
θυσίαν ἐπηρώτησαν λέγοντες ταῦτα ‖ 426 Τιτὰν Φοῖβ᾽ Th χ E: Τιτὰν Φοῖβε
Σ Ox Dindorf Erbse Φοῖβε Τιτάν T Buresch ‖ 427 τίνος ἔσται δόμος οὗτος
Th: τί ἔσται <ἢ> τίνος ἔσται Σ τίνος ἔσται δόμος οὗτος ἢ τί δ᾽ ἔσται χ τίνος
ἔσται δόμος οὗτος εἰ τί δὲ ἔσται Ox Dindorf εἰ τί δὲ ἔσται *om.* Cedr. τί
ἐστι τίνι τε εἴη μετά σε δόμος οὗτος E τί ἐστι τίνος τε εἴη π τίνος ἄρα ἔσται
μ τίνος ἂν εἴη T Buresch Erbse   **55.** 428 ὄρωρε: ὤρωρεν Th ‖ ἐγὼ γὰρ
Th T Buresch Erbse: ἐγὼ δὲ Σχ Ox Dindorf ἐγὼ δ᾽ π πλὴν ἐγὼ μ ‖ ἐφετμεύω:
'ἤγουν μετὰ ἀληθείας προσαγορεύω' T mg. ἐφετμέω Cedr. Dindorf ἐπεθνεύω
Ox ‖ 429 τρὶς ἕνα Th Ox χ: τρεῖν ἕνα Cedr. Dindorf τρεῖς ἕνα Σπ P
τρισένα TL᾽ Buresch Erbse ‖ μοῦνον Σ T Buresch Erbse: μόνον χ *om.* Th
π ἐν τρισὶν ἕνα μόνον μ ‖ οὗ λόγος Σ Th TPQ᾽: οὗ ὁ λόγος B᾽ZS ‖ ἀδαεῖ:
'τουτέστιν ἀπειρογάμῳ' T mg. Chron. Cedr. E Dindorf ἀδαῆ Ox ‖ κόρη
Th Ox Cedr. χπμ E Dindorf *om. cett.* ‖ ἐγκύμων Σ: ἔγκυμος Ox Th T χπ
E Buresch Erbse ἔγκυος Chron. Cedr. Dindorf μ ‖ 430 ὅστις T Buresch
Erbse: ὃς Th χ ‖ ὅστις ὥσπερ: οὗτος ὥσπερ Ox Dindorf ὥσπερ γὰρ π οὗτος
γὰρ μ ‖ πυρφόρον Σ Th T Buresch Erbse: πυριφόρον Ox Cedr. Dindorf χ
‖ πυρφόρον τόξον E ‖ κόσμον ἄπαντα: ἄπαντα κόσμον Th Ox Dindorf

ζωγρήσας πατρὶ προσάξει δῶρον· αὐτῆς ἔσται δόμος οὗτος, Μυρία δὲ τὸ ὄνομα αὐτῆς.

56. Ἐκ τῶν Σκαμάνδρου.

Εἷς πρὸ αὐγῶν θεὸς γεννηθείς, ὁ πρὸ οὐρανῶν καὶ γῆς καὶ πάσης κτίσεως καὶ κατασκευῆς κόσμου ὤν, ὡς τρισεὶς θεός, λόγος ἐκ Μαρίας [τινος],   435
παρθένου τινὸς Ἑβραΐδος, τίκτεται [ἐκ παρθένου].

57. Ἐκ τοῦ κατὰ Λουκᾶν ἁγίου εὐαγγελίου.

Ἀνέβη δὲ καὶ Ἰωσὴφ ἀπὸ τῆς Γαλιλαίας πόλεως Ναζαρὲθ εἰς τὴν πόλιν
Ἰούδα ἥτις καλεῖται Βηθλέεμ, ἀπογράψασθαι σὺν Μαριὰμ τῇ ἐμνηστευμένῃ
αὐτῷ, οὔσῃ ἐγκύῳ (p).   440

58. Ἐκ τῆς πρὸς Γάλατας ἐπιστολῆς Παύλου.

Ὅτε δὲ ἦλθεν τὸ πλήρωμα τοῦ χρόνου, ἐξαπέστειλεν ὁ θεὸς τὸν υἱὸν αὐτοῦ,
γενόμενον ἐκ γυναικός, γενόμενον ὑπὸ νόμον, ἵνα τοὺς ὑπὸ νόμον ἐξαγοράσῃ,
ἵνα τὴν υἱοθεσίαν ἀπολάβωμεν (q).

59. Ἐκ τοῦ κατὰ Ἰωάννην εὐαγγελίου.   445

Ὅταν ὑψωθῶ πάντας ἑλκύσω πρὸς ἐμαυτόν (r).

60. Ἐκ τῆς α΄ καθολικῆς ἐπιστολῆς Πέτρου τοῦ ἁγίου ἀποστόλου.

Κρεῖττον γὰρ ἀγαθοποιοῦντας, εἰ θέλοι τὸ θέλημα τοῦ θεοῦ, πάσχειν ἢ
κακοποιοῦντας. Ὅτι καὶ Χριστὸς ἅπαξ περὶ ἁμαρτιῶν ὑπὲρ ἡμῶν ἀπέθανεν,
δίκαιος ὑπὲρ ἀδίκων, ἵνα ἡμᾶς προσαγάγῃ τῷ θεῷ (s).   450

61. Ἐκ τοῦ κατὰ Μάρκον εὐαγγελίου.

Καὶ ἐξεπλήσσοντο δὲ οἱ ὄχλοι ἐπὶ τῇ διδαχῇ αὐτοῦ λέγοντες· Πόθεν τούτῳ
ταῦτα, καὶ τίς ἡ σοφία ἡ δοθεῖσα τούτῳ, καὶ δυνάμεις τοιαῦται διὰ τῶν
χειρῶν αὐτοῦ γίνονται; οὐχ οὗτός ἐστι ὁ υἱὸς τοῦ τέκτονος καὶ Μαρίας (t);

56–62. cod. Σ

p) Lc. 2,4–5   q) Gal. 4,4–5   r) Io. 12,32   s) I Pt. 3,17–18
t) Mc. 6,2–3

55. 431 ζωγρεύσας Ox Dindorf ‖ αὐτῆς ἔσται δόμος οὗτος T Buresch Erbse:
οὗτος ἔσται δόμος Th ‖ οὗτος om. Σ Ox Dindorf ‖ Μυρία Σχπ PT Erbse
'forte Μαρία' Tmg. Μαρία Th Ox Cedr. E Buresch Μηρία Q' ‖ 431–432
τὸ ὄνομα: τοὔνομα Σχπ Th Ox E Dindorf   **56.** 434 πρὸ αὐγῶν θεὸς Σ
Pitra: θεὸς πρὸ αὐγῶν transp. Erbse ‖ 435 τρισεὶς (vel τρὶς εἷς) Erbse: τρεῖς
ἕνα Σ ‖ ἐκ Μαρίας Erbse: ἀπὸ Μαρίας Σ Pitra ‖ 436 <ἐκ> παρθένου coni.
Erbse ‖ τινος Ἑβραΐδος corr. Erbse: τιτος εραιδος Σ τις ἀίδιος Pitra ‖ verba
τινος (post Μαρίας) et ἐκ παρθένου (post τίκτεται) exp. Erbse

62. Ἐκ τῶν Σκαμάνδρου. 455

Φῶς ἐκ φωτὸς ὁ ὕψιστος, ὁ αἰώνιος, ὁ ἄφθαρτος φρικτὸς καὶ <ἐν> ξύλῳ
τρισμακαρίστῳ τανυσθείς, νύκτωρ τριήμερος φανείς, εἰς Ὄλυμπον ἑπτά-
ζωνον ἀνδρόδμητος ἀνεξιχνίαστος <ἔχων τε> αὐτεξούσιον ἀρχαγγελικὸν
ἐφ᾽ ἅρματος τέτρασι ζῴοις πολυομμάτοις ἑξαπτερύγοις <ἐπαρθεὶς τῷ>
προγεννήτορι πατρὶ καὶ ὁμοουσίῳ πνεύματι συγκάθηται <ἐν τῷ> θρόνῳ, 460
ὁ πρὸ ὢν καὶ <νῦν> ὢν καὶ ἀεὶ διαμένων θεὸς εἰς τοὺς αἰῶνας· ἀμήν.

---

62. 455 Σκαμάνδρου *corr.* Pitra: σκαμάντρου Σ ‖ 458 ἀνδρόδμητος *em.* Erbse:
ἀνδρίδμητος Σ ‖ 459 ἐφ᾽ *corr.* Erbse: ἐπὶ Σ ‖ τέτρασι ζῴοις πολυομμάτοις
ἑξαπτερύγοις *cf.* Apoc. 4,6.8: Καὶ ἐν μέσῳ τοῦ θρόνου καὶ κύκλῳ τοῦ θρόνου
τέσσαρα ζῷα γέμοντα ὀφθαλμῶν ἔμπροσθεν καὶ ὄπισθεν... καὶ τὰ τέσσαρα
ζῷα, ἓν καθ᾽ ἓν αὐτῶν ἔχων ἀνὰ πτέρυγας ἕξ, κυκλόθεν καὶ ἔσωθεν γέμου-
σιν ὀφθαλμῶν κτλ. ‖ 460 συγκάθηται *em.* Erbse: συγκάθεται Σ ‖ *omnia sup-
plementa add.* Erbse

⟨ΒΙΒΛΙΟΝ Β′

ΘΕΟΛΟΓΙΑΙ ΤΩΝ ΠΑΡ᾽ ΕΛΛΗΣΙ ΚΑΙ ΑΙΓΥΠΤΙΟΙΣ ΣΟΦΩΝ⟩

1. Συμφωνία ἐκ τῶν παλαιῶν φιλοσόφων τῶν Ἑλλήνων πρὸς τὴν ἁγίαν
καὶ θεόπνευστον νέαν γραφὴν ἤγουν ἀπόδειξις καὶ ἔλεγχος παρ᾽ αὐτῶν
περὶ τῆς ἁγίας ὁμοουσίας καὶ ὑπερουσίας, ἀδιαιρέτου δημιουργοῦ, ζω-   5
αρχικῆς τε καὶ προσκυνητῆς τριάδος, πατρὸς λέγω καὶ υἱοῦ καὶ ἁγίου
πνεύματος, καὶ <περὶ> τῆς ὑπεραγάθου καὶ φιλανθρώπου ἐνσάρκου
οἰκονομίας τοῦ ἑνὸς τῆς αὐτῆς πανσέπτου καὶ πανυμνήτου μακαρίας τριάδος, θεοῦ λόγου <καὶ περὶ τῆς τιμίου καὶ σωτηριώδους αὐτοῦ σταυρώσεως>.

2. Ὅτι Ὀρφεύς, ὁ Οἰάγρου τοῦ Θρακός, πρότερον μὲν ὕμνους τινὰς εἰς   10
τοὺς ἐξαγίστους θεοὺς ἐξυφάνας καὶ τὰς μιαρὰς γενέσεις αὐτῶν διηγη-
σάμενος, εἶτα συνεὶς ὥσπερ τὸ δυσσεβὲς τοῦ πράγματος, μετέθηκεν ἑαυτὸν
ἐπὶ τὸ μόνον καλόν, καὶ τὸν ὄντως ὑμνῶν θεὸν καὶ τὴν τῶν πάλαι Χαλδαίων
σοφίαν [δηλαδὴ τὴν τοῦ Ἀβραάμ] ἐπαινῶν παραινεῖ τῷ ἰδίῳ παιδὶ Μουσαίῳ
τοῖς μὲν φθάσασι μυθευθῆναι μὴ πείθεσθαι, τοῖς δὲ ῥηθήσεσθαι μέλλουσι   15
προσέχειν τὸν νοῦν. Ἔστι δὲ τὰ ἔπη ταῦτα·

3.   Φθέγξομαι οἷς θέμις ἐστί· θύρας δ᾽ ἐπίθεσθε, βέβηλοι,
        φεύγοντες δικαίων θεσμοὺς θεῖόν τε νόημα

---

1. cod. Σ
2–6. cod. Τ

1–2. ΒΙΒΛΙΟΝ Β′ ΘΕΟΛΟΓΙΑΙ ΤΩΝ ΠΑΡ᾽ ΕΛΛΗΣΙ ΚΑΙ ΑΙΓΥΠΤΙΟΙΣ ΣΟΦΩΝ
planitatis causa inserui
1. 3 ἐκ *exp.* Scott-Ferguson ‖ 4 παρ᾽ αὐτῶν *em.* Erbse: κατ᾽ αὐτῶν Σ Scott-
Ferguson ‖ 7 περὶ *ins.* Erbse ‖ 9 *verba post* λόγου *add.* Erbse   **2.** Cf.
Theoph., Ad Autol. III,2; Ps.Iust., Coh. 36,4; Lact., Div. Inst. I,7,6–7; Cyr.
Al., C.Iul. I,35 ‖ 14 *verba* δηλαδὴ τὴν τοῦ Ἀβραάμ *corrupta ex margine in tex-*
tum irrepsisse suspicatus sum et delenda existimavi   **3.** Vv. 4–8. 10–12. 14. 16.
17. 21. 22. 24. 33–37 cf. Ps.Iust., De Mon. 2,4; vv. 1. 2–8. 14. 15. 17.
21. 22. 24. 33–37 cf. Ps.Iust., Coh. 15,1 et Cyr. Al., C. Iul. I,35 (= Orph.
fr. 245 Kern); vv. 1. 3–9. 10–12 cf. Clem. Al., Protr. 7,74,4–6; vv. 14. 16.
35. 36 a. 34 b cf. Clem. Al., Strom. V, 14, 126,5– 127,2; vv. 5–9 cf. Clem.
Al., Strom. V, 14,123,1; vv. 10–12. 21–23 cf. Clem. Al., Strom. V, 12,78,4–5;
v. 17 cf. Clem. Al., Strom. V, 14,133,1–2 (= Orph. fr. 246 Kern); vv.
27–31. 33–36. 38–40. 43. 44 cf. Clem. Al., Strom. V,14,123,2–124,1; vv.
1–12. 14–21. 25–36. 38–46 cf. Eus., P.E. XIII,12,5; v. 1 cf. Eus., P.E.
III,7,1 et III,13,4 et Thdrt., Graec. aff. cur., I,86 et I,115; vv. 10–12. 21.
23. 33–36. 38–40 cf. Thdrt., Graec. aff. cur., II,30–31 (= Orph. fr. 247
Kern) ‖ 17 φθέγξομαι—βέβηλοι 'quaere in Iustino et confer' T mg.

πάντες ὁμῶς. Σὺ δ᾽ ἄκουε, φαεσφόρου ἔγγονε Μήνης,
Μουσαῖ᾽, ἐξερέω γὰρ ἀληθέα, μηδέ σε τὰ πρὶν   20
5 ἐν στήθεσσι φανέντα φίλης αἰῶνος ἀμέρσῃ.
Εἰς δὲ λόγον θεῖον βλέψας τούτῳ προσέδρευε
ἰθύνων κραδίης νοερὸν κύτος· εὖ δ᾽ ἐπίβαινε
ἀτραπιτοῦ, μοῦνον δ᾽ ἐσόρα κόσμοιο τυπωτὴν
ἀθάνατον. Παλαιὸς δὲ λόγος περὶ τοῦδε φαείνει·   25
10 εἷς ἔστ᾽ αὐτογενής, <Διὸς> ἔκγονα πάντα τέτυκται,
ἐν δ᾽ αὐτοῖς αὐτὸς περινίσσεται οὐδέ τις αὐτὸν
εἰσοράᾳ θνητῶν, αὐτὸς δέ γε πάντας ὁρᾶται.
[αὐτὸν δ᾽ οὐχ ὁρόωσι· περὶ γὰρ νέφος ἐστήρικται.]
Οὗτος δ᾽ ἐξ ἀγαθῶν θνητοῖς κακὸν οὐκ ἐπιτέλλει   30
15 ἀνθρώποις, αὐτοῖς δὲ κέρις καὶ μῖσος ὀπηδεῖ
καὶ πόλεμος καὶ λοιμὸς ἰδ᾽ ἄλγεα δακρυόεντα.
Οὐδέ τις ἔσθ᾽ ἕτερος, τῷ κεν ῥέα πάντ᾽ ἐσορῇται.
Οὔ κεν ἴδοις αὐτόν, πρὶν δή ποτε δ <εὖρ>᾽ ἐπὶ γαῖαν,
τέκνον ἐμόν, δείξω σοι, ὁπηνίκα δέρκομαι αὐτοῦ   35
20 ἴχνια καὶ χεῖρα στιβαρὴν κρατεροῖο θεοῖο.
Αὐτὸν δ᾽ οὐχ ὁρόω, περὶ γὰρ νέφος ἐστήρικται·
πᾶσι γὰρ θνητοῖς <θνηταὶ> κόραι εἰσὶν ἐν ὄσσοις
μικραί, ἐπεὶ σάρκες <τε> καὶ ὀστέα ἐμπεφύασιν,
ἀσθενέες τ᾽ ἰδέειν Δία τὸν πάντων μεδέοντα.   40

---

3. 19 πάντες ὁμῶς Ps.Iust. Clem. T Buresch Erbse: πᾶσιν ὁμοῦ Eus. ‖
ἔγγονε Eus. (*codd.* ION) T Buresch Holladay: ἔκγονε Ps.Iust. Clem. Eus. (*cod.*
B) Cyr. Erbse ‖ 20 Μουσαῖε T *em.* Buresch ‖ μὴ δέ σε T: *em.* Buresch ‖
24 τυπωτὴν Eus. T Buresch Erbse: ἄνακτα *cett.* ‖ 25 *ad* παλαιὸς δὲ λόγος
verba 'ὁ τοῦ Μωσέως καὶ τῶν ἄλλων προφητῶν' *asterisco referuntur* T mg. ‖ 26
αὐτογενής Ps.Iust. Clem., Protr. Cyr. T Buresch Erbse: αὐτοτελής Clem.,
Strom. Eus. ‖ Διὸς: *cf.* Orph. fr. 168,2 Kern Διὸς δ᾽ ἐκ πάντα τέτυκται *et*
infra v. 24 Δία τὸν πάντων μηδέοντα; τοῦ δ᾽ *suppl.* Kroll ἑνὸς Ps.Iust. Buresch
Erbse Riedweg Holladay αὐτοῦ Eus. ‖ ἔκγονα πάντα τέτυκται T Buresch
Erbse: δ᾽ ὕπο πάντα τελεῖται Eus. πέφυκεν Clem., Strom. ‖ 27 περινίσσεται Clem., Protr. Eus. T Buresch Erbse: περιγίνεται Ps.Iust. Cyr. ‖ 28
εἰσοράᾳ Ps.Iust. Clem. Eus. Thdrt. Kern Erbse Riedweg: εἰσοράει T Buresch
Holladay ‖ 29 αὐτὸν—ἐστήρικται *del.* Kern Erbse *def.* Buresch Riedweg
Holladay; *vide infra* v. 21 ‖ 30 οὗτος T: αὐτὸς Eus. ‖ 31 αὐτοῖς δὲ κέρις
Erbse: κ᾽ ἔρις T Buresch Holladay δὲ τ᾽ ἔρις Schenkl (*ad Eus. ante codicis T*
editionem) αὐτῷ (*cod.* D᾽ *et* Mras) δὲ χάριν Eus. χάρις Stephanus Mras ‖ 33
οὐδέ τις Ps.Iust. Clem. Eus. Cyr. Riedweg: οὐδεὶς T Buresch Erbse Holladay
‖ τῷ κεν ῥέα πάντ᾽ ἐσορῇται T Buresch Erbse: σὺ δέ κεν ῥέα πάντ᾽ ἐσορήσω
Eus. (*em.* Mras: ἐσόρησο *codd.*) ‖ 34 οὔ κεν ἴδοις *em.* Buresch Kern Erbse:
οὔκουν ἴδησ᾽ T αἴ κεν ἴδῃς Eus. οὔ κεν ἴδῃς Elter Holladay ‖ πρὶν: 'πρὸ
τοῦ σαρκωθῆναι καὶ ἐπὶ γῆν ὀφθῆναι' Tmg. ‖ δήποτε T: *em.* Buresch ‖ δ
[1 cm]᾽ ἐπὶ T: *em.* Buresch ‖ 36 ἴχνια: 'ὅτε τῶν θυρῶν κεκλεισμένων ἔδειξε
τὰς χεῖρας καὶ τοὺς πόδας' (*cf.* Io. 20,26) T mg. ‖ στιβαρὴν χεῖρα T Holladay:
b *supra* στιβαρὴν *et* a *supra* χεῖρα *in* T ‖ 38 θνηταὶ *ins.* Buresch ‖ 39 τε
ins. Buresch ‖ 40 Δία τὸν πάντων Ps.Iust., Coh. *edd.* Erbse: τὸν διὰ πάντων
Ps.Iust., Coh. Mon. q Stephanus τὸν ἀεὶ πάντων Ps.Iust., Mon. s τὸν δὴ
πάντα T Holladay τὸν δὴ πάντων Buresch διὰ πάντων τὸν Burkert *ap.* Riedweg

25 Λοιπὸν ἐμοὶ καὶ πᾶσι δεκάπτυχον ἀνθρώποισιν·
οὐ γάρ κέν τις ἴδοι θνητῶν μερόπων κρείοντα,
εἰ μὴ μουνογενής τις ἀπορρὼξ φύλου ἄνωθεν
Χαλδαίων· ἴδρις γὰρ ἔην ἄστρων τε πορείης
καὶ σφαίρης, ἥ τ᾽ ἀμφὶς ὀχῆος ἀεὶ περιτέλλει   45
30 κυκλοτερὴς ἴση τε κατὰ σφέτερον κνώδακα.
Πνεύματα δ᾽ ἡνιοχεῖ περί τ᾽ ἠέρα καὶ περὶ χεῦμα,
ἐκφαίνει δὲ πυρὸς σέλατα, διαφεγγέα πάντῃ.
Αὐτὸς δὴ μέγαν αὖθις ἐπ᾽ οὐρανὸν ἐστήρικται
χρυσέῳ εἰνὶ θρόνῳ· γαίη δ᾽ ὑπὸ ποσσὶ βέβηκε,   50
35 χεῖρα δὲ δεξιτερὴν ἐπὶ τέρμασιν ὠκεανοῖο
πάντοθεν ἐκτέτακεν, ὀρέων δὲ τρέμει βάσις αὐτὸν
ἐν θυμῷ πολιῆς τε βάθος χαροποῖο θαλάσσης
οὐδὲ φέρειν δύναται κρατερὸν μένος. Ἔστι δὲ πάντῃ
αὐτὸς ἐπουράνιος καὶ ἐπὶ χθονὶ πάντα τελευτᾷ   55
40 ἀρχὴν αὐτὸς ἔχων, ᾗ δ᾽ αὖ μέσον, ᾗ δὲ τελευτήν,
ὡς λόγος ἀρχαίων, ὡς ὑδογενὴς διέταξεν
ἐκ θεόθεν γνώμην τε λαβὼν καὶ δίπλακα θεσμόν.
Ἄλλως οὐ θεμιτόν σε λέγειν, τρομέω δὲ τελίην,
ἐκ νόου ἐξ ὑπάτου κραίνει περὶ πάντ᾽ ἐνὶ τάξει.   60

41 λοιπὸν· 'ἀντὶ τοῦ καὶ ἐμοὶ καὶ πᾶσι τοῖς ἀνθρώποις' Τ mg. || δεκάπτυχον: 'ἡ μωσαϊκὴ δεκάλογος διδάσκαλος ἔσται' Τ mg. || 42 κρείοντα Τ Buresch Erbse Holladay: κραίνοντα Eus. || 44 Χαλδαίων κτλ.: 'ὁ γὰρ τὴν δεκάπτυχον γράψας Μωσῆς τῶν Χαλδαίων ἔμπειρος ἦν καὶ τῆς ἀστρονομίας' Tmg. || ἄστρων τε πορείης Τ Buresch Erbse: ἄστροιο πορείης Clem. Eus. || 45 ἥτ᾽ Τ Holladay 'ἥτις ἐξ ἀμφοτέρωθεν τοῦ ὁρίζοντος ἢ τοῦ ἄξονος ἀεὶ κινεῖται' Τ mg. || 46 κυκλοτερὲς τ᾽ ἐν ἴσῳ, κατὰ δὲ (τε, κατὰ Clem.) σφέτερον κνώδακα Clem., Strom. Eus. || 47 πνεύματα Eus. Buresch Erbse: πνεύματι Clem. Τ Riedweg Holladay || ἡνιοχεῖ: Τ supra lin. 'εὐτάκτως ἄγει <περὶ> (ins. Buresch) τὸν ἀέρα καὶ (em. Buresch: ἢ Τ) τὰ τῆς γῆς πέρατα, τὸ ὕδωρ' || 48 πυρὸς σέλατα: Τ supra lin. 'τῆς θεότητος ἀπαυγάσματα' et Τ mg. 'in antigr. πυροσέλευτα' || 50 χρυσέῳ· 'in antigr. χρυσέων' Τ mg. || εἰνὶ Ps.Iust., Mon. q Eus. Cyr.: ἐνὶ Clem. Ps.Iust. Coh. Mon. s || γαίη δ᾽ ὑπὸ Clem., Strom. 124 Eus. Thdrt. Τ Buresch Erbse Holladay: γαίης δ᾽ ἐπὶ Ps.Iust., Coh. Mon. γαίη δ᾽ ἐπὶ Clem., Strom. 127 γαίη δ᾽ ἐπὶ Cyr. || 52–53 πάντοθεν—θαλάσσης Τ: πάντοθεν ἐκτέτακεν· περὶ γὰρ τρέμει οὔρεα μακρὰ Ps.Iust., Coh. Mon., Cyr. πάντοθεν ἐκτέτακεν, γαίη δ᾽ ἐπὶ (ὑπὸ) ποσ(σ)ὶ βέβηκεν Clem., Strom. 127 Eus. ἐκτέτακεν, ὀρέων δὲ τρέμει βάσις ἔνδοθι θυμοῦ (θυμῷ) Clem., Strom. 124 Eus. || 54 πάντῃ Τ Clem.: πάντων codd. Eus. πάντως Stephanus Mras || 57 ὑδογενὴς coni. Scaliger appr. Mras Riedweg: ὑλογενὴς Τ Buresch Erbse Holladay; 'ὁ τὴν τῶν ἐνύλων γένεσιν γράψας Μωσῆς' Τ mg. || 58 δίπλακα: 'forte δυσί· διὸ γὰρ ἔλαβε τὸν νόμον ἐν πλαξί' Tmg. || 59 ἄλλως Clem. Eus. Riedweg: ἀλλ᾽ ὡς Τ Buresch Erbse Holladay || σε Clem. Riedweg: δὲ Eus. Τ Holladay με Buresch Erbse || τρομέω: 'φρίττω τὸ μυστήριον λογιζόμενος' Tmg. || δὲ τελίην Τ Buresch Holladay: δέ τε (γε Eus.) γυῖα Clem. Eus. δέ γε λίην em. Erbse || 60 ὑπάτου Τ: em. Buresch || πάντ᾽ ἐνὶ: 'in antigr. πάντες' Τ mg.

45 Ὦ τέκνον, σὺ δὲ σοῖσι νόοις πέλας ἴσθι ἐς αὐτόν
μηδ᾽ ἀπόδος, μάλ᾽ ἐπικρατέων στέρνοις θεοφήμην.

4. Ὅτι θεὸς ἀρχὴν μὲν ἔχει τὸν οὐρανόν, μέσον δὲ τὴν γῆν, τέλος δὲ τὰ
ὑποχθόνια. Τὸ δὲ 'ἔχων' εἴληπται ἀντὶ τοῦ κρατῶν καὶ ἄρχων. Ἢ ὅτι 'ἀρχὴν
μὲν ἔχει' λέγεται ὡς γενεσιουργὸς τῶν ἄλλων, 'μέσον' δὲ ὡς τὰ μεταξὺ   65
γεγονότα δημιουργήματα συνέχων, 'τέλος' δὲ ὡς μετὰ τὴν πάντων παρέλευσιν
ἀϊδίως διαμένων.

5. Ὅτι δύο δεκάλογοι ὑπὸ Μωσέως ἐγράφησαν προ<σ>τάξει τοῦ ὄντως
θεοῦ, ὧν ὁ πρῶτός ἐστιν οὗτος· 'τοὺς βωμοὺς αὐτῶν καθελεῖτε καὶ τὰς
στήλας <αὐτῶν> συντρίψετε καὶ τὰ ἄλση <αὐτῶν> ἐκκόψετε καὶ τὰ   70
γλυπτὰ τῶν θεῶν αὐτῶν κατακαύσετε πυρί· οὐ γὰρ μὴ προσκυνήσητε θεῷ
ἑτέρῳ· ὁ γὰρ κύριος ὁ θεὸς ζηλωτὸν ὄνομα, θεὸς ζηλωτής ἐστι', καὶ τὰ
ἑξῆς (a). Ὁ δὲ ἕτερος δεκάλογός ἐστιν οὗτος· 'ἐγώ εἰμι κύριος, ὁ θεός σου,
ὁ ἐξαγαγών σε ἐκ γῆς Αἰγύπτου, ἐξ οἴκου δουλείας. Οὐκ ἔσονταί σοι θεοὶ
ἕτεροι πλὴν ἐμοῦ', καὶ τὰ ἐξῆς (b).   75

6. Ὅτι ἐν τῷ τεσσαρεσκαιδεκάτῳ ψαλμῷ ἐξ ἐπερωτήσεως ἀπόκρισις θεία
φέρεται δεκάλογον ἔχουσα (c).

7. Ὅτι ὁ Πλάτων οὕτως εὔχεσθαι διδάσκει·

Ζεῦ βασιλεῦ, τὰ μὲν ἐσθλὰ καὶ εὐχομένοις καὶ ἀνεύκτοις
ἄμμι δίδου, τὰ δὲ λυγρὰ καὶ εὐχομένων ἀπερύκοις.   80

Τουτέστι· καὶ σιωπῶσιν ἡμῖν χαρίζου, ἅπερ οἶδας χρηστά· εἰ δέ τι τῶν
ἀσυμφόρων εὐξόμεθα τὸ μέλλον ἀγνοοῦντες, κώλυσον ὡς ἀγαθός.

8. Ὅτι ὁ Πλάτων ποτέ τινι θέλοντι περὶ οὐρανοῦ καὶ κινήσεως ἄστρων
διαλέγεσθαι ἔφη καταγινώσκων· Ἑταῖρε, πόσον ἔχεις ἀπὸ τοῦ οὐρανοῦ;'

---

7. codd. Tv: *om.* Steuchus Piccolos
8–31. cod. T

7. 79–80 Ps. Plat., Alcib. sec. 143a 1–2; cf. Procl., In Plat. Remp., Kroll
I, p. 188

a) Ex. 34,13–14   b) Ex. 20,1–3   c) Ps. 14,1–5

62 ἀπόδος *corr.* Buresch: ἄπογος T   **5.** 68 προτάξει T Buresch: *em.* Erbse
|| 70 αὐτῶν *utroque loco ins.* Buresch: *om.* T || συντρίψατε *et* ἐκκόψατε T:
em. Buresch || 71 προσκυνήσετε T: *em.* Buresch || 75 καὶ τὰ ἑξῆς Erbse:
et caetera T Buresch   **7.** 78 ὅτι ὁ T: ὁ δὲ v Wolff || 79 ζεῦ: ὦ BL Wolff
|| 80 λυγρὰ—ἀπερύκοις: λυγρὰ καὶ εὐχομένων ἀπέρυκε Procl. δειλὰ (*vel*
δεινὰ) καὶ εὐχομένοις ἀπαλέξειν κελεύει Ps. Plat. || 81–82 τουτέστι—ἀγαθός
om. v   **8.** Dictum spurium aliunde ignotum || 84 πόσον *em.* Buresch
Erbse: πόστον T

9. Ὅτι ἐν πολλοῖς Φάνητα φερωνύμως ὁ Ὀρφεὺς προσαγορεύει τὸν μονο-   85
γενῆ, τὸν υἱὸν τοῦ θεοῦ· οἴεται γὰρ αὐτῷ πρέπειν τὸ ὄνομα ὡς ἀϊδίως καὶ
ἀοράτως πανταχοῦ φαίνοντι καὶ ὡς πᾶσι τὸ ἐκ μὴ ὄντων φανῆναι παρα-
σχομένῳ. Μεμνημένος οὖν πολλαχῇ τοῦ μυθευομένου Διὸς καὶ τοῦ Διονύσου,
ὃν Φάνητα προσαγορεύει, δημιουργὸν πάντων αὐτὸν εἰσάγει τὸν Φάνητα
ὡσανεὶ τὸν τοῦ θεοῦ υἱόν, δι᾽ οὗ τὰ πάντα ἐφάνη. Διὸ καὶ ἐν τῇ τετάρτῃ   90
ῥαψῳδίᾳ πρὸς Μουσαῖον οὕτω λέγει·

ταῦτα νόῳ πεφύλαξο, φίλον τέκος, ἐν πραπίδεσσιν
εἰδώς περ μάλα πάντα παλαίφατα τἀπὸ Φάνητος.

10. Ὅτι τοῦ Ἀπόλλωνος εἰπόντος ‘πάντων δ᾽ ἀνθρώπων Σωκράτης
σοφώτατος’ ἐκεῖνος μετριοφρονῶν καὶ ἀπ᾽ ἐναντίας τῶν ἄλλων φερόμενος   95
οἷον προσποιουμένων εἰδέναι ἃ μὴ ἴσασιν ἔφη· ‘ἔοικα <οὖν> αὐτῷ τούτῳ
τῷ σμικρῷ σοφώτατος εἶναι, ὅτι ἃ μὴ οἶδα οὐδὲ οἴομαι εἰδέναι.’

11. Ὅτι ὁ Πλάτων τὰ περὶ θεολογίας μυστήρια μὴ καταπιστεύων ἀκαθάρ-
τοις ἀκοαῖς ἐν τῇ πρὸς Διονύσιον ἐπιστολῇ φησιν οὕτως· ‘φραστέον δή σοι
δι᾽ αἰνιγμῶν, ἵν᾽, ἄν τι ἡ δέλτος ἢ πόντου ἢ γῆς ἐν πτυχαῖς πάθη, ὁ ἀναγνοὺς   100
μὴ γνῷ.’

12. Ὅτι ἡ τριὰς ἀρχὴν καὶ μέσον καὶ τέλος ἔχει καὶ δῆλον ὅτι πάντα τὰ
ὄντα διὰ τριάδος συνέστηκε· διὸ ἐπὶ τοῦ ‘δύο’ ἀριθμοῦ ‘ἄμφω’ μὲν
λέγομεν καὶ ‘ἀμφότεροι’, ‘πάντες’ δὲ οὐ λέγομεν, ἀλλὰ κατὰ τῶν τριῶν
κυρίως καὶ τῶν ἐφεξῆς ἐξ αὐτῶν ταττομένων τὴν προσηγορίαν ταύτην   105
φέρομεν.

9. 92–93 Ἱεροὶ λόγοι ἐν ῥαψῳδίαις κδ᾽ (IV Rhapsodia ad Musaeum, Orph.
fr. 61 Kern)   **10.** 94–97 Ps.Iust., Coh. 36,1; 96–97 Plat., Apol. 21 d
6–7   **11.** 99–101 Plat., Ep. 2,312 d   **12.** 102–106 Arist., De caelo
A, 1, 268a 10–13; 15–19, pp. 1–2 Moraux: Καθάπερ γάρ φασι καὶ οἱ
Πυθαγόρειοι, τὸ πᾶν καὶ τὰ πάντα τοῖς τρισὶν ὥρισται· τελευτὴ γὰρ καὶ μέσον
καὶ ἀρχὴ τὸν ἀριθμὸν ἔχει τὸν τοῦ παντός, ταῦτα δὲ τὸν τῆς τριάδος (. . .)
Ἀποδίδομεν δὲ καὶ τὰς προσηγορίας τὸν τρόπον τοῦτον· τὰ γὰρ δύο ἄμφω
μὲν λέγομεν καὶ τοὺς δύο ἀμφοτέρους, πάντας δ᾽ οὐ λέγομεν, ἀλλὰ κατὰ τῶν
τριῶν ταύτην τὴν κατηγορίαν (προσηγορίαν T et codd. FO Aristotelis) κατά-
φαμεν (φέρομεν T φαμὲν seu εἰλήφαμεν codd. nonnulli) πρῶτον. De hac
Aristotelis sententia vide P. Moraux in “Hermes” 82 (1954), pp. 166 sqq.

9. 86 πρέπειν *em.* Buresch: τρέπειν T ‖ 87–88 παρασχομένου T: *em.* Buresch
‖ 88 μεμνημένου T: *em.* Buresch ‖ 93 τἀπὸ *coni.* Erbse: κἀκ T κἀπὸ
Buresch Kern   **10.** 95 σοφώτατος Ps.Iust. Buresch Erbse diss. Marcovich
Riedweg: σοφώτερος T Erbse ‖ ἀπ᾽ ἐναντίας *em.* Erbse: ἀπεναντίας
T Riedweg ‖ 96 προσποιουμένων Ps.Iust. Buresch Erbse: προσποιοῦνται
T ‖ οὖν *addidi* ‖ 97 σοφώτατος Ps.Iust. T Buresch Erbse Riedweg: σοφώτερος Plat. Marcovich ‖ οἴομαι Plat. Ps.Iust. Buresch: οἶμαι T Erbse
11. 99 δή Plat.: οὖν T Buresch Erbse ‖ 100 ἵν᾽, ἄν τι *em.* Buresch: ἵναν
τι T ‖ πόντου *em.* Buresch: πόντος T ‖ 100–101 πάθη *et* γνῷ T: *em.* Buresch

13. Ὅτι Πορφύριος ὁ Φοῖνιξ, ὁ Ἀμελίου μὲν συμφοιτητής, μαθητὴς δὲ Πλωτίνου, φησὶν οὕτως· ἹΠερὶ τοῦ πρώτου αἰτίου οὐδὲν ἴσμεν· οὔτε γὰρ ἁπτὸν οὔτε γνωστόν, ἀλλ᾽ ἔστιν αὐτοῦ γνῶσις ἡ ἀγνωσία.'

14. Ὅτι Ἰάμβλιχος ὁ Χαλκιδεὺς Πορφυρίου μαθητής.   110

15. Ὅτι ὁ Ἐφέσιος Ἡράκλειτος αἰνιττόμενος τὸ ῾<ὁ> ἔχων ὦτα ἀκούειν ἀκουέτω᾽ (d) φησίν· 'Ἀξύνετοι ἀκούσαντες κωφοῖσιν ἐοίκασι· φάτις αὐτοῖσι μαρτυρεῖ [λέγουσα] παρεόντας ἀπεῖναι.'

16. Ὅτι Ἡράκλειτος μεμφόμενος τοὺς θύοντας τοῖς δαίμοσι ἔφη· ῾Καθαίρονται δ᾽ ἄλλως αἵματι μιαινόμενοι, ὁκοῖον εἴ τις ἐς πηλὸν ἐμβὰς   115
πηλῷ ἀπονίζοιτο· μαίνεσθαι δ᾽ ἂν δοκέοι εἴ τίς μιν ἀνθρώπων ἐπιφράσαιτο οὕτω ποιέοντα. Καὶ τοῖς ἀγάλμασι δὲ τουτέοισιν εὔχονται, ὁκοῖον εἴ τις <τοῖς> δόμοισι λεσχηνεύοιτο οὔ τι <γινώσκων θεοὺς οὐδ᾽ ἥρωας, οἵτινές εἰσι>.'

17. Ὁ αὐτὸς πρὸς Αἰγυπτίους ἔφη· Ἱεἰ θεοί εἰσιν, ἵνα τί θρηνεῖτε αὐτούς;   120
εἰ δὲ θρηνεῖτε αὐτούς, μηκέτι τούτους ἡγεῖσθε θεούς.'

13. 108–109 Porph., Com. Parm. IX, lin.1–X, lin. 35, Hadot II, pp. 90–98; cf. fr. 427 Smith. De theologia apophatica huius fragmenti vide Saffrey, in Gonimos, 1988, pp. 1–20   **15.** 112–113 Heracl. fr. 2 Marcovich; cf. Clem. Al., Strom. V,14,115,3; Eus., P.E. XIII,13,42; Thdrt., Graec. aff. cur. I,70   **16.** 115–119 Heracl. fr. 86 Marcovich; cf. Clem. Al., Protr. IV,50,4; cf. Orig., C. Cels. I,5; VII,62   **17.** 120–121 Heracl. fr. 119 spur. Marcovich; cf. Plut., De Is. 379 B; Clem. Al., Protr. II,24,3; Epiph., Ancor. 104,1

d) Lc. 8,8; 14,35; cf. Mc. 4,9.23; Matth. 11,15; 13, 43

14. Vide fr. 33 c Smith   **15.** 111 ὁ ins. Neumann: om. T || 112 κωφοῖσιν Eus.: κωφοῖς Clem. Thdrt. || αὐτοῖσι Eus. (codd. IO) Thdrt.: αὐτοῖσιν Clem. αὐτοῖς Eus. (codd. ND) || 113 μαρτυρεῖ Clem. Eus. Thdrt. T: μαρτυρέει Buresch || λέγουσα T: exp. Neumann || ἀπεῖναι Eus. Thdrt.: ἀπιέναι Clem. **16.** 115 ὁκοῖον Neumann Buresch Erbse: οἷον T || ἐς Neumann Buresch Erbse: εἰς T Marcovich || 116 δοκέοι Buresch Erbse Marcovich: δοκοίη T Neumann || μιν Snell Erbse Marcovich: ἀυτον T αὐτὸν Neumann Buresch Diels || ἀνθρώπων del. Wilamowitz || 117 ποιέοντα Neumann Buresch Diels Erbse Marcovich: ποιοῦντα T || δὲ T: om. Clem. Orig. del. Wilamowitz || τοῦ τέοισιν T Clem. (cod. A") || ἔχονται T || ὁκοῖον Clem. Orig. VII: ὡς Orig. I οἶον T || 118 τοῖς Orig. (utroque loco) Erbse Marcovich: om. Clem. T Buresch || δόμοισι Orig. VII Erbse Marcovich: δόμοις Clem. Orig. I T Buresch || οὔ τι Orig. Diels Erbse Marcovich: θύειν T exp. Neumann Buresch || 118–119 γινώσκων—εἰσι ex Orig.VII add. Neumann Diels Erbse Marcovich   **17.** 120–121 θρενεῖτε (utroque loco) et ἡγεῖσθε T Erbse Marcovich: θρενέετε et ἡγέεσθε Neumann Buresch

18. Ὅτι Διαγόρας ὁ φιλόσοφος εἰς ναὸν Ἡρακλέους ἑσπέρας κατ<ὰ δείλην ἐπι>βάσης εἰσελθὼν ἔλαβε τὸν Ἡρακλέα ἐκ πρίνου κατεσκευασμένον καὶ χλευάζων εἶπεν· 'εἶα δή, ὦ Ἥρακλες, νῦν σοι ἤδη καιρός, ὥσπερ Εὐρυσθεῖ ἀτὰρ δ<ὴ καὶ> ἡμῖν ὑπουργῆσαι τὸν τρισκαιδέκατον τοῦτον ἆθλον   125 ἐκτελοῦντα καὶ τὴν ἐμὴν φακῆν ἕψοντα.' Καὶ τοῦτο εἰπὼν εἰς τὸ πῦρ αὐτὸν ἐνέθηκεν.

19. Ὅτι Διονύσιος, ὁ Σικελίας τύραννος, νικήσας τὴν Ἑλλάδα τοὺς θεοὺς αὐτῆς ἐσκύλευσε χλευάζων. Καὶ τοῦ μὲν Διὸς ἀφελόμενος τὸ χρυσοῦν περιβόλαιον ἐκέλευσεν ἐρεοῦν αὐτῷ ἐπιτεθῆναι, φάσκων κἂν τῷ θέρει   130 αὐτῷ τὸν χρυσὸν βαρὺν εἶναι κἂν τῷ χειμῶνι ψυχρόν, τὸ δὲ ἔριον ἐν ἀμφοτέροις τοῖς καιροῖς ἁρμόδιον.

20. Καὶ τοῦ Ἀσκληπιοῦ χρυσοῦ ὄντος τὸν πώγωνα λαβών, ἀσύμφωνον καὶ ἀπαράδεκτον εἶναι ἔφη τὸν μὲν πατέρα αὐτοῦ Ἀπόλλωνα ἀγένειον ἱστορεῖσθαι, τοῦτον δὲ γενειήτην.   135

21. Καὶ πάντων τῶν ξοάνων ἐκτεταμέναις χερσὶ χρυσᾶς φιάλας βασταζόντων ἀφείλετο, λαμβάνειν μᾶλλον λέγων ἢ ἀφαιρεῖσθαι· 'εὔηθες γάρ, φησί, πάνυ τὸ μὴ δέχεσθαι παρὰ τῶν προτεινόντων τὰς χεῖρας καὶ ἑκοντὶ διδόντων.'

22. Ὅτι ὁ Ἡράκλειτος ὁρῶν τοὺς Ἕλληνας γέρα τοῖς δαίμοσιν ἀπονέμοντας εἶπεν· 'Δαιμόνων ἀγάλμασιν εὔχονται οὐκ ἀκούουσιν, ὅκωσπερ <εἰ>   140 ἀκούοιεν, οὐκ ἀποδιδοῦσιν, ὅκωσπερ <εἰ> οὐκ ἀπαιτέοιεν.'

23. Ὅτι κατὰ Πίνδαρον ἀπίστοις πιστὸν οὐδέν.

24. Ὅτι Σιμωνίδης ἐρωτηθεὶς ὑπό τινος περὶ τοῦ θείου ἐπὶ πολλὰς ἡμέρας ἀνεβάλλετο καὶ αὖθις ἐρωτηθεὶς τὴν αἰτίαν τῆς ὑπερθέσεως· ''Οσον, ἔφη, μᾶλλον σκοπῶ περὶ τοῦ θείου, τοσοῦτον ἀπέχω εἰδέναι.'   145

25. Ὅτι ὁ Πορφύριος εἷς ἐγένετο παρὰ τὴν ἀρχὴν ἐξ ἡμῶν, διὰ δὲ τὰς

---

22. 141–142 Heracl. fr. 86 g¹ Marcovich   **23.** 143 Pind. fr. 233 Maehler: πιστὸν δ᾽ ἀπίστοις οὐδέν; cf. Clem. Al., Paed. III,12,92,4

---

18. Narratiuncula Diagorae adsignanda est: vide T. 29 Winiarczyk; cf. Clem. Al., Protr. II,24,4; Epiph., Ancor. 103,8 ‖ 122 Διαγόρας *scripsi* (*vide infra* Chron. VI,2,16): Διογένης *cett.* ‖ 122–123 κατὰ δείλην ἐπιβάσης *scripsi duce* Erbse: κατ [lac. 1,5 cm] βάσης T καταβάσης *suppl.* Buresch κατ᾽ οὐρανοῦ προβάσης Erbse diss. ‖ 123 πρίνου *scripsi duce* Erbse: ξύλου Clem. τρίχων T τρίχων ξύλῳ Buresch ‖ 125 δ [lac. 1 cm] T: *suppl.* Buresch *sec.* Clem. ‖ 126 ἕψοντα *em.* Buresch: ἕλοντα T   **19.** Cf. Clem. Al., Protr. IV,52,2; Lact., Div. Inst. II,4,16–17 ‖ 130 ἐρεοῦν Clem.: ἔριον T Buresch Erbse **20–21.** Cf. Lact., Div. Inst. II,4,18–19   **20.** 134 ἀπαράδεκτον Erbse: ἄδεκτον T Buresch   **22.** 141–142 ὅκωσπερ <εἰ> (*utroque loco*) Erbse: ὥσπερ T Buresch Marcovich ‖ 142 ἀπαιτέοιεν Buresch Erbse: ἀπαιτοῖεν T Marcovich **24.** Vide narratiunculam ap. Cic., Nat. deor. I,22,60, Pease I, pp. 349–350 **25.** Vide fr. 10 T. Smith; cf. Lact., Div. Inst. V,2,3; Eunap., Vitae soph. IV,2,5; Socr., H.E. III,23,38;

ἐπενεχθείσας αὐτῷ, ὡς ἱστόρησαν ἅγιοι, ὑπό τινων Χριστιανῶν ἐν Καισαρείᾳ τῆς Παλαιστίνης πληγὰς ἐν ἰδιωτικοῖς πράγμασιν ἀπέστη ἀφ᾽ ἡμῶν. Φιλοχρήματος δὲ ὢν πλουσίαν ἔγημε γυναῖκα πέντε παίδων μητέρα,   150 γεγηρακυῖαν ἤδη καὶ Ἑβραίαν.

26. Ὅτι Εὐριπίδης ἐν ΟΙΔΙΠΟΔΙ τῷ δράματί [αὐτοῦ] φησι·

κακὸν <γὰρ> ἄνδρα χρὴ κακῶς πάσχειν ἀεί.

27. Ὅτι Μένανδρος παραινεῖ·

ἄνθρωπος ὢν τοῦτ᾽ ἴσθι καὶ μέμνησ᾽ ἀεί.   155

Καὶ πάλιν·

εἰ θνητὸς εἶ, βέλτιστε, θνητὰ καὶ φρόνει.

Καὶ αὖθις·

ὑπὲρ εὐσεβείας καὶ λάλει καὶ μάνθανε.

28. <Καὶ πάλιν·>   160

ἔα κεκρύφθαι λανθάνουσαν ἀτυχίαν·
τὸ γὰρ ἐξελέγχειν τὴν ὕβριν διττὴν φέρει.

29. Καὶ τοῦτο τὸ δὴ λεγόμενον· ὄνου ἀποθανόντος ὠνὰς μὴ ἀναγίνωσκε.

30. Ὅτι Ἀντισθένης φησί·

αἰσχρὸν τό γ᾽ αἰσχρόν, κἂν δοκῇ, κἂν μὴ δοκῇ.   165

31. Ὅτι Τίμων ὁ Φλιάσιος, ὁ τοῦ Πύρρωνος μαθητής, οὕτω γράφει·

σχέτλιοι ἄνθρωποι, κάκ᾽ ἐλέγχεα, γαστέρες οἶον,
τοίων ἔκ τ᾽ ἐρίδων ἔκ τε στοναχῶν πέπλασθε.

---

26. 153 Euripides, TrGF 1049,4 Nauck-Snell; cf. Stob., Anth. IV,5,11, v.4 **27.** 155 Menander fr. 944 Koerte-Thierfelder sec. Stob., Anth. III,21,1 Philemonis est; 157 Menander fr. 945 Koerte-Thierfelder = Mon. 246 Jaekel sec. Stob., Anth. III,21,4 Antiphanis est; 159 Menander fr. 946 Koerte-Thierfelder = Mon. 781 Jaekel **28.** 161–162 Menander fr. 947 Koerte-Thierfelder novum distichon est **30.** 165 Antisthenes fr. novum: cf. Plut., Mor. 33c (De aud. poet. 12) **31.** 167–168 Timo Phliasius fr. 784 Suppl. Hell.; 170 fr. 785. Cf. Eus., P.E. XIV,18,28; Thdrt., Graec. aff. cur. II,20–21

---

150 φιλοχρήματος: de Porphyrii avaritia vide Beatrice, 'Antistes philosophiae' (1993), p. 41 ‖ πέντε παίδων: θυγατέρων μὲν πέντε, δυοῖν δὲ ἀρρένων οὖσαν μητέρα Porph., Ad Marc.1 ‖ 152 αὐτοῦ exp. Erbse ‖ 153 γὰρ Stob. ins. Buresch ‖ πάσχειν Stob.: πράσσειν T Buresch Erbse **28.** 160 Καὶ πάλιν: lac. [ca. 6 litt.] expl. Buresch ‖ 162 διττὴν φέρει τὴν ὕβριν T: transp. Buresch **29.** Fortasse paroemia valde obscura quam Erbse sic interpretatus est: 'noli pactum emptionis relegere (h.e. noli recordari, quanti illum asinum emeris), ne detrimento frustra movearis' **31.** 168 τοίων Eus. Thdrt. Buresch Erbse: τοῖον T ποίων Wilamowitz ‖ πέπλασθε Eus. (codd. ON): πεπλάνησθε T Eus. Thdrt. (codices nonnulli) πέπλησθε Thdrt. (codd. cett.)

Καὶ πάλιν·

ἄνθρωποι κενεῆς οἰήσιος ἔμπλεοι ἀσκοί.   170

32. Ἑρμοῦ <ἐν λόγῳ τρίτῳ τῶν> ΠΡΟΣ ΑΣΚΛΗΠΙΟΝ περὶ θεοῦ.

Οὐ γὰρ ἐφικτόν ἐστιν εἰς ἀμυήτους τοιαῦτα μυστήρια παρέχεσθαι, ἀλλὰ
τῷ νοῒ ἀκούσατε· ἓν μόνον ἦν φῶς νοερὸν πρὸ φωτὸς νοεροῦ καὶ ἔστιν ἀεί,
νοῦς νοὸς φωτεινός· καὶ οὐδὲν ἕτερον ἦν ἢ ἡ τούτου ἑνότης. Ἀεὶ ἐν ἑαυτῷ
ὤν, ἀεὶ τῷ ἑαυτοῦ νοῒ καὶ φωτὶ καὶ πνεύματι πάντα περιέχει.   175

33. Τοῦ αὐτοῦ ἐκ τοῦ αὐτοῦ λόγου.

Ἐκτὸς τούτου, οὐ θεός, οὐκ ἄγγελος, οὐ δαίμων, οὐκ οὐσία τις ἄλλη·
πάντων γάρ ἐστι κύριος καὶ πατὴρ καὶ θεὸς καὶ πηγὴ καὶ ζωὴ καὶ δύναμις
καὶ φῶς καὶ νοῦς καὶ πνεῦμα, καὶ πάντα ἐν αὐτῷ καὶ ὑπ' αὐτόν ἐστι.

34. Τοῦ αὐτοῦ <ἐκ τοῦ τῶν> ΠΡΟΣ ΤΑΤ ΔΙΕΞΟΔΙΚΩΝ πρώτου λόγου περὶ   180
θεοῦ.

Ὁ τοῦ δημιουργοῦ Λόγος, ὦ τέκνον, ἀΐδιος, αὐτοκίνητος, ἀναυξής, ἀμείωτος,
ἀμετάβλητος, ἄφθαρτος, μόνος ἀεὶ ἑαυτῷ ὅμοιός ἐστιν, <ἴσος δὲ καὶ ὁμαλός,
εὐσταθής, εὔτακτος,> εἷς ὢν μετὰ τὸν προεγνωσμένον θεόν.

35. <Τοῦ αὐτοῦ περὶ θεοῦ>.   185

Ὁ γὰρ λόγος αὐτοῦ προελθών, παντέλειος ὢν καὶ γόνιμος, καὶ δημιουργός,
ἐν γονίμῳ φύσει πεσὼν ἐπὶ γονίμῳ ὕδατι ἔγκυον τὸ ὕδωρ ἐποίησε.

32–33. 172–175 et 177–179 CH fr. 23, Nock-Festugière IV,
p. 126; cf. Didym., De Trin. II,27; Cyr., C.Iul. I,48; Malalas II, pp. 26–27
Dindorf   **34.** 182–184 CH fr. 30, Nock-Festugière IV, p. 135; cf. Cyr.,
C.Iul. I,46   **35.** 186–187 CH fr. 27, Nock-Festugière IV, p. 132; cf.
Cyr., C.Iul. I,46; Malalas II, p. 27 Dindorf

170 κενῆς οἰήσεως T   **32.** 171 *titulum ampl.* Erbse *Cyrilli verbis* (556 A)
usus ‖ 172 *verba* εἰ μὴ πρόνοιά τις ἦν τοῦ πάντων κυρίου ὥστε με τὸν λόγον
τοῦτον ἀποκαλύψαι, οὐδὲ ὑμᾶς τοιοῦτος ἔρως κατεῖχεν, ἵνα περὶ τούτου ζητήσητε
ante οὐ γὰρ ἐφικτόν *falso, ut videtur, posuit* Erbse, *Malalae ordinem secutus. Iuxta
Didymi et Cyrilli textum, secretiore loco edenda putavi: vide infra caput* 42 ‖ 172–173
οὐ—ἀκούσατε *om.* χ Cedr. ‖ 172 ἐστιν *om.* Σ ‖ 173 ἦν Cyr. Σ: ἐστὶ τὸ Ox
‖ ἔστιν Cyr.: ἦν Ox ‖ 174 φωτινός Ox ‖ ἢ *om.* Ox ‖ ἡ *om.* Cyr. ‖
174–175 ἑαυτῷ ὤν Cyr. Chron.: αὐτῷ ὤν Did., Ox, Cedr. αὐτῷ ὤν P̈
Dindorf αυτωι ὄν Σ *om.* Su. χ ‖ 175 τῷ ἑαυτοῦ Did. Cyr. Cedr.: τῷ αὐτῷ
Ox ἐν τῷ αὐτῷ Chron. τῷ αὐτοῦ Dindorf   **33.** 176 Τοῦ αὐτοῦ—λόγου
Σ: Καὶ μεθ' ἕτερά φησι Cyr. ‖ 178 πάντων γὰρ κύριος καὶ θεὸς Ox ‖
178–179 καὶ πηγή—πνεῦμα Cyr. Σ: *om.* cett. ‖ 179 ἐν αὐτῷ καὶ ὑπ' (ἐπ' Cyr.
codd. nonnulli) αὐτὸν Did. Cyr. codd. nonnulli Chron. Σ: ὑπ' αὐτὸν καὶ ἐν αὐτῷ
Ox   **34.** 180 ἐκ τοῦ τῶν *ins.* Erbse e Cyr.: *om.* Σ ‖ Τὰτ Scott-Ferguson
Erbse e Cyr. suppl.: τὰ Σ ‖ 182 Ὁ τοῦ—τέκνον *om.* Erbse ‖ ἀμείωτος Cyr.
Σ Pitra Scott-Ferguson: ἀσώματος Erbse ‖ 183–184 ἴσος—εὔτακτος *ins.* Erbse
e Cyr.: om. Σ   **35.** 185 *titulum suppl.* Erbse *Cyrilli verbis* (552 D) *usus:* Ὁ δὲ
Τρισμέγιστος Ἑρμῆς οὕτως φθέγγεται περὶ Θεοῦ ‖ 187 γονίμῃ φύσει Steuchus
Nock ‖ ἐπὶ Cyr.: ἐν Ox Chron. Cedr. Erbse

36. Καὶ μὴν καὶ Ὀρφεὺς αὖθις οὕτω πού φησι·

Οὐρανὸν ὁρκίζω σε, θεοῦ μεγάλου σοφὸν ἔργον·
αὐδὴν ὁρκίζω σε Πατρός, ἢν φθέγξατο πρώτην,   190
ἡνίκα κόσμον ἅπαντα ἑαῖς στηρίξατο βουλαῖς.

'Αὐδὴν δὲ Πατρός ἢν φθέγξατο πρώτην' τὸν μονογενῆ Λόγον αὐτοῦ φησι.

37. Ἑρμοῦ μεγίστου περὶ παντοκράτορος.

Ἀκοιμήτου πυρὸς ὄμματι ἐγρήγορε, δρόμον αἰθέρος ζωογονῶν, ἡλίου θέρμην
κρατύνων, λαίλαπι μεθιστῶν νέφη, τοὔνομα μὴ χωρῶν ἐν κόσμῳ· ἄφθιτον   195
ἀέναον πανεπίσκοπον ἐπίφοβον ὄμμα, πατέρα τῶν ὅλων, θεὸν ὄντα μόνον,
ἀπ' οὐδενὸς ἔχοντα ἀρχήν, ἔγνωκα. Ἕνα μετὰ σὲ ὄντα μόνον ἐκ σοῦ γεραίρω
υἱόν, ὃν ῥώμῃ ἀπορρήτῳ καὶ ὀξυτέρα νοῦ καὶ φωνῆς ἴδιον εὐθὺς ἀφθόνως
καὶ ἀπαθῶς ἀγένητον λόγον ἐγέννησας, θεὸν ὄντα τὴν οὐσίαν ἐκ τῆς σῆς
οὐσίας, ὃς σοῦ τοῦ πατρὸς τὴν εἰκόνα τὴν ἄφθαρτον καὶ πᾶν ὁμοίαν φέρει,   200
ὥστε εἶναι ἐκεῖνον ἐν σοί, σὲ δὲ ἐν ἐκείνῳ, κάλλους ἔσοπτρον, ἀλληλ-
ευφραντὸν πρόσωπον.

---

37. codd. Σ χ V'M'. Fragmentum novum dubitanter rec. Nock IV, p. 147.

---

36. 189–191 Orph. fr. 299 Kern; cf. Ps.Iust., Coh. 15,2; Cyr., C.Iul. I,46; Malalas II, p. 27 Dindorf

---

36. 188 Καὶ μὴν—φησι e Cyrilli verbis (552 C) supplevi: καὶ ταῦτα εἰρηκὼς ηὔξατο λέγων (scil. Hermes Trismegistus) Ox Erbse || 189 Οὐρανὸν ὁρκίζω σε Ps.Iust., Coh. Cyr. Erbse: ὁρκίζω σέ, οὐρανέ Ox Chron. Cedr. χ || σοφὸν: σοφοῦ A" || 190–191 αὐδὴν—βουλαῖς e Ps.Iust. et Cyr. supplevi || 190 ἢν: τὴν Ps. Iust., Coh. || πρώτην: πρῶτον Ps.Iust., Coh. || ἵλαος ἔσο· ὁρκίζω σε, φωνὴν Πατρός, ἢν ἐφθέγξατο πρώτην, ἡνίκα κόσμον ἅπαντα ἐστηρίξατο βουλῇ Ox Chron. Cedr. Erbse ἡνίκα τὸν πάντα κόσμον ἐστηρίξατο χ capitulum om. S L' || 192 αὐδὴν Cyr.: φωνὴν Ox || φησίν om. Ox Chron. || add. Malalas, loc. laud.: ταῦτα δὲ καὶ ἐν τοῖς κατὰ Ἰουλιανοῦ τοῦ βασιλέως ὑπὸ τοῦ ὁσιωτάτου Κυρίλλου συναχθεῖσιν ἐμφέρεται, ὅτι καὶ ὁ Τρισμέγιστος Ἑρμῆς ἀγνοῶν τὸ μέλλον τριάδα ὁμοούσιον ὡμολόγησεν
37. 193 Ἑρμοῦ—παντοκράτορος χ: μεγίστου om. P Q' M' παντοκρατορίας P Q' titulum om. S τοῦ αὐτοῦ ἐκ τοῦ ὕμνου πρὸς τὸν παντοκράτορα Σ Ἑρμοῦ τρισμεγίστου V' || 194–197 verba ἀκοιμήτου—ἔγνωκα decurtavit, in tituli formam convertit et oraculi parti secundae praeposuit Σ: πατέρα τῶν ὅλων καὶ θεὸν ὄντα μόνον ἀπ' οὐδενὸς ἔχοντα τοῦτο ὅπερ ἔχει ἀεὶ ἔγνωκα || 196 θεὸν χ: καὶ θεὸν Σ M' V' || 197 μετὰ σὲ ὄντα μόνον χ: μετὰ σοῦ ὥστε τὸν Σ ὡς αἴτιον V' || 198 νοῦ καὶ φωνῆς Σ V': φωνῇ χ Nock om. M' || 199 ἀγένητον Erbse: ἀγεννήτως PQ'SL' ἀπογεννήτως B' ἀγενοῦς Σ V' om. M' || σῆς Σ Pitra Scott-Ferguson: om. χ Nock Erbse || 200 τὴν ante εἰκόνα om. Σ M' V' || τὴν ἄφθαρτον om. χ || πανόμοιαν Pitra Nock πανόμοιον Scott-Ferguson || 201 εἶναι om. χ M' || κάλλους Σ M' Erbse: κάλλος χ καλὸν V' || 201–202 ἀλληλέφραστον PQ'S ἀνέκφραστον Pitra Scott-Ferguson

38. Πορφυρίου Πλάτωνος ἐκτιθεμένου δόξαν.

Ἄχρι γὰρ τριῶν ὑποστάσεων, ἔφη Πλάτων, τὴν τοῦ θείου προελθεῖν οὐσίαν,
εἶναι δὲ τὸν μὲν ἀνωτάτω θεὸν τἀγαθόν, μετ' αὐτὸν δὲ καὶ δεύτερον τὸν   205
δημιουργόν, τρίτον δὲ καὶ τὴν τοῦ κόσμου ψυχήν· ἄχρι γὰρ ψυχῆς τὴν
θειότητα προελθεῖν.

39. Πλάτωνος.

Γεννητὸς οὐδεὶς ἱκανὸς γνώμης ἀφανοῦς ἰδεῖν αἰσθητήριον· φύσις γὰρ
μόνου θεοῦ, ὡς αἰτίου τοῦ παντός, γυμνὴν ψυχὴν δυναμένη ἰδεῖν. Εἷς γὰρ   210
αἴτιος τοῦ παντός, εἷς καὶ ἐξ αὐτοῦ ἄλλος [ὁ εἷς] καί ποτε οὗτος ὁ εἷς οὐκ
ἐν χρόνῳ· ἀΐδιος γὰρ ὁ εἷς καὶ <ἄλλος αὐτῷ> συναΐδιος <καὶ οὐδὲν τούτοις συναΐδιον>.

40. Ἀριστοτέλους.

Ἀκάματος φύσις θεοῦ γεννήσεως οὐκ ἔχουσα ἀρχήν· ἐξ αὐτῆς δὲ ὁ   215
πανσθενὴς οὐσίωται λόγος.

41. Πλουτάρχου.

Τοῦ ὑπερτάτου, τῶν ὅλων αἰτίου, προεπινοεῖται οὐδέν· ὅλος δὲ ἐξ ὅλου,
ἄλλος δὲ ἐξ αὐτοῦ ὡς αὐτός, ἀλλ' οὐκ ἀλλοῖος καὶ μέσον οὐδέν.

42. Ἑρμοῦ ἐκ τοῦ ΠΡΟΣ ΑΣΚΛΗΠΙΟΝ λόγου τρίτου.   220

Εἰ μὴ πρόνοιά τις ἦν τοῦ πάντων Κυρίου ὥστε με τὸν λόγον τοῦτον
ἀποκαλύψαι, οὐδὲ ὑμᾶς νῦν ἔρως τοιοῦτος κατεῖχεν ἵνα περὶ τούτου
ζητήσητε· νῦν δὲ τὰ λοιπὰ τοῦ λόγου ἀκούετε. Τούτου τοῦ πνεύματος οὗ

---

38. 204–207 Porph., Hist. phil. IV, fr. 221, pp. 242–244 Smith; cf. Didym.,
De Trin. II,27; Cyr., C.Iul. I,47; VIII,271   **42.** 221–226 CH fr. 24,
Nock-Festugière IV, p. 128; cf. Didym., De Trin. II,27; Cyr., C.Iul. I,49;
Malalas II, p. 26 Dindorf

38. 203 Πλάτωνος ἐκτιθεμένου *cf.* Did. Cyr. I : ἐκτιθεμένου Πλάτωνος Σ
Erbse ‖ 204 θείου: θεοῦ Cyr. VIII ‖ 206 τρίτον Cyr. I: τρίτην Did. Cyr.
(*codd. nonnulli*) Σ Steuchus Erbse ‖ δὲ καὶ: δὲ Cyr. VIII ‖ 207 θειότητα
Did. Cyr. I: θεότητα Cyr. VIII Σ Steuchus   **39.** Dictum spurium aliunde
ignotum ‖ 208 Πλάτωνος V': τοῦ αὐτοῦ Σ Πλάτωνος φιλοσόφου PQ'L'
φιλοσόφου *om.* B'ZS Τοῦ αὐτοῦ Πλάτωνος Erbse ‖ 209 γεννητὸς Σ V': γενετὸς
M' γενετὸς χ ‖ 209–210 ἰδεῖν: κατιδεῖν M' V' *utroque loco* ‖ 210 γυμνὴν
ψυχὴν Σ B'ZS : γνώμην ψυχῆς PQ' ‖ δυναμένη *scripsi*: δυναμένου *cett.* ‖
211 ἄλλος Σ M'V': ἀλλ' οἷος ὁ B'ZS ἀλλ' υἱὸς PQ' ‖ ὁ εἷς *delevi* ‖ 212–213
ἀΐδιος γὰρ ὁ εἷς καὶ συναΐδιος χ V' Erbse: ἀΐδιος γὰρ ὁ εἷς καὶ ἀναΐδιος ὁ
εἷς καὶ οὐδὲν τούτοις συναΐδιον Σ ἀΐδιος γὰρ ὁ εἷς καὶ συναΐδιος ὁ υἱὸς καὶ
οὐδὲν τούτοις συναΐδιον Scott-Ferguson, *sed omnia incerta*   **40.** Dictum
spurium aliunde ignotum ‖ 215 γεννήσεως Σ π M' V': γενέσεως χ   **41.**
Dictum spurium aliunde ignotum ‖ 219 ἀλλοῖος V' Erbse: ἀλλοίως Σ
42. 221 με Cyr.: μοι Did. Ox Chron. ‖ 222 νῦν ἔρως τοιοῦτος Cyr.: τοιοῦτος
ἔρως Did. Ox Chron. Cedr. τοσοῦτος ἔρως Scott-Ferguson ‖ 223 ζητήσητε
Cyr.: ζητήσετε Ox ζητήσεται Chron. ζητήσαιτε Dindorf

πολλάκις προεῖπον, πάντα χρῄζει· τὰ πάντα βαστάζον, κατ᾽ ἀξίαν τὰ
πάντα ζωοποιεῖ καὶ τρέφει, καὶ ἀπὸ τῆς ἁγίας πηγῆς ἐξήρτηται, ἐπίκουρον   225
πνεῦμα καὶ ζωῆς ἅπασιν ἀεὶ ὑπάρχον γόνιμον, ἓν ὄν.

43. Ἐκ τοῦ κατὰ Ἰωάννην εὐαγγελίου.

Ὅταν δὲ ἔλθῃ ἐκεῖνος, τὸ πνεῦμα τῆς ἀληθείας, ὃ ἐκπορεύεται παρὰ τοῦ
πατρός, ἐκεῖνος ὑμᾶς διδάξει πάντα καὶ ἀναγγελεῖ πάντα (e).

44. Ἐκ τῆς πρὸς Κορινθίους α΄ ἐπιστολῆς Παύλου τοῦ ἁγίου ἀποστόλου.   230

Ἑκάστῳ δὲ δίδοται ἡ φανέρωσις τοῦ πνεύματος πρὸς τὸ συμφέρον. ᾯ
μὲν γὰρ δίδοται διὰ τοῦ πνεύματος λόγος σοφίας, ἄλλῳ δὲ λόγος γνώσεως
κατὰ τὸ αὐτὸ πνεῦμα, ἑτέρῳ δὲ πίστις ἐν τῷ αὐτῷ πνεύματι, ἄλλῳ δὲ
χαρίσματα ἰαμάτων ἐν τῷ ἑνὶ πνεύματι, ἄλλῳ δὲ ἐνεργήματα δυνάμεων,
ἄλλῳ δὲ προφητεία, ἄλλῳ δὲ διακρίσεις πνευμάτων, ἑτέρῳ δὲ ἑρμηνεία   235
γλωσσῶν· πάντα δὲ ταῦτα ἐνεργεῖ τὸ ἓν καὶ τὸ αὐτὸ πνεῦμα διαιροῦν ἰδίᾳ
ἑκάστῳ καθὼς βούλεται (f).

45. Τοῦ ἁγίου Κυρίλλου ἐπισκόπου Ἀλεξανδρείας ἐκ τῆς γραφείσης παρ᾽
αὐτοῦ α΄ βίβλου ΥΠΕΡ ΤΗΣ ΧΡΙΣΤΙΑΝΩΝ ΘΡΗΣΚΕΙΑΣ ΚΑΙ ΚΑΤΑ ΙΟΥ-
ΛΙΑΝΟΥ ΤΟΥ ΠΑΡΑΒΑΤΟΥ ἑρμηνεία πρὸς τὴν χρῆσιν Πλάτωνος διὰ   240
Πορφυρίου καὶ Ἑρμοῦ.

46. Νοῦν μὲν γὰρ ἐκ νοῦ᾽, καθάπερ ἐγῷμαι, φησὶ τὸν Υἱὸν καὶ ὡς ᾽φῶς
ἐκ φωτός᾽· μέμνηται δὲ καὶ τοῦ Πνεύματος, ὡς πάντα περιέχοντος· οὔτε δὲ
ἄγγελον, οὔτε δαίμονα, οὔτε μὴν ἑτέραν τινὰ φύσιν ἢ οὐσίαν ἔξω κεῖσθαί
φησι τῆς θείας ὑπεροχῆς ἤγουν ἐξουσίας, ἀλλ᾽ ὑπ᾽ αὐτῇ τὰ πάντα καὶ δι᾽   245
αὐτὴν εἶναι διορίζεται.

43–45. cod. Σ

---

46. 242–246 Cyr., C.Iul. I,49, p. 204 Burguière

---

e) Io. 16,13 + 14,26   f) I Cor. 12,7–11

223–226 νῦν δὲ τὰ λοιπὰ—ἓν ὄν om. Ox ‖ 224 τὰ πάντα βαστάζον Cyr.:
πάντα γὰρ βαστάζων Σ πάντα γὰρ βαστάζον Erbse τὰ πάντα γὰρ βαστάζον
Did. Nock τὰ πάντα γὰρ βαστάζων Steuchus ‖ 226 πνεῦμα scripsi: πνεύμασι
Did. Steuchus Nock Burguière πνεύματι Cyr. πνεῦμα ἦν Σ Erbse ‖ ζωῆς:
ζῴοις Steuchus   **45.** 239–240 Ὑπὲρ τῆς Χριστιανῶν θρησκείας καὶ κατὰ
Ἰουλιανοῦ τοῦ παραβάτου Cyrilli contra Iulianum operis titulum fortasse genuinum
praebet Σ: Ὑπὲρ τῆς τῶν Χριστιανῶν εὐαγοῦς θρησκείας πρὸς τὰ τοῦ ἐν ἀθέοις
Ἰουλιανοῦ cett.   **46.** 242 ἐγὼ οἶμαι Σ ‖ τὸν Υἱὸν φησὶ Σ ‖ ὡς om. Σ ‖
243 ὡς πάντα: τοῦ πάντα Σ ‖ 243–244 οὐδὲ ἄγγελον οὐδὲ δαίμονα Σ ‖ 244
ἔξω κεῖσθαι om. Σ

47. Καὶ μεθ᾽ ἕτερα πρὸς τὰ Πλάτωνος·

Ἰδοὺ δὴ σαφῶς ἐν τούτοις ἄχρι τριῶν ὑποστάσεων τὴν τοῦ θείου προελθεῖν οὐσίαν ἰσχυρίζεται· εἷς μὲν γάρ ἐστιν ὁ τῶν ὅλων Θεός, κατευρύνεται
δὲ ὥσπερ ἡ περὶ αὐτοῦ γνῶσις εἰς ἁγίαν τε καὶ ὁμοούσιον Τριάδα, εἷς τε   250
Πατέρα φημὶ καὶ Υἱὸν καὶ ἅγιον Πνεῦμα, ὃ καὶ ᾽ψυχὴν τοῦ κόσμου᾽ φησὶν
ὁ Πλάτων· ζωοποιεῖ δὲ τὸ Πνεῦμα καὶ πρόεισιν ἐκ ζῶντος Πατρὸς δι᾽ Υἱοῦ,
καὶ ἐν αὐτῷ ζῶμεν καὶ κινούμεθα καὶ ἐσμέν.

48. Καὶ αὖθις πρὸς τὰ Ἑρμοῦ ΔΙΕΞΟΔΙΚΑ τοῦ αὐτοῦ·

Σημαίνει δέ, οἶμαι, διά γε τουτουῒ τὸν Πατέρα. Ἀπόχρη μὲν οὖν ταυτὶ πρὸς   255
ἐντελεστάτην ἀπόδειξιν τοῦ, ὅτι τὸν μονογενῆ τοῦ Θεοῦ Λόγον ἐννενοήκασι
καὶ αὐτοί.

49. Καὶ πάλιν πρὸς τὰ τοῦ αὐτοῦ Ἑρμοῦ <ἐκ τοῦ> ΠΡΟΣ ΑΣΚΛΗΠΙΟΝ
λόγου τρίτου.

Οἶδεν οὖν αὐτὸ καὶ ὑπάρχον ἰδιοσυστάτως, καὶ τὰ πάντα ζωοποιοῦν καὶ   260
τρέφον, καὶ ὡς ἐξ ἁγίας πηγῆς ἠρτημένον τοῦ Θεοῦ καὶ Πατρός. Πρόεισι
γὰρ ἐξ αὐτοῦ κατὰ φύσιν, καὶ δι᾽ Υἱοῦ χορηγεῖται τῇ κτίσει.

50. Σόλωνος Ἀθηναίου τοῦ νομοθέτου περὶ λόγου ἐγκωμίου ἀπόφθεγμα.

Ὀψέ ποτέ τις ἐπὶ τὴν πολυσχιδῆ ταύτην ἐλάσει γῆν καὶ διὰ πετάσματος
σὰρξ γενήσεται· ἀκαμάτοις τε θεότητος ὅροις ἀνιάτων παθῶν λύσει φθοράν·   265
κατὰ τούτου φθόνος ἀπίστῳ γενήσεται λαῷ καὶ πρὸς ὕψος κρεμασθεὶς ὡς
θανάτου κατάδικος πραέως πείσεται παρ᾽ αὐτῶν, θανὼν δὲ εἰς πόλον
ἀρθήσεται.

47. 248–253 Cyr., C.Iul. I,47, p. 200 Burguière   **48.** 255–257 Cyr.,
C.Iul. I,46–47, p. 200 Burguière   **49.** 260–262 Cyr., C.Iul. I,49, pp.
204–206 Burguière

47. 247 Καὶ μεθ᾽ ἕτερα πρὸς τὰ Πλάτωνος Σ ‖ 248 τούτοις ἄχρι: ἀρχῇ διὰ
Σ ‖ 249 ἐστιν *om.* Σ ‖ 251 ἅγιον Πνεῦμα: Πνεῦμα ἀληθείας Σ ‖ ὅ: ἦν Σ
‖ 253 *cf.* Act. 17,28   **48.** 254 Καὶ αὖθις—τοῦ αὐτοῦ Σ ‖ 255 ταυτὶ
πρός: ὥστε ταύτην ὡς Σ   **49.** 258–259 Καὶ πάλιν—τρίτου Σ ‖ 258 ἐκ τοῦ
inserui: *om.* Σ ‖ 260 Οἶδε μὲν οὖν Σ   **50.** Dictum spurium aliunde ignotum
‖ 263 Σόλωνος *em.* Erbse: Σώλονος Σ τοῦ αὐτοῦ (Πλάτωνος) Β΄ Πλάτωνα Cath.
‖ 264 τις *om.* Σ ‖ πολυσχιδῇ Cath. Pitra Bratke Erbse: πολυσχεδῆ Σ χ π
Pers. ‖ ταύτην *om.* Σ ‖ ἐλάσει Σ Erbse: ἐλάσειε *cett.* ‖ διὰ πετάσματος Σ
Pers.: δίχα σφάλματος χ π E Cath. Pitra Bratke Erbse ‖ 265 τε Σ: δὲ Erbse
om. cett. ‖ 266 κατὰ τούτου Σ: καὶ τούτου Ρ τοῦτο Β΄ Q᾽ τούτῳ S Pitra
Erbse ‖ φθόνον Σ ‖ ἐγέννησε Σ ‖ ἀπίστῳ λαῷ Σ: ἐξ ἀπίστου λαοῦ Β΄ Erbse
ἀπίστου λαοῦ Pitra λαοῦ π ‖ κρεμασθεὶς Σ π Pers.: κρεμασθήσεται χ Cath. Pitra
Bratke Erbse ‖ 267 *post* κατάδικος *add.* καὶ πάντα Erbse πάντα Β΄ π ταῦτα
δὲ πάντα ἑκὼν προσπείσεται φέρων Pitra ‖ πραέως Σ Ρ Q᾽: πράως S πρά-
σας Β΄ ‖ παρ᾽ αὐτῶν Σ Pers.: *om. cett.* ‖ φέρειν *add.* Cath. Bratke ‖ 267–268
θανὼν—ἀρθήσεται Pitra

51. Ἐκ τοῦ κατὰ Ἰωάννην εὐαγγελίου.

Καὶ ὁ λόγος σὰρξ ἐγένετο καὶ ἐσκήνωσεν ἐν ἡμῖν, καὶ ἐθεασάμεθα τὴν   270
δόξαν αὐτοῦ, δόξαν ὡς μονογενοῦς παρὰ πατρός, πλήρης χάριτος καὶ
ἀληθείας (g).

52. Ἐκ τῆς πρὸς Ἑβραίους ἐπιστολῆς.

Ἔχοντες οὖν, ἀδελφοί, παρρησίαν εἰς τὴν εἴσοδον τῶν ἁγίων ἐν τῷ αἵματι
Ἰησοῦ, ἣν ἐνεκαίνισεν ἡμῖν ὁδὸν πρόσφατον καὶ ζῶσαν διὰ τοῦ κατα-   275
πετάσματος, τοῦτ᾽ ἔστιν τῆς σαρκὸς αὐτοῦ, καὶ ἱερέα μέγαν ἐπὶ τὸν οἶκον
τοῦ θεοῦ, προσερχώμεθα μετὰ ἀληθινῆς καρδίας ἐν πληροφορίᾳ πίστεως
ρεραντισμένοι τὰς καρδίας ἀπὸ συνειδήσεως πονηρᾶς καὶ λελουσμένοι τὸ
σῶμα ὕδατι καθαρῷ· κατέχωμεν τὴν ὁμολογίαν τῆς ἐλπίδος ἀκλινῆ (h).

53. Πλάτωνος.   280

Ὁ παλαιὸς νέος καὶ ὁ νέος ἀρχαῖος· ὁ πατὴρ γόνος καὶ ὁ γόνος πατήρ· τὸ
ἓν τρία καὶ τὰ τρία ἕν, ἄσαρκον σαρκικόν· γῆ τέτοκε τὸν οὐρανοῦ γεννήτορα.
Θεὸν νοῆσαι μὲν χαλεπόν, φράσαι δὲ ἀδύνατον· ἔστι γὰρ τρισυπόστατος,
ἀνερμήνευτος οὐσία καὶ φύσις, οὐκ ἔχουσα παρὰ βροτοῖς ἐξομοίωσιν· οὓς
δὲ θεοὺς ὀνομάζουσιν ἄνθρωποι, πολὺ τὸ μυθῶδες καὶ σφαλερὸν ἐφ᾽ ἑαυτοὺς   285
ἐπεσπάσαντο.

54. Σοφοκλέους.

Εἷς ταῖς ἀληθείαισιν, εἷς ἐστιν θεός,
ὃς οὐρανόν τ᾽ ἔτευξε καὶ γαῖαν μακράν,
πόντου τε χαροπὸν οἶδμα, κἀνέμων βίας.   290

---

54. 288–296 Ps. Sophocles, TrGF adesp. 618 Kannicht-Snell; cf. Clem.
Al., Protr. VII,74,2; Clem. Al., Strom. V,14, 113,2; Ps.Iust., Mon. 2,2;
Ps.Iust., Coh. 18,2; Eus., P.E. XIII,13,40; Cyr., C.Iul. I,44; Thdrt., Graec.
aff. cur. VII,46; Malalas II, pp. 40–41 Dindorf. Versus oraculi oratione
pedestri a scriptoribus et in codicibus byzantinis redditi sunt.

---

g) Io. 1,14   h) Hebr. 10,19–23

---

53. Dictum spurium aliunde ignotum; aliam sententiam theologicam de
Trinitate attribuit Platoni comico Didym., De Trin. II,27 (PCG fr. 302).
|| 280 Πλάτωνος πμ: *verba* ὁ παλαιὸς—πατήρ *Plutarcho, verba* τὸ ἕν—γεννήτορα
Thucydidi attr. χ || 281 ὁ παλαιὸς—ἀρχαῖος *om.* W || ὁ γόνος πατὴρ καὶ ὁ
πατὴρ γόνος W || 282 τὰ τρία ἕν, ἓν τρία W || σαρκικόν: προσωπικόν χ ||
ἄσαρκος σαρκικὸς γῆν τέτοκε τῶν οὐρανῶν γεννήτωρ Ε || 283–284 Θεὸν
νοῆσαι—ἐξομοίωσιν Ε Ν Art. || Θεὸν νοῆσαι μὲν χαλεπόν, φράσαι δὲ ἀδύνατον:
cf. CH, Exc. I,1 *ap.* Stob., Anth. II,1,26; Ps.Iust., Coh. 38,2; Greg. Naz.,
Or. 28,4; Cyr., C.Iul. I, 43 || 284–286 οὓς δὲ θεοὺς—ἐπεσπάσαντο *ex* Art.
Pass. 28 *supplevi*   **54.** Fragmentum addubitatum || 288 εἷς ταῖς: ἐν ταῖς
Cyr. (*codd. nonnulli*) *om.* Ox Cath. || ὡς ἕνα τῆς Y || ἀληθείας εἶναι Ox Y
|| 289 τ᾽ ἔτευξε: τέτευχε A" Ps.Iust., Mon. s Cedr. τέτευξαι B || μακρήν
Clem. Eus. || 290 δὲ χαρωποῦ Ox τε χαροποῦ Dindorf || κἀνέμων Sylburg
|| βίαν Clem., Strom. βία B

Θνητοὶ δὲ πολλοὶ καρδίᾳ πλανώμενοι
5   ἱδρυσάμεσθα πημάτων παραψυχὰς
θεῶν ἀγάλματ' ἐκ λίθων τε καὶ ξύλων,
ἢ χρυσοτεύκτων ἢ ἐλεφαντίνων τύπους,
θυσίας τε τούτοις καὶ κενὰς πανηγύρεις   295
τεύχοντες, οὕτως εὐσεβεῖν νομίζομεν.

55. Ὀστάνου φιλοσόφου περὶ τῆς θεοτόκου.

Τιμήσωμεν τὴν Μαρίαν ὡς καλῶς κρύψασαν τὸ μυστήριον.

56. Μενάνδρου.

Θεὸν σέβου καὶ μάνθανε, μὴ ζήτει δὲ τίς ἐστιν ἢ πῶς ἐστιν· εἴτε γὰρ ἔστιν   300
εἴτε οὐκ ἔστιν, ὡς ὄντα τοῦτον καὶ σέβου καὶ μάνθανε· ἀσεβὴς γὰρ τὸν
νοῦν ὁ θέλων μανθάνειν θεόν.

---

56. codd. thesauri π et cod. E; cf. Didym., De Trin. III,2; Comp. Menandri
et Philistionis, II, 77–82, p. 106 Jaekel

---

291 πολλοὶ Ps.Iust. Clem. Cyr. A" Y πολλὰ P" Erbse πολὺ Ps.Iust., Mon.
s Ox Cath. ‖ καρδίᾳ Clem., Protr. Ps.Iust., Coh. Cyr. Ox A" καρδίαν
Ps.Iust., Mon. q Clem., Strom. Eus. Thdrt. ‖ 292 ἱδρυσάμεσθα Cyr.:
ἱδρυσάμεθα Β Erbse ἱδυσάμεθα Ox ‖ πημιμάτων Ox ‖ παραψυχὰς Ps.Iust.,
Mon. Cyr. Ox Cath.: παραψυχὴν Clem. Ps.Iust, Coh. Eus. παρὰ ψυχὴν A"
‖ 293 θεῷ Ox ‖ τε καὶ ξύλων Ps.Iust., Coh. Cyr. A" Steuchus τε om. Ox
Cath. Y: ἢ χαλκέων Ps.Iust., Mon. Clem. Eus. Thrdt. ‖ 295 κενὰς Clem.,
Protr. Cyr. Ox B: καινὰς Cath. καλὰς Ps.Iust. Thdrt. Cedr. A" Steuchus
κακὰς Clem., Strom. Eus. κοινὰς Y ‖ 296 τεύχοντες Ps.Iust. Cyr. Ox Cedr.
A": στέφοντες Clem., Strom. Eus. νέμοντες Clem., Protr. ‖ οὕτως om. Ox
Y   **55.** Dictum spurium aliunde ignotum: cf. fr. A 12 Bidez-Cumont ‖
297 ὀστάνου em. Bentley: ἀστάνου Β' ἱστάνου Q' ‖ φιλοσόφου Q': om. Β'
‖ περὶ τῆς θεοτόκου om. Q' ‖ 298 τιμήσωμεν Bidez-Cumont: τιμήσομεν Q'
Erbse ‖ μαρίαν Q' Erbse: μαριάμ Β' Bidez-Cumont   **56.** 302 θεὸν: περὶ
θεοῦ E

Fragm. Α

I

1. Ἐπειδὴ δὲ τῶν προσφάτων λόγων ἡ παράθεσις τῶν παλαιῶν ἱκανωτέρα πρὸς τὰς ἐναντιώσεις ἐστίν, οὐ πρὸς μονοειδῆ τινα μαρτυρίαν τὸ βιβλίον φέρειν σπουδάζω, πολυχουστέραν δὲ μᾶλλον τῶν ἄλλων καὶ ποικιλωτέραν 5 τὴν περὶ τῆς πραγματείας ἀπόδειξιν ποιούμενος.

2. Σίβυλλαι τοίνυν, ὡς πολλοὶ ἔγραψαν, γεγόνασιν ἐν διαφόροις τόποις καὶ χρόνοις τὸν ἀριθμὸν δέκα. Σίβυλλα δὲ Ῥωμαϊκὴ λέξις, ἑρμηνευομένη προφῆτις εἴτ᾽ οὖν μάντις· ὅθεν ἑνὶ ὀνόματι αἱ θήλειαι μάντιδες ὠνομάσθησαν. 10

3. Πρώτη οὖν ἡ Χαλδαία εἴτ᾽ οὖν ἡ Περσὶς ἡ κυρίῳ ὀνόματι καλουμένη Σαμβήθη ἐκ τοῦ γένους τοῦ μακαριωτάτου Νῶε, ἡ τὰ κατ᾽ Ἀλέξανδρον τὸν Μακεδόνα λεγομένη προειρηκέναι, ἧς μνημονεύει Νικάνωρ ὁ τὸν Ἀλεξάνδρου βίον ἱστορήσας. Δευτέρα ἡ Λίβυσσα, ἧς μνήμην ἐποιήσατο Εὐριπίδης ἐν τῷ προλόγῳ τῆς ΛΑΜΙΑΣ. Τρίτη ἡ Δελφὶς ἡ ἐν Δελφοῖς τεχθεῖσα, 15

---

3. 13 Nicanor, FGrHist 146,1; 15 Euripides, TrGF pp. 506–507 Nauck-Snell; 16 Chrysippus, De divinatione (cf. Lact., Div. Inst. I,6 = SVF II, 1216); 19–20 Apollodorus Erythr., FGrHist 422,1; 21 Eratosthenes, FGrHist 241,26; 22 Verg., Aen. VI,35–36; 26 Heraclides Pont., fr. 131c Wehrli

---

1–2. ΒΙΒΛΙΟΝ Γ΄ ΧΡΗΣΜΟΙ ΤΩΝ ΣΙΒΥΛΛΩΝ *planitatis causa inserui; titulum* ἐκ τῶν Φιρμιανοῦ Λακταντίου τοῦ Ῥωμαίου περὶ Σιβύλλης καὶ τῶν λοιπῶν *spurium esse recte cont.* Mras
1. 3 *lac. ante verba* ἐπειδὴ δὲ κτλ. *nequiquam susp.* Mras Erbse ‖ 6 ποιούμενος *scripsi:* ποιούμενον D λ Mras Erbse   **2.** 7–10 Σίβυλλαι τοίνυν—δέκα. Σίβυλλα—ὠνομάσθησαν D λ Erbse: Σίβυλλα—ὠνομάσθησαν. Σίβυλλαι τοίνυν—δέκα Geffcken Ὅτι τὸ Σίβυλλα ὄνομα Ῥωμαϊστὶ τὴν προφῆτιν δηλοῖ· ὅθεν ἑνὶ ὀνόματι αἱ θήλειαι μάντεις πᾶσαι ὠνομάσθησαν Τ ‖ 7–8 τόποις καὶ χρόνοις D λ Erbse: χρόνοις καὶ τόποις Φ Su. Ο Geffcken ‖ 9 εἴτ᾽ οὖν D λ Erbse: ἤγουν Φ Su. Ο Geffcken   **3.** 11 εἴτ᾽ οὖν ἡ D λ Erbse: ἤγουν Φ Geffcken ἡ καὶ Su. Ο ‖ κυρίως Φ ‖ 12 γένους D λ Erbse: γένους οὖσα Φ Geffcken ‖ κατ᾽ D λ Erbse: κατὰ Φ Ο Geffcken ‖ 13 Νικάνωρ: ἱκανῶς Φ ‖ 14 ἡ *ante* Λίβυσσα Su. Ο: *om.* D Φ schol. ‖ 15 ἡ *ante* Δελφὶς Ο: *om.* D Φ Su. schol.

περὶ ἧς εἶπε Χρύσιππος ἐν τῷ ΠΕΡΙ ΘΕΟΤΗΤΟΣ βιβλίῳ. Τετάρτη ἡ Ἰταλικὴ
ἡ ἐν Κιμμερίᾳ τῆς Ἰταλίας, ἧς υἱὸς ἐγένετο Εὔανδρος ὁ τὸ ἐν Ῥώμῃ τοῦ
Πανὸς ἱερὸν τὸ καλούμενον Λουπέρκιον κτίσας. Πέμπτη ἡ Ἐρυθραία ἡ
καὶ περὶ τοῦ Τρωϊκοῦ προειρηκυῖα πολέμου, περὶ ἧς Ἀπολλόδωρος ὁ
Ἐρυθραῖος διαβεβαιοῦται. Ἕκτη ἡ Σαμία ἡ κυρίῳ ὀνόματι καλουμένη   20
Φοιτώ, περὶ ἧς ἔγραψεν Ἐρατοσθένης. Ἑβδόμη ἡ Κυμαία ἡ λεγομένη
Ἀμάλθεια, ἡ καὶ Ἡροφίλη, παρά τισι δὲ Ταραξάνδρα· Βεργίλιος δὲ τὴν
Κυμαίαν Δηιφόβην καλεῖ, Γλαύκου θυγατέρα. Ὀγδόη ἡ Ἑλλησποντία
τεχθεῖσα ἐν κώμῃ Μαρμησσῷ περὶ τὴν πολίχνην Γεργίθιον, ἥτις ἐνορίᾳ
ποτὲ Τρωάδος ἐτύγχανεν, ἐν καιροῖς Σόλωνος καὶ Κύρου, ὡς ἔγραψεν   25
Ἡρακλείδης ὁ Ποντικός. Ἐνάτη ἡ Φρυγία, πολλῷ πρότερον τῆς Ἑλλησ-
ποντίας, καὶ αὕτη χρησμώδης. Δεκάτη ἡ Τιβουρτία ὀνόματι Ἀλβουναία,
καὶ αὕτη πολλῷ πρότερον.

4. Φασὶ δέ, ὡς ἡ Κυμαία ἐννέα βιβλία χρησμῶν ἰδίων προσεκόμισε
Ταρκυνίῳ Πρίσκῳ τῷ τηνικαῦτα βασιλεύοντι τῶν Ῥωμαϊκῶν πραγμάτων   30
τριακοσίους φιλιππείους ὑπὲρ αὐτῶν ζητοῦσα. Καταφρονηθεῖσα δὲ καὶ
οὐκ ἐρωτηθεῖσα τίνα ἐστὶ τὰ ἐν αὐτοῖς περιεχόμενα, πυρὶ παρέδωκεν ἐξ
αὐτῶν τρία. Αὖθις δὲ ἐν ἑτέρᾳ προσόδῳ τοῦ βασιλέως προσήνεγκε τὰ ἓξ

---

16 περὶ θεότητος: *perperam titulum Chrysippi operis 'De divinatione' ex Latino in
Graecum sermonem vertit* ‖ ἡ ante Ἰταλικὴ Φ: *om. cett.* ‖ 17 Κιμμερίᾳ D λ Su.
O Geffcken Erbse: μερίᾳ Φ ἐρημίᾳ schol. ‖ 18 λουπέρκιον Mras Erbse:
λουπερκί D λ λούπερκον Φ schol. Geffcken *om.* Su. Ο λουπερκάλιον Maass
‖ ἡ ante Ἐρυθραία Φ schol.: *om.* D λ O Su. ‖ 20 ἡ ante Σαμία Φ schol.:
om. D λ O Su. ‖ 21 Φοιτώ D λ Τ Erbse: φυτώ Φ O Su. schol. Geffcken
‖ 22 Ἀμάλθεια schol. Τ Geffcken Erbse: ἀμαλθεία Ο ἀμαλθία D λ Φ
ἀμαλθαία Su. ‖ Ἡροφίλη Erbse: ἱεροφίλη D λ O ἐροφίλη Su. Geffcken
ἐρωφίλην schol. ‖ Ταραξάνδρα λ Geffcken Erbse: παραξάνδρα D W' ‖
Βιργήλιος W' Βεργήλιος S' παρὰ Βεργιλίῳ τῷ Ῥωμαίῳ Τ ‖ 23 δηιφόβης W'
δηιφόβοις S' διιφόβην λ ‖ 24 κώμῃ: κύμῃ D λ ‖ Μαρμησσῷ D Geffcken
Erbse (*Marmesso* Lact.): μαρμήσσω Su. μαρμισσῷ schol. μαρμίσω S' μαρσίσω
W' μαρπεσσῷ Maass Wehrli *om.* λ ‖ πολίχνην Geffcken Mras Erbse: τι
πολίχνιον λ ‖ Γεργίθιον Erbse Wehrli (*Gergithium* Brandt): Gergithum Maass
γεργήτιον D λ γεργιτίονα Φ Geffcken γεργετίωνα schol. γεργίτων Ο γεργίτιον
malit Mras (*Gergitium* Lact.) ‖ 24–25 ἥτις ἐνορίᾳ ποτὲ Τρωάδος ἐτύγχανεν Φ
Geffcken *sim.* schol. Mras: αἱ τῆς ἐνορίας ποτὲ τῆς τρωάδος ἐτύγχανον D λ
Su. Erbse ‖ 26 ἡ ante Φρυγία Φ schol.: *om.* D O Su. ‖ 26–27 πολλῷ—
χρησμώδης D λ Erbse: *om.* O Su. schol. Geffcken ‖ 27 Τιβουρτία D λ schol.
Geffcken Erbse: τιγουρτία Φ Su. τιγούρτη Ο αἰγυπτία Τ ‖ Ἀλβουναία schol.
Mras Erbse (*Albuneam* Lact.): ἀμμουναία D λ ἀβουναία Φ O Su. Τ Geffcken
‖ 28 καὶ αὕτη—πρότερον D λ: *om. cett.* **4–5.** Vide Lact., Div. Inst.
I,6,10–11 **4.** 29 προσεκόμισε: προεκόμισεν D λ ‖ 30 πρίσκῳ: πρίσκυνι
D λ ‖ 31 φιλιππείους Τ Alexandre Geffcken Erbse: φιλιππαίους D λ Φ *om.*
cett. ‖ ὑπὲρ αὐτῶν Φ Τ Geffcken Erbse: ὑπὲρ ἑαυτῆς D λ ‖ ζητοῦσα Τ
Erbse: ζητήσασα D Φ Geffcken ‖ 32 οὐκ Τ Geffcken Erbse: οὔτε D λ Φ
‖ τίνα ἐστὶ Φ Geffcken Erbse: εἰσὶ D λ τίνα ταῦτά ἐστι Τ ‖ 33 προσόδῳ
em. Alexandre (προσελθοῦσα Io. Lyd., De mens. IV,47): προόδῳ D λ Φ
προήνεγκε D λ

βιβλία τὴν αὐτὴν ὁλκὴν ἐπιζητοῦσα. Οὐκ ἀξιωθεῖσα δὲ λόγου πάλιν ἔκαυσεν ἄλλα τρία. Εἶτα ἐκ τρίτου ἐπιφερομένη τὰ περιλειφθέντα τρία 3 προσῆλθεν αἰτοῦσα οὐδὲν ἧττον τὸ αὐτὸ τίμημα καὶ λέγουσα, εἰ μὴ λάβοι, καίειν καὶ αὐτά.

5. Τότε, φασίν, ὁ βασιλεὺς ἐντυχὼν αὐτοῖς καὶ θαυμάσας ἔδωκε μὲν ὑπὲρ αὐτῶν ἑκατὸν φιλιππείους καὶ ἐκομίσατο αὐτά, παρεκάλει δὲ περὶ τῶν ἄλλων ἕξ· τῆς δὲ ἀπαγγειλάσης μήτε τὰ ἴσα τῶν ἐμπρησθέντων ἔχειν μήτε 4 τι δίχα ἐνθουσιασμοῦ τοιοῦτον εἰδέναι, ἔσθ' ὅτε δέ τινας ἐκ διαφόρων πόλεων καὶ χωρίων ἐξειληφέναι τὰ νομισθέντα αὐτοῖς ἀναγκαῖα καὶ ἐπωφελῆ καὶ δεῖν ἐξ αὐτῶν συναγωγὴν ποιήσασθαι, τοῦτο τάχιστα πεποίηκε.

6. Τὸ γὰρ ἐκ θεοῦ δοθὲν ὡς ἀληθῶς μυχῷ κείμενον οὐκ ἔλαθεν. Ἀνατέλλει δὲ πρόπαρ ἄλλων καὶ πασῶν τῶν Σιβυλλῶν τὰ βιβλία <ἃ> ἐν τῇ βιβλιοθήκῃ 4 τοῦ Καπετωλίου τῆς πρεσβυτέρας Ῥώμης ἀπετέθησαν, τῶν μὲν τῆς Κυμαίας κατακρυφθέντων καὶ οὐ διαδοθέντων εἰς πολλούς, ἐπειδὴ τὰ συμβησόμενα ἐν Ἰταλίᾳ ἰδικώτερον καὶ τρανότερον προανεφώνησεν, τῶν δὲ ἄλλων γνωσθέντων ἅπασιν. Ἀλλὰ τὰ μὲν τῆς Ἐρυθραίας προγεγραμμένον ἔχει τοῦτο τὸ ἀπὸ τοῦ χωρίου ἐπικεκλημένον αὐτῇ ὄνομα· τὰ δέ γε ἄλλα οὐκ 5 ἐπιγραφέντα, ποῖα ποίας εἰσίν, ἀδιάκριτα καθέστηκε.

7. Φιρμιανὸς τοίνυν, οὐκ ἀθαύμαστος φιλόσοφος καὶ ἱερεὺς τοῦ προ- λεχθέντος Καπετωλίου γενόμενος, πρὸς τὸ αἰώνιον ἡμῶν φῶς, τὸν Χριστόν, βλέψας ἐν ἰδίοις πονήμασι τὰ εἰρημένα ταῖς Σιβύλλαις περὶ τῆς ἀρρήτου δόξης παρέθηκε καὶ τὴν ἀλογίαν τῆς Ἑλληνικῆς ὑπολήψεως καὶ ἀντι- 5 δοξίας δυνατῶς ἀπήλεγξεν. Καὶ ἔστιν ἡ μὲν αὐτοῦ ἔντονος ἐξήγησις τῇ Αὐσονίᾳ γλώττῃ, οἱ δὲ Σιβυλλιακοὶ στίχοι Ἑλλάδι φωνῇ, ὡς καὶ ἐξηνέχθη-

---

34 ἐπιζητοῦσα Erbse: ζητοῦσα Τ ἐπιζητήσασα Φ Geffcken ἐπερωτήσασα D λ ‖ 36 οὐδὲν ἧττον et καὶ ante λέγουσα D λ Erbse: om. Φ Geffcken 5. 38 φασίν Φ Geffcken Erbse: φησίν D λ ‖ 39 φιλιππαίους D λ ‖ 40 ἕξ D λ Erbse: om. Φ Geffcken ‖ τῆς D λ Erbse: αὐτῆς Φ Geffcken ‖ 41 εἰδέναι Φ Geffcken Erbse: εἶναι D λ ‖ 42 αὐτοῖς Φ Τ Geffcken Erbse: αὐταῖς D λ ‖ 43 πεποίηκε D λ Erbse: καὶ πεποιήκασι Φ Geffcken 6. 44–46 ἀνατέλλει—ἀπετέθησαν D λ Erbse: ἃ ins. Mras πασῶν δὲ τῶν σιβυλλῶν τὰ βιβλία ἀπετέθησαν ἐν τῷ καπιτωλίῳ Ῥώμης τῆς πρεσβυτέρας Φ Geffcken ‖ 47 κατακρυφθέντων D λ Erbse: κατακρυβέντων Φ Geffcken ‖ 48 ἰδικώτερον καὶ τρανότερον προανεφώνησεν D λ Erbse: ἰδικώτερα καὶ τρανότερον (τρανώτερον Φ) ἀνεφώνησε (ἀνεφώνησεν S') Geffcken ‖ 49 προγεγραμμένον D λ Erbse: προγεγραμμένα Φ Geffcken ‖ 50 τὸ D λ Τ Erbse: om. cett. ‖ 51 ἐπιγραφέντα Buresch Erbse: ἐπιγράφοντα D λ Τ ἐπιγράφονται Φ Geffcken ‖ ποῖα D λ Erbse: ποία Geffcken ‖ ποίας: ποίοις S' ‖ δὲ post ἀδιάκριτα Φ Geffcken ‖ καθέστηκε: καθέστησα W' 7. 53 φῶς Φ Geffcken Erbse: ὄφελος D λ ‖ 54 πονήμασι: ποιήμασι λ ‖ 55 τῆς ἀλογίας W' ‖ 55–56 ὑπολήψεως καὶ ἀντιδοξίας D λ Erbse: πλάνης Φ Geffcken ‖ 56 δυνατῶς om. Erbse ‖ ἔστιν om. Φ Geffcken ‖ 57 ὡς καὶ om. Φ Geffcken

σαν. Ἵνα δὲ τοῦτο μὴ ἄπιστον φαίνηται, μαρτυρίαν τοῦ μνημονευθέντος πολυμαθοῦς ἀνδρὸς παρέξομαι ἔχουσαν τόνδε τὸν τρόπον·

8. Harum omnium Sibyllarum carmina et feruntur et habentur,   60
praeterquam Cymaeae, cuius libri a Romanis occultantur nec eos
ab ullo nisi <a quindecimuiris inspici fas habent. Et sunt singularum
singuli libri: quos, quia Sibyllae nomine inscribuntur, unius esse cre-
dunt, suntque confusi nec discerni ac suum cuique adsignari potest
nisi Erythraeae, quae et nomen suum uerum carmini inseruit et   65
Erythraeam se nominatuiri praelocuta est, cum esset orta Babylone.
Sed et nos confuse Sibyllam dicemus, sicubi testimoniis earum fuerit
abutendum>.

9. Ἐπεὶ οὖν τὰ παρ᾽ ἡμῖν εὑρισκόμενα Σιβυλλιακὰ οὐ μόνον ὡς εὐπόριστα
παρὰ τοῖς νοσοῦσι τὰ τῶν Ἑλλήνων εὐκαταφρόνητά ἐστιν—τὰ γὰρ σπά-   70
νια τίμια δοκεῖ—, ἀλλὰ καὶ ὡς πάντων τῶν στίχων μὴ σῳζόντων τὴν
ἀκρίβειαν τοῦ μέτρου ἀγροτέραν ἔχει τὴν πίστιν—αἰτία δὲ αὐτῶν τῶν
ταχυγράφων οὐ συμφθασάντων τῇ ῥύμῃ τοῦ λόγου ἢ καὶ ἀπαιδεύτων
γενομένων, οὐ τῆς προφήτιδος· ἅμα γὰρ τῇ ἐπινοίᾳ ἐπέπαυτο τῶν λεχθέντων
ἡ μνήμη· καὶ πρὸς τοῦτο βλέψας ὁ Πλάτων ἔφη· ὅταν κατορθῶσι   75
<λέγοντες> πολλὰ καὶ μεγάλα πράγματα, μηδὲν εἰδότες ὧν λέγουσιν᾽—,

---

8. 60–68 Lact., Div. Inst. I,6,13–14, pp. 22–23 Brandt. Verba Lactantii
genuina ‘Harum—nisi’ in solo codice D leguntur, cuius in margine verba
haecce scripta sunt: ‘verba Lactantii cap. VI de falsa religione feruntur
extr.’. Verba ‘a quindecimuiris inspici fas habent’ suppl. Erbse, sed auctorem Theosophiae totum caput in testimonium adduxisse suspicari licet
9. 71–76 Ps. Iust., Coh. 37, 2–3; 75–76 Plat., Men. 99 d 4–5; 80 Aesch.,
Arm. iud, TrGF 176 Radt. Capita 9–12 falso Lactantio attribuit Brandt,
in CSEL 27, pp. 158–160 (fragm. VIII spurium)

---

58 μνημονευθέντος D λ: προμνημονευθέντος *cett.* || 59 πολυμαθοῦς D λ Erbse:
om. cett. || *post* τόνδε τὸν τρόπον *lac. quattuor linearum continet* λ, *sex autem lin-
eae vacant in* λ₁   **8.** 60 feruntur Lact.: ειruntur D || 61 cymaeae Lact.:
cum. D Lact. (*codd.* HMPV) || libri a Lact.: libriaria D || occultantur Lact.
(*cod.* M) Brandt Monat: occuluntur Lact. (*codd.* PV) D Erbse absconduntur
Lact. (*codd. cett.*)   **9.** 70 νοσοῦσι D λ Φ Brandt Mras: νοοῦσι *coni.* Rzach
Geffcken Erbse Riedweg || τὰ τῶν Ἑλλήνων W´: τὰ Ἑλλήνων Geffcken τῶν
Ἑλλήνων D λ Brandt Mras Erbse || τοῖς νοσοῦσι τὰ τῶν Ἑλλήνων: *de morbo
paganismi vide Theodoreti opus* Ἑλληνικῶν θεραπευτικὴ παθημάτων || 72 ἀγροτέραν
scripsi: ἀργοτέραν *cett.* || 72–73 αὐτῶν τῶν ταχυγράφων Erbse: αὐτῶν ταχυ-
γράφων D λ αὐτη τῶν ταχυγράφων Φ Geffcken || 74 *post* γενομένων *add.*
Lyd. O Su. καὶ ἀπείρων γραμματικῶν || 74–75 τῶν λεχθέντων ἡ μνήμη D
λ Erbse: ἡ τῶν λεχθέντων μνήμη *cett.* || 75 καὶ—ἔφη D λ Erbse: πρὸς ἃ καὶ
ὁ Πλάτων βλέψας ἔφη Φ Geffcken || ὅταν κατορθῶσι Plat. Ps.Iust.: κατορθώσωσι
D λ Erbse ὅτι κατορθώσουσι Φ Geffcken || 76 λέγοντες *e Platone suppl.* Erbse

διὰ τοῦτο οὖν, ὅπερ ἔφην, ἐκ τῶν κομισθέντων ἐν Ῥώμῃ ὑπὸ τῶν πρέσβεων καὶ ληφθέντων ὕστερον ἀπὸ τοῦ Καπετωλίου παραθέσομαι νῦν ὅσ᾽ ἂν συνειδῶ. Καὶ γὰρ Αἰσχύλος ἀπεφήνατο εἰπών·

ἁπλᾶ γάρ ἐστι τῆς ἀληθείας ἔπη.

10. Ἐμαρτύρησε τοίνυν ἡ <Σίβυλλα> περὶ τοῦ ἑνὸς ἀνάρχου θεοῦ ταῦτα·

Εἷς θεός, ὃς μόνος ἄρχει, ὑπερμεγέθης, ἀγένητος.

11. <Καὶ> τῷ τῆς θεολογίας λόγῳ προσαποδιδοῦσα τὸν τῆς κοσμογενείας τῷ ἀρρητοτάτῳ καὶ τεχνικωτάτῳ τούτῳ θεῷ τὸ πᾶν ἔδωκεν εἰποῦσα·

Ἀλλὰ θεὸς μόνος εἷς πανυπέρτατος, ὃς πεποίηκεν
οὐρανὸν ἠέλιόν τε καὶ ἀστέρας ἠδὲ σελήνην
καρποφόρον γαῖάν τε καὶ ὕδατος οἴδματα πόντου,
ὃς μόνος ἐστὶ θεὸς κτίστης, ἀκράτητος ὑπάρχων,
αὐτὸς στήριξεν μερόπων μορφήν τε τύπον τε
<καὶ θῆρας ποίησε καὶ ἑρπετὰ καὶ πετεηνά.>
Αὐτὸς ἔμιξε φύσιν πάντων, γενέτης βιότοιο.

12. 'ἔμιξε δὲ φύσιν πάντων', καθὸ ἐκ τῆς πλευρᾶς τοῦ ἀνδρὸς ἡ γυνὴ ἐπλάσθη καὶ καθὸ συνερχόμενοι εἰς σάρκα μίαν πατέρες γίνονται καὶ

---

10. 82 Orac. Sib. fr. 1,7 Geffcken; cf. Theoph., Ad Autol. II,36; Lact., Div. Inst. I,6,15; Ps.Iust., Coh. 16,1 **11.** 85–91 Orac. Sib. fr. 3,3–5+ fr. 5 Geffcken; cf. Theoph., Ad Autol. II,36; Lact., Div. Inst. I,6,15; II,11,18

77–79 διὰ τοῦτο—συνειδῶ (ὅσα συνείδω D λ) Mras Erbse: ἡμεῖς οὖν ἐκ τῶν κομισθέντων ἐν Ῥώμῃ ὑπὸ τῶν πρέσβεων ὅσα δυνατὸν παραθήσομαι Φ Geffcken || 79 καὶ γὰρ Αἰσχύλος Erbse: καὶ Αἰσχύλος γὰρ D λ || 79–80 αἰσχύλος ὅπλα γάρ ἐστι τῆς ἀληθείας ἔπη D mg. καὶ γὰρ—ἔπη om. Φ Geffcken || 80 ἁπλᾶ em. Mras: ὅπλα D λ **10.** 81 ἐμαρτύρησε—ταῦτα Erbse (τοιαῦτα λ): σίβυλλα om. D λ Φ Geffcken suppl. Mras σίβυλλα θεολόγος D mg. ἐξηγήσατο τοίνυν περὶ τοῦ ἀνάρχου θεοῦ τάδε Φ Geffcken || 82 ὃς μόνος ἄρχει Lact. (μόνος ὃς Φ ὃς om. Theoph.) Geffcken: ἐστιν ἄναρχος D λ Mras Erbse μόνος ἐστίν Ps.Iust. (cod. A") ὃς μόνος ἔστιν Marcovich ἐστίν, μόναρχος Riedweg || ἀγένητος Lact. Φ: ἀγέννητος D λ **11.** 83–84 καὶ τῷ τῆς θεολογίας— εἰποῦσα D λ (καὶ add. Erbse): om. Φ Geffcken || 85 πανυπέρτατος: πάντων ὑπέρτατος Φ || 87 ὕδατος οἴδματα Theoph. Lact. Φ Geffcken: ὑγρὰ κύματα D λ ὑγροῦ κύματα Erbse || 89 αὐτὸς—τύπον τε coni. Struve: αὐτὸς δ᾽ ἐστήριξε τύπον μορφῆς μερόπων τε Lact. Rzach Brandt Geffcken Kurfess᾽ μορφῆς τε τύπον Φ μορφὴν τύπον Orac. Sib. III,27 W᾽ τύπον μορφὴν Ψ μορφῆς τύπον D λ Erbse || 90 καὶ θῆρας—πετεηνά ex Orac. Sib. III,28 addidi: om. cett. || 91 αὐτὸς ἔμιξε em. Rzach e Lact. appr. Geffcken Erbse: αὐγὰς μῖξε Φ || γενέτης em. Stadtmüller appr. Geffcken Erbse: γενεῆς Lact. D λ Φ **12.** 92–93 ἔμιξε—καὶ D λ Erbse: ὅπερ εἴρηκεν ἢ Φ Geffcken || καθὸ ἐκ τῆς πλευρᾶς τοῦ ἀνδρὸς ἡ γυνὴ ἐπλάσθη: cf. Gen. 2,21–22 || 93 πατέρες γίνονται D λ appr. Mras Erbse: πρσ γίνονται Φ προσγίνονται Alexandre Brandt προγίνονται Rzach πατρὸς γίνονται Geffcken πατρὸς < ἑνὸς > γίνονται Hartel || καθὸ συνερχόμενοι εἰς σάρκα μίαν πατέρες γίνονται: cf. Gen. 2,24

καθὸ ἐκ τῶν τεσσάρων στοιχείων ἐναντίων ὄντων ἀλλήλοις καὶ τὸν
ὑπουράνιον κόσμον καὶ τὸν ἄνθρωπον ἐδημιούργησεν.   95

13. Ἐξηγεῖται δὲ καὶ τὴν γένεσιν τοῦ ἀνθρώπου καὶ τὴν ἐκ τοῦ παραδείσου
ἔξοδον, ἥτις οὐ μόνον πρόσκαιρον, ἀλλὰ καὶ μοχθηρὰν τὴν ζωὴν αὐτῶν
πεποίηκε, λέγουσα οὕτως·

    Ἄνθρωπον πλασθέντα θεοῦ παλάμαις ἁγίαισιν,
    ὃν κἐπλάνησεν ὄφις δολίως, ἐπὶ μοῖραν ἀνελθεῖν   100
    τοῦ θανάτου γνῶσίν τε λαβεῖν ἀγαθοῦ τε κακοῦ τε.

14. Ἐπεὶ οὖν, φησί, μόνος ἐστὶ ποιητὴς καὶ προνοητὴς τῶν ἀπάντων καὶ
ἀρχιτέκτων τῶν πραγμάτων, μόνος σεπτὸς καὶ προσκυνητὸς ἔστω, φησί·

    Αὐτὸν τὸν μόνον ὄντα σέβεσθ᾽, ἡγήτορα κόσμου,
    ὃς μόνος εἰς αἰῶνα καὶ ἐξ αἰῶνος ἐτύχθη.   105

15. Συνάπτει δὲ τοῖς ἐγκειμένοις, ὅτι ὁ σωτὴρ πάντων περὶ ἑαυτοῦ διὰ
σοφῶν αἰνιγμάτων πρὸς τὸν Νῶε λέγει τοιάδε·

    Εἰμὶ δ᾽ ἐγὼ τοῖος· <σὺ δ᾽ ἐνὶ φρεσὶ σῇσι νόησον·
    οὐρανὸν ἐνδέδυμαι,> περιβέβλημαι δὲ θάλασσαν,
    γαῖα δέ μοι στήριγμα ποδῶν, περὶ σῶμα κέχυται   110
    ἀήρ, ἠδ᾽ ἄστρων με χορὸς περιδέδρομε πάντη.
    Ἐννέα γράμματ᾽ ἔχω, τετρασύλλαβός εἰμι· νόει με·
    αἱ τρεῖς αἱ πρῶται δύο γράμματ᾽ ἔχουσιν ἑκάστη,
    ἡ λοιπὴ δὲ τὰ λοιπὰ καί εἰσιν ἄφωνα τὰ πέντε·
    τοῦ παντὸς δ᾽ ἀριθμοῦ ἑκατοντάδες εἰσὶ δὶς ὀκτώ,   115

---

13. 99–101 Orac. Sib. VIII, 260–262; cf. Lact., Div. Inst. II,12,20   **14.**
104–105 Orac. Sib. fr. 1,15–16 Geffcken; cf. Lact., Div. Inst. I,6,16   **15.**
108–117 Orac. Sib. I,137–146

---

13. 99 ἄνθρωπον πλασθέντα Lact. Φ Ψ Geffcken Erbse: οὐράνιον ἄνθρωπον
πλασθέντα Ω ‖ θεοῦ παλάμαις ἁγίαισιν *om.* Φ Ψ θεοῦ παλάμησιν Ω ‖ 100
κἐπλάνησεν Erbse: κ᾽ ἐπλάνησε Lact. Ω καὶ πλάνησεν D λ Ψ τ᾽ ἐπλάνησεν
Φ Geffcken Mras ‖ δόλιος Ψ ‖ ἀνελθεῖν Lact. D λ Erbse: ἀπελθεῖν ΦΨ
Geffcken Mras ἐλθεῖν Ω ‖ 101 ἀγαθοῦ τε κακοῦ τε D λ Geffcken Mras
Erbse: ἀγαθοῦ τε καὶ κακοῦ B" ἀγαθοῦ κακοῦ τε R   **14.** 104 σέβεσθ᾽
Lact. D Geffcken Mras Erbse: σέβεσθαι λ σέβεσθε Η   **15.** 108 εἰμὶ δ᾽
ἐγὼ τοῖος D λ Mras Erbse: εἰμὶ δ᾽ ἔγωγε ὁ ὢν Τ Ψ Geffcken εἰμὶ δ᾽ ἐγὼ ὁ
ὢν Φ ‖ 108–109 σὺ δ᾽ ἐνὶ φρεσὶ—ἐνδέδυμαι *ex* Orac. Sib. (= T) *ins.* Erbse:
om. D λ ‖ 110 δέ μοι Φ Geffcken Erbse: δέ μου D λ Mras *versum om.* T
Ψ ‖ 111 ἠδ᾽ D λ Τ Geffcken Mras Erbse: δ᾽ ἠδ᾽ ΦΨ ‖ περιδέδρομε Τ Φ
Geffcken Mras Erbse: περιδέδραμε D λ περιδέδραμαι Ψ ‖ πάντα W᾽ Ψ ‖
114 τὰ *ante* πέντε *om.* Τ: δὲ *coni.* Alexandre *appr.* Buresch

τρεῖς τρισκαιδεκάδες τρίς θ᾽ ἑπτά· γνοὺς δὲ τίς εἰμι
οὐκ ἀμύητος ἔσῃ σοφίης πολυήρατος ἀνήρ.

16. Ἐννεαγράμματον <οὖν> ὄνομα τετρασύλλαβον, οὗ αἱ πρῶται τρεῖς
συλλαβαὶ ἀπὸ δύο στοιχείων εἰσίν, ἡ δὲ τελευταία τριῶν 'μ ο ν ο γ ε ν ή ς'
ἐστιν· εἰς δὲ τὰ ἐννέα ταῦτα στοιχεῖα ἔστιν ἄφωνα πέντε μ̅ ν̅ γ̅ ν̅ ϛ̅· τοῦ   1?
παντὸς δ᾽ ἀριθμοῦ τῶν γραμμάτων, τουτέστιν τοῦ 'μονογενὴς υἱὸς θεοῦ',
συνάγονται ψῆφοι ‚αχξ᾽. Καὶ Ἐμμανουὴλ δὲ τοσαύτας ἔχει συλλαβὰς καὶ
γράμματα· οὐκ ἄπορον τοίνυν ἡμῖν ἐγένετο τὸ νόημα, ἀλλ᾽ ἔγνωμέν σε,
δέσποτα, καὶ ἑαυτούς σοι μετ᾽ ἰσχυρᾶς ἐλπίδος παρεθέμεθα καὶ πρὸς σὲ
ἔχομεν ἑαυτούς, μᾶλλον δὲ αὐτὸς σὺ πρὸς ἑαυτὸν ἔχεις ἡμᾶς, καὶ ὑμνοῦμέν   1?
σε· ἡ ἐξουσία σου ἐξουσία ἀΐδιος καὶ ἡ βασιλεία σου βασιλεία αἰώνιος.

17. Εἶτα τῶν ἐπῶν τοῦ δευτέρου αὐτῆς τόμου ἐπαίωμεν τῶν μηνυόντων
τὴν ἐκ παρθένου πάναγνον γέννησιν τοῦ ἁγίου τῶν ἁγίων Ἐμμανουὴλ
ἐχόντων ὧδε·

Ὀπ<π>ότ᾽ ἂν ἡ δάμαλις λόγον ὑψίστοιο θεοῖο   1?
τέξεται, ἡ δ᾽ ἄλοχος φῶς <τῷ> λόγῳ οὔνομα δώσει,
καὶ τότ᾽ ἀπ᾽ ἀντολίης ἀστὴρ ἐνὶ ἤμασι μέσσοις
λαμπρὸς παμφαίνων <τε> ἀπ᾽ οὐρανόθεν προφανεῖται
σῆμα μέγ᾽ ἀγγέλλων θνητοῖς μερόπεσσι βροτοῖσι,

---

17. 130–146 Orac. Sib. I, 323a–e + 324–335.

---

116 τρεῖς τρισκαιδεκάδες D λ Mras Erbse: καὶ τρεῖς τρισκαιδεκάδες Ψ Τ
καὶ τρεῖς, τρὶς δεκάδες Geffcken ‖ τρὶς θ᾽ ἑπτά *em.* Mras *appr.* Erbse: καὶ
τρὶς ἑπτά D λ καὶ δὶς ἑπτά Τ δίς θ᾽ ἑπτά Buresch σὺν τοῖς ἑπτά Ψ σὺν γ᾽
ἑπτά Φ (γὰρ *cod.* Β") Geffcken σὺν τοῖς δυσὶ Alexandre ‖ 117 σοφίης
πολυήρατος ἀνήρ D λ Mras Erbse: τῆς παρ᾽ ἐμοὶ σοφίης Τ Φ (παρ᾽ ἐμοῦ Ψ)
Geffcken ‖ οὗτος μὲν οὖν ὁ τὴν Θεοσοφίαν Σιβύλλης γεγραφὼς ἔδοξέν εἰς
λύσιν τοῦ ζητημένου τὸ 'μονογενοῦς' ὄνομα καὶ τὸ 'Ἐμμανουὴλ' εὑρεῖν. ἔοικε
δὲ μὴ εἰδέναι τὴν λύσιν *add.* Τ   **16.** 118 οὖν *ins.* Erbse ‖ 120 εἰς δὲ D
Erbse: εἰ δὲ λ Mras ‖ 126 ἡ *ante* ἐξουσία D Mras Erbse: ἡ ἡ λ   **17.**
130–134 *versus* 323 a–e ὁππότ᾽ ἂν—βροτοῖσι *in solis codd.* D, λ, α, Q" et O'
inveniuntur ‖ 130 ὁππότ᾽ *em.* Mras *appr.* Erbse: ὁπότ᾽ *codd.* ‖ δάμαλις *cf.*
Apocr. Ezech. *ap.* Tert., De carne Christi 23,6: *legimus apud Ezechielem de
vacca illa, quae peperit et non peperit* Epiph., Pan. 30,30,3: καὶ τέξεται ἡ δάμαλις
καὶ ἐροῦσιν, οὐ τέτοκεν Ps.Greg. Nyss., Test. adv. Jud. 3: ἰδοὺ ἡ δάμαλις
τέτοκε καὶ οὐ τέτοκε. Τοῦτο δὲ δηλοῖ τὴν Παρθένον ‖ λόγον ὑψίστοιο θεοῖο
transp. et em. Mras *appr.* Erbse: θεοῦ λόγον ὑψίστοιο *codd.* Kurfess ‖ περὶ τῆς
γεννήσεως τοῦ δεσπότου Χριστοῦ ἐκ τῆς ἀειπαρθένου καὶ ἀχράντου Μαρίας
καὶ τῆς ὀνομασίας αὐτοῦ ἤγουν τὸ Ἰησοῦς ὅ τι ἐκλήθη D mg. ‖ 131 τέξεται—
δώσει *om.* α Q" O' ‖ ἄλοχος Mras Kurfess J.B. Bauer: ἄλαλος D Erbse ‖
φῶς *em.* Mras: φῶς D λ φω<τὸ>ς *coni.* Rzach Kurfess J.B. Bauer Erbse ‖
τῷ *ins.* Mras: θεοῦ Snell Erbse ‖ 132 καὶ τότ᾽ D λ Mras Erbse: δὴ τότ᾽ α
Q" O' ‖ ἀντολίης D Mras Erbse: ἀνατολίης α Q" O' ἀπανατολίης λ ‖
ἤμασι Mras Kurfess: ἤμασι Erbse ‖ 133 τε *ins.* Mras ‖ 134 μερόπεσσι:
μερίπασσι Kurfess

δὴ τότε τοῦ μεγάλοιο θεοῦ παῖς ἀνθρώποισιν   135
ἥξει σαρκοφόρος θνητοῖς ὁμοιούμενος ἐν γῇ,
τέσσαρα φωνήεντα φέρων, τὰ δ᾽ ἄφωνα ἐν αὐτῷ
δισσῶς· ἐγὼ δέ κέ τοι ἀριθμόν γ᾽ ὅλον ἐξονομήνω.
᾽Οκτὼ γὰρ μονάδας, τόσσας δεκάδας δ᾽ ἐπὶ ταύταις
ἠδ᾽ ἑκατοντάδας ὀκτὼ ἀπιστοκόροις ἀνθρώποις   140
οὔνομα δηλώσει· σὺ δ᾽ ἐνὶ φρεσὶ σῇσι νόησον
ἀθανάτοιο θεοῦ Χριστὸν παῖδ᾽ ὑψίστοιο.
Αὐτὸς πληρώσει δὲ θεοῦ νόμον, οὐ καταλύσει,
ἀντίτυπον μίμημα φέρων καὶ πάντα διδάξει.
Τούτῳ προσκομίσουσ᾽ ἱερεῖς χρυσόν, προφέροντες   145
σμύρναν, ἀτὰρ λίβανον· καὶ γὰρ τάδε πάντ᾽ ἐθελήσει.

18. Δάμαλιν τὴν ἀπειρόγαμον παρθένον λέγει· ῾Εβραϊστὶ γὰρ παρθένος
καὶ δάμαλις τῷ ἑνὶ ὀνόματι προσαγορεύονται, καθὰ οἱ τὰς θείας γραφὰς
ἀπὸ τῆς ῾Εβραΐδος φωνῆς εἰς τὴν ῾Ελλάδα μεταθέντες ἡρμήνευσαν. Δάμαλις
γὰρ καλεῖται ἡ ἀδάμαστος καὶ μήπω ταύρῳ μιγεῖσα· μετὰ τὸ σκυλῆναι   150
γὰρ οὐκέτι δάμαλις, ἀλλὰ βοῦς ὀνομάζεται. Διὸ ἐπήγαγεν·

ἡ <δ᾽> ἄλοχος φῶς <τῷ λόγῳ οὔνομα δώσει>,

τουτέστιν ἡ ἄλοχος ἄνθρωπος τῷ λόγῳ τοῦ θεοῦ ὄνομα ὡς μήτηρ ἐπιθήσει.

19. Καταγινωσκόμενοι οὖν οἱ ᾽Ιουδαῖοι, ὅτι τῷ μακαριωτάτῳ ῾Ησαΐᾳ οὐκ
ἐπίστευσαν εἰπόντι· ῾῾Ιδοὺ ἡ παρθένος ἐν γαστρὶ ἕξει καὶ τέξεται υἱὸν καὶ   155
καλέσουσιν τὸ ὄνομα αὐτοῦ ᾽Εμμανουήλ, ὅ ἐστι <μεθερμηνευόμενον>
῾῾μεθ᾽ ἡμῶν ὁ θεός᾽᾽᾽ (a), ψυχρὰν ἀπολογίαν προΐσχονται, ὅτι ἔνιοι τῶν

---

a) Matth. 1,23; cf. Is. 7,14 et 8,8.10 LXX

135 δὴ D λ Φ Ψ Mras Erbse: καὶ α Q" O' ‖ 135–141 δὴ τότε—νόησον
T ‖ 135 τοῦ D Ψ T Erbse: καὶ Φ Geffcken Mras *om. cett.* ‖ 136 θνητοῖσιν
Ψ ‖ 137 φέρει Φ ‖ 137–138 τὰ δ᾽ ἄφωνα—ἐγὼ δέ κέ τοι *ego*: τὸ δ᾽ ἄφωνον
ἐν (ἐν Erbse) αὐτῷ δισσόν T Geffcken Kurfess τὰ δ᾽ ἄφωνα (τὰ δ᾽ ἀφώνων
λ) ἑαυτῶν (ἑαυτὸν Mras ὃν αὐτῷ Φ) δισσῶς ἀγγέλλων D Φ τὰ δ᾽ ἄφωνα ὄντα
ἐν αὐτῷ δισσόν τ᾽ ἀγγέλῳ Ψ ‖ 138 γ᾽ ὅλον T Erbse: δ᾽ ὅλον Ψ δόλον Φ ‖
139 δ᾽ *ante* ἐπὶ Ψ Geffcken Erbse: *om. cett.* ‖ ταύταις Ψ T Geffcken Erbse:
τούτοις *cett.* ‖ 140 ἠδ᾽ ἑκατοντάδας: ἡ διεκατοντάδας λ ‖ 141 *post* νόησον
add. T: οὗτος ὁ τῆς Θεοσοφίας συγγραφεὺς τὸ ῾῾Ιησοῦς᾽ ὄνομα παρατίθεται εἰς
τὴν τοῦ ζητουμένου λύσιν, καὶ ὡς οἶμαι, τοῦτο ἀσφαλῶς ‖ 143 δὲ *post* πληρώσει
Φ: *om. cett.* ‖ 145 προσκομίσουσ᾽ Φ Geffcken Mras Erbse: προσκομίσουσιν
D λ Ψ Q" O' προσκυνήσουσι α ‖ ἱερεῖς D λ Φ Ψ Geffcken Mras Erbse:
μάγοι α Q" O' ‖ προφέροντες D α λ Geffcken Mras Erbse: προσφέροντες
Φ Ψ Q" O' ‖ 146 πάντ᾽ ἐθελήσει Q" O' Erbse: πάντα θελήσει α πάντα
ποιήσει D λ Φ Ψ Geffcken Mras   **18.** 149 ἡρμήνευσαν λ Mras Erbse:
εἱρμήνευσαν D ‖ 151 οὐκέτι *em.* Erbse: οὐκ ἔτι D λ Mras ‖ 152 δ᾽ *ins.*
Mras ‖ ἄλοχος Mras: ἄλαλος D λ Erbse ‖ φὼς *em.* Mras: φῶς D λ ‖ τῷ
λόγῳ οὔνομα δώσει *suppl.* Mras: θεοῦ λόγῳ οὔνομα δώσει Erbse ‖ 153 ἄλοχος
Mras: ἄλαλος D λ Erbse   **19.** 156 μεθερμηνευόμενον *ex evangelio sec.*
Matthaeum ins. Erbse ‖ 157 μεθ᾽ Erbse: μετὰ D λ Mras

παρ' αὐτοῖς ἑρμηνευτῶν δάμαλιν ἀντὶ τῆς παρθένου εἰρήκασιν, οὐ θεωροῦντες, τί τὸ ὄνομα τοῦ ἐξ αὐτῆς τεχθέντος, Ἐμμανουήλ, σημαίνει.

20. Ὁ προαιώνιος οὖν, φησίν, υἱὸς τοῦ θεοῦ ἀπὸ τῆς παρθένου ἐν τῇ ἀνα- 16̇
τολῇ τεχθήσεται ἐν ὁμοιώματι σαρκός, ὡς γέγραπται, καὶ ὑπὸ ἀστέρος μηνυθήσεται, οὗτινος τὰ στοιχεῖα τοῦ ὀνόματος τέσσαρα φωνήεντά εἰσι, τουτέστιν ō ō ē ῆ, ἄφωνα δὲ ἄλλα τοσαῦτα, τουτέστι μ̄ ν̄ γ̄ ξ̄, ἅτινα συναπτόμενα σημαίνει 'μονογενής'. — Καὶ πάλιν φωνήεντα ῑ ῆ ō ῡ, ἄφωνα σ̄ σ̄, ἅτινα συναπτόμενα δηλοῖ ''Ιησοῦς'· ὅπερ ὄνος συνάγει ψήφους· 16̣
ὀκτάκις ἑκατὸν ἕνδεκα, τουτέστιν ωπη' ὡς εἶπεν μονάδας η' ἀντὶ τοῦ ἅπαξ η', τόσσας δεκάδας <δ'> ἐπὶ ταύταις ἀντὶ τοῦ ὀκτάκις δέκα, π', ἠδ' ἑκατοντάδας η' ἀντὶ τοῦ ὀκτάκις ρ', ω'.—'Κύριος' δὲ συνάγει ψήφους ω' ὡς γίνεσθαι πάλιν ἑτέρῳ τρόπῳ κατὰ τὸ εἰρημένον ὀκτάκις ἑκατὸν ἕνδεκα, τουτέστιν ''Ιησοῦς Κύριος' ψήφῳ ωπη'. Ἀπὸ τούτων τοίνυν νόησον τὸ 17̇
ὄνομα καὶ τὴν μεγαλοπρέπειαν τοῦ προφητευομένου καὶ εἰρηκότος· 'οὐκ ἦλθον καταλῦσαι τὸν νόμον, ἀλλὰ πληρῶσαι' (b), ἀντὶ τοῦ παῦσαι· ᾧ καὶ προσεκομίσθη χρυσὸς μὲν ὡς βασιλεῖ βασιλέων, λίβανος δὲ ὡς θεῷ καὶ ἀμίσθῳ οἰκονόμῳ, ὡς ἀποθανουμένῳ δὲ οὐκ ἄνευ τοῦ ζῆν σμύρνα.

21.   Ἀλλ' ὁπότ' ἂν φωνή τις ἐρημαίης διὰ χώρης   17
ἥξη ἀπαγγέλλουσα βροτοῖς καὶ πᾶσι βοήσῃ,
εὐθείας ἀτραποὺς ποιησέμεν ἠδ' ἀποριψαι
ἐκ κραδίης κακίας καὶ ὕδασι φωτίζεσθαι
πᾶν δέμας ἀνθρώπων, ἵνα γεννηθέντες ἄνωθεν
μηκέτι μηθὲν ὅλως γε παρεκβαίνωσι δικαίων—   18̇
τὴν δ' αὖ βαρβαρόφρων, πεπιεσμένος ὀρχηθμοῖσιν,
ἐκκόψας δώσει μισθόν—, τότε σῆμα βροτοῖσιν

---

21. 175–198 Orac. Sib. I, 336–359

---

b) Matth. 5,17

---

158 ὅ ἐστι μετὰ ἡμῶν ὁ θεὸς *post* εἰρήκασιν *iter.* D et λ: *del.* Mras *et* Erbse **20.** 164 ιηου *em.* Mras: αηου D λ ‖ 167 δ' *ins.* Erbse ‖ ταύταις Erbse: τούτοις D λ Mras ‖ 169 ὀκτάκις ἑκατὸν ἕνδεκα *corr.* Mras: ὀκτωκαίδεκα εἰς ἑκατὸν ια D λ ‖ 170 ωπη *corr.* Mras: ωχπη D λωχπη λ   **21.** 175 ὁπότ' ἂν D λ Mras Erbse: ὁπόταν Φ Ψ Geffcken ‖ 176 ἥξη Geffcken *appr.* Mras Erbse: ἥξη Ψ ἥξει Φ D λ ‖ βοήσῃ Ψ βοήσει Φ ‖ 177 ἀπορρῖψαι D ἀπορρίψῃ Ψ ‖ 178 κραδίης ΦΨ Mras Erbse: καρδίης D λ ‖ κακίην Ψ ‖ 180 γε Φ Geffcken Mras Erbse: *om.* D λ Ψ ‖ παρὸς ἐκβαίνωσι Ψ ‖ 181 τὴν D ΦΨ Geffcken Erbse: τῆς λ Mras ‖ πεπιεσμένος D λ Mras Erbse: πεπεισμένος Ψ πεπεδημένος Φ Geffcken ‖ ὀρχηθμοῖσιν Φ Ψ Geffcken Erbse: ὀρχηθμοῖο D λ Mras

ἔσσεται ἐξαίφνης, ὁπότ᾽ ἂν πεφυλαγμένος ἥξῃ
ἐκ τῆς Αἰγύπτοιο καλὸς λίθος. Ἐν δ᾽ ἄρα τούτῳ
λαὸς προσκόψει Ἑβραίων, ἔθνη δ᾽ ἀγερο͂νται   185
αὐτοῦ ὑφηγήσει· καὶ γὰρ θεὸν ὑψιμέδοντα
γνώσονται διὰ τοῦδε καὶ ἀτραπὸν ἐν φαῒ κοινῷ·
δείξει γὰρ ζωὴν αἰώνιον ἀθρώποισιν
ἐκλεκτοῖς, ἀνόμοις δὲ τὸ πῦρ αἰῶσιν ἐποίσει.
Καὶ τότε δὴ νοσεροὺς ἰήσεται ἠδ᾽ ἐπιμώμους   190
πάντας, ὅσοι τούτῳ πίστιν ἐνιποιήσονται.
Βλέψουσιν δέ τε τυφλοί, ἀτὰρ βαδίσουσί τε χωλοί,
κωφοὶ τ᾽ εἰσαΐσουσι, λαλήσουσ᾽ οὐ λαλέοντες·
δαίμονας ἐξελάσει, νεκρῶν δ᾽ ἐπανάστασις ἔσται·
κύματα πεζεύσει καὶ ἐρημαίῃ ἐνὶ χώρῃ   195
ἐξ ἄρτων <ἅμα> πέντε καὶ ἰχθύος εἰναλίοιο
χιλιάδας κορέσει πέντε, τὰ δὲ λείψανα τούτων
δώδεκα πληρώσει κοφίνους εἰς ἐλπίδα λαῶν.

22. Διὰ τούτων προεφῆκεν αὐτολεξεὶ σχεδὸν τὸ κήρυγμα τοῦ ὁσιωτάτου
Ἰωάννου διαλαλοῦν· ʽφωνὴ βοῶντος ἐν τῇ ἐρήμῳ· ἑτοιμάσατε τὴν ὁδὸν   200
Κυρίουʼ καὶ τὰ ἑξῆς (c).

23. Καὶ ἄλλη δὲ Σίβυλλα, ἥτις ποτέ ἐστιν, λόγους τοῦ ἀεὶ ὄντος θεοῦ καὶ
πατρὸς πρὸς ἀνθρώπους διεκόμισεν ἔχοντας ὧδε·

     Μοῦνος γὰρ θεός εἰμι, καὶ οὐκ ἔστιν θεὸς ἄλλος.

---

23. 204 Orac. Sib. VIII,377; cf. Lact., Div. Inst. I,6,16

22. c) Matth. 3,3; Mc. 1,3; Lc. 3,4 = Is. 40,3

183 ὁπότ᾽ ἂν D λ Mras Erbse: ὁπόταν ΦΨ Geffcken ‖ 185 ἀγερο͂νται Φ
Ψ Geffcken: ἐγερο͂νται D λ Mras Erbse ‖ 187 καὶ ἀτραπὸν Ψ Erbse:
ἀταρπιτὸν D λ Mras Geffcken ἀταρπητὸν τ᾽ Φ ‖ φαῒ Geffcken: φάει Φ Ψ
λ ‖ κοινῷ *om.* Φ ‖ 188 αἰώνιον ζωὴν Φ ‖ 189 ἐποίσει D λ Geffcken Mras
Erbse: ἀποίσει ΦΨ ‖ 191 πίστιν *om.* λ ‖ 192 τε Φ Geffcken Erbse: γε Ψ
om. D λ Mras ‖ βαδίσουσι *em.* Mras: βαδίσωσι D λ βαδιοῦσί Ψ ‖ 193
εἰσαΐσουσι Φ Geffcken Mras Erbse: εἰσακούσουσι Ψ εἰσακούσωσι D λ ‖
λαλήσουσ᾽ Sʼ Mras Erbse: λαλήσουσι δ᾽ D λ Ψ Wʼ λαλήσʼ Bʼʼ ‖ οὐ λαλέοντες:
δʼ ἄφωνοι Wʼ ‖ 195 κύματα—χώρῃ *om.* Ψ ‖ ἐρημαίῳ ἐνὶ χώρῳ Geffcken
‖ 196 ἅμα *ex* Orac. Sib. VIII, 275 *ins.* Castalio *appr.* Erbse ‖ ἰχθύων
ἐναλίων Ψ λ ‖ 198 δώδεκα: δέκα δύο Ψ ‖ ἐλπίδα λαῶν Rzach Geffcken
(*cf.* Lact., Div. Inst. IV,15,18 *et* Orac. Sib. VIII,278): παρθένον ἀγνήν D λ
Φ Ψ Mras Erbse   **23.** 204 εἰμι Lact. D Ω Geffcken Mras Erbse: ἐστι Φ
Ψ ‖ ἔστιν Lact. Bʼʼ D Mras Erbse: ἐστι *cett.*

24. Ταῦτα μὲν περὶ τοῦ αὐτοπάτορος πατρός, τοῖς ὁμοίοις δὲ καὶ ἴσοις καὶ 205 περὶ τοῦ μονογενοῦς υἱοῦ αὐτοῦ· εὐθὺς γὰρ περὶ τῆς ἐνανθρωπήσεως αὐτοῦ ὅμοιόν τι λέγουσα τῷ προφήτῃ Ἡσαΐᾳ· 'ἐξελεύσεται ῥάβδος ἐκ τῆς ῥίζης Ἰεσσαὶ καὶ ἄνθος ἐξ αὐτῆς ἀναβήσεται' (d), ἡ Ἐρυθραία ἐπιθειαζομένη Σίβυλλα προεῖπεν οὕτως·

Ἀνθήσει δ' ἄνθος καθαρόν, βρίσουσι δὲ πάντα.   210
Δείξει δ' ἀνθρώποισιν ὁδούς, δείξει δὲ κελεύθους
οὐρανίας, πάντας δὲ σοφοῖς μύθοισι διδάξει.
Ἄξει δ' ἔς τε δίκην καὶ πείσει λαὸν ἀπεχθῆ,
πάντα λόγῳ πράσσων πᾶσάν τε νόσον θεραπεύων·
τοὺς ἀνέμους παύσειε λόγῳ, στρώσει δὲ θάλασσαν   215
μαινομένην ποσὶν εἰρήνης πίστει τε πατήσας.

25. Καὶ περὶ τοῦ πάθους τοῦ Χριστοῦ αὖθις·

Οὐδὲ γὰρ ἐν δόξῃ, ἀλλ᾽ ὡς βροτὸς εἰς κτίσιν ἥξει
οἰκτρὸς ἄτιμος ἄμορφος, ἵν᾽ οἰκτροῖς ἐλπίδα δώσει.

26. Ὡς ἀφελκύσασα τὴν Ἡσαΐου προφητείαν (e) οὕτως καὶ τοῦδε 220 προαπήγγειλε τοὺς στίχους·

---

24. 210–216 Orac. Sib. VI,8–11 + VIII,272–274   **25.** 218–219 Orac. Sib. VIII,256–257   **26.** 222–225 Orac. Sib. VIII,287–290; cf. Lact., Div. Inst. IV,18,13.15; August., De Civ. Dei XVIII,23

---

d) Is. 11,1   e) Is. 50,6

---

24. 207 ἐξελεύσεται: καὶ ἐξελεύσεται LXX ‖ 208 ἐξ αὐτῆς: ἐκ τῆς ῥίζης LXX ‖ 210 βρίσουσι *scripsi*: βρίθουσι D λ Mras Erbse βρύσουσι Ω Geffcken βρύουσι Φ Ψ ‖ πάντα D λ Mras Erbse: πηγαί Ω Geffcken ‖ 212 οὐρανίους Φ Ψ ‖ σοφοῖς Φ Ψ Ω Geffcken: σοφούς D λ Mras Erbse ‖ 213 ἄξει Φ Ψ D λ Mras Erbse: ἤξει Ω Geffcken ὤξει W' ‖ πείσει: πιάσει Ω ‖ ἀπεχθῆ Φ Ψ Ω: ἀπειθῆ *coni.* Alexandre *appr.* Geffcken ‖ ἄξει δ' εἴς (ἐς Erbse) τε δίκην καὶ δείξει πλοῦτον ἀπεχθῆ D λ Mras Erbse ‖ 214–216 *verba* πάντα—θεραπεύων *laudat* Lact., Div. Inst. IV,15,9, τοὺς ἀνέμους—πατήσας *ibid.* IV,15,24 *leguntur* ‖ 214 τε Lact. D λ Mras Erbse: δὲ Ω Geffcken *om.* Φ Ψ ‖ νόσον: νοῦσον Φ ‖ 215 ἀνέμους: ἀνόμους Ω Ψ ‖ στρώσει δὲ Lact. D λ Mras Erbse: στορέσει δὲ Φ Geffcken στορέσειε (στορέσεις R) δὲ Ψ παύσει δὲ Ω ‖ 216 εἰρήνης Lact. D λ Geffcken Mras Erbse: εἰρήνη Ψ εἰρήνην Ω εἰρήνη Φ ‖ πίστει τε πατήσας Lact. D λ Φ Ψ Geffcken Mras Erbse: ποτὶ δὲ κρατήσει Ω
25. 218 ἀλλ᾽ ὡς Ω Geffcken Mras Erbse: ἄλλως Φ Ψ κάλλους D λ ‖ βροτὸς Ω Geffcken Mras Erbse: χριστὸς D λ ‖ βροτὸς—ἥξει *om.* Φ (*in* B" λείπει) Ψ ‖ κτίσιν *ex* Orac. Sib. VIII,269 *coni.* Mendelssohn *appr.* Geffcken: κρίσιν D λ Ω Mras Erbse *om.* Φ Ψ ‖ 219 *verba* οἰκτρὸς—δώσει *in* Lact., Div. Inst. IV,16,17 *leguntur* ‖ οἰκτρὸς Lact. Φ Ψ Ω Geffcken Mras Erbse: ἀλλ᾽ οἰκτρὸς D λ ‖ ἄτιμος ἄμορφος Lact. (*sed* ἄμορφος ἄτειμος Lact. *cod. Bonon.*) Φ Ψ Ω Geffcken: ἄμορφος ἵν᾽ ἄτιμοσιν D λ ἄμορφος ἄτιμος ἵν᾽ Mras Erbse ‖ δώσει Lact. Ω Geffcken Mras: δώσῃ D λ Erbse (—ῃ) ἵν᾽—δώσει *om.* Φ Ψ

Εἰς ἀνόμους χεῖρας καὶ ἀπίστων ὕστερον ἥξει.
Δώσουσιν δὲ θεῷ ῥαπίσματα χερσὶν ἀνάγνοις
καὶ στόμασιν μιαροῖς ἐμπτύσματα φαρμακόεντα.
Δώσει δ᾽ εἰς μάστιγας ἁπλῶς ἁγνὸν τότε νῶτον.   225

27. Εἶτα περὶ τοῦ ἐθελοντὴν ἅπαντα ὑπομένοντα τὸν Σωτῆρα σιγὴν ἀσκεῖν ὡς πρόβατον ἐπὶ σφαγὴν ἑλκόμενον καὶ ὡς ἀμνὸν ἐναντίον τοῦ κείροντος αὐτόν (f)· ἄφωνος, λέγει,

καὶ κολαφιζόμενος σιγήσει, μή τις ἐπιγνῷ
τίς λόγος, ἤ πόθεν ἦλθεν, ἵνα φθιμένοισι λαλήσει   230
καὶ στέφανον φορέσει τὸν ἀκάνθινον, ἐκ γὰρ ἀκανθῶν
τὸ στέφος ἐκλεκτῶν ἁγίων αἰώνιον ἥξει.

28. Πάλιν οὐκ ἀπᾴδοντα τοῦ ἑξηκοστοῦ ὀγδόου ψαλμοῦ (g) χαριέντως διεξέρχεται·

Εἰς δὲ τὸ βρῶμα χολὴν κεἰς δίψαν ὄξος ἔδωκαν·   235
τῆς ἀφιλοξενίης ταύτην δείξουσι τράπεζαν.

---

27. 229–232 Orac. Sib. VIII,292–295; cf. Lact., Div. Inst. IV,18,16–17
28. 235–236 Orac. Sib. VIII,303–304; cf. Lact., Div. Inst. IV, 18,18–19

---

f) Is. 53,7   g) Ps. 68,22–23

---

26. 222 ἀνόμους Lact. D λ Mras Erbse: ἀνόμων Φ Ψ Ω Geffcken || ὕστερον Lact. D λ Ω Geffcken Mras Erbse: ὕστατον Φ Ψ || 223 δώσουσιν δὲ Lact. Geffcken Mras Erbse: δώσουσι δὲ Lact. (*cod. Bonon.*) D λ Ω καὶ δώσουσι Φ δώσουσι Ψ || 224 στόμασιν Lact. (*cod. Bonon.*) Geffcken Mras Erbse: στόμασι Lact. (*cett. codd.*) D λ Ω om. Φ Ψ || ἐμπτύσματα φαρμακόεντα Lact. Ω Ψ Geffcken Mras Erbse: εἰς ἐκπτύσματα φαρμακόεντα παρειὰς αὐτοῦ Φ || 225 δώσει κ᾽ εἰς (κεἰς W᾽) Φ δώσει τ᾽ εἰς Ψ || ἁπλῶς ἁγνὸν τότε Lact. Rzach Mras Erbse: ἁπλώσας D λ ἀναπλώσας τότε Ω Geffcken ἁπλώσει θ᾽ ἁγνὸν Φ Ψ || ἁγνὸν om. Ω Geffcken   **27.** 229–232 *versus Sibyllinos scripsi testimonio Lact. nisus* || 229 σιγήσει, μή τις Geffcken: ἐσίγησεν, ἵνα μήτις D λ Mras Erbse || 230 τίς λόγος ἤ πόθεν: ὀπ<π>όθεν D λ *suppl.* Mras *appr.* Erbse τίς τίνος ὢν πόθεν Φ Geffcken τίς τίνος ὃς Ψ τίς τίνος ἤ Ω || λαλήσει Lact. L᾽ Geffcken: λαλήσῃ D λ Mras Erbse || 231 φορέσει Lact. D λ Ω Geffcken Mras Erbse: φορέσῃ Φ Ψ || 231–232 ἐκ γὰρ ἀκανθῶν—ἥξει *om.* Lact. || 232 ἐκλεκτῶν—ἥξει Φ Ψ ἔξει D λ Mras Erbse ἐκλεκτὸν (-ῶν *em.* Buresch) αἰώνιόν ἐστι ἄγαλμα Ω Geffcken   **28.** 233 ἀπᾴδοντα *em.* Mras *appr.* Erbse: ἀπάιδοντα D ἀπαείδοντα λ || 235 κεἰς δίψαν Lact. Mras Erbse: καὶ εἰς δίψαν D λ καὶ πιεῖν Φ Ψ Ω Geffcken || 236 τῆς ἀφιλοξενίης Lact. Ω D λ Geffcken Mras Erbse: δὲ φιλοξενίης Φ Buresch τῆς φιλοξενίης Ψ || ταύτην δείξουσι τράπεζαν Lact. D λ (τραπέζουσαν) Geffcken Mras Erbse: ταύτης τίσουσι τράπεζαν Ω Φ Ψ

29. Καὶ μετὰ βραχέα·

Ὦ ξύλον ὦ μακαριστόν, ἐφ᾽ ᾧ θεὸς ἐξετανύσθη,
<οὐχ ἕξει σε χθών, ἀλλ᾽ οὐρανοῦ οἶκον ἐσόψει,
ἡνίκα ἀστράψειε τὸ σόν, θεός, ἔμπυρον ὄμμα.>   24(

30. Καὶ αὖθις·

Καὶ θανάτου μοῖραν τελέσει τρίτον ἦμαρ ὑπνώσας·
<καὶ τότ᾽ ἀπὸ φθιμένων ἀναλύσας εἰς φάος ἥξει,>
πρῶτος ἀναστάσεως κλητοῖς ἀρχὴν ὑποδείξας,

ἵνα ᾖ ἐν πᾶσι πρωτεύων᾽, ὡς ὁ ἱερώτατος Παῦλος ἐπιστέλλει (h).   24:

31. Ὡς δὲ σύμφωνός τις οὖσα ἡ πρόμαντις τῶν ὁσίων προφητῶν καὶ τὴν
ἔντρομον ἀγανάκτησιν καὶ συμπάθειαν τῆς κτίσεως αὐτῆς τε τῆς τότε
ἡμέρας τὸ ἀκαλλὲς ὁρατῶς οἷον καὶ ἀκουστῶς δηλοῖ·

Ναοῦ δὲ σχισθῇ τὸ πέτασμα καὶ ἤματι μέσσῳ
νὺξ ἔσται σκοτόεσσα πελώριος ἐν τρισὶν ὥραις.   25(
Ἀλλ᾽ ὅτε δὴ ταῦτα πάντα τελειωθῇ, ἅπερ εἶπον,
εἰς αὐτὸν τότε πᾶς λύεται νόμος, ὅσπερ ἀπ᾽ ἀρχῆς
<δόγμασιν ἀνθρώποις ἐδόθη διὰ λαὸν ἀπειθῆ.>

---

29. 238–240 Orac. Sib. VI,26–28; cf. Sozom., H. E. II,1,10; Io. Lyd., De
mens. IV,47   **30.** 242–244 Orac. Sib. VIII, 312–314; cf. Lact., Div. Inst.
IV,19,10   **31.** 249–253 Orac. Sib. VIII,305–306 + 299–301; cf. Lact.,
Div. Inst. IV,19,5 + IV,17,4

---

h) Col. 1,18

---

29. 238 ὦ ξύλον, ὦ μακαριστόν Io. Lyd. D λ Φ Ω α E O Buresch Geffcken
Mras Erbse: ὦ μακάριστόν γ᾽ ὦ ξύλον Ψ ὦ ξύλον μακαριστόν Soz. τρισμακάριστον T ‖ ἐφ᾽ ᾧ D λ Φ α Mras Erbse: ᾧ Ψ ἐφ᾽ οὗ Ω Soz. Geffcken
ὑφ᾽ οὗ Io. Lyd. O ἐν ᾧ E T Buresch ‖ 239–240 οὐχ—ὄμμα addidi ex Orac.
Sib. ‖ 239 οὐχ ἕξει σε χθών Castalio Geffcken: οὐχ ἕξει σ᾽ (ἕξεις B") οὐ
χθών Φ οὐχ ἕξεις οὐκέτι χθών Ψ οὐχ ἕξεις ἐχθρὸν Ω οὐκ ἕξει σε χθών E ‖
240 οὐρανοῦ Rzach Buresch Kurfess: οὐρανὸν cett. ‖ 240 ἡνίκα ἀστράψειε
Geffcken: ἡνίκα δ᾽ ἀστράψει Ω ἡνίκ᾽ ἀστράψεις Ψ ἡνίκα ἀστράψῃ Φ ἡνίκ᾽
ἀπαστράψειε Kurfess ‖ τὸ σόν, θεός Alexandre Geffcken Kurfess τόσον
(τόσσον H) θεός Ω τὸ νέον θεοῦ Φ Ψ   **30.** 242 περὶ τῆς ἀναστάσεως D
λ mg. ‖ καὶ θανάτου—ὑπνώσας om. Φ Ψ ‖ ἦμαρ Geffcken Mras: ἤμαρ D
λ Erbse ‖ 243 καὶ τότ᾽—ἥξει add. Erbse e Lact. et codd. Φ Ψ (om. L") Ω:
om. D λ Mras ‖ ἀναλύσας: ἀναστήσας Ω ‖ 244 κλητοῖς (κλυτοῖς λ) ἀρχὴν
ὑποδείξας: ἀρχὴν θνητοῖς (Lact. cod. Bonon.) ἐπιδείξας Ω ‖ 245 ἵνα γένηται
ἐν πᾶσιν αὐτὸς πρωτεύων Paulus   **31.** 247 τε om. λ Mras ‖ 249 τὸ
πέτασμα καὶ Lact. Geffcken Mras Erbse: τὸ καταπέτασμα καὶ D λ Φ Ψ τὰ
πετάσματα Ω ‖ ἤματι D λ Erbse ‖ 251 δὴ ταῦτα πάντα Lact.: δὴ τάδε
πάντα D λ Mras Erbse ταῦτά γε πάντα Φ Geffcken ταῦτα πάντα Ψ Ω ταῦτα
ἅπαντα Brandt ‖ 252 τότε—νόμον Lact. Φ D λ Geffcken Mras Erbse: τε
πᾶς λύεται νόμος Ψ τότε πᾶς τε νόμος λύεται Ω ‖ 252–253 ὅσπερ—ἀπειθῆ
om. Lact. ‖ 252 ὅσπερ D λ Mras Erbse: ὅστις Φ Ψ Geffcken τίς Ω ‖
253 verba δόγμασιν—ἀπειθῆ ex Orac. Sib. addidi: om. cett. ‖ ἀνθρώποις:
ἀνθρώπων Φ Ψ

32. Καὶ ἄλλη Σίβυλλα θεοφορουμένη προανεφώνησε περὶ τοῦ τὸν θεὸν
πατέρα πέμπειν τὸν ἴδιον υἱόν, δι᾽ οὗ τὰ ἄπαντα καὶ ὑφίστησι καὶ κυβερνᾷ,   255
ἐπὶ τὸ πᾶν ἀποπαῦσαι κακόν·

   Καὶ τότ᾽ ἀπ᾽ ἠελίοιο θεὸς πέμψει βασιλῆα,
   ὃς πᾶσαν γαῖαν παύσει πολέμοιο κακοῖο.

33. Καὶ ἵνα μὴ τοῦ πέμψαντος κἂν πρὸς ὀλίγον ἐξαλλαγὴν ἔχων νομισθῇ
ὁ τὰ σύμπαντα ποιήσας τε καὶ διέπων, ἀπήγγειλαν σαφῶς καὶ διαρρήδην   260
αἱ Σίβυλλαι, τίς ἐστιν οὗτος ἐκεῖνος·

   αὐτόν σου γίνωσκε θεὸν θεοῦ υἱὸν ἐόντα,
  ὃς δι᾽ οἶκτον ἄνθρωπος γενόμενος καὶ ταπεινὸς φανεὶς

    κύματα πεζεύσει, νόσον ἀνθρώπων ἀπολύσει,
    στήσει τεθνηῶτας, ἀπώσεται ἄλγεα πολλά,   265
    ἐκ δὲ μιῆς πήρης ἄρτου κόρος ἔσσεται ἀνδρῶν.

34. Ὅτι δ᾽ ἐν ἡμέρᾳ σκότος ἡλίου τε καὶ <ἔγερσις> ἀνθρωπείων ψυχῶν
διὰ τὸ σωτήριον πάθος τὸ πάσης γέμον ἀθανασίας ἐγένετο, ἐν δὲ μεσονυκτίῳ
φῶς ταῖς ψυχαῖς ἀνήφθη διὰ τὴν ἐκ νεκρῶν ἀνάστασιν τοῦ Σωτῆρος τὴν
ὑπόδειγμα καὶ αἰτίαν ἀναστάσεως οὖσαν τῷ ἡμετέρῳ γένει, συντόμως   270
καταλέγει ἐν τοῖσδε τοῖς ἔπεσι·

              ὁππόταν   ἔλθῃ,
  πῦρ ἔσται σκοτόεντι μέσῃ <τ᾽> ἐνὶ νυκτὶ μελαίνῃ.

---

32. 257–258 Orac. Sib. III,652–653; cf. Lact., Div. Inst. VII,18,5   **33.**
262 Orac. Sib. VIII, 329 (cf. Lact., Div. Inst. IV,6,5); 264–266 Orac. Sib.
VI, 13–15 (cf. Lact., Div. Inst. IV,15,25)   **34.** 272–273 Orac. Sib. fr. 6
Geffcken; cf. Lact., Div. Inst. VII,19,2

---

32. 257 ἀπ᾽ ἠελίοιο Lact. Φ Ψ Geffcken: *om.* Ω ἀφ᾽ ἡλίου Steuchus ἀπ᾽
ὀλύμποιο D λ ἀπ᾽ οὐλύμποιο Mras Erbse   **33.** 262 αὐτόν σου Lact. (*praeter*
cod. S) D Ω (*praeter cod.* H) Mras Erbse: αὐτόν σοι Lact. (*cod.* S) αὐτόν συ
λ || 264 πεζεύσει νόσον ἀνθρώπων Lact. D λ Geffcken Mras Erbse: πεζεύσειε
νόσους δ᾽ ἀνδρῶν Φ πεζεύσει νόμους δ᾽ ἀνδρῶν Ψ πεζεύσειε νόμοις (νόμους
Η) τ᾽ ἀνθρώπους Ω || ἀπολύσει Lact. Φ Ψ Geffcken Mras: ἀπολύει Ω ἀπελά-
σει D λ ἀπελάσ<σ>ει Erbse || 265 τεθνηῶτας ἀπώσεται Lact. Geffcken
Mras Erbse: τεθνηῶτας ἀποίσεται Ω τεθνεῶτας κἀπώσεται Ψ *fere* Φ τεθνεῶτας
ἀπώσεται D λ || ἄλγεα Lact. Φ Ψ Ω Geffcken Mras Erbse: δ᾽ ἄλγεα D λ
|| πολλά Lact. D λ Ω Geffcken Mras Erbse: λυγρά Φ Ψ || 266 ἐκ δὲ μιῆς:
μιᾶς Ψ ἐκ δεμνῆς λ || πήρης Lact. D λ Geffcken Mras Erbse: σπείρης Ω
ῥίζης Φ Ψ Buresch Wilamowitz   **34.** 267 ἔγερσις *suppl.* Erbse: ἀνάστασις
Mras || 272 ὁππόταν ἔλθῃ *e Lact. supplevi* || 273 σκοτόεντι Lact. Geffcken
Mras Erbse: σκότος, ἔν τε D λ ψολόεν τι Stadtmüller Brandt || τ᾽ *ante* ἐνὶ
ins. Mras *appr.* Erbse || μελαίνῃ Lact. Geffcken: γαλήνῃ D λ Mras Erbse

35. Οὕτω γὰρ ηὐδόκησεν ἡ αἰώνιος ζωή, ἡ πηγὴ τῆς ἀθανασίας· ὁ ἔχων πλῆθος οἰκτιρμῶν τὴν ἀνθρωπείαν φύσιν δι᾽ οἰκείαν παρακοὴν συν- 27? τετριμμένην καὶ τεταπεινωμένην καὶ ἐν ἁμαρτίαις καθεύδουσαν ἐξεγεῖραι, τὸν δὲ εὑρετὴν τῆς ἀπάτης, τὸν σκελίσαντα τὴν Εὔαν, τὸν χειμάσαντα τὸ ἀνθρώπειον γένος, τὸν ἀμνη <***>

II

1.]οὕτως ἔφη·

Ἥξει καὶ μακάρων ἐθέλων πόλιν ἐξαλαπάξαι.
Καὶ κέν τις θεόθεν βασιλεὺς πεμφθεὶς ἐπὶ τοῦτον
πάντας ὀλεῖ βασιλεῖς μεγάλους καὶ φῶτας ἀρίστους.
Εἶθ᾽ οὕτως κρίσις ἔσται ὑπ᾽ ἀφθίτου ἀνθρώποισιν.

Ἐν φόβῳ οὖν, φησί, τὸν τῆς παροικίας ἡμῶν χρόνον ἀναστραφῶμεν, πτερωθέντες τὴν αἴσθησιν καὶ εὐμενιζόμενοι τὸν μόνον νομοθέτην καὶ κριτὴν καὶ τῶν ἀνθρώπων κηδόμενον διὰ ἱεροπρεποῦς βίου.

2. Εἶτα καὶ ἄλλη Σίβυλλα τὴν ἔνδοξον καὶ φιλάνθρωπον δευτέραν ἐπιδημίαν τοῦ πλησίον ἀεὶ πάντων παρόντος καὶ πάντα ἐφορῶντος 1(πολυσέπτου θεοῦ προαναφωνοῦσά φησιν·

<ὅς ῥά κε πραῢς ἰδοὺ ἥξει,> ἵνα τὸν ζυγὸν ἡμῶν
δοῦλον δυσβάστακτον ἐπ᾽ αὐχένι κείμενον ἄρη
καὶ θεσμοὺς ἀθέους λύσει δεσμούς τε βιαίους.

3. Καὶ μετὰ βραχέα πάλιν περὶ τῶν αὐτῶν· 15

Ταρτάροεν δὲ χάος δείξει τότε γαῖα χανοῦσα,
ἥξουσιν δ᾽ ἐπὶ βῆμα θεοῦ βασιλῆος ἅπαντες.
Ῥεύσει δ᾽ οὐρανόθεν ποταμὸς πυρὸς ἠδὲ θ<ε>είου.

---

1. 2–5 Orac. Sib. V,107–110; cf. Lact., Div. Inst. VII,18,5   **2.** 12–14 Orac. Sib. VIII,326–328; cf. Lact., Div. Inst. VII,18,8   **3.** 16–18 Orac. Sib. VIII,241–243; cf. Lact., Div. Inst. VII,20,3

35. 278 *litteris* αμνη *in cod.* D *textus abrumpitur; lac. septem linearum habet cod.* λ
1. 2 καὶ Lact. D λ Geffcken Mras Erbse: δ᾽ αὖ Φ Ψ ‖ ἐθέλων Lact. Φ Geffcken Erbse: *om.* Ω ἐθνῶν D λ Mras πόλιν ἐθέλων Ψ ‖ 3 καὶ κέν τις Lact. D λ Ω Geffcken Mras Erbse: κἀκεῖ τις Φ Ψ ‖ βασιλεὺς—τοῦτον: σθε- ναρὸς βασιλεὺς ἐκπεμφθεὶς Φ Ψ ‖ τοῦτον: *om.* Ω τοῦτο D λ Mras ‖ 4 φῶτας: ἄνδρας Φ Ψ ‖ 5 κρίσις ἔσται ὑπ᾽ ἀφθίτου: τέλος ἔσται ἄφθιτον Φ Ψ   **2.** 12 ὅς ῥά κε πραῢς ἰδοὺ ἥξει, *supplevi*: *om.* D λ ‖ ἵνα τὸν ζυγὸν ἡμῶν D λ Geffcken Mras Erbse: ἵνα τοι ζυγὸν ὅνπερ ὑπῆμεν Φ Ψ ‖ 13 δοῦλον: δούλειον Ω ‖ δυσβάστακτον ἐπ᾽ αὐχένι Lact. Φ Ψ Ω Geffcken Mras Erbse: δυσβάσταυρον ἐπαυχένιον D λ ‖ 14 ἀθέους: ἀθέσμους Φ Ψ ‖ λύσει Lact.: λύσῃ *cett.*   **3.** 16 ταρτάροεν Lact.: ταρτάρεον *cett.* ‖ 17 ἥξουσι Lact. Φ Geffcken Mras Erbse: ἥξουσι D λ Ω ‖ βασιλῆος Lact. D λ Geffcken Mras Erbse: βασιλῆες Ω Φ Ψ ‖ ἅπαντες Lact. Φ Ψ Ω Geffcken: ἁπάντων D λ Mras Erbse ‖ 18 θεείου *suppl.* Alexandre *appr.* Geffcken Mras Erbse: θείου D λ ‖ ῥεύσει—θεείου *om.* Lact.

4. Καὶ ἐν ἄλλῳ τόπῳ ἡ αὐτὴ οὐχ ἁμαρτάνουσα τοῦ σαφοῦς καὶ ἀληθοῦς
τάσδε ἀφίησι φωνάς·   20

> Οὐρανὸν εἱλίξω, γαίης κευθμῶνας ἀνοίξω,
> καὶ τότ᾽ ἀναστήσω νεκροὺς μοῖραν ἀναλύσας
> καὶ θανάτου κέντρον, καὶ ὕστερον εἰς κρίσιν ἄξω
> κρίνων εὐσεβέων καὶ δυσσεβέων βίον ἀνδρῶν.

5. Ὀρθῶς οὖν ὁ Ἡσαΐας προεκήρυξεν· ʼὁ οὐρανὸς ἑλιγήσεται ὡς βιβλίονʼ   25
(i), ὀρθῶς δὲ ὁ Δανιὴλ προεφήτευσε τὸ αὐτοφυὲς τῆς ἀληθείας· ʼἐθεώρουν,
φησίν, ἕως οὗ θρόνοι ἐτέθησαν καὶ βίβλοι ἀνεῴχθησαν καὶ παλαιὸς ἡμερῶν
ἐκάθητο ἐν ἐκείνῳ τῷ μεγίστῳ φόβῳʼ (j) οὗ μείζων οὐκ ἔστιν αὐτοῖς.

6. Ὡς πέφυκας, ἀναλλοίωτε δέσποτα, καὶ ὡς ἐποίησας ἡμῖν ἀεί, μνήσθητι
τῆς σῆς ἀγαθότητος καὶ τῆς φωνῆς σου ἧς ἀφῆκας ἡμῖν, ὅτι τὰ παρὰ   30
ἀνθρώποις ἀδύνατα δυνατά σοι τῷ θεῷ ἐστι, καὶ ἱλάσθητι ἕνεκεν τοῦ
ὀνόματός σου, ὁ μόνος ἀναμάρτητος καὶ μόνος πολυέλεος· καὶ σὺ δέ, ἁγία
θεοτόκε παρθένε Μαρία, ἧς ἐγγύτερον ἐν ἀγάπῃ μετὰ τὸν σύναρχον αὐτοῦ
πατέρα καὶ τὸ ἅγιον πνεῦμα οὐκ ἔχει <ὁ υἱὸς>, μία ἐξ ἡμῶν κατὰ τὴν
φύσιν, οὐ κατὰ τὰς ἁμαρτίας ἡμῶν ὑπάρχουσα, συμπάθησον καὶ τὸν πρὸ   35
αἰώνων ἐκ τοῦ θεοῦ, ἐπ᾽ ἐσχάτων δὲ ἐκ σοῦ γεννηθέντα ἱκέτευσον ὑπὲρ
πάντων προβαλλομένη τὸν τόκον σου καὶ τὰς καθαρὰς καὶ πανάγνους
ἀγκάλας σου, αἳ αὐτὸν ἐβάστασαν, ὅπως τὰς ἡμετέρας πρόσ<σ>χῃ δεήσεις,
φθάσῃ δὲ πάντη καὶ πάντως ἐφ᾽ ἡμᾶς τὸ ἄφατον αὐτοῦ ἔλεος καὶ ῥυσθῶμεν
ἐκ τῆς ἐπερχομένης τοῖς ἁμαρτωλοῖς δικαίας ὀργῆς ἐν τῇ φρικτῇ καὶ φοβερᾷ   40
ἐλεύσει αὐτοῦ.

7. Καὶ ἄλλη δὲ Σίβυλλα ὥσπερ μαινομένη ἐκβοᾷ·

> Κλῦτε δέ μου, μέροπες, βασιλεὺς αἰώνιος ἄρχει.

---

4. 21–24 Orac. Sib. VIII,413–416; cf. Lact., Div. Inst. VII,20,4   **7.** 43
Orac. Sib. fr. 4 Geffcken; cf. Lact., Div. Inst. VII,24,2

i) Is. 34,4   j) Dan. 7,9–10; cf. 10,7

---

4. 21 εἱλίξω Lact. H D λ Geffcken Mras Erbse: εἱλήξω Ω (*praeter* H) εἱλίξει
Φ Ψ ‖ κεθμῶνας Φ ‖ ἀνοίξει Φ Ψ ‖ 22–23 καὶ τότ᾽–ἄξω *om.* Ω ‖ 22
ἀναστήσει Φ Ψ ‖ νεκροὺς: νέκυας Φ Ψ ‖ ἀναλύσας: καταλύσας Φ Ψ ‖ 23
ἄξω Lact. D λ Mras Erbse: ἥξω *coni.* Struve *appr.* Geffcken ἥξει Φ Ψ ‖ 24
κρίνω Ω ‖ βίον *om.* Ω   **5.** 25 ὁ οὐρανὸς ἑλιγήσεται Mras Erbse (εἱληγήσεται
D ἑλιγήσεται λ): καὶ ἑλιγήσεται ὁ οὐρανός LXX ‖ 27 οὗ D λ Mras Erbse:
ὅτε LXX ‖ ἀνεῴχθησαν D λ Mras Erbse: ἠνεῴχθησαν LXX   **6.** 33
παρθένε *ante* Μαρία D Erbse: *om.* λ Mras ‖ σύναρχον λ Mras Erbse: συνά-
ναρχον D ‖ αὐτοῦ *em.* Erbse: αὐτοῦ D λ Mras ‖ 34 ὁ υἱός *ins.* Erbse:
δεσπότης (*vel* Χριστός) *prop.* Mras ‖ 38 πρόσ<σ>χῃ *suppl.* Erbse: πρόσχῃ D
λ πρόσχῃς λ₁ Mras ‖ 39 πάντη *ego*: πάντι *cett.*

Δεδιότες, φησί, τὸν κριτὴν πυκτεύσατε εὐσεβῶς τῷ βίῳ πολλὰς ἔχοντες
ἀφορμάς, ἵνα τὸν ἀκήρατον δέξησθε στέφανον, πρὶν <ἂν> ἡ ἀνυπέρβατος   4⋮
ἔλθῃ συντέλεια καὶ ἡ εὐκταία ἀνάστασις, καταδράξασθε τοῦ θεοῦ καὶ
τοῖς δάκρυσι κατασβέσατε τὸ πῦρ τῆς γεέννης, δυσὶν ὀβολοῖς τὸν παμβασι-
λέα καὶ χορηγὸν τῆς ἀθανασίας ὀφειλέτην κτήσασθε καὶ ἐναδήσασθε τὴν
ἐγκράτειαν, περιπτύξασθε τὴν πίστιν τοῦ θεοῦ λόγου, τὰς ἐντολὰς πληρώ-
σατε καὶ οὐ μὴ γεύσησθε θανάτου· δι' ἐγκράτειαν γὰρ Ἡλίας ἀνελήφθη   5(
καὶ διὰ πίστεως Ἐνὼχ μετετέθη εἰς τὸν ἀειθαλῆ παράδεισον [καὶ διὰ τοῦ
ἀγαπῆσαι τὸν τοῦ θεοῦ λόγον Ἰωάννης ὁ εὐαγγελιστὴς μένει ὡς οἱ προλεχθέντες ἕως τῆς δευτέρας τοῦ Κυρίου παρουσίας θανάτου ἄμοιρος].

8. Ἄλλη δὲ πάλιν προφῆτις καταθέλγεσθαι τοὺς θεοφιλεῖς καὶ τῆς ἄκρας
ἀπολαύειν ζωῆς τῇ ὑπερβολῇ τοῦ περὶ αὐτοὺς θείου φίλτρου τοῦτον   55
προαγορεύει τὸν τρόπον·

> Εὐσεβέων δὲ μόνων ἁγία <χθὼν> πάντα τάδ᾽ οἴσει,
> νᾶμα μελισταγέης ἀπὸ πέτρης ἠδ᾽ ἀπὸ πηγῆς
> καὶ γλάγος ἀμβροσίης ῥεύσει πάντεσσι δικαίοις.

9. Ἡ δὲ Ἐρυθραία προορῶσα τῶν Ἑλληνικῶν ψυχῶν τὸ τυφλὸν καὶ   60
ἄλαλον καὶ πολλὴν καταγινώσκουσα μανίαν αὐτῶν οὕτως πρὸς αὐτοὺς
διαλέγεται·

> εἰ δ᾽ ἄρα γεννητὸν καὶ φθείρεται, οὐ δύνατ᾽ ἀνδρὸς
> ἐκ μηρῶν μήτρας τε θεὸς τετυπωμένος εἶναι.

10. Ὡς ἀληθῶς γὰρ μόνος ὕψιστος ἀγέννητος, τἆλλα δὲ πάντα γεννητά·   65
ἀγεννήτῳ δὲ πρὸς γεννητὸν ποῖα μῖξις; εἰ δὲ μίγνυται, οὐ θεὸς οὐδ᾽ ἀνώλε-
θρος φύσις· εἰ δὲ καὶ ἀθάνατος ὁ θεὸς καὶ ἄυλος, οὐκ ἀναγκαία ὑπεισέλευσις

---

8. 57–59 Orac. Sib. V,281–283; cf. Lact., Div. Inst. VII,24,14   **9.** 63–64
Orac. Sib. fr. 3,1–2 Geffcken; cf. Theoph., Ad Autol. II,36; Hippol., Ref.
V,16,1; Lact., Div. Inst. I,8,3

---

7. 45 ἂν ins. Mras appr. Erbse ‖ 49 cum codd. D λ et Mras post λόγου inter-
punxi: post πίστιν Erbse ‖ 51–53 verba καὶ διὰ τοῦ ἀγαπῆσαι—θανάτου ἄμοιρος
probabiliter expungenda ‖ 52 τὸν τοῦ θεοῦ λόγον prop. Erbse: τὸν λόγον τοῦ
θεοῦ λόγου D λ Mras   **8.** 54 καταθέλγεσθαι D Erbse: καταλέγεσθαι λ
Mras ‖ 56 προαγορεύει D Mras Erbse: προσαγορεύει λ ‖ 57 εὐσεβέων δὲ
μόνων ἁγία χθὼν Lact. Geffcken Mras Erbse (χθὼν om. D λ): ἑβραίων δὲ
χθὼν ἁγία ἔστι (ἐστὶ W᾽) Φ ἑβραίων δὲ μόνων ἡ χθὼν ἁγία ἐστὶ Ψ ‖ πάντα
τάδ᾽ οἴσει Lact. D λ W᾽ Geffcken Mras Erbse: πάντα δ᾽ οἴσει cett. ‖ 58
νᾶμα Lact. Φ Ψ Geffcken Mras Erbse: ἅμα D λ ‖ μελισταγέης Lact. D λ
Mras Erbse: μελισταγέουσ᾽ Alexandre μελισταγέος Φ Ψ Geffcken ‖ ἠδ᾽ ἀπὸ
πηγῆς: καὶ διὰ γλώσσης Φ Ψ ‖ 59 γλάγος Lact. Geffcken Mras Erbse: γάλακ-
τος D λ γάλα τ᾽ Φ μάλα τ᾽ Ψ ‖ ἀμβροσίης Lact. D λ Mras Erbse: ἀμβρόσιον Φ
Ψ Geffcken   **9.** 63 εἰ δ᾽ ἄρα—φθείρεται D λ Mras Erbse: om. Lact. εἰ
δὲ γενητὸν ὅλως καὶ φθείρεται Theoph. Geffcken εἰ γάρ τι γεννητὸν ὅλως
καὶ φθείρεται Hippol. ‖ ἀνδρὸς: ἄνδρες Theoph. H   **10.** 66 μῖξις em.
Mras: μίξις D λ Erbse

γονῆς θεοῦ εἰς ἀεὶ διαμένοντος καὶ ὡσαύτως ἔχοντος. Κατὰ τοῦτο <ἄρα
ἀνάγκη τὸν> ἄϋλον καὶ ἀνείδεον ἄρ<ρ>ευστον εἶναι, τῷ δὲ ἀρ<ρ>εύστῳ
καὶ ἀνειδέῳ μηδὲν κοινὸν μετὰ τῶν ἐκ μίξεως καὶ εἰδοποιῶν.   70

11. Κατὰ φύσιν μὲν οὖν οὕτως, κατὰ χάριν δὲ καὶ φιλανθρωπίαν ἡνώθη
ὁ θεὸς λόγος ἀνθρώπῳ σὰρξ γενόμενος δίχα ῥεύσεως ἀνδρὸς καὶ συγχύσεως
καὶ τροπῆς. Ἐν τούτῳ γάρ ἐστι τὸ μυστήριον ἐν τῷ νενικῆσθαι τὴν
ἀνθρωπείαν φύσιν καὶ γενέσθαι τὸν μὲν θεὸν λόγον ἑκουσίως καὶ ἀτρέπτως
ἄνθρωπον καὶ μεῖναι ἕνα καὶ τὸν αὐτόν, τὸν δὲ ἄνθρωπον κατὰ χάριν τῇ   75
ἑνώσει θεόν.

12. Εἰ δὲ καὶ ποιητὴς παντοδύναμος ὁ θεός, λόγῳ ἢ θελήσει μόνῃ, ὅσα καὶ
οἷα βούλεται, παράγει. Καὶ ὡς τοῖς ἀνθρώποις καὶ τοῖς ἀλόγοις ζῴοις ἢ
φύλλοις καὶ πόαις, οὐ χρεία <τῷ θεῷ> διαδοχῆς γένους· ἔχει μὲν γὰρ
[καὶ] ὁ θεὸς καὶ πατὴρ τὸν μονογενῆ υἱὸν καὶ λόγον, δι᾽ οὗ πάντα, καὶ τὸ   80
ἓν ἁγιαστικὸν καὶ ζωοποιὸν πνεῦμα ἐν ἰδίᾳ ὑποστάσει, ἀλλ᾽ ἔχει ἐξ αὐτοῦ
μόνως καὶ συνυφεστώτως καὶ διὰ παντὸς ἀχωρίστως καὶ ἀρρήτως. Καὶ ἐν
τούτῳ εἷς θεὸς καὶ μία οὐσία ἡ ἁγία καὶ ἁγιαστικὴ Τριάς, καθὰ εὐθὺς ἀπὸ
πρώτου βιβλίου καὶ ἐφεξῆς μέχρις ὑστάτου σὺν θεῷ φάναι ἀβιάστῳ λόγῳ
ἀπὸ Γραφῶν ἐταξάμεθα.   85

13. Αἰνιττομένη δὲ ἡ αὐτὴ τῶν δαιμόνων τὴν πρὸς ἀνθρώπους ἔχθραν καὶ
ὡς ἀπ᾽ αὐτῶν μαγείαις, ἀστρολογίαις, οἰωνοσκοπίαις, μαντείαις τε καὶ
νεκυομαντείαις καὶ εἴ τινα ἄλλα κακὰ ἐνεργεῖται, διὰ συντόμων ἐδήλωσεν
οὕτως·

ἐπεὶ πλάνα πάντα τάδ᾽ ἐστιν,   90
ὅσσαπερ ἄφρονες ἄνδρες ἐρευνῶσι κατὰ ἦμαρ.

---

13. 90–91 Orac. Sib. III,228–229; cf. Lact., Div. Inst. II,16,1

---

68 εἰς *em.* Mras *appr.* Erbse: ἐς D λ ‖ κατὰ *scripsi:* μετὰ *cett.* ‖ τοῦτο *em.*
Mras *appr.* Erbse: τούτῳ D λ ‖ 68–69 ἄρα *add.* Erbse *ante verba* ἀνάγκη τὸν
quae suppl. Mras ‖ 69 ἄρευστον et ἀρεύστῳ D λ: *em.* Mras *appr.* Erbse
11. 72 ὁ θεὸς λόγος D λ: ὁ θεοῦ λόγος Mras Erbse ‖ 74 τὸν μὲν θεὸν λόγον
scripsi: τὸν μὲν θεοῦ λόγον *cett.*   **12.** 79 τῷ θεῷ *inserui* ‖ 80 καὶ *ante* ὁ
θεὸς *delevi* ‖ 81 αὐτοῦ *em.* Mras ‖ 84 μέχρι Erbse   **13.** 90 ἐπεὶ Lact.:
ἔρρει D λ Mras Erbse τὰ γὰρ Φ Geffcken καὶ γὰρ R L″ *om.* Ω ‖ πλάνα
πάντα Lact. Φ Geffcken Mras Erbse: πλάνη πάμπαν D λ πλάνα ταῦτα R
L″ ‖ τάδ᾽ ἐστιν Lact. D λ Mras Erbse: πέφυκεν Φ R L″ Geffcken *om.* Ω
‖ 91 ὅσσαπερ Lact. D λ Mras Erbse: ὅσσα κεν *cett.* ‖ ἐρευνῶσι Lact. (*praeter
cod.* P: ἐρευνώωσι) D λ Φ Ψ: ἐρευνώωσι Rzach Geffcken Mras Erbse ἐνεργοῦσι
F″ ἐρευνῶσι F″ *mg.* ‖ κατὰ ἦμαρ Lact. (*praeter cod.* P: κατ᾽ ἦμαρ) D λ Φ
Ψ: κατ᾽ ἦμαρ Rzach Geffcken Mras: καθ᾽ ἦμαρ Erbse

14. Καὶ ἄλλη Σίβυλλα ἀπεχθανομένη τῷ Ἑλλήνων ἔθ<ν>ει διὰ τὴν καταφρόνησιν καὶ ἀμέλειαν τῆς ἀληθείας, καὶ τὸν ἐντεῦθεν ὄλεθρον, τὰ τασσόμενα σκώπτουσα, αὐτῷ βοᾷ·

Ἑλλὰς δή, τί πέποιθας ἐπ' ἀνδράσιν ἡγεμόνεσσιν   95
<θνητοῖς, οἷς οὐκ ἔστι φυγεῖν θανάτοιο τελευτήν;>
Πρὸς τί τε δῶρα μάταια καταφθιμένοισι πορίζεις
θύεις τ' εἰδώλοις; Τίς σοι πλάνον ἐν φρεσὶ θῆκεν
ταῦτα τελεῖν προλιπόντα θεοῦ μεγάλοιο πρόσωπον;
Ἀλλὰ τί δὴ θνητοῖσιν ὀνείδεα ταῦτ' ἐπιβάλλω;   100

15. Καὶ μεθ' ἕτερα[

Fragm. B

[Ἐπιγραφή· Τῆς Σιβύλλης, ἥτις δι' ἀποκαλύψεως τὸ ὅραμα τῶν ἑκατὸν κριτῶν τῆς μεγάλης πόλεως Ῥώμης διεσάφησεν]

1. Παραγενομένης τῆς Σιβύλλης ἐν τῇ Ῥώμῃ ὑπήντησεν αὐτῇ πᾶσα ἡ πόλις ἀπὸ μεγάλου ἕως μικροῦ. Οἱ δὲ ἑκατὸν κριταὶ ὑπήντησαν αὐτῇ λέγοντες· ''Ἡ σοφία καὶ ἡ σύνεσις τῆς βασιλείας σου μεγάλη ἐστίν. Νῦν   5
διασαφήνισον ἡμῖν τὸ ὅραμα ὃ εἴδαμεν σήμερον [οἱ ἑκατὸν κριταί]· καὶ οὐ δυνάμεθα διασαφηνίσαι αὐτὸ καὶ τὴν σύγκρισιν αὐτοῦ οὐ δυνάμεθα γνωρίσαι'. Ἀποκριθεῖσα δὲ ἡ Σίβυλλα ἔφη αὐτοῖς· ''Ἀπέλθωμεν ἐν τῷ Καπετωλίῳ τῆς μεγάλης πόλεως Ῥώμης· καὶ γενηθήτω τὸ τριβουνάλιον'. Καὶ ἐγένετο καθῶς συνέταξεν αὐτοῖς.   10

---

14. 95–100 Orac. Sib. III,545–549 + versus novus; cf. Lact., Div. Inst. I,15,15

---

14. 92 ἔθνει *suppl.* Mras *appr.* Erbse: ἔθει D λ ‖ 94 σκώπτουσα *em.* Mras *appr.* Erbse: σκόπτουσα D λ ‖ 95 ἡγεμόνεσσιν: ἡγεμόσιν D λ ‖ 96 *versum* θνητοῖς—τελευτήν; *inserui ex* Orac. Sib.: *om. cett.* ‖ 97 τί τε Lact. Φ Ψ Geffcken: τί δὲ D λ Mras Erbse *om.* Ω ‖ 98 θύεις *vel* θύεις τ' Lact.: θύεις τ' Φ Ψ Geffcken *om.* Ω θύεις δ' D λ Mras Erbse ‖ τίς σοι Lact. Erbse: τίς τοι Φ Ψ Geffcken Mras *om.* Ω τί D λ ‖ 99 τελεῖν Lact. Φ Ψ Geffcken: *om.* Ω ποιεῖν D λ Mras Erbse ‖ προλιπόντα Lact. D λ Mras Erbse: προλιποῦσα Φ Geffcken προλιποῦσι Ψ προλιπεῖν τε Brandt ‖ 100 *versus* ἀλλὰ—ἐπιβάλλω *in solis codd.* D *et* λ *invenitur* ‖ ὀνείδεα *em.* Erbse: ἀνείδεα D λ Mras
15. 101 *post* ἕτερα D *et* λ *abrumpuntur*

1–2 *titulum spurium expungendum putavi; verbum* ἐπιγραφή *tantum uncis incl.* Alexander
1. 6 ἡμῖν A K: *om.* Q Alexander ‖ εἴδαμεν *em.* Alexander: οἴδαμεν K Q ‖ οἱ ἑκατὸν κριταί Q: *secl.* Alexander ‖ 9 τῆς μεγάλης πόλεως *em.* Alexander: τῆς μεγαλοπόλεως Κ ἐν μεγάλη πόλη (*sic*) Q ‖ καὶ—τριβουνάλιον *om.* A

2. Καὶ ἔφη πρὸς αὐτούς· ''Απαγγείλατέ μοι τὸ ὅραμα ὃ εἴδατε, καὶ τὴν σύγκρισιν αὐτοῦ διασαφηνίσω ὑμῖν'. Καὶ καθίσασα ἡ Σίβυλλα ἐν τῷ Καπετωλίῳ ἔσωθεν τῶν ἐλαιῶν ἀπεκρίθη αὐτοῖς λέγουσα· 'Τί εἴδατε ἀπαγγείλατέ μοι'. Καὶ ἀποκριθέντες οἱ ἑκατὸν κριταὶ λέγουσι πρὸς αὐτὴν· 'Εἴδαμεν ὅτι ἐννέα ἥλιοι ἔλαμψαν ἐπὶ τὴν γῆν'. Καὶ ἀποκριθεῖσα ἡ Σίβυλλα 15 ἔφη αὐτοῖς· 'Οἱ ἐννέα ἥλιοι ἐννέα γενεαί εἰσιν'. Λέγουσι πρὸς αὐτὴν· 'Οὕτως δεῖ γενέσθαι, κυρία ἡμῶν, πάντα ὅσα εἴδαμεν ἐν τῷ ὁράματι ἀπαγγελῶμέν σοι'. Καὶ ἀποκριθεῖσα ἡ Σίβυλλα εἶπεν· 'Οὕτως δεῖ γενέσθαι. [Καὶ λέγουσιν αὐτῇ οἱ κριταί· 'ὡς εἴδαμεν τὸ ὅραμα, οὕτως καὶ ἀπαγγελῶμέν σοι'. Λέγει αὐτοῖς ἡ Σίβυλλα·] Πῶς γὰρ εἴδατε;' 20

3. Λέγουσιν αὐτῇ ἐκεῖνοι· 'Εἴδαμεν οὕτως· ὅτι ὁ πρῶτος ἥλιος πολυποίκιλος, ἀκτινολαμπής, φωτεινότατος, παμμεγέθης, λαμπρὸς σφόδρα. Ὁ δεύτερος ἥλιος ὑπέρλαμπρος, παμμεγέθης, πολυποίκιλος, ἀκτινολαμπής. Ὁ τρίτος ἥλιος αἱματοειδής, ταρταροειδής, παμμεγέθης, πῦρ φλέγον. Ὁ τέταρτος ἥλιος αἱματοειδής, ταρταροειδής. Ὁ πέμπτος ἥλιος αἱματοειδής, φω- 25 τεινότατος, ἀπαστράπτων ὡς ἐν βροντῇ ὑετοῦ. Ὁ ἕκτος ἥλιος ὀμιχλοφανής, χιονοειδής, αἱματοειδής. Ὁ ἕβδομος ἥλιος ταρταροειδής, αἱματοειδής, φοβερός. Ὁ ὄγδοος ἥλιος ἀκτινολαμπὴς ὥστε ἔχειν αὐτὸν ἐν μέσῳ χρόας. Ὁ ἔνατος ἥλιος ὑπὲρ τοὺς ἄλλους ταρταροειδής, ἀπαύγασμα ἔχων'.

4. Καὶ ἀποκριθεῖσα ἡ Σίβυλλα εἶπεν· 'Οἱ ἐννέα ἥλιοι ἐννέα γενεαί εἰσιν. 30 Ὁ μὲν πρῶτος ἥλιος πρώτη γενεά ἐστιν· ἄνθρωποι ἄκακοι, πολυχρόνιοι, ἐλεύθεροι, ἀληθεῖς, πραεῖς, ἐπιεικεῖς, ἀγαπῶντες ἀλήθειαν. Ὁ δεύτερος ἥλιος δευτέρα γενεά ἐστιν, καὶ αὐτοὶ ἄνθρωποι ἀληθινοί, πραεῖς, φιλόξενοι, ἄκακοι, ἀγαπῶντες τῶν ἐλευθέρων τὸ γένος. Ὁ τρίτος ἥλιος τρίτη γενεά ἐστιν· ἀναστήσεται βασιλεία ἐπὶ βασιλείαν, ἔθνος ἐπὶ ἔθνος, γενήσονται 35 πόλεμοι [πλὴν φιλόξενοι καὶ ἐλεήμονες ἔσονται] ἐν τῇ Ῥωμαίων πόλει.

---

2. 11 εἴδατε *corr.* Alexander: οἴδατε Κ Q || 12 διασαφηνίσω *em.* Alexander: ἀπαγγελῶ Κ διασαφηνῆσω Q σαφηνίσω Α || καθήσασα Κ καθεστῆσα Q || 13 εἴδατε *corr.* Alexander: οἴδατε Κ Q Α || 15 εἴδαμεν Alexander: οἴδαμεν Κ Q Α || 17–18 ἀπαγγελῶμέν σοι Alexander: *om.* Κ ἀπαγγέλομέν σοι Q ἀπαγγέλομέν σοι Α || 18–20 *verba* καὶ λέγουσιν—ἡ Σίβυλλα *expungenda existimavi* **3.** 21 πολυποίκιλος *om.* Κ Α || 22 φωτεινότατος: φοβερός Q || παμμεγέθης *om.* Α || 24–25 ὁ τέταρτος—ταρταροειδής *om.* Α || 26 ὡς ἐν βροντῇ Alexander (sicut in tonitruo w¹): ὡς βροντὴν Κ ὦσι Q ὡσεὶ Α || 28 χρόας (*vel* χροιάς) *scripsi Latinis versionibus nisus* (*vide codd.* w³ w⁴ w⁵: colorem): χεῖρας Α Q Alexander || ἐν μέσῳ χρόας: ἐπιχεῖρας Κ **4.** 31 πρώτη *om.* Q || ἄκακοι: κακοι (*sic*) Q || 32 *ante* ἀλήθειαν *add.* πᾶσαν Α Q || 33 δευτέρα: δευτέρη Κ *om.* Q || 34 τῶν ἐλευθέρων τὸ γένος: τὸ ἐλεύθερον γένος Q || 35 ἀναστήσονται βασιλεῖς ἐπὶ βασιλεῖς Α || 35–36 γενήσονται πόλεμοι ἐν τῇ Ῥωμαίων πόλει (τιρήμι πόλεως Q) *scripsi Latinis versionibus nisus* (erunt pugne multe in Roma w¹; erunt pugne nimium multe in Roma w⁴ *et* w⁵) || 36 *verba* πλὴν—ἔσονται *delenda putavi*

5. Ὁ τέταρτος ἥλιος τετάρτη γενεά ἐστιν· θεότης πολλὴ φανήσεται ἐν
μεσημβρίᾳ· ἐγερθήσεται γὰρ γυνὴ ἐκ τῆς Ἑβραΐδος χώρας ὀνόματι Μαρία
καὶ τέξεται υἱόν, καὶ καλέσουσι τὸ ὄνομα αὐτοῦ Ἰησοῦν. Καὶ λύσει τὸν
νόμον τῶν Ἑβραίων καὶ ἴδιον νόμον στήσει, καὶ βασιλεύσει ὁ νόμος αὐτοῦ.   40
Καὶ ἀνοιγήσονται αὐτῷ οἱ οὐρανοί, καὶ φωνὴν λήψεται, καὶ στρατιαὶ
ἀγγέλων τὸν θρόνον αὐτοῦ βαστάσουσιν, καὶ τὰ ἐξαπτέρυγα τὰ ἴχνη τῶν
ποδῶν αὐτοῦ προσκυνήσουσιν. Καὶ λήψεται ἄνδρας ἀπὸ τῆς Γαλιλαίας
καὶ νομοθετήσει αὐτοῖς καὶ εἴπῃ πρὸς αὐτούς· Τὸν λόγον, ὃν ἐλάβετε παρ᾽
ἐμοῦ, κηρύξατε αὐτὸν τοῖς ἔθνεσι τῶν ἑβδομήκοντα δύο γλωσσῶν᾽.   45

6. Καὶ λέγουσιν αὐτῇ οἱ ἱερεῖς τῶν Ἑβραίων· Φρικωδεστάτη δέσποινα
ἡμῶν, ἐρωτῆσαί σε ζητοῦμεν᾽. Καὶ ἀποκριθεῖσα ἡ Σίβυλλα λέγει πρὸς
αὐτούς· Ὃ βούλεσθε ἀπαγγείλατέ μοι. Καὶ λέγουσι πρὸς αὐτὴν ἐκεῖνοι·
Ἀκοὴν ἠκούσαμεν ἀπὸ τῶν ἐθνῶν ὅτι ὁ θεὸς τῶν οὐρανῶν υἱὸν μέλλει
τίκτειν. Πιστεύεις ὅτι τοῦτο γίνεται, κυρία ἡμῶν;᾽ Λέγει ἡ Σίβυλλα πρὸς   50
αὐτούς· Ὑμεῖς οὐ πιστεύετε ὄντες ἱερεῖς τῶν Ἑβραίων;᾽ Λέγουσιν αὐτῇ·
Ἡμεῖς οὐ πιστεύομεν ὅτι ὁ θεὸς υἱὸν μέλλει τίκτειν. Καὶ γὰρ λόγον ἔδωκε
τοῖς πατράσιν ἡμῶν τοῦ μὴ ἆραι τὴν χεῖρα αὐτοῦ ἀφ᾽ ἡμῶν᾽. Λέγει αὐτοῖς
ἡ Σίβυλλα· Ὁ νόμος οὗτος σκόλοψ ὑμῖν ἐστιν᾽. Καὶ λέγουσιν αὐτῇ· Καὶ
τί λέγεις, δέσποινα ἡμῶν, περὶ τοῦ ζητήματος τούτου;᾽   55

7. Καὶ ἀποκριθεῖσα ἡ Σίβυλλα εἶπε πρὸς αὐτούς· Ὁ θεὸς τοῦ οὐρανοῦ
υἱὸν μέλλει τίκτειν, ὃς ὅμοιος τῷ πατρὶ ἔχει εἶναι καὶ ὁμοίωμα νηπίου
λήψεται. Καὶ ἀναστήσονται κατ᾽ αὐτοῦ βασιλεῖς, Ἀλέξανδρος, Σέλευκος
καὶ Ἡρώδης, οἱ μὴ δυνάμενοι σῶσαι ἑαυτούς. Ποιήσουσι διωγμοὺς πολλοὺς
εἰς τὴν Ἰουδαίαν χώραν καὶ φονεύσουσι νήπια μετὰ τῶν γονέων αὐτῶν   60
ὥστε τὸν Ἰορδάνην ποταμὸν αἵματι συγκερασθῆναι· καὶ οὐδὲν ὠφελήσουσιν.
Καὶ μετὰ ταῦτα πολλὰς θεραπείας ποιήσει ὁ ἐπὶ ξύλου μέλλων σταυρωθῆναι. Καὶ ὡς θυσιάσουσι <***> τοὺς βωμοὺς αὐτῆς, ἀκούσωσι τὰ
σημεῖα αὐτοῦ ἃ ἐποίησεν εἰς τὴν Ἰουδαίαν χώραν.

---

5. 37 θεότης πολλὴ *scripsi*: θεότης πολλῇ K A θεότητος · πολλᾶ Q θεότητος
γονὴ Alexander ‖ 38 ἑβραίδων K ‖ 39 *post* τέξεται *add.* κατὰ τὰ νομικὰ
παραγγέλματα A ‖ 42 *post* ἀγγέλων *add.* καὶ ἐξουσίαι ἀρχαγγέλων Q ‖ βαστά-
ζουσι K A ‖ 43 προσκυνοῦσιν K ‖ 44 αὐτοῖς *post* νομοθετήσει *inserui*: αὐτοὺς
(*sic*) A *om. cett.* ‖ εἴπῃ *corr.* Alexander: εἴποι K εἴπει A   **6.** 47–48 πρὸς
αὐτούς: αὐτοῖς Q ‖ 49 ἀκοὴν *om.* K ‖ ἐθνῶν: ἑβραίων (*sic*) A ‖ 51–52
πιστεύετε—οὐ *om.* Q   **7.** 56 εἶπε πρὸς αὐτούς *om.* Q ‖ τοῦ οὐρανοῦ Q
(*vide etiam* Deus celi w[1] *et* dominus celi w[4] *et* w[5]): τῶν οὐρανῶν *cett.* ‖ 57 ὅς:
ὃ K ‖ ὁμοίως A ‖ ἔχει εἶναι καὶ: ἔχειν · ἤνεγκεν Q (similis erit patri suo
w[1] est w[4] *et* w[5]) ‖ 58 λήψεται *om.* Q ‖ βασιλεῖς κατ᾽ αὐτοῦ K ‖ 59 διωγμοὺς
prop. Alexander: δὲ λιμοὺς K A δὲ λοιμοῦς Q ‖ 60 τοὺς γονεῖς K ‖ 62
πολλοὺς θεράπους K ‖ 63 θυσιάσωσι K Q: *lac. post hoc verbum susp.* Alexander
‖ ἀκούσαντες A

8. Καὶ ἀναστήσεται βασιλεὺς ὀνόματι Αὔγουστος ἀπὸ τῆς Φρυγίας καὶ   65
βασιλεύσει ἐν τῇ Ῥώμῃ· καὶ ὑποταγήσεται αὐτῷ πᾶσα ἡ οἰκουμένη. Καὶ
ἕκαστος βασιλεὺς Ῥωμαίων τὸ ὄνομα αὐτοῦ κληθήσεται [Αὔγουστος]. Τὸ
ξύλον τὸ τρισμακάριστον, ἐν ᾧ Χριστὸς μέλλει τανύεσθαι <***> καὶ μετὰ
ταῦτα συναχθήσονται τῶν Ἰουδαίων οἱ ὄχλοι, καὶ ὁ μέλλων ἐπὶ ξύλου
κρεμασθῆναι ποιήσει σημεῖα καὶ θεραπεύσει πολλούς. Κρεμάσουσι τρεῖς   70
ἐξ αὐτῶν ἐπὶ ξύλου καὶ καλάμῳ νύξουσιν αὐτοῦ τὴν πλευρὰν καὶ οὐδὲν
ἀδικήσουσιν αὐτόν.

9. Ἐν δὲ τῇ πέμπτῃ γενεᾷ ἀναστήσονται τρεῖς βασιλεῖς, Ἀντίοχος, Τιβέριος
καὶ Γάϊος, καὶ πολλοὺς διωγμοὺς ποιήσουσι διὰ τὸν ἐν ξύλῳ σταυρωθέντα.
Καὶ ἀνοικοδομήσουσι τὰ ἱερὰ Ἡλίου πόλεως καὶ τοὺς βωμοὺς τοῦ Λιβάνου.   75
Καὶ οἱ ναοὶ τῆς πόλεως ἐκείνης παμμεγέθεις εἰσὶ καὶ εὐπρεπεῖς ὑπὲρ πάντα
ναὸν τῆς οἰκουμένης.

10. Ἐν δὲ τῇ ἕκτῃ γενεᾷ ἀναστήσονται δύο βασιλεῖς ὀλιγοχρόνιοι καὶ
ποιήσουσι διωγμοὺς πολλοὺς κατὰ τῶν Χριστιανῶν. Καὶ οἱ ἄρχοντες αὐτῶν
κρινοῦσι καὶ ἀπολέσουσι τὰ τάγματα τῶν συγκλητικῶν καὶ θανατώσουσιν   80
αὐτοὺς διὰ τὸ ὄνομα τοῦ Χριστοῦ καὶ οὐδὲν ὠφελήσουσιν.

11. Καὶ μετὰ ταῦτα ἀναστήσεται βασιλεὺς ὀνόματι Κωνσταντῖνος, φοβερὸς
καὶ κραταιὸς πολεμιστής, καὶ λύσει πάντας τοὺς ναοὺς τῶν ἐθνῶν καὶ τοὺς
βωμοὺς τοῦ Λιβάνου καὶ τὰς θυσίας αὐτῶν καὶ ταπεινώσει τοὺς Ἕλληνας.
Καὶ φανήσεται αὐτῷ σημεῖον ἐν τῷ οὐρανῷ, καὶ ἐπιζητήσει ἡ μήτηρ αὐτοῦ   85
Ἑλένη τὸ ξύλον τοῦ σταυροῦ, ὅπου ὁ Χριστὸς μέλλει σταυρωθῆναι, ὁ υἱὸς
τοῦ Θεοῦ τοῦ ζῶντος, εἰς τὴν Ἰουδαίαν γῆν. Καὶ ἀνοικοδομήσει Βυζάντιον,
καὶ ἀλλαγήσεται τὸ ὄνομα τῆς πόλεως ἐκείνης, καὶ κληθήσεται εὐδοκῶν
πόλις Κωνσταντίνου. Καὶ ἐνοικήσουσιν ἐν αὐτῇ πᾶσαι αἱ φυλαὶ τῶν

---

8. 66 βασιλεύσει: βασιλεύσι Q δουλεύσει A || πᾶσα *om.* K, *sed vide* omnem
terram w¹ w³ w⁴ w⁵ || 67 κληθήσεται: λαληθήσεται Q || Αὔγουστος *uncis
recte incl.* Alexander || 68 *lac. post* τανύεσθαι *stat.* Alexander || 68-69 καὶ
μετὰ ταῦτα *om.* Q || 69-70 ὁ μέλλων—πολλούς *om.* Q || 70-71 τρεῖς ἐξ
αὐτῶν A: τρεῖς μετ᾽ αὐτοῦ K Alexander τρεῖς μετ᾽ αὐτὸν Q || 71-72 οὐδὲν
αὐτὸν ἀδικήσουσι ποιήσει δὲ σημεῖα *(sic)* πολλὰ Q   **9.** 73 τρεῖς: ε̄ (= πέντε)
A || 74 διὰ τὸν ἐν ξύλῳ σταυρωθέντα: τω ἐπιξύλου κρεμασθέντι K τῶν ἐπὶ
ξύλου κρεμασθέντων A || 75 ἀνοικοδομήσουσι: ὠνοίξουσι Q || τὰ ἱερὰ Ἡλίου
πόλεως: τὴν ἱερακλείου πόλεως K τὰ ἱερὰ ἰλιουπόλεως A || 76 ναοί: βωμοι
(sic) Q || *verba* εἰσὶ καὶ εὐπρεπεῖς *om.* K A   **10.** 79 πολλοὺς κατὰ *om.* K
A || 80 ἀπολέσουσι: λύσουσι Q || τὰ τάγματα τῶν συγκλητικῶν: στρατεύματα
κατοικῶν *(sic)* Q στρατεύματα συγκλητικῶν A   **11.** 82 *ante* βασιλεὺς *add.*
ἄλλος K || 83 ναούς: θεοὺς K || 84 καὶ τὰς θυσίας αὐτῶν *om.* Q || αὐτῶν
καὶ ταπεινώσει *om.* A || 86 σταυρωθῆναι *em.* Alexander: σταυρωθίναι Q
ἐσταυρώθη K A || 87 Ἰουδαίαν γῆν: ἰδίαν αὐτοῦ γῆν K ἰδίαν αὐτοῦ A ||
88 τὸ ὄνομα *om.* A || 88-89 εὐδοκῶν πόλις Κωνσταντίνου *scripsi:* εὐδοκῶν
πόλις K A Κωνσταντίνου πόλις *om.* K Εὐδοκόπολις Κωνσταντίνου πόλις
Alexander || 89-90 γλωσσῶν ἐνοικήσουσι *transp.* A

ἐβδομήκοντα δύο γλωσσῶν. Μὴ καυχῶ, Βυζαντία πόλις, τρὶς γὰρ ἑξηκοστὸν   90
τῶν ἐτῶν σου οὐ μὴ βασιλεύσεις.

12. Καὶ μετὰ ταῦτα ἀναστήσονται τρεῖς βασιλεῖς, Οὐάλης, ἔγγων
Κωνσταντίνου, Οὐαλεντ<ιν>ιανὸς καὶ Ἰουβιανός, καὶ ποιήσουσι διωγμοὺς
πολλούς· καὶ ἐξ αὐτῶν εἰς πῦρ<ὶ> ἀναλωθήσεται, καὶ οὐ μὴ ἀδικήσουσιν
οἱ βάρβαροι τὰς πόλεις τῆς Ῥωμανίας. Καὶ μετὰ ταῦτα ἀναστήσονται   95
βασιλεῖς δύο, Γρατιανὸς καὶ Θεοδόσιος, δυνάσται κραταιοί, πολεμισταὶ
καὶ δικαιοκρίται, διδάσκαλοι τῆς πίστεως, καὶ λύσουσι τοὺς καταλειφθέντας
ναοὺς τῶν Ἑλλήνων, καὶ γενήσονται οἱ ναοὶ τῶν ἐθνῶν εἰς τάφους τῶν
ἁγίων.

13. Ἐν δὲ τῇ ἑβδόμῃ γενεᾷ βασιλεύοντος Ἀρκαδίου καὶ Ὀνωρίου, γίνεται   100
Ῥώμη ῥύμη καὶ πόλις ῥύμης. Ἐν Φρυγίᾳ αἱματοχυσίαι γίνονται, Παμφυλία
ἐρημωθήσεται. Καὶ μετὰ ταῦτα ἀναστήσονται δύο βασιλεῖς, Θεοδόσιος
καὶ Οὐαλεντινιανός, πραεῖς, ἐπιεικεῖς, καὶ ἀναστήσουσιν ἐπ᾽ αὐτῶν πόλεμον
ἐπὶ πόλεμον. Συρία αἰχμαλωτισθήσεται, εἶθ᾽ οὕτως ἀναστήσεται τυράν-
νων γένος ἰσχυρόν, καὶ ληστεύσουσιν τὸν Ταῦρον τῆς Ἀνατολῆς καὶ τὸν   105
Ἀντίταυρον τῆς Ἀρμενίας καὶ τὸν Λίβανον, καὶ οὐ μὴ ἀνανεωθῶσιν αἱ
πόλεις αἷς παρῴκησαν τὸ πρότερον. Καὶ ἀναστήσονται οἱ Πέρσαι πρὸς
κραταιὸν πόλεμον καὶ ὀλισθήσονται ὑπὸ Ῥωμαίων καὶ δώσουσιν εἰρήνην
ἐπὶ ἔτη τεσσαράκοντα.

14. Καὶ εἰσέλθῃ ἀνὴρ †πρόπιος† πολεμιστής <εἰς Ἱερόπολιν> καὶ συν-   110
τρίψει τὰ ἱερὰ τῶν πόλεων καὶ τοὺς βωμοὺς τοῦ Λιβάνου. Καὶ ἔλθῃ ἀκρὶς

---

90 βύζαντι πόλεις Q πόλις βυζαντία A ‖ τρὶς γὰρ ἑξηκοστὸν *em.* Alexander:
Γ ΧΧΧ (*id est* τρὶς ἑξακοσιοστὸν = 1800) Κ Γ γὰρ Χ Α   **12.** 92 Οὐάλης
corr. Alexander: οὐάλις Κ ιοὑλης Q ιουλήν Α ‖ ἔγγων: ἐκγον (*sic*) Q ἔγγονος Α
‖ 93 Κωνσταντίνου Κ: κων^τιν *vel* κων^τιου Q κω^ου Α Κωνσταντίου Alexander ‖
Οὐαλεντινιανὸς *scripsi:* βαλλεντιανὸς Κ βαλεντιανὸς (*sic*) Q βαλεντιανὸς Α
βαλεντ<ιν>ιανὸς *coni.* Alexander ‖ ϊουβένιος Q ἰουβῖνος Α ‖ 94 πυρὶ ἀναλωθήσεται *prop.* Alexander (conburebitur in igne w³ igni conburetur w⁴ w⁵):
πῦρ ἀναλωθήσεται Κ Α ὑπεραναλωθήσονται Q ‖ 96 Γρατιανὸς *scripsi:* Μαρκιανὸς *cett.* ‖ 97 καταληφθέντας Κ ‖ 98 *post* Ἑλλήνων *add.* καὶ τοὺς βωμοὺς
τοῦ λιβάνου Κ Α   **13.** 100 *cod.* Κ *haec verba transp. et falso post* γενεᾷ *coll.*:
ἀναστήσεται τύραννον γένος βασιλεύοντες ἐνισχύι (*sic*) καὶ ληστεύσουσιν τὸν
σταυρὸν τῆς ἀρμενίας καὶ τὸν λίβανον· καὶ οὐ μὴ ἀνανεωθῶσιν αἱ πόλεις·
συρία αἰχμαλωτισθησεται (*sic*) ὑπὸ ‖ 101 Ῥώμη (*vide* Orac. Sib. III,364 *et*
VIII, 165; Roma w¹) : ῥωμανία Q ‖ ῥύμη: ῥύμης ἐν Φρυγίᾳ Α ‖ πόλις ῥύμης:
πάλιν ῥώμη Κ Α ‖ αἱματοχυσίαι *scripsi:* αἱματοχυσεῖαι Κ Α αἰχμαλωσίαι Q
Alexander ‖ 103 Οὐαλεντινιανός: οὐαλέντιος Κ ουαλεᾶνος (*sic*) Q ‖ ἀναστήσονται Q Α ‖ αὐτῶν: αὐτοὺς Κ αὐτῆς Q ‖ 103–104 πόλεμος ἐπὶ πόλεμον
Α ἐπὶ πόλεμις (*sic*) Q ‖ 104–108 Συρία—πόλεμον *om.* Κ ‖ 105 Ταῦρον *corr.*
Alexander: σταυρὸν *codd.* ‖ 106 Ἀντίταυρον *corr.* Alexander: ἀντίσταυρον
Q *om.* Α   **14.** 110–111 καὶ εἰσέλθῃ—πόλεων *scripsi versioni Latinae* w¹ *confisus:*
et intrabit vir belligerator rex Graecorum in Iheropolim (*variae lectiones:*
hierapolim, hierapolium, ierapolym, neapolim, aepolim) et destruet templa ydol-
orum (*vide etiam* tunc surget rex generatus sanguine Grecorum super Hiero-
solimam, et destruentur templa idolorum apoca Libani w²): καὶ ἀνέλθῃ ἀνηρ
(*sic*) πρόπιος πολεμιστὴς· καὶ συντρίψει τὰ ἱερὰ τῶν πόλεων Κ εἰσέλθῃ (*sic*) μὴρ
προκαταπολεμηστὴν καὶ ἐπιστρέψει τακατα τῶν πόλεων Q εἰσέλθῃ ἀνὴρ πρόπιος·
πολεμιστὴς (*sic*) καὶ στρέψει τὰ ἱερὰ τῆς πόλεως Α ‖ 110 εἰς Ἱερόπολιν *add.*
Alexander *om. codd.* ‖ 111 βουμος των (*sic*) λιβάνων Q

καὶ βροῦχος πολύς, καὶ καταφάγωσι τὸν καρπὸν τῆς Συρίας καὶ Καππαδοκίας, καὶ λιμάξει Καππαδοκία. Καὶ μετὰ ταῦτα γενήσεται εὐθηνία. Τότε γονεῖς τέκνα ἀρνήσονται καὶ τέκνα γονεῖς. Ἀδελφὸς ἀδελφὸν παραδώσει εἰς θάνατον. Ἀδελφὸς ἀδελφῇ συγκοιμηθήσεται καὶ πατὴρ θυγατρὶ 115 συγγενήσεται, νεώτεροι γραίας λάβωσιν. Ἐπίσκοποι φάρμακοι ἔσονται καὶ πρεσβύτεροι πορνεύσουσιν. Καὶ αἱματοχυσίαι γενήσονται εἰς <τὴν γῆν καὶ> τοὺς ναοὺς τῶν ἁγίων στρατιαὶ καὶ ἐξουσίαι <βδελύξουσιν>. Καὶ ἔσονται μοιχεῖαι, πορνεῖαι, ἀνδρομανίαι, καὶ τὰ σχήματα αὐτῶν εἰς ἀτιμίαν καλέσουσιν. Ἔσονται δὲ πλεονέκται, ἅρπαγες, φιλόχρυσοι, ὑπερήφανοι 120 καὶ ἀλαζόνες. Καὶ κατὰ τόπον προβάτων καὶ βοῶν θνῆσις γενήσεται.

15. Θρᾴκη ἐρημωθήσεται ὑπὸ βαρβάρων προδοσίᾳ τῶν Ῥωμαίων καὶ διὰ τὴν πολλὴν αὐτῶν φιλαργυρίαν. Καὶ μετὰ ταῦτα ἀναστήσεται Μαρκιανὸς καὶ γενήσονται πόλεμοι. Καὶ ἀναστήσεται ἀπὸ Ἀφρικῆς τύραννος ὀνόματι Γιζέριχος καὶ αἰχμαλωτεύσει τὴν Ῥώμην καὶ οὐκ ἀποφθαρῇ ἀπὸ τῶν 125 προμάχων ἕως πληρωθῇ ὁ χρόνος τῆς ζωῆς αὐτοῦ· σταθήσεται δὲ ἡ βασιλεία αὐτοῦ ἔτη τριάκοντα. Καὶ ταπεινώσει τὴν Ῥώμην διὰ τὴν πολλὴν αὐτῆς φιλαργυρίαν. Καὶ οὐ βασιλεύσει ἡ Ῥώμη ἕως τοῦ καιροῦ τοῦ χρόνου αὐτῆς. Δαλματία καταποντισθήσεται πάνυ, Καμπανία καὶ Καλαβρία αἰχμαλωτισθήσονται. 130

---

112 καρπὸν K A: κόπον Q Alexander *cf.* arbores (*seu* labores) et fructus w¹ labores et fructus w² ‖ 113 καὶ λιμάξει Καππαδοκία *om.* Q *cf.* fame cruciabuntur w¹ fame peribunt w² ‖ 114 ἀδελφὸς ἀδελφὸν: ἀδελφῇ ἀδελφοὺς K ‖ 114–115 ἀδελφὸς—θάνατον *om.* A ‖ 115 ἀδελφὸς ἀδελφῇ συγκοιμηθέσεται *om.* Q ἀδελφαὶ ἀδελφῷ συγκοιμηθήσονται A ‖ 116 γραίας *corr.* Alexander: γρέας *codd.* ‖ 117–118 τὴν γῆν καὶ *ins.* Youtie *appr.* Alexander ‖ 118 τοὺς ναοὺς τῶν ἁγίων K: τὸν ναὸν τοῦ ἁγιάσματος αὐτῶν Q A ‖ καὶ ἐξουσίαι *codd.*: *om.* Youtie Alexander ‖ βδελύξουσιν *add.* Youtie *appr.* Alexander: *om.* *codd.* templa sanctores (*sic*) polluent w¹ ‖ 119 ἀνδρομανίαι: ἀνδρομαχεῖαι K sodomiticum scelus w¹ ‖ 120–121 φιλόχρυσοι—γενήσεται: ἄσπλαγχνοι γενήσοντε· ἐλάστορες καταπόλιν καὶ χώραν (*sic*) K **15.** 122 προδοσίᾳ τῶν Ῥωμαίων καὶ *om.* K ‖ 125 Γιζέριχος *em.* Alexander *e.g.* *Procopium secutus:* δύσαρχος K δίρχος Q σιδήρχος A ‖ ἀποφθαρῇ *scripsit* Alexander: *om.* K A ἀποθάνη Q ‖ 125–126 ἀπὸ τῶν προμάχων *em.* Alexander: ἀπὸ προμάχων K απο τον προμάχων (*sic*) Q ἀπὸ προμάχων A ‖ 126 πληρωθῇ ὁ χρόνος: ἔλθοι τὸ τέλος K ‖ 127 ἔτη λ K: ἔτι Γ Q A ‖ ταπεινώσει: οὐ μὴ βοηθήσει Q A ‖ 128 καὶ—Ῥώμη *om.* Q ‖ 129 Δαλματία *corr.* Alexander: δαλμάτου Q δελματία A ‖ Δαλματία—πάνυ *om.* K ‖ Καμπανία καὶ Καλαβρία: καὶ καλαβρία καὶ σπανία A ‖ 130 αἰχμαλωτισθήσονται: ἐρημωθήσεται K αἰχμαλωτισθήσεται A

16. Ἐν δὲ τῇ ὀγδόῃ γενεᾷ ἀναστήσεται βασιλεὺς θηριώνυμος. Ἄρχονται ὠδῖνες τοῦ κόσμου ἐν τοῖς καιροῖς αὐτοῦ, σεισμοί, καταποντισμοὶ πόλεων καὶ χωρῶν, καὶ ἔσονται πόλεμοι καὶ καύσεις πόλεων. Θρᾴκη ἐρημωθήσεται καὶ οὐκ ἔστιν ὁ διοικῶν ἢ ὁ διατάσσων τὴν Ῥωμανίαν. Ταυροκιλικία ὑψώσει τράχηλον, ἀναστήσεται δὲ Σκύλλα, γυνὴ τοῦ θηρίου τοῦ βασι- 135 λεύοντος, καὶ γεννήσει δύο κοιλίας, ἐξ ὧν μία ἄρρενα <γεννᾷ>, καὶ καλέσουσι τὸ ὄνομα τοῦ πατρός. Καὶ ἔσται καὶ αὐτὸς συγκαθήμενος τῇ θηριωνυμίᾳ τοῦ πατρὸς [αὐτοῦ], μίαν ὁμοίωσιν ἐπὶ τῆς γῆς βασιλείας ἔχοντες.

17. Ἐν δὲ τῇ βασιλείᾳ αὐτοῦ φαίνεται Ἴσαυρος. Καὶ προσκυνεῖται οὗτος 140 ὑπὸ τοῦ πατρός. Καὶ τότε εἴπωσιν ἐκεῖνοι λόγον βλασφημίας εἰς τὸν υἱὸν καθὼς ἔστιν. Καὶ διὰ τοῦ λόγου αὐτοῦ κατενεχθῇ σφόδρα ἀπὸ τοῦ θρόνου αὐτοῦ ὁ πατὴρ [αὐτοῦ], κρατήσει δὲ ἡ ἐξουσία καὶ ἡ δυναστεία τῆς κοιλίας ἔτη τριάκοντα δύο. Καὶ μετὰ ταῦτα γενηθῇ Ἴσαυρος βασιλεὺς καὶ ἔσται μισῶν τοὺς τῆς πόλεως αὐτοῦ καὶ φύγῃ <εἰς> τὴν χώραν αὐτοῦ. 145

18. Καὶ ἀναστήσεται ἄλλος βασιλεύς, οὗτινος τὸ ὄνομά ἐστι τοῦ θηρίου συρτοῦ. Γράφεται δὲ τὸ ὄνομα τοῦ θηρίου ἀπὸ τοῦ δευτέρου γράμματος· ὅ ἐστι Βασιλίσκος. Καὶ λαλήσει βλασφημίαν κατὰ τοῦ θεοῦ τοῦ ὑψίστου, καὶ διὰ τὴν βλασφημίαν αὐτοῦ ἀπὸ γυναικὸς χλευασθεὶς κακῶς ἀπολεῖται καὶ αὐτὸς καὶ πᾶσα ἡ συγγένεια αὐτοῦ. 150

19. Καὶ μετὰ ταῦτα ὑποστρέψει Ἴσαυρος εἰς τὴν βασιλείαν αὐτοῦ, πλὴν οὐκ ἔστι διδομένη ἐξ οὐρανοῦ ἡ βασιλεία αὐτοῦ. Ἔστι δὲ τὸ ὄνομα αὐτοῦ ἐν γράμμασι Ῥωμαϊκοῖς εἰς τὸ τέλος τοῦ ἀλφαβήτου, γραφόμενον δὲ Γραικῶς

---

16. 131 θεριώνυμος: *scholium* ὅ ἐστι λέων *add.* Q (ὅ) A ‖ ἄρχονται *em.* Alexander: ἀρχὴ K A αρχι (*sic*) Q ‖ 132–133 πόλεων καὶ χωρῶν: πόλις καὶ χώρα καταποντισθήσεται K πόλεις καὶ χώραι καταποντισθήσονται A ‖ 133 *post* πόλεμοι *add.* μεγάλοι ἐμπρισμοὶ καὶ K ‖ *post* πόλεων *add.* καὶ αἰχμαλωσεῖαι πολλαὶ K ‖ 135 ὑψώσει τράχηλον: ἐρημωθήσεται K ‖ 136 γεννᾷ *add.* Youtie *appr.* Alexander ‖ 137 *post* πατρὸς *falso add.* αὐτοῦ K Q ‖ 137–139 καὶ αὐτὸς—ἔχοντες: καθήμενος καὶ αὐτὸς μία ὁμοιώμασιν μετὰ τοῦ θηρίου εἰς τὴν βασιλείαν αὐτοῦ K A ‖ 138 αὐτοῦ *post* πατρὸς *expungendum existimavi* **17.** 140 Ἴσαυρος *em.* Alexander: καιρὸς *codd.* ‖ 141 υἱὸν: ιῡ (= Ἰησοῦν) A ‖ 142 κατενεχθῇ: καταβήσεται K κατενεχθεῖ Q ‖ θρόνου: φόνου A ‖ 143 αὐτοῦ *post* πατὴρ *omittendum putavi* ‖ κοιλίας (*scil. Ariadnes*): *falso scribit* σκύλλας (*scil. Verinae*) K ‖ 144 τριάκοντα δύο *dubitanter scripsi*: νβ̄ K Q A πεντήκοντα δύο Alexander ‖ 144–145 καὶ ἔσται μισῶν: μέσον K ‖ 145 εἰς *add.* Alexander **18.** 146–147 θηριόσυρον (*sic*) Q ‖ 148 ὅ ἐστι Βασιλίσκος: *fortasse scholium secludendum* ‖ λαλήσει βλασφημίαν: λέγοσην φλασφημίας (*sic*) Q ‖ 149 χλευασθεὶς: χλεβάσθη (*sic*) καὶ Q ‖ 150 αὐτὸς—συγγένεια: μετὰ τῆς συγγενίας Q ‖ *post* αὐτοῦ *add.* μετ᾽ αὐτοῦ K A **19.** 152 ἔστι διδομένη ἐξ οὐρανοῦ *scripsit* Alexander: ἔστιν (*sic*) διδόναι ἐξ οὐνο̄ῦ K ἔστι διδονεξᾶνω Q ἔστι διδόναι ἐξ ἀνο̄ῦ A ‖ 153 ρωμαίοις K A ‖ ἀλφαβήτου *em.* Alexander: αβ K ἄλφα καὶ του (*sic*) βήτα Q α᾽β᾽ A ‖ δὲ Γραικῶς Alexander: δὲ τὸ γρίκον K *om.* Q δὲ γραίκων A

ἀπὸ τοῦ ἑβδόμου γράμματος· οὗτινος τὸ ὄνομά ἐστι Γραικολατῖνον. Καὶ
ἔσται ἡ βασιλεία αὐτοῦ δυνατή, ἀρέσκουσα παντὶ τῷ λαῷ. Φιλῶν τοὺς 155
πένητας, δυνάστας καὶ πλουσίους ταπεινώσει.

20. Καὶ μετὰ ταῦτα ἀναστήσεται ἄλλος βασιλεὺς ἀπὸ δυσμῶν πόλεως
Ἐπιδάμνου, ὅ ἐστι Λατίνως Δυρραχίου· τὸ δὲ ὄνομα τοῦ βασιλέως
κεκρυμμένον ἐστὶ τοῖς ἔθνεσιν, ὁμοιοῖ δὲ τὸ ὄνομα αὐτοῦ τῇ ἡμέρᾳ τῇ
ἐσχάτῃ, γράφεται δὲ ἀπὸ τοῦ γράμματος τοῦ ὀκτωκαιδεκάτου. Ὅταν δὲ 160
λάβῃ τὴν βασιλείαν αὐτοῦ κληθήσεται Ἀναστάσιος. Ἔστι δὲ φαλακρός,
εὐπρεπής, ὡς ἄργυρος τὸ μέτωπον αὐτοῦ, τὴν δεξιὰν χεῖραν ἔχων μακράν,
γενναῖος, φοβερός, μεγαλόψυχος καὶ ἐλεύθερος, μισῶν πάντας τοὺς πτωχούς.
Πολλοὺς δὲ τοῦ λαοῦ ἀπολέσει δικαίως ἀδίκως καὶ καθελεῖ τοὺς τρώσαντας
θεοσέβειαν. Καὶ ἀναστήσονται ἐν τοῖς καιροῖς αὐτοῦ οἱ Πέρσαι καὶ 165
καταστρέψουσι τὰς πόλεις τῆς Ἀνατολῆς μετὰ τοῦ πλήθους τῶν στρα-
τιωτῶν τῆς Ῥωμανίας μαχαίρᾳ. Καὶ βασιλεύσει ἔτη ἕνδεκα.

21. Καὶ μετὰ ταῦτα ἔσονται οἱ ἄνθρωποι ἅρπαγες, πλεονέκται, τύραννοι,
βάρβαροι, μισομήτορες [τὰς ἰδίας πατρίδας] καὶ <ἀντὶ> τῆς ἀρετῆς καὶ
τῆς ἐπιεικείας καὶ τῆς ἀληθείας πάσης ἐπιστήμης, βαρβάρων σχῆμα 170
ἀναλαβόντες. Λῃστεύσουσι τὰς ἰδίας πατρίδας, καὶ οὐκ ἔστιν ὁ ἀντεχόμενος
τοῖς ποιήμασι καὶ τοῖς ἔργοις αὐτῶν, ἐργαζόμενοι τὴν γῆν αὐτῶν διὰ τὴν
πολλὴν αὐτῶν φιλαργυρίαν.

22. Ἐν δὲ τῇ ἐνάτῃ γενεᾷ κολοβωθήσονται τὰ ἔτη ὡσεὶ μῆνες καὶ οἱ μῆνες
ὡσεὶ ἑβδομάδες καὶ ἑβδομάδες ὡς ἡμέραι καὶ ἡμέραι ὡσεὶ ὧραι. Καὶ 175

154 τοῦ ἑβδόμου γράμματος Alexander: τῶν ε̄ζ γραμμάτων Κ τον ἕπτα γραμ-
μάτων (sic) Q τῶν ἑπτὰ γραμμάτων Α || Γραικολατῖνον em. Alexander:
γρεκολάτινον Κ Γρικολάτιος Q γραικολατεῖνον Α || 156 δυνάστας καὶ
πλουσίους: δυνᾶστ (ας ?) πλουτῶν (sic) Q δύναται πλουτεῖν δυνάστας Α **20.**
158 Ἐπιδάμνου em. Alexander: ἐπιδαμῶς Κ Α ἐπίδαμος (sic) Q || Λατίνως
Δυρραχίου Alexander: λάτε ἐδωρακίου Κ λατήνος ἐν δυρραχίῳ Q λατίναι
δορακίῳ Α || 160 ὀκτωκαιδεκάτου Alexander: ῑΝ Κ ἰώτα (sic) καὶ ἦτα Q ||
163 ante πτωχούς add. πένητας καὶ Κ || 164–165 τοὺς τρώσαντας θεοσέβειαν
vel quid aliud huiusmodi conieci: τοὺς θεοροῦντας (sic) θεοσέβειαν Κ τοὺς θεοὺς
τοὺς θεωροῦντας πάντας πλησίον· φυλάττον θεοσέβειαν καὶ προφήτας Q τοὺς
θεοὺς τοὺς θεωροῦντας πάντας πλὴν φυλάττον θεοσέβειαν καὶ προφήτειαν Α
τηροῦντας θεοσέβειαν prop. Youtie appr. Alexander || 167 ἕνδεκα scripsi chrono-
graphica computatione compulsus: λ̄α Κ λ̄ καὶ ἕν Α om. Q τριάκοντα ἕν Alexander
|| de duabus ultimis emendationibus (τρώσαντας et ἕνδεκα) vide Beatrice in RQ 92
(1997), p. 182 et 185   **21.** 169 μισομήτορες: μηκρομήτριοι Κ Α || τὰς ἰδίας
πατρίδας recte uncis incl. Alexander || ἀντὶ ins. Alexander || 169–170 τῆς
ἀρετῆς—ἐπιστήμης scripsi: τας ἀρετας καὶ τὰς ἐποϊηκίας καὶ τας ἀληθοίας
πάσης ἐπὶ στήμης (sic) Q τῆς ἐπιεικείας καὶ τῆς ἀληθείας πάσης ἐπιστήμης Α
τῆς ἀρετῆς καὶ τῆς ἐπιεικείας Alexander || 171 ἀνεχόμενος Q Α sed vide non
est in terra qui eis resistat w¹ || 172 lac. ante ἐργαζόμενοι vel post φιλαργυρίαν
fortasse statuendam exist. Alexander   **22.** 174 ὡσεὶ em. Alexander: ὡς ἡ Κ ωση
(sic) Q ὡς οἱ Α || 175 ἑβδομάδες pr. em. Alexander: ἑβδομάδαι Κ εὐδομάδες
Q -άδες Α || καὶ ἡ ἑβδομᾶς ὡς ἡμέρα Κ οἱ εὐδομάδες ὡς ἡμέραι Α || ἡμέραι
alt. em. Alexander: ἡ ἡμέρα Κ ημέραις (sic) Q αἱ ἡμέραι Α || ὡσεὶ ὧραι: ὡς
ὥρα Κ ὡς αἱ ὧραι Α

ἀναστήσονται δύο βασιλεῖς ἀπὸ Ἀνατολῆς καὶ δύο ἀπὸ Συρίας, καὶ ἔσον
ται οἱ Ἀσσύριοι ὡς ἡ ἄμμος τῆς θαλάσσης ἀναρίθμητοι καὶ παραλάβωσι
πόλεις καὶ χώρας τῆς Ἀνατολῆς ἕως Χαλκηδονίας. Καὶ γενήσονται αἱμα
τοχυσίαι πολλαὶ ὥστε γενέσθαι τὸ αἷμα εἰς τὸ στῆθος τῶν ἵππων τοῦ συγ
κερασθῆναι τὴν θάλασσαν. Καὶ αἰχμαλωτεύσουσι καὶ ἐμπυρίσουσι τὰς   180
πόλεις καὶ σκυλεύσουσι τὴν Ἀνατολήν.

23. Καὶ μετὰ ταῦτα ἀναστήσεται ἄλλος βασιλεὺς ἀπὸ Ἀνατολῆς, οὗτινος
τὸ ὄνομά ἐστι † Ὀλιβός†. Οὗτος λαμβάνει τοὺς τέσσαρας βασιλεῖς τοὺς
πρὸ αὐτοῦ καὶ ἀποκτενεῖ αὐτούς. Καὶ δώσει ἀτέλειαν τοῦ μὴ παρασχέσθαι
δημόσιον τέλος καὶ ἀνανεώσει πάντας τοὺς λαοὺς τῆς Ἀνατολῆς πάσης   185
καὶ τῆς Παλαιστίνης.

24. Καὶ μετὰ ταῦτα ἀναστήσεται ἄλλος βασιλεὺς μορφὴν ἔχων ἠλλοιω
μένην καὶ βασιλεύσει ἔτη τριάκοντα καὶ ἀνοικοδομήσει τοὺς βωμοὺς τῆς
Αἰγύπτου. Καὶ πολεμήσει τὸν βασιλέα τῆς Ἀνατολῆς καὶ θανατώσει αὐτὸν
καὶ πᾶσαν τὴν στρατιὰν αὐτοῦ καὶ κρατήσει παῖδας ἀπὸ δώδεκα ἐτῶν.   190
Καὶ κρατήσουσιν ἀσπίδας καὶ θηλάσουσι τὰς ἐχούσας τὰ βρέφη καὶ αἱμάσ
σουσι διὰ τὰ φάρμακα τῶν βελῶν καὶ τὰς ἀνάγκας τῶν πολέμων. Οὐαὶ
ταῖς ἐν γαστρὶ ἐχούσαις καὶ ταῖς θηλαζούσαις ἐν ταῖς ἡμέραις ἐκείναις.
Καὶ γενήσονται αἱ πόλεις τῆς Ἀνατολῆς ὄρη.

25. Καὶ σταθήσεται ἀπὸ τοῦ μιαροῦ ἔθνους τῶν Καππαδόκων καὶ συρίσει   195
καὶ εἴπη· ἀρά ποτε ὦδε πόλις ἦτο; Καὶ μετὰ ταῦτα ἀναστήσονται πόλεμοι
ἀπὸ ἀνατολῶν ἕως δυσμῶν. Καὶ μετὰ ταῦτα ἀναστήσεται γυνή· ἀπὸ δυσμῶν

176 ἀνατολῶν Q ‖ 177 παραλάβωσι corr. Alexander: παραλάβουσι Κ
παραδώσει Α ‖ 178 πόλεις καὶ scripsi Latina versione nisus civitates et wⁱ: πολ
λὰς cett. ‖ Ἀνατολῆς: τῆς ρωμανίας Q ρωμανίας Α ‖ Χαλκηδονίας scripsit
Alexander Latinae versioni confisus Calcedoniam wⁱ: εἰς χαλκιδῶνος Κ χαλκιδωνίας
Q χαλκηδόνος Α ‖ 178–179 γενήσεται αἱματοχυσία πολλὴ Α ‖ 180
ἐμπηρήσουσι Q om. Κ ‖ 181 καὶ σκυλεύσωσι Κ om. Q ‖ τὴν Ἀνατολήν:
τὰς ἀνατολὰς πάσας Κ   **23.** 182 Καὶ μετὰ ταῦτα: εἰθούτως Q ‖ 183
Ὀλιβός verbum desperanter corruptum: ἴολβος Κ ολιβὸς (sic) Q ἴοὐλίβος Α ‖
οὗτος: οὕτως Κ τουτέστη Q ‖ λαμβάνει em. Alexander: ἀναλαμβάνεται Κ
λαμβανη (sic) Q λᾱμβάσυει Α ‖ 184 ἀτέλειαν: τελείαν Κ ‖ παρασχέσθαι
corr. Alexander: ἐξέρχεσθαι Κ παρέσχεσθαι Q παρέρχεται Α ‖ 185 δημοσία
τέλη Α ‖ 186 παλαιστίνης πάσης Q Α   **24.** 187–188 ἠλλοιομένην Κ
ἠλληωμένην (sic) Q ‖ 188–189 post τῆς Αἰγύπτου (τῶν Αἰγυπτίων Q) add. εἰς
μορφὴν (sic) Q -ήν Α ‖ 190 παιδίον Α ‖ ἀπὸ δώδεκα ἐτῶν em. Alexander:
ἀπὸ ἰβ ἐτῶν Κ Α ἀποιτῶν δώδεκα Q ‖ 191 ἀσποίδας Q ἀσπίδα Α ‖ 191–192
αἱμάσσουσι em. Alexander: ξηράσουσι Κ (add. τὸν ἰὸν) Q ἐμέσουσι Α ‖ 192
τὰ φάρμακα τῆς ἀνάγκης Κ ‖ τὰς ἀνάγκας om. Κ   **25.** 195 μιαροῦ ἔθνους:
μιαροῦ εἴδους Κ μικροῦ ἔθνος Q ‖ συρίσει em. Alexander: συρήσει Κ συρῆσει
Q συριάσει Α ‖ 196 πόλεις (sic) ὦδε (ὦδε Q) Q Α ‖ ἦτο scripsit Youtie
appr. Alexander: εἶτον Κ ἤτον Q ἦτον Α ‖ 196–197 ἀναστήσονται—μετὰ
ταῦτα scripsi: ἀναστήσοντε πόλεμοι ἀπὸ ἀνατολῶν ἕως δυσμῶν. καὶ μετὰ ταῦτα
Κ ἀναστήσονται πόλεμοι ἀποδυσμῶν ἕως ἀνατολῆς καὶ (sic) Α om. Alexander

ἕως ἀνατολῆς ἡλίου δράμῃ καὶ οὐ μὴ ἴδῃ ἄνθρωπον, καὶ ἐπιθυμήσει ἴχνος
ἀνθρώπου καὶ οὐ μὴ εὕρῃ. Καὶ εὑροῦσα ἄμπελον καὶ ἐλαίαν εἴπῃ· ἆρα
ποῦ ἐστιν ὁ φυτεύσας ταῦτα; Καὶ περιπλακεῖσα τοῖς δένδροις τούτοις   200
ἀποδώσει τὸ πνεῦμα· καὶ φάγωσιν αὐτὴν λύκοι.

26. Καὶ μετὰ ταῦτα ἀναστήσεται βασιλεὺς ἀπὸ Ἡλίου πόλεως καὶ
πολεμήσει τὸν βασιλέα τῆς Ἀνατολῆς καὶ θανατώσει αὐτόν. Καὶ δώσει
ἀτέλειαν εἰς ὅλας τὰς χώρας ἐπὶ ἔτη τρία καὶ μῆνας ἕξ, καὶ δώσει ἡ γῆ
τοὺς καρποὺς αὐτῆς, καὶ οὐκ ἔστιν ὁ ἐσθίων.   205

27. Καὶ ἥξει ὁ ἄρχων τῆς ἀπωλείας <ὁ> ἠλλοιωμένος καὶ πατάξει καὶ
θανατώσει αὐτόν. Καὶ ποιήσει σημεῖα καὶ τέρατα ἐπὶ τῆς γῆς. Τὸν ἥλιον
ἐπιστρέψει εἰς σκότος καὶ τὴν σελήνην εἰς αἷμα. Καὶ μετὰ ταῦτα αἱ πηγαὶ
καὶ οἱ ποταμοὶ ξηρανθήσονται, καὶ ὁ Νεῖλος Αἰγύπτου εἰς αἷμα μετα-
στραφήσεται. Καὶ ὀρύξουσι λάκκους οἱ περιλειφθέντες ἄνθρωποι ζητοῦντες   210
ὕδωρ ζωῆς καὶ οὐχ εὑρήσουσιν.

28. Καὶ τότε φανήσονται δύο ἄνδρες, οἵτινες οὐκ ἔγνωσαν πεῖραν θανάτου, Ἐνὼχ καὶ Ἡλίας, καὶ πολεμήσουσι τὸν ἄρχοντα τῆς ἀπωλείας. Καὶ
εἴπῃ· ἤγγικεν ὁ καιρός μου, καὶ θυμωθεὶς θανατώσει αὐτούς. Καὶ τότε ὁ
ἐπὶ ξύλου σταυρωθεὶς ἥξει ἐξ οὐρανῶν ὡς φωστὴρ μέγας καὶ ἀστράπτων   215
καὶ ἀναστήσει τοὺς δύο ἄνδρας ἐκείνους.

29. Καὶ πολεμήσει ὁ ἐπὶ σταυροῦ κρεμασθεὶς τὸν υἱὸν τῆς ἀπωλείας καὶ
θανατώσει αὐτὸν καὶ πᾶσαν τὴν στρατιὰν αὐτοῦ. Τότε καήσεται ἡ γῆ τῆς
Αἰγύπτου πήχεις δώδεκα, καὶ ἡ γῆ βοήσει πρὸς τὸν θεόν· κύριε, παρθένος

198 ἕως ἀνατολῶν καὶ Κ ‖ ἴδῃ: δεῖ Κ ἤδη (*sic*) Q ‖ 198–199 καὶ ἐπιθυμήσει—
εὕρη *om.* Α ‖ 199 εἴπῃ *em.* Alexander: εἴποι Κ καὶ εἰπει (*sic*) Q καὶ εἴπῃ Α
‖ 200 ποῦ Alexander: ποῦ Κ ‖ ταῦτα: τὴν ἄμπελον καὶ τὴν ἐλαίαν ταύτην
Α ‖ 200–201 τοῖς—πνεῦμα: τῇ ἐλαίᾳ καὶ τῇ ἀμπέλῳ τελευτήσει (*sic*) Κ τοῖς
αὐτῆς γόνασι καὶ ἀποδώσει τὸ πνεῦμα Α ‖ 201 φάγωσιν *corr.* Alexander:
φάγουσιν *codd.* ‖ αὐτὴν λύκοι: η λυκη αὐτὴν (*sic*) Q αὐτὸν λύκοι (*sic*) Α
26. 202 *ante* βασιλεὺς *add.* ἕτερος Κ *add.* ἄλλος Α ‖ ἱλιοῦ πόλεως Α ‖ 203
παραδώσει Κ δόσει Q ‖ 204 τέλεια Κ ‖ ἐπὶ ἔτη τρία καὶ μῆνας ἕξ: ἐπὶ
ἔτη Γ καὶ μήνας (*sic*) ἕξ Κ ετι (*sic*) γῆν ? Q ἐπὶ γ̄ χρόνους καὶ μῆνας ϛ΄ Α
‖ 205 τὸν καρπὸν Κ   **27.** 206 ὁ *ante* ἠλλοιωμένος *add.* Alexander ‖
ἠλλοιωμένος Κ ηλοιωμένος (*sic*) Q ‖ 208 εἰς αἷμα: εἰσέμα (*sic*) Q ‖ μετὰ
ταῦτα *om.* Q ‖ 209 Νεῖλος: ἥλιος Α ‖ αἴγυπτον Q ‖ 209–210 ἀποστραφήσεται
Α ‖ *post* μεταστρα- *explicit* Q ‖ 210 περιληφθέντες Κ ‖ ἄνθρωποι ζητοῦντες:
ἀναζητοῦντες Α ‖ 211 ζωῆς: εἰς ζωὴν αὐτῶν Α ‖ οὐχ εὑρήσουσιν: οὐ μὴ
εὕρωσι Α   **28.** 212 ἄνθρωποι Κ ‖ 213 πολεμήσωσι Κ ὀνειδίσουσι Α ‖
post ἀπωλείας *add.* Α: καὶ ἐν τούτῳ θανατώσει αὐτοὺς (*sic*) · καὶ βρύξει ὁ
ἄρχων τῆς ἀπωλείας ‖ 214 θανατώσει—τότε *om.* Α ‖ 214–215 ὁ—σταυρωθεὶς *om.* Κ ‖ 215 οὐρανοῦ Α ‖ *post* μέγας *add.* λαμπρῶς Α ‖ *post* ἀστράπτων
periit Α *qui tamen finem doxologiae servat*: πάντων τῶν ἁγίων· νῦν καὶ ἀεὶ
καὶ εἰς τοὺς αἰῶνας τῶν αἰώνων, ἀμήν   **29.** 218 καήσεται *corr.* Alexander:
καίσεται Κ ‖ 219 πήχεις *corr.* Alexander: πήχας Κ ‖ δώδεκα: ιβ̄ Κ

εἰμί. Καὶ πάλιν καήσεται ἡ γῆ τῆς Ἰουδαίας πήχεις ὀκτωκαίδεκα, καὶ ἡ   22(
γῆ βοήσει πρὸς τὸν θεόν· κύριε, παρθένος εἰμί. Καὶ τότε ἥξει ὁ υἱὸς τοῦ
θεοῦ μετὰ δυνάμεως καὶ δόξης πολλῆς εἰς τὸ κρῖναι τὰς ἐννέα γενεάς. Καὶ
τότε βασιλεύσει ὁ Χριστός, ὁ υἱὸς τοῦ θεοῦ ζῶντος, μετὰ τῶν ἁγίων ἀγγέλων
αὐτοῦ. Ἀμήν, γένοιτο, ἀμήν.'

---

220 καίσεται K: *iterum corr.* Alexander || πήχας K: *iterum corr.* Alexander ||
ὀκτωκαίδεκα: ι̅η̅ K

1. Sitting near the spring of waters at Glousa of Hurîn, at the place chosen for bathing by the ancient kings, Zoroaster opened his mouth and spoke thus to his disciples Hystaspes, Sassan and Mahman.   5

2. "I address you, my friends and my sons, whom I have nourished with my doctrine. Listen to me, and I shall reveal to you the wondrous mystery about the great king who must come into the world. Indeed, at the end of times, at the moment of dissolution which puts an end to them, a child will be conceived and will be formed with   10 all his limbs in the womb of a virgin untouched by man. He will be like a tree with fine branches and laden with fruits, standing on arid ground.

3. The inhabitants of that land will oppose his growth and strive to uproot him from the ground, but they will not succeed. Then they   15 will seize him and kill him on the scaffold; the earth and the sky will go into mourning for his violent death and all the families of nations will weep for him. He will open the descent into the depths of the earth; and from the depth he will rise towards the Most High. Then he will be seen coming with the army of light, borne on white   20 clouds, because he is the son conceived by the Word which generates all things".

4. Hystaspes said to Zoroaster:

"He of whom you said all that, whence comes his power? Is he greater than you, or are you greater than he?"   25

5. Zoroaster said to him:

"He will arise from my family and my lineage. He is I and I am he. He is in me and I am in him. When the beginning of his coming is made manifest, great wonders will appear in the sky. A bright

---

1–6. 3–43 Ps. Hystaspis Liber Sapientiae, fr. ap. Theod. Bar-Koni, Liber Scholiorum, Mimrā VII,21, Scher, II, pp. 74 sq.

1–2 BIBΛION Δ′ ΧΡΗΣΕΙΣ ΥΣΤΑΣΠΟΥ *planitatis causa inserui*

star will be seen in the middle of the sky, its light will be greater   30
than that of the sun. Now, my sons, you the seed of life, issued from
the treasure of light and of the spirit, which has been sown in the
soil of fire and water, you will have to be on your guard and watch
out for what I have told you, waiting for it to come about, because
you will know in advance of the coming of the great king, whom   35
captives await so that they may be set free.

6. So now, my sons, guard the mystery that I have revealed to you;
let it be written in your heart and preserved in the treasure of your
souls. And when the star of which I spoke arises, let messengers be
sent by you, laden with gifts, to adore him and make offers to him.   40
Do not neglect him, lest he makes you perish by the sword, for he
is the king of kings and it is from him that all receive the crown. I
and he are one".

<XPONIKON>

I

1,1. Ἧι ἡμέρᾳ ἐποίησεν ὁ θεὸς τὸν Ἀδάμ, κατ᾽ εἰκόνα θεοῦ ἐποίησεν αὐτόν, uxor autem eius Aeua. Ab Adam usque ad diluuium Noe generationes X, anni autem duo milia ducenti quadraginta duo.
2. Ἔζησε δὲ Ἀδὰμ ἔτη σλ᾽ καὶ ἐγέννησε τὸν Σήθ. Mortuus est autem   5
Adam annorum noningentorum treginta.
3. Καὶ ἔζησε Σὴθ ἔτη σε᾽: fiunt simul anni quadringenti XXXV, καὶ ἐγέννησε τὸν Ἐνώς. Mortuus est autem Seth annorum noningentorum duodecim.
4. Καὶ ἔζησε Ἐνὼς ἔτη ρϞ᾽: fiunt simul anni sexcenti uiginti quinque,   10
καὶ ἐγέννησε τὸν Καϊνάν. Mortuus est autem Enos annorum noningentorum quinque.
5. Καὶ ἔζησε Καϊνὰν ἔτη ρο᾽: fiunt simul anni DCC nonaginta quinque,
καὶ ἐγέννησε τὸν Μαλελεήλ. Mortuus est autem Cainan annorum noningentorum X.   15
6. Καὶ ἔζησε Μαλελεὴλ ἔτη ρξε᾽: fiunt simul anni noningenti sexaginta,
καὶ ἐγέννησε τὸν Ἰάρεδ. Mortuus est autem Malelehel annorum octin-
gentorum nonaginta <quinque>.
7. Καὶ ἔζησε Ἰάρεδ ἔτη ρξβ᾽: fiunt simul anni mille centum uiginti
duo, καὶ ἐγέννησε τὸν Ἐνώχ. Mortuus est autem Iared annorum no-   20
ningentorum LXII.
8. Καὶ ἔζησε Ἐνὼχ ἔτη ρξε᾽: fiunt simul anni mille ducenti octuaginta
VII, καὶ ἐγέννησε τὸν Μαθουσάλα. Placuit autem Enoch deo factus
annorum tricentorum sexaginta quinque et translatus est.
9. Καὶ ἔζησε Μαθουσάλα ἔτη ρξζ᾽: fiunt simul anni mille quadringenti   25

1,1–5,8. 2–96 Hippolyti Συναγωγὴ χρόνων καὶ ἐτῶν ἀπὸ κτίσεως κόσμου ἕως τῆς ἐνεστώσης ἡμέρας 23–43, pp. 8–10 Bauer-Helm

1 XPONIKON *planitatis causa inserui; in marg. sup. fol. 1r cod.* E᾽ *legitur:* Cronica georgii ambionensis epi uel sicut alii dicunt uictoris turonensis epi *et in marg. inf.:* cronica georgii ambione
1,4. 10 uiginti *scripsi:* quinquaginta E᾽   **1,5.** 14–15 noningentorum X *scripsi:* noningentorum XC E᾽   **1,6.** 18 quinque *addidi: om.* E᾽

LIIII, καὶ ἐγέννησε τὸν Λάμεχ. Mortuus est autem Mathusalam annorum noningentorum LXVIIII.
10. Καὶ ἔζησε Λάμεχ ἔτη ρπη΄: fiunt simul anni mille DCXLII, καὶ
ἐγέννησε τὸν Νῶε. Mortuus est autem Lamech annorum septingento-
rum <LIII>.   30

2,1. Καὶ ἦν Νῶε ἐτῶν φ΄: fiunt simul anni duo milia CXLII, καὶ ἐγέννησε
τρεῖς υἱοὺς τὸν Σὴμ τὸν Χὰμ τὸν Ἰάφεθ.
2. Et factum est cum homines multiplicarentur super terram et filias
procreassent. Videntes autem angeli dei filias hominum quod essent
pulchrae, acceperunt sibi uxores ex omnibus quas elegerant.   35
3. Et dixit dominus deus: Non permanebit spiritus meus in hominibus
istis in aeternum quia caro sunt, eruntque dies eorum annorum CXX.
4. Gigantes autem erant super terram in diebus illis et ultra. Cumque
introissent angeli dei ad filias hominum, illaeque genuerunt, illi fuerunt
gigantes a seculo homines nominati.   40
5. Corrupta est autem terra coram deo et repleta est terra iniquitate. Et uidit dominus deus terram quia corrupta erat: omnis quippe
caro corruperat uiam suam super terram.
6. Et dixit dominus deus ad Noe: Tempus omnium rerum uenit
coram me. Et quia repleta est terra iniquitate eorum, et ecce cor-   45
rumpam eos et terram. Fac autem tibi arcam de lignis quadratis et
linies eam intrinsecus et extrinsecus asfaltu bitumini. Et quod sequitur.

3,1. Et fecit Noe omnia quae praeceperat illi dominus deus. Μετὰ
δὲ ἔτη ρ΄ τοῦ τεχθῆναι τὸν Σὴμ γίνεται ὁ κατακλυσμὸς ὄντος τοῦ Νῶε ἐτῶν
χ΄: fiunt autem simul anni duo milia ducenti quadraginta duo, et   50
diluuium aquarum factum est super terram quadraginta diebus et
quadraginta noctibus.
2. Et mortua est omnis caro quique habuit spiritum uitae in semet
ipso super terram, ab homine usque ad pecus et reptile et ferarum et
omnium quod erat super terram habens spiritum uitae in semet ipso.   55
3. Post haec autem in sexcentesimo primo anno exiit Noe et omnes
qui cum eo erant de arca. Γίνονται οὖν ἀπὸ Ἀδὰμ ἕως τοῦ κατακλυσμοῦ γενεαὶ δέκα ἔτη ‚β<σ> μβ΄.
4. Et a diluuio Noe usque ad turris aedificationem et confusione<m>
linguarum generationes sex, anni autem quingenti quinquaginta octo.   60

1,10. 30 LIII *addidi: om.* E'   **2,3.** 37 eruntque *em.* Frick: erunt que E'
2,4. 39 illaeque *scripsi:* ille que E' illeque Frick   **2,5.** 42 quia *em.* Frick:
quia quia E'   **2,6.** 45 iniquitate *emendaui:* iniquitates E' Frick   **3,3.** 58
σ *ins.* Bauer-Helm: ‚βμβ΄ H'   **3,4.** 59 confusionem *emendaui:* confusione E'

4,1. Hii sunt autem filii Noe, Sem, Cham et Iafeth <***> post diluuium sic. Αὗται αἱ γενέσεις Σήμ· Σὴμ ὢν ἐτῶν ρ΄ ἐγέννησε τὸν Ἀρφαξὰδ
ἔτους δευτέρου μετὰ τὸν κατακλυσμόν: fiunt simul anni duo milia tre-
centi quadraginta tres.

2. Καὶ ἔζησεν Ἀρφαξὰδ ἔτη ρλε΄: fiunt simul anni duo milia quadrin- 65
genti septuaginta octo, καὶ ἐγέννησε τὸν Καϊνάν.

3. Καὶ ἔζησε Καϊνὰν ἔτη ρλ΄: fiunt simul anni duo milia sexcenti octo,
καὶ ἐγέννησε τὸν Σάλα.

4. Καὶ ἔζησε Σάλα ἔτη ρλ΄: fiunt simul anni duo milia septingenti
treginta octo, καὶ ἐγέννησε τὸν Ἔβερ. 70

5. Καὶ ἔζησεν Ἔβερ ἔτη ρλδ΄: fiunt simul anni duo milia octingenti
septuaginta duo καὶ ἐγέννησε τὸν Φάλεγ [et Ragau fratrem eius]. Ἐπὶ
τούτου γενεαὶ πέντε ἔτη φκε΄, ἀπὸ δὲ Ἀδὰμ γενεαὶ ιε΄ ἔτη ͵βψξζ΄. Sub
ipso facta est dispersio.

5,1. Et fuit omnis terra labia et uox una omnibus. Et factum est 75
dum mouerent ab oriente, inuenerunt planum, quod est terra fruc-
tifera, in terra Sennaar et habitauerunt ibi.

2. Et dixit homo ad proximum suum: Venite, faciamus nobis lateres
et coquamus eas igne. Et facta est eis ipsa latera quasi lapis, et bitu-
men erat illis lutus. 80

3. Et dixerunt: Venite, aedificemus nobis ciuitatem et turrem, cuius
capud sit usque ad caelum, et faciamus nobis nomen, antequam dis-
persi fuerimus super omnem faciem terrae.

4. Et descendit dominus deus uidere ciuitatem et turrem, quam
aedificauerant filii hominum. 85

5. Et dixit dominus deus: Ecce labia et uox omnibus una, et hoc
initiarunt facere. Et nunc non minuitur ex ipsis omnia, quaecumque
proposuerunt facere. Venite, descendentes dispersas faciamus ibi
eorum linguas, ut non obaudiat unusquisque uocem proximi sui.

6. Et dispersit illos dominus deus inde super faciem omnis terrae, et 90
cessauerunt aedificantes ciuitatem et turrem.

7. Propter hoc uocatum est nomen eius Confusio, quia ibi confudit
dominus labia omnis terrae et exinde dispersit eos dominus deus
super omnem faciem terrae.

8. Γίνονται οὖν ὁμοῦ ἀπὸ Ἀδὰμ ἕως τῆς πυργοποιίας καὶ συγχύσεως τῶν 95
γλωσσῶν γενεαὶ μὲν ιε΄, ἔτη δὲ ͵βω΄.

4,1. 61 *lac. post* Iafeth *stat.* Frick || 61–62 diluuium *em.* Frick: dilu um E'
4,5. 71 ρλδ΄ *scripsi; cf.* centu XXXIIII E': ρλ΄ H' || 71–72 octingenti
duodecim E' || 72 et Ragau fratrem eius *exp.* Frick || 74 facta *emendaui:*
factum E' Frick   **5,1.** 76 planum *scripsi:* paneum E'   **5,8.** 95 *ante*
Γίνονται *verba* Ἀρχὴ τοῦ χρονογράφου· ἀλλ᾽ ἐν ἄλλοις βίβλοις εὑρήσεις
πλατυτέρως τὴν ἀρχήν, ἡμεῖς δὲ τὸν διαμερισμὸν μόνον ἐν συντόμῳ γεγρά-
φαμεν *om.* E'

II

1,1. Διαμερισμὸς τῆς γῆς εἰς τοὺς τρεῖς υἱοὺς τοῦ Νῶε. Τῆς γῆς ὁ διαμερισμὸς τοῖς τρισὶν υἱοῖς τοῦ Νῶε μετὰ τὸν κατακλυσμὸν ἐγένετο οὕτως τῷ Σὴμ τῷ Χὰμ καὶ τῷ Ἰάφεθ.

2. Τῶν τριῶν ἀδελφῶν αἱ φυλαὶ διεμερίσθησαν, καὶ τῷ μὲν Σὴμ τῷ πρωτοτόκῳ ἀπὸ Περσίδος καὶ Βάκτρων ἕως Ἰνδικῆς τὸ μῆκος, πλάτος δὲ ἀπὸ τῆς Ἰνδικῆς ἕως Ῥινοκορούρων, Χὰμ δὲ τῷ δευτέρῳ ἀπὸ Ῥινοκορούρων ἕως Γαδείρων τὰ πρὸς νότον, Ἰάφεθ δὲ τῷ τρίτῳ ἀπὸ Μηδίας ἕως Γαδείρων τὰ πρὸς βορρᾶν.

3. Ἔχει δὲ Ἰάφεθ ποταμὸν Τίγριν τὸν διορίζοντα Μηδίαν καὶ Βαβυλωνίαν in terra Assyriorum, ὁ δὲ Χὰμ ἔχει ποταμὸν Γηὼν τὸν καλούμενον Νεῖλον [χρυσορρόαν], ὁ δὲ Σὴμ ἔχει [ποταμοὺς δύο] τὸν Εὐφράτην [καὶ τὸν Φισών].

4. Συνεχύθησαν δὲ αἱ γλῶσσαι μετὰ τὸν κατακλυσμὸν ἐπὶ τῆς γῆς· ἦσαν οὖν αἱ συγχυθεῖσαι γλῶσσαι οβ', οἱ δὲ τὸν πύργον οἰκοδομήσαντες ἦσαν ἔθνη ο', οἳ καὶ ἐν γλώσσαις αὐτῶν ἐπὶ προσώπου τῆς γῆς διεμερίσθησαν.

5. Νεβρὼδ δὲ ὁ γίγας, υἱὸς Χοὺς τοῦ Αἰθίοπος, οὗτος εἰς τὴν βρῶσιν αὐτοῖς κυνηγῶν ἐχωρήγει θηρία φαγεῖν. Τὰ δὲ ὀνόματα τῶν ἑβδομήκοντά ἐστι ταῦτα·

2,1. Υἱοὶ Ἰάφεθ τοῦ τρίτου υἱοῦ Νῶε· Γάμερ, ἀφ' οὗ Καππάδοκες, Μαγώγ, ἀφ' οὗ Κελτοὶ καὶ Γαλάται, Μαδάι, ἀφ' οὗ Μῆδοι, Ἰωύαν, ἀφ' οὗ Ἕλληνες καὶ Ἴωνες, Θωβέλ, ἀφ' οὗ οἱ Θετταλοί, Μοσόχ, ἀφ' οὗ οἱ Ἰλ<λ>υριοί, Θήρας, ἀφ' οὗ οἱ Θρᾷκες, Χαταΐν, ἀφ' οὗ οἱ Μακεδόνες.

2. Υἱοὶ Γάμερ τοῦ υἱοῦ τοῦ Ἰάφεθ τοῦ υἱοῦ τοῦ Νῶε· Ἀσχανάθ, ἀφ' οὗ Σαρμάται, Ἐρισφάν, ἀφ' οὗ οἱ Ῥόδιοι, Θωργαμά, ἀφ' οὗ Ἀρμένιοι.

3. Υἱοὶ Ἰωύαν υἱοῦ Ἰάφεθ τοῦ υἱοῦ τοῦ Νῶε· Ἐλισσά, ἀφ' οὗ οἱ Σικελοί, Θαρσεῖς, ἀφ' οὗ Ἴβηρες <οἱ> καὶ Τυρ<ρ>ηνοί, καὶ Κίτιοι, ἀφ' οὗ Ῥωμαῖοι <οἱ> καὶ Λατῖνοι.

1,1–7,7. 1–263 Hippolyti Συναγωγὴ χρόνων καὶ ἐτῶν ἀπὸ κτίσεως κόσμου ἕως τῆς ἐνεστώσης ἡμέρας 44–237, pp. 10–42 Bauer-Helm

1,1. 1 εἰς τοὺς τρεῖς υἱοὺς τοῦ Νῶε V" *om.* H' Bauer-Helm   **1,2.** 7 Γαδείρων H' Bauer-Helm: Γαρίρων V"   **1,3.** 10 in terra Assyriorum E': *om.* H' ‖ 11 χρυσορρόαν *exp.* Bauer-Helm ‖ ποταμοὺς δύο *exp.* Bauer-Helm ‖ καὶ τὸν Φισών *exp.* Bauer-Helm   **2,1.** 20 Ἰλυριοί H' Bauer-Helm   **2,3.** 25 οἱ *post* Ἴβηρες *ins.* Bauer-Helm: *om.* H' ‖ Τυρηνοί H' Bauer-Helm ‖ 26 οἱ *post* Ῥωμαῖοι *ins.* Bauer-Helm *om.* H'

4. Πάντες οὗτοι υἱοὶ Ἰάφεθ τοῦ τρίτου υἱοῦ Νῶε· ἐκ τούτων ἀφωρίσθησαν νῆσοι τῶν ἐθνῶν. Εἰσὶ δὲ καὶ οἱ Κύπριοι ἐκ τῶν Κιτιέων ἐκ τῶν υἱῶν Ἰάφεθ. Ὁμοῦ ἔθνη ιε΄.

5. Ἔτι δὲ εὑρίσκομεν καὶ τοὺς ἐν βορρᾷ ὄντας ἐξ αὐτῶν ὁμοφύλους τῶν   30
Κιτιέων.

6. Ἔστι δὲ καὶ τὰ ἐκ τῆς Ἑλλάδος ἔθνη πάντα ἐξ αὐτοῦ ἐκτὸς τῶν
μετῳκηκότων ὕστερον ἐκεῖ, οἷον Σαιτῶν, οἳ κατῴκησαν τιμωμένην πόλιν
τὴν καλουμένην Ἀθήνας, καὶ τὰς <Θήβας, οἳ Σιδωνίων ἄποικοί εἰσιν ἐκ
Κάδμου Ἀγή>νορος, καὶ οἱ Χαλκηδόνιοι δὲ τῶν Τυρρηνίων εἰσὶν ἄποικοι,   35
καὶ εἴ τινες ἄλλοι εἰς Ἑλλάδα μετῴκησαν.

7. Ταῦτα δὲ τὰ τοῦ Ἰάφεθ ἔθνη ἀπὸ Μηδίας ἕως τοῦ ἑσπερίου κατέσπαρται
ὠκεανοῦ βλέποντα πρὸς βορρᾶν· Μῆδοι, Ἀλβανοί, Γαργανοί, Ἑρραῖοι,
Ἀρμένιοι, Ἀμαζόνες, Κῶλοι, Κορζηνοί, Δενναγηνοί, Καππάδοκες,
Παφλαγόνες, Μαριανδηνοί, Ταβαρηνοί, Χάλυβες, <Μοσσύνοικοι,   40
Σαρμάται, Σαυρομάται, Μαιῶται, Σκύθες, Ταύριοι,> Θρᾷκες, Βασταρνοί,
Ἰλ<λ>υριοί, Μακεδόνες, Ἕλληνες, Λίγυρες, <Ἴστροι, Οὐεννοί, Δαυνεῖς,
Ἰάπυγες, Καλαβροί, Ὀππικοί, Λα>τῖνοι οἱ καὶ Ῥωμαῖοι, Τυρρηνοί, Γάλλιοι
<οἱ καὶ> Κελτοί, Λυγιστινοί, Κελτίβηρες, Ἴβηρες, Γάλλοι, <Ἀ>κουατινοί,
<Ἰλλυρικοί>, Βάσαντες, Κυρ<τανοί, Λυσιτάνιοι, Οὐακκαῖοι, Κόννιοι,   45
Βρεττανοί, οἱ ἐν νή>σοις οἰκοῦντες.

8. Οἱ δὲ ἐπιστάμενοι αὐτῶν γράμματά εἰσιν Ἴβηρες, Λατῖνοι οἷς χρῶνται
οἱ Ῥωμαῖοι, Σπάνοι, Ἕλληνες, Μῆδοι, Ἀρμένιοι.

9. Ἔστι δὲ τὰ ὅρια αὐτῶν ἀπὸ Μηδίας ἕως Γαδείρων τὰ πρὸς βορρᾶν,
εὖρος δὲ ἀπὸ Τανάϊδος ποταμοῦ ἕως Μαστουσίας τῆς κατὰ Ἴλιον.   50

10. Αἱ δὲ χῶραί εἰσιν αὗται· Μηδία, Ἀλβανία, Ἀμαζονίς, Ἀρμενία μικρὰ
καὶ μεγάλη, Καππαδοκία, Παφλαγονία, Γαλατία, Κολχίς, Σινδικὴ Ἀχαΐα,
Βοσπορινή, Μαιῶτις, Δέρρης, Σαρματίς, Ταυριανή, Βασταρνίς, Σκυθία,
Θράκη, Μακεδονία, Δελματία, Μολχίς, Θεσσαλία, Λωκρίς, Βοιωτία,
Αἰτωλία, Ἀττική, <Ἀχαΐα>, Πελοπόννησος, <Ἀκαρνία>, Ἠπειρώτης,   55
Ἰλλυρίς, ἡ Λυχνῖτις, Ἀδριακή, ἀφ᾽ ἧς τὸ Ἀδριακὸν πέλαγος, Γαλλία,
Θουσκηνή, Λυσιτανία, Μεσαλία, Ἰταλία, Κελτίς, Σπανογαλία, Ἰβηρία,
Σπανία ἡ μεγάλη. Ὁμοῦ μα΄. Ἐνταῦθα καταλήγει τὰ ὅρια τοῦ Ἰάφεθ ἕως
Βρεταννικῶν νήσων πᾶσαί τε πρὸς βορρᾶν βλέπουσαι.

11. Εἰσὶ δὲ αὐτοῖς καὶ νῆσοι ἐπίκοιναι αὗται· Σικελία, Εὔβοια, Ῥόδος,   60

2,6. 34–35 Θήβας-Ἀγή *ins.* Bauer-Helm   **2,7.** 40–41 Μοσσύνοικοι-Ταύριοι
ins. Bauer-Helm: *om.* Η' ‖ 42 Ἰλυριοί Η' Bauer-Helm ‖ 42–43 Ἴστροι-
Λα *ins.* Bauer-Helm: *om.* Η' ‖ 44 οἱ καὶ *post* Γάλλιοι *ins.* Bauer-Helm: *om.*
Η' ‖ Ἀκουατινοί *em.* Bauer-Helm ‖ 45 Ἰλλυρικοί *ins.* Bauer-Helm ‖ 45–46
τανοί-ἐν νή *ins.* Bauer-Helm   **2,9.** 50 Τανάϊδος *lectionem genuinam praebet*
Syncellus p. 55 Mosshammer: Ποταμίδος Η' Bauer-Helm ‖ Ἴλιον *scripsi*: ἥλιον
Η' 'solem' *per itacismum vertit Barbarus*   **2,10.** 52 Σινδικὴ: Ἰνδικὴ Η' ‖ 55
Ἀχαΐα *et* Ἀκαρνία *ins.* Bauer-Helm: *om.* Η'

Χῖος, Λέσβος, Κυθήρα, Ζάκυνθος, Κεφαληνία, Ἰθάκη, Κέρκυρα καὶ αἱ Κυκλάδες καὶ μέρος τι τῆς Ἀσίας τὸ καλούμενον Ἰωνία. [Αὗται αἱ νῆσοι τῷ μέρει τοῦ Ἰάφεθ.]

12. Ποταμὸς δέ ἐστιν αὐτοῖς <Τίγρις> διορίζων Μηδίαν <καὶ> Βαβυλωνίαν. Ταῦτά ἐστι τὰ ὅρια τοῦ Ἰάφεθ τοῦ τρίτου υἱοῦ Νῶε.

6

3,1. Γενεαλογία τοῦ Χὰμ <τοῦ> δευτέρου υἱοῦ τοῦ Νῶε. Οἱ δὲ υἱοὶ Χὰμ τοῦ δευτέρου υἱοῦ τοῦ Νῶε πρῶτος Χούς, ἐξ οὗ Αἰθίοπες, <καὶ> Μεστραείμ, ἐξ οὗ Αἰγύπτιοι, καὶ Φούδ, ἐξ οὗ Τρωγλοδύται, καὶ Χανάν, ἐξ οὗ <Ἄφροι> καὶ Φοίνικες.

2. Οἱ δὲ υἱοὶ Χοὺς τοῦ Αἰθίοπος <τοῦ υἱοῦ Χὰμ τοῦ δευτέρου> υἱοῦ Νῶε   7(
Σαβὰ καὶ Εὐηλὰτ καὶ Σεβακαθὰθ καὶ Ῥεγμὰ καὶ Σεκαθά.

3. Οὗτοι Αἰθίοπες πρῶτοι κατὰ τὰς φυλὰς αὐτῶν. Καὶ υἱοὶ Ῥεγμὰ τοῦ υἱοῦ Χοὺς τοῦ Αἰθίοπος <τοῦ υἱοῦ Χὰμ> τοῦ <δευτέρου> υἱοῦ Νῶε Σάβατον καὶ Ἰουδὰδ καὶ Νεβρὼδ ὁ γίγας ὁ Αἴθιοψ.

[**4.** Γέγραπται γάρ· 'καὶ Χοὺς ἐγέννησε τὸν Νεβρὼδ τὸν Αἰθίοπα γίγαντα   7:
κυνηγόν—ὡς Νεβρὼδ γίγας κυνηγός' (a)].

5. Καὶ Αἰγυπτίων πατριαὶ σὺν Μεστραεὶμ τῷ πατρὶ αὐτῶν ὀκτώ. Λέγει γὰρ οὕτως· 'Καὶ Μεστραεὶμ ἐγέννησε τοὺς Λυδιείμ', ἐξ οὗ ἐγένοντο Λύδιοι, 'καὶ τοὺς Ἐνεμετείμ', ἐξ οὗ Πάμφυλοι, 'καὶ τοὺς Λαβιείμ', ἐξ οὗ Λίβυες, 'καὶ τοὺς Νεφθαλείμ', ἐξ οὗ Φρύγες, 'καὶ τοὺς Πατροσωνιείμ', ἐξ οὗ <Κρῆτες,   8(
'καὶ τοὺς Χασλωνιείμ', ἐξ οὗ> Λύκιοι, 'καὶ τοὺς Φυλιστιείμ', ἐξ οὗ Φιλιστιαῖοι, 'καὶ τοὺς Καφθοριείμ', ἐξ οὗ Κίλικες' (b).

6. Χαναναίων δὲ πατριαὶ σὺν Χαναὰν τῷ πατρὶ αὐτῶν εἰσι ιβʹ. Λέγει γὰρ οὕτως· 'Καὶ Χανάαν ἐγέννησε τὸν Σιδῶνα πρωτότοκον καὶ τὸν Χετταῖον καὶ τὸν Ἀμορραῖον καὶ τὸν Γεργεσσαῖον καὶ τὸν Εὐαῖον καὶ τὸν Ἀρου-   8:
καῖον, ἐξ οὗ Τριπολῖται, καὶ τὸν Ἀσενναῖον, ἐξ οὗ Ὀρθωσιασταί, καὶ τὸν Ἀράδιον, ἐξ οὗ Ἀράδιοι, καὶ τὸν Σαμορραῖον, ἐξ οὗ Σαμαρεῖται, <καὶ τὸν Φερεζαῖον, ἐξ οὗ Φερεζαῖοι>, καὶ τὸν Ἀματθῆ, ἐξ οὗ Ἀμαθούσιοι' (c).

---

a) Gen. 10,8–9   b) Gen. 10,13–14   c) Gen. 10,15

2,11. 62–63 αὗται- Ἰάφεθ *exp.* Bauer-Helm   **2,12.** 64 Τίγρις *et* καὶ *ins.* Bauer-Helm   **3,1.** 66–68 τοῦ—καὶ—Ἄφροι *ins.* Bauer-Helm: *om.* Η᾽ **3,2.** 70 τοῦ υἱοῦ Χὰμ τοῦ δευτέρου *ins.* Bauer-Helm: *om.* Η᾽   **3,3.** 73 *verba* τοῦ υἱοῦ Χὰμ *et* δευτέρου *ins.* Bauer-Helm: *om.* Η᾽   **3,4.** 75–76 γέγραπται-κυνηγός *exp.* Bauer-Helm   **3,5.** 79 Ἐνεμετείμ *scripsi:* Enemigim Ε᾽ Τενιείμ Η᾽ Bauer-Helm ‖ 80 Φρύγες *scripsi:* Φυγάδες Η᾽ Bauer-Helm Fygabii Ε᾽ ‖ Πατροσωνιείμ *scripsi:* Πατροσονιείμ Η᾽ Bauer-Helm ‖ 80–81 Κρῆτες—ἐξ οὗ *inserui* ‖ 81–82 καὶ τοὺς Φυλιστιείμ ἐξ οὗ Φιλιστιαῖοι (Φοίνικες Η᾽) *om.* Ε᾽   **3,6.** 87–88 καὶ τὸν-Φερεζαῖοι *ins.* Bauer-Helm

7. Ἔστι δὲ καὶ αὐτῶν ἡ κατοικία ἀπὸ Ῥινοκορούρων ἕως Γαδείρων τὰ 90
πρὸς νότον ἐπὶ μῆκος.

8. Τὰ δὲ ἐκ τούτων γεννηθέντα ἔθνη. Αἰθίοπες, Τρωγλοδύται, Ἀγγαῖοι,
Ταγηνοί, Ἰσακηνοί, Ἰχθυοφάγοι, Ἑλλανικοί, Αἰγύπτιοι, Φοίνικες, Λίβυες,
Μαρμαρίδες, Κᾶρες, Ψυλλῖται, Μυσοί, Μοσυνοί, Φρύγες, Μάκονες, Βιθυνοί,
Νομάδες, Λύκιοι, Μαριανδηνοί, Πάμφυλοι, <Μοσοσυνοί>, Πισιδηνοί, 95
Αὐγαλαῖοι, Κίλικες, Μαυρούσιοι, Κρῆτες, Μαγάρται, Νούμιδες, <Μάκρω-
νες>, Νασαμῶνες. Οὗτοι διακατέχουσιν ἀπὸ Αἰγύπτου ἕως τοῦ νοτιαίου
ὠκεανοῦ.

9. Οἱ δὲ ἐπιστάμενοι αὐτῶν γράμματα Φοίνικες, Αἰγύπτιοι, Πάμφυλοι,
Φρύγες. 100

10. Ἔστι δὲ τὰ ὅρια τοῦ Χὰμ ἀπὸ Ῥινοκορούρων τῆς ὁριζούσης Συρίαν
καὶ Αἴγυπτον καὶ Αἰθιοπίαν ἕως Γαδείρων ἐπὶ μῆκος.

11. Τὰ δὲ ὀνόματα τῶν χωρῶν ἐστι ταῦτα· Αἴγυπτος σὺν τοῖς περὶ αὐτὴν
πᾶσιν, Αἰθιοπία ἡ βλέπουσα κατὰ Ἰνδούς, καὶ ἑτέρα Αἰθιοπία, ὅθεν
ἐκπορεύεται Γηὼν ὁ <τῶν Αἰθιόπων> ποταμὸς ὁ καλούμενος Νεῖλος, 105
Ἐρυθρὰ ἡ βλέπουσα κατὰ ἀνατολάς, Θηβαῒς ὅλη, Λιβύη ἡ παρεκτείνουσα
μέχρι Κορκυρίνης, Μαρμαρὶς καὶ τὰ περὶ αὐτὴν πάντα, Σύρτις ἔχουσα
ἔθνη τρία, Νασαμῶνας Μάκας Ταυταμαίους, Λιβύη ἑτέρα ἡ παρεκτείνουσα
<ἀπὸ Λέπτεως> μέχρι μικρᾶς Σύρτεως, Νουμίδα, Μασσυρίς, Μαυριτανία
ἡ παρεκτείνουσα μέχρι Ἡρακλείων στηλῶν κατέναντι Γαδείρων. Ἔχει δὲ 110
ἐν τοῖς κατὰ βορρᾶν τὰ πρὸς θάλασσαν, Κιλικίαν, Παμφυλίαν, Πισιδίαν,
Μυσίαν, Λυγδονίαν, Φρυγίαν, Καμηλίαν, Λυκίαν, Καρίαν, Λυδίαν, Τρῳάδα,
Αἰολίαν, Βιθυνίαν, τὴν ἀρχαίαν καλουμένην Φρυγίαν.

12. Εἰσὶ δὲ αὐτοῖς καὶ νῆσοι ἐπίκοινοι αἵδε· Κόρσυλα, Λαπάδουσα, Γαῦλος,
Μελίτη, Κέρκινα, Μηνίς, Ταυριανίς, Σαρδανίς, Γαλάτη, Γορσύνη, Κρήτη, 115
Γαυλορίδη, Θήρα, Καρίαθος, Ἀστυπάλια, Χίος, Λέσβος, Τένεδος, Ἴμβρος,
Ἰασός, Σάμος, Κῶος, Κνίδος, Νίσυρος, μεγίστη Κύπρος, ὁμοῦ νῆσοι κε΄.
Αὗται αἱ νῆσοι δουλεύουσι τῷ Χὰμ καὶ τῷ Ἰάφεθ τοῖς δύο υἱοῖς τοῦ Νῶε.

13. Ἔχει δὲ Χὰμ ποταμὸν Γηὼν τὸν καλούμενον Νεῖλον τὸν κυκλοῦντα
πᾶσαν τὴν Αἴγυπτον <καὶ> Αἰθιοπίαν· ὁρίζει δὲ μεταξὺ τοῦ Χὰμ καὶ τοῦ 120
Ἰάφεθ τὸ στόμα τῆς ἑσπερινῆς θαλάσσης. Αὕτη τοῦ Χὰμ ἡ γενεαλογία
<τοῦ δευτέρου υἱοῦ τοῦ Νῶε>.

4,1. Γενεαλογία τοῦ Σὴμ τοῦ πρωτοτόκου υἱοῦ Νῶε. Ἐκ δὲ τοῦ Σὴμ τοῦ
πρωτοτόκου υἱοῦ Νῶε εἰσὶ φυλαὶ κε΄ · οὗτοι πρὸς ἀνατολὰς ᾤκησαν.

3,8. 94 Φρύγες *scripsi*: Φυγάδες Η᾽ Bauer-Helm ǁ 95 Μοσοσυνοί *ins.* Bauer-
Helm: *om.* Η᾽ ǁ 96–97 Μάκρωνες *scripsi*: Μακάριοι Η᾽ ǁ 97 Νασαμῶνες
scripsi: Νασαμίδες Η᾽ Νασαμ<ων>ίδες Bauer-Helm **3,11.** 105 τῶν Αἰθιόπων
ins. Bauer-Helm: *om.* Η᾽ ǁ 108 Νασαμόνας Η᾽ ǁ 109 ἀπὸ Λέπτεως *ins.* Bauer-
Helm: *om.* Η᾽ **3,13.** 120 καὶ *ins.* Bauer-Helm ǁ 122 τοῦ δευτέρου υἱοῦ
τοῦ Νῶε *add.* Bauer-Helm

2. Ἐλάμ, ὅθεν οἱ Ἐλυμαῖοι, καὶ Ἀσούρ, ὅθεν οἱ Ἀσσύριοι, καὶ Ἀρφαξάδ,   1⸱
ὅθεν οἱ Χαλδαῖοι, καὶ Λούδ, ὅθεν οἱ Ἀλαζονεῖς, [καὶ Φούδ, ὅθεν οἱ Πέρσαι]
καὶ Ἀράμ, ὅθεν οἱ Αἰΐται.

3. Καὶ υἱοὶ Ἀρὰμ υἱοῦ Σὴμ υἱοῦ Νῶε· Ὡς καὶ Οὔλ, ὅθεν γεννῶνται Λυδοί,
καὶ Γαθέρ, ὅθεν Γασφηνοί, καὶ Μοσόχ, ὅθεν Μοσυνοί.

4. Καὶ Ἀρφαξὰδ ἐγέννησε τὸν Καϊνάν, ὅθεν γίνονται οἱ πρὸς ἀνατολὰς   1⸱
Σαμῖται, καὶ Καϊνὰν ἐγέννησε τὸν Σαλαθιήλ, ὅθεν γεννῶνται οἱ Σαλαθιαῖοι,
καὶ Σαλαθιὴλ ἐγέννησε τὸν Ἔβερ, ὅθεν γεννῶνται Ἑβραῖοι. Καὶ τῷ Ἔβερ
ἐγεννήθησαν υἱοὶ δύο· πρῶτος Φάλεχ, ὅθεν κατάγεται τὸ γένος τοῦ Ἀβραάμ,
καὶ Ἰεκτὰν ὁ ἀδελφὸς αὐτοῦ.

5. Ἰεκτὰν δὲ [ὁ ἀδελφὸς Φάλεχ] ἐγέννησε τὸν Ἐλμωδάδ, ὅθεν γεννῶνται   1⸱
οἱ Ἰνδοί, καὶ τὸν Σαλέφ, ὅθεν οἱ Βακτριανοί, καὶ τὸν Ἀράμ, ὅθεν οἱ Ἀρά-
β<ι>ες, καὶ Ἰ<δ>ουράμ, ὅθεν Καρμήλιοι, καὶ Αἰθήλ, ὅθεν οἱ Ἀρειανοί,
καὶ Ἀβιμεήλ, ὅθεν Ὑρκάνιοι, καὶ Δεκλάμ, ὅθεν Κεδρούσιοι, καὶ Γεβάλ,
ὅθεν οἱ Σκύθες, καὶ Σαβάτ, ὅθεν οἱ Ἀλαμοσινοί, καὶ [Π]Οὐήρ, ὅθεν Ἐμηραῖοι,
καὶ Εὐεαί, ὅθεν Γυμνοσοφισταί. Οὗτοι πάντες ἐκ τοῦ Σὴμ τοῦ πρωτοτόκου   1⸱
υἱοῦ Νῶε.

6. Πάντων δὲ τῶν υἱῶν τοῦ Σήμ ἐστιν ἡ κατοικία ἀπὸ Βάκτρων ἕως
Ῥινοκορούρων τῆς ὁριζούσης Συρίαν καὶ Αἴγυπτον καὶ τὴν ἐρυθρὰν θάλασσαν ἀπὸ στόματος τοῦ κατὰ τὸν Ἀρσινοΐτην τῆς Ἰνδικῆς.

7. Ταῦτα δὲ τὰ ἐξ αὐτῶν γενόμενα ἔθνη· Ἑβραῖοι <οἱ> καὶ Ἰουδαῖοι,   1⸱
Πέρσαι, Μῆδοι, Παίονες, Ἀρειανοί, <Ἀσσύριοι>, Ὑρκάνιοι, Ἰνδοί,
Μαγαρδοί, Πάρθοι, Γερμανοί, Ἐλυμαῖοι, Κοσσαῖοι, Ἄραβες, [οἱ] πρῶτοι
οἱ καλούμενοι Κεδρούσιοι, Ἄραβες δεύτεροι [οἱ καλούμενοι], Γυμνοσοφισταί. Παρεκτείνε<ι> δὲ αὐτῶν ἡ κατοικία ἀπὸ Ἡλιουπόλεως τῆς ἔσω
ἕως Ῥινοκορούρων καὶ τῆς Κιλικίας.   1⸱

8. Οἱ δὲ ἐπιστάμενοι αὐτῶν γράμματα οὗτοί εἰσιν· Ἑβραῖοι οἱ καὶ Ἰουδαῖοι,
Πέρσαι, Μῆδοι, Χαλδαῖοι, Ἰνδοί, Ἀσσύριοι.

9. Ἐστὶ δὲ ἡ κατοικία τῶν υἱῶν τοῦ Σὴμ τοῦ πρωτοτόκου υἱοῦ Νῶε μῆκος
μὲν ἀπὸ τῆς Ἰνδικῆς ἕως Ῥινοκορούρων, πλάτος δὲ ἀπὸ τῆς Περσίδος καὶ
Βάκτρων ἕως τῆς Ἰνδικῆς.   1⸱

10. Τὰ δὲ ὀνόματα τῶν χωρῶν τῶν υἱῶν τοῦ Σήμ ἐστι ταῦτα· Περσὶς σὺν
τοῖς ἐπικειμένοις αὐτῇ ἔθνεσιν, Βακτριανή, Ὑρκανία, Βαβυλωνία,
Κορδυλία, Ἀσσυρία, Μεσοποταμία, Ἀραβία ἡ ἀρχαία, Ἐλυμαΐς, Ἰνδική,

---

4,2. 126 *verba* καὶ Φούδ, ὅθεν οἱ Πέρσαι *omittenda putavi quia Fud supra* (3,1)
inter filios Cham numeratur   **4,5.** 135 ὁ ἀδελφὸς Φάλεχ *exp.* Bauer-Helm ‖
136–137 Ἀράβ<ι>ες *em.* Bauer-Helm ‖ 137 Ἰ<δ>ουράμ *em.* Bauer-Helm
‖ 139 Οὐήρ *em.* Bauer-Helm ‖ Ἐμηραῖοι *scripsi:* Ἑρμαῖοι H' Armenii E'
4,7. 145 οἱ *post* Ἑβραῖοι *ins.* Bauer-Helm ‖ 146 Ἀσσύριοι *ins.* Bauer-Helm:
om. H' ‖ 147 οἱ *ante* πρῶτοι *exp.* Bauer-Helm ‖ 148 οἱ καλούμενοι *exp.*
Bauer-Helm ‖ 149 παρεκτείνει *em.* Bauer-Helm

Ἀραβία ἡ εὐδαίμων, <Κοίλη Συρία>, Κομμαγηνή καὶ ἡ Φοινίκη ἥπερ
ἐστὶ τῶν υἱῶν τοῦ Σήμ.   160

11. [Τοῦ δὲ Χὰμ τοῦ δευτέρου υἱοῦ Νῶέ ἐστιν ἡ κατοικία ἀπὸ Ῥινοκορούρων
τῆς ὁριζούσης Συρίαν καὶ Αἴγυπτον καὶ Αἰθιοπίαν ἕως Γαδείρων. Τοῦ δὲ
Ἰάφεθ τοῦ τρίτου υἱοῦ Νῶε ἀπὸ Μηδίας ἕως Γαδείρων τὰ πρὸς βορρᾶν
μέρη καὶ νῆσοι ἐπίκοινοι].

12. Αἱ πᾶσαι ἐκ τῶν τριῶν υἱῶν τοῦ Νῶε ὁμοῦ φυλαὶ οβ΄.   165

5,1. Τὰ δὲ ἔθνη, ἃ διέσπειρε κύριος ὁ θεὸς ἐπὶ προσώπου πάσης τῆς γῆς
ἐν ταῖς ἡμέραις Φαλὲκ καὶ Ἰεκτὰν τῶν δύο ἀδελφῶν κατὰ τὰς ἰδίας γλώσσας
αὐτῶν ἐν τῇ πυργοποιίᾳ, ὅτε συνεχύθησαν αἱ γλῶσσαι αὐτῶν, ἐστὶ ταῦτα·
2. Ἑβραῖοι οἱ καὶ Ἰουδαῖοι, Ἀσσύριοι, Χαλδαῖοι, Μῆδοι, Πέρσαι,
<Ἄραβες πρῶτοι καὶ δεύτεροι>, Μαδιηναῖοι πρῶτοι καὶ δεύτεροι,   170
Ἀδιαβηνοί, Ταιηνοί, Σαλαμοσηνοί, Σαρακηνοί, Μάγοι, Κάσπιοι, Ἀλβανοί,
Ἰνδοὶ πρῶτοι καὶ β΄, Αἰθίοπες πρῶτοι καὶ δεύτεροι, Αἰγύπτιοι καὶ Θηβαῖοι,
Λίβυες [πρῶτοι καὶ β΄], Χετταῖοι, Χαναναῖοι, Φερεζαῖοι, Εὐαῖοι, Ἀμορραῖοι,
Γεργεσαῖοι, Ἰεβουσσαῖοι, Ἰδουμαῖοι, Σαμαρρεῖοι, Φοίνικες, Σύροι, Κίλικες
οἱ καὶ Θαρσεῖς, Καππάδοκες, Ἀρμένιοι, Ἴβηρες, Βιβρανοί, Σκύθαι, Κόλχοι,   175
Σαῦνοι, Βοσπορανοί, Ἀσιανοί, Ἰσαυροί, Λυκάονες, Πισίδες, Γαλάται,
<Παφλαγόνες, Φρύγες>, Ἕλληνες οἱ καὶ Ἀχαῖοι, Θεσσαλοί, Μακεδόνες,
Θρᾷκες, Μυσοί, Βεσσοί, Δάρδανοι, Σαρμάται, Γερμανοί, Παννόνιοι οἱ καὶ
Παίονες, Νωρικοί, Δελμάται, Ῥωμαῖοι οἱ καὶ Λατῖνοι καὶ Κιτιαῖοι, Λίγυρες,
Γάλ<λ>οι οἱ καὶ Κελταῖοι, Ἀκ<ο>υατινοί, Βριτανοί, Σπάνοι <οἱ> καὶ   180
Τυρρηνοί, Μαῦροι, Μακουακοί, Γαίτυλοι, Ἄφροι, Μάζικες, Ταράμαντες
οἱ ἐξώτεροι, Σποράδες, Κελτίονες, Ταράμαντες ἐσώτεροι, οἳ ἕως τῆς
Αἰθιοπίας ἐκτείνουσι.
3. Ταῦτα τὰ ἔθνη, ἃ διέσπειρε κύριος ὁ θεὸς ἐπὶ προσώπου πάσης τῆς γῆς
κατὰ τὰς ἰδίας γλώσσας αὐτῶν ἐν ταῖς φυλαῖς αὐτῶν καὶ ἐν ταῖς χώραις   185
αὐτῶν καὶ ἐν ταῖς πόλεσιν αὐτῶν.

6,1. Ἀναγκαῖον δὲ ἡγησάμην καὶ τὰς ἀποικίας αὐτῶν τῶν ἀναγνωσθέντων
ἐθνῶν καὶ τὰς προσηγορίας αὐτῶν δηλῶσαί σοι καὶ τὰ κλίματα αὐτῶν,
πῶς οἰκοῦσι καὶ ποῖον ἔθνος πλησίον τίνος ἐστίν, ὅπως μηδὲ καὶ τούτων
ἄπειρος ὑπάρχῃς. Ἄρξομαι δὲ διαγράφειν ἀπὸ ἀνατολῆς καὶ μέχρι δύσεως   190
<κατὰ τάξιν>.

4,10. 159 Κοίλη Συρία *ins.* Bauer-Helm: *om.* Η'   **4,11.** 161–164 τοῦ δὲ
Χάμ—ἐπίκοινοι *om.* Ε' *exp.* Bauer-Helm   **5,2.** 170 Ἄραβες πρῶτοι καὶ
δεύτεροι *ins.* Bauer-Helm ‖ 173 πρῶτοι καὶ β΄ *exp.* Bauer-Helm ‖ 177
Παφλαγόνες Φρύγες *ins.* Bauer-Helm ‖ 180 Γάλλοι *em.* Bauer-Helm ‖
Ἀκυατινοί Η' ‖ οἱ *ins.* Bauer-Helm   **6,1.** 187 ἀναγνωσθέντων Η' Helm:
ἀγνώστων Bauer *interpretatione Barbari inepte confisus* ignotas gentes ‖ 191 κατὰ
τάξιν *add.* Bauer-Helm

2. Τῶν Περσῶν καὶ Μήδων ἄποικοι γεγόνασι Πάρθοι καὶ τὰ πέριξ ἔθνη τῆς Εἰρήνης ἕως τῆς Κοίλης Συρίας.

3. Ἀράβων δὲ ἄποικοι γεγόνασιν Ἄραβες οἱ εὐδαίμονες· τούτῳ γὰρ τῷ ὀνόματι προσαγορεύεται εὐδαίμων Ἀραβία.   19

4. Χαλδαίων δὲ ἄποικοι γεγόνασιν οἱ Μεσοποταμῖται.

5. Μαδιηναίων δὲ ἄποικοι γεγόνασιν οἱ Κιναιδοκολπῖται <καὶ Τρωγλο-δύται> καὶ Ἰχθυοφάγοι.

6. Ἑλλήνων δὲ ἔθνη καὶ προσηγορίαι εἰσὶ πέντε· Ἴωνες, Ἀρκάδες, Βοιωτοί, Αἰολεῖς, Λάκωνες. Τούτων δὲ ἄποικοι γεγόνασι· Ποντικοὶ καὶ Βιθυνοί,   20 Τρῷες, Ἀσιανοί, Κᾶρες, Λύκιοι, Πάμφυλοι, Κυρηναῖοι καὶ νῆσοι δὲ πλεῖσται αἱ καλούμεναι Κυκλάδες ια΄, αἳ τὸ Μυρταῖον πέλαγος περιέχουσι.

7. Εἰσὶ δὲ αὗται· Ἄνδρος, Τῆνος, Τήω, Νάξος, Κέως, Κοῦρος, Δῆλος, Σίφνος, Νήρεα, Κύρνος, Μαραθών [ὁμοῦ ια΄].

8. Εἰσὶ δὲ αὐτοῖς καὶ ἕτεραι νῆσοι μείζονες ιβ΄, αἵτινες καὶ πόλεις ἔχουσι   20 πλείστας αἱ καλούμεναι Σποράδες, ἐν αἷς ἀπῳκίσθησαν Ἕλληνες. Εἰσὶ δὲ αὗται· Εὔβοια, Κρήτη, Σικελία, Κύπρος, Κῶος, Σάμος, Ῥόδος, Χῖος· Θάσος, Λῆμνος, Λέσβος, Σαμοθράκη [ὁμοῦ ιβ΄].

9. Ἐστὶν οὖν ἀπὸ τῶν Βοιωτῶν Εὔβοια ὥσπερ ἀπὸ τῶν Ἰώνων Ἰωνί-δες πόλεις ις΄ ὀνομασταί. Εἰσὶ δὲ αὗται· Κλαζομεναί, Μιτυλήνη, Φωκ<α>ία,   21 Πριήνη, Ἐρυθραί, Σάμος, Τέως, Κολοφών, Χῖος, Ἔφεσος, Σμύρνα, Πέρινθος, Βυζάντιον, Χαλκηδών, Πόντος, Ἀμισὸς ἐλευθέρα [πᾶσαι ις΄].

10. Ῥωμαίων δὲ τῶν καὶ Κιτιέων [τῶν καὶ Λατίνων κεκλημένων] ἔθνη καὶ ἀποικίαι εἰσὶν ἑπτά· <Τοῦσκοι>, Αἰμηλίσιοι, Σικηνοί, Κα<μ>πανοί, Ἀπουλούσιοι, Καλαβροί, Λουκανοί.   21

11. Ἄφρων δὲ ἔθνη καὶ ἀποικίαι εἰσὶ πέντε· Νεβληνοί, Κνίθιοι, Νούμιδες, Σάιοι, Νασαμῶνες. Εἰσὶ δὲ αὐτοῖς καὶ νῆσοι πέντε πόλεις ἔχουσαι· Σαρδανία, Κόρσι<κ>α, Γίρβα, Κέρκινα, Γαλάτη.

12. Μαύρων δὲ ἔθνη καὶ ἀποικίαι εἰσὶ τρεῖς· Μοσσουλαμοί, Τι<γγι>τανοί, Καισαρηνσεῖς.   22

13. Σπάνων δὲ τῶν καὶ Τυρρηναίων, καλουμένων δὲ Ταρακωννησίων, ἔθνη καὶ ἀποικίαι εἰσὶ πέντε· Λυσιτανοί, Βαιτικοί, Αὐτρίγονοι, Βάσκωνες, Καλλαϊκοὶ οἱ καλούμενοι Ἄσπορες.

14. Γάλλων δὲ τῶν καὶ Να<ρ>βουδησίων καλουμένων ἔθνη καὶ ἀποικίαι εἰσὶ τέσσαρες· Λουγδουνοί, Βελσικοί, Σικανοί, Ἔδνοι.   22

15. Γερμανῶν δὲ ἔθνη καὶ ἀποικίαι εἰσὶ πέντε· Μαρκόμανοι, Βάρδουλοι, Κουᾶδροι, Βέρδηλοι, Ἑρμόνδουλοι.

6,5. 197–198 καὶ Τρωγλοδύται *ins.* Bauer-Helm   **6,7.** 204 ὁμοῦ ια΄ *exp.* Bauer-Helm   **6,8.** 208 ὁμοῦ ιβ΄ *exp.* Bauer-Helm   **6,9.** 210 Φωκαία *em.* Bauer-Helm ‖ 212 πᾶσαι ις΄ *exp.* Bauer-Helm   **6,10.** 213 τῶν καὶ Λατίνων κεκλημένων *exp.* Bauer-Helm ‖ 214 Τοῦσκοι *ins.* Bauer-Helm ‖ Καμπανοί *em.* Bauer-Helm   **6,11.** 217 Νασαμόνες Η᾽ ‖ 218 Κόρσικα *em.* Bauer-Helm   **6,12.** 219 Τιγγιτανοί *em.* Bauer-Helm   **6,14.** 224 Ναρβουδησίων *em.* Bauer-Helm

16. Σαρματῶν δὲ ἔθνη καὶ ἀποικίαι εἰσὶ δύο· Ἀμαξόβιοι καὶ Γρικοσαρμάτα<ι>.

17. Ταῦτα τὰ ἔθνη καὶ αἱ ἀποικίαι αὐτῶν.   230

7,1. Καὶ τοῦτο δὲ ἀναγκαῖον ἔδοξέ μοι δηλῶσαί σοι· τὰ κλίματα τῶν ἀναγνωσθέντων ἐθνῶν καὶ τὰ ὀνομαστὰ ὄρη καὶ τοὺς ἐπισήμους ποταμοὺς τοὺς ἀποχέοντας εἰς τὴν θάλασσαν, ὅπως μηδὲ τούτων ἄπειρος ὑπάρχῃς.

2. Ἄρξομαι οὖν λέγειν περὶ τῶν ἀναγνωσθέντων ἐθνῶν ἀπὸ ἀνατολῶν καὶ μέχρι δυσμῶν, πῶς οἰκοῦσι.   235

3. Ἀδιαβηνοὶ πέραν τῶν Ἀράβων, Ταϊνοὶ καταντικρὺς αὐτῶν, Ἀλαμοσινοὶ <δὲ πέραν τῶν Ἀράβων, Σακκηνοὶ> δὲ πέραν τῶν Ταϊνῶν, Ἀλβανοὶ δὲ πέραν τῶν Κασπίων πυλῶν, Μαδιηναῖοι δὲ οἱ μείζονες οἱ πολεμηθέντες ὑπὸ Μωϋσέως ἐντὸς τῆς ἐρυθρᾶς θαλάσσης οἰκοῦσιν· ἡ γὰρ μικρὰ Μαδιὰμ πέραν ἐστὶ τῆς ἐρυθρᾶς θαλάσσης, ὅπου ἐβασίλευσε Ῥαγουὴλ καὶ Ἰώθωρ   240 ὁ πενθερὸς Μωϋσέως.

4. Καὶ πέραν δὲ τῶν Καππαδόκων εἰς τὰ δεξιὰ μέρη οἰκοῦσιν Ἀρμένιοι καὶ Ἴβηρες καὶ Βηρανοί, εἰς δὲ τὰ εὐώνυμα μέρη οἰκοῦσι Σκύθες καὶ Κόλχοι καὶ Βοσπορανοί, Σαῦνοι δὲ οἱ λεγόμενοι Σάνιγγες, οἱ ἕως τοῦ Πόντου ἐκτείνοντες, ὅπου ἐστὶ παρεμβολὴ Ἄψαρος <καὶ Σεβαστόπολις> καὶ   245 Ὕσσου λιμὴν καὶ Φάσις ποταμός. Καὶ ἕως Τραπεζοῦντος οἰκοῦσι καὶ παρεκτείνεται τὰ ἔθνη ταῦτα.

5. Ὄρη δὲ ὀνομαστά εἰσιν ἐν τῇ γῇ δώδεκα· Λίβανος ἐν τῇ Συρίᾳ μεταξὺ Βύβλου καὶ Βηρυτοῦ, Καύκασος ἐν τῇ Σκυθίᾳ, Ταῦρος ἐν τῇ Κιλικίᾳ καὶ Καππαδοκίᾳ, Ἄτλας ἐν τῇ Λιβύῃ ἕως τοῦ μεγάλου ποταμοῦ, Παρνασὸς ἐν   250 τῇ Φωκίδι, Κιθαιρὼν ἐν τῇ Βοιωτίᾳ, Ἑλικὼν ἐν τῇ Τελμισῷ, Παρθένιον ἐν τῇ Εὐβοίᾳ, Ναυσαῖον τὸ καὶ Σινᾶ ἐν τῇ Ἀραβίᾳ, Λυκάβαντος ἐν Ἰταλίᾳ καὶ Γα<λ>λίᾳ, Πίνιον ὁ καὶ Μίμας ἐν τῇ Χίῳ, Ὄλυμπος ἐν τῇ Μακεδονίᾳ.

6. Δεδειγμένων οὖν τῶν ὀνομάτων τῶν δώδεκα ὀρέων τῆς γῆς ἀναγκαῖόν ἐστι καὶ τοὺς ἐπισήμους ποταμοὺς δηλῶσαί σοι.   255

7. Ποταμοὶ οὖν εἰσιν ὀνομαστοὶ τεσσαράκοντα ἐν τῇ γῇ οὗτοι· Ἰνδὸς ὁ καλούμενος Φισών, Νεῖλος ὁ καλούμενος Γηών, Τίγρις, Εὐφράτης, Ἰορδάνης, Κηφισσός, Τάναϊς, Ἰσμηνός, Ἐρύμανθος, Ἅλυς, Αἰσωπός, Θερμώδων, Ἐρασῖνος, Ῥεῖος, Βορυσθένης, Ἀλφειός, Ταῦρος, Εὐρώτας, Μέανδρος, Ἄξιος, Πύραμος, Ὀρέντης, Ἕβρων, Σαγγάριος, Ἀχελῷος, Πινειός, Εὔηνος,   260 Σπερχιός, Κάϋστρος, Σιμόεις, Σκάμανδρος, Στρυμών, Παρθένιος, Ἴστρος, Ῥῆνος, Βαίτης, Ῥόδανος, Ἠριδανός, Βαῖος, Θούβηρος ὁ νῦν καλούμενος Τιβέρης· ὁμοῦ ποταμοὶ μʹ.

6,16. 228–229 Γρικοσαρμάται *em.* Bauer-Helm   **7,1.** 231–232 ἀναγνωσθέντων Η' *iterum scripsi sicut supra* (6,1): ἀγνώστων Bauer   **7,2.** 234 ἀναγνωσθέντων Η': ἀγνώστων Bauer   **7,3.** 237 δὲ πέραν—Σακκηνοὶ *ins.* Bauer-Helm   **7,4.** 245 καὶ Σεβαστόπολις *ins.* Bauer-Helm   **7,5.** 253 Γαλλία *em.* Bauer-Helm

III

1,1. Significantes autem his omnibus tempus aduenit ad textum chronicae currere annos.

2. Sicut prius demonstrauimus dicentes, ab Adam usque ad diluuium Noe generationes quidem X, anni duo milia ducenti quadraginta duo, et a diluuio Noe usque ad turris edificationem et confusione\<m\> 5
diuisarum linguarum generationes quidem sex, anni autem quingenti quinquaginta octo. Fiunt simul anni duo milia octingenti.

2,1. Et a diuisione terrarum usque dum genuit Abraham Isaac generationes quidem sex, anni autem sexcenti tredecim sic. Post diuisionem terrarum factus est Falec annorum C: fiunt simul anni duo 10
milia noningenti, et genuit Ragau. Sub isto diuisio facta est. Falec enim in\<ter\>praetatur diuisio.

2. Vixit autem Ragau annos centum treginta II: fiunt simul anni trea milia treginta II, et genuit Seruch.

3. Vixit autem Seruch annos centum treginta duos: fiunt simul anni 15
trea milia CLXIIII, et genuit Nachor.

4. Vixit autem Nachor annos septuaginta nouem: fiunt simul anni trea milia CCXLIII, et genuit Tharam.

5. Vixit autem Thara annos LXX: fiunt simul anni trea milia CCCXIII, et genuit Abraham. 20

6. Factus est autem Abraham annorum LXXV: fiunt simul anni trea milia CCCLXXXVIII, quando praecepit illi deus exire de domo patris sui et uenire in terram Chanaan.

7. Habitauit autem Abraham in terra Chanaan alios annos XXV: fiunt anni centum, et sic genuit Isaac. Fiunt simul ab Adam usque 25
quod genuit Abraham Isaac omnes anni trea milia quadringenti XIII.

8. Temporibus uere Abrahae quando genuit Isaac Syrorum primus regnauit Bilus annos LXII, Sicyoniorum autem regnauit Egialeus, in Egyptios regnauit Necherocheus Farao.

9. Fiunt simul ab Adam usque dum genuit Abraham Isaac genera- 30
tiones XXI, anni trea milia quadringenti XIII, et ab Abraham usque ad exitum filiorum Israhel per Moysen generationes quidem VI, anni autem quadringenti quadraginta tres.

3,1. Abraham autem erat annorum centum, quando genuit Isaac: fiunt simul ab Adam anni trea milia quadringenti XIII. 35

1,2. 5 confusione E'   **2,1.** 9 tredecim *scripsi*: tres E' || 12 inpraetatur
E'   **2,8.** 29 Necherocheus; cf. *infra* Chron. VII, 3,5: Arouth E' Frick
2,9. 33 quadraginta *secl.* Frick *ex antecedente* quadringenti *ortum credens*

2. Vixit autem Isaac annos sexaginta: fiunt anni trea milia quadringenti septuaginta tres, et genuit Iacob.

3. Vixit autem Iacob annos octuaginta tres: fiunt simul anni trea milia quingenti quinquaginta sex, et genuit Leui et fratres eius.

4. Vixit autem Leui annos XLV: fiunt simul anni trea milia DCI, et sic genuit Caath.

5. Vixit autem Caath annos LX: fiunt simul anni trea milia DCLXI, et genuit Ambram.

6. Vixit autem Ambram annos LXXV, fiunt simul anni trea milia septingenti XXXVI, et genuit Moysen et Aaron et Mariam sororem eorum.

7. Factus est autem Moyses annorum LXXX: fiunt simul anni trea milia octingenti XVI, quando intrauit ad Faraonem regem Egypti. Et fecit dominus deus signa et prodigia per manum Moysi, mittens decem plagas in Egypto. Et eduxit filios Israhel de Egypto in manu forte, et transierunt mare Rubrum pedibus sicut per aridam.

8. Fecerunt autem et in herimo Sinai filii Israhel comedentes manna annos XL: fiunt simul anni trea milia octingenti LVI. Fiunt ab Adam usque ad mortem Moysi anni trea milia octingenti LVI.

9. In diebus autem Moysi F<o>roneus Argion regnauit post Inachum, Leucyppus autem Siceis regnauit, Eretheus Athineis regnauit, Belochus autem Assyriis regnauit, Petissonius autem Farao in Egypto. Occiduum enim sine regno erat.

4,1. Fiunt simul ab Adam usque ad mortem Moysi generationes quidem XXVI, anni autem trea milia octingenti LVI, et a morte Moysi usque ad mortem Hiesu Naue et Finees sacerdotis anni LIIII sic.

2. Post mortem autem Moysi et Aaron suscitauit dominus deus spiritum suum super Hiesu filium Naue, et transmeauit populum filiorum Israhel Iordanis fluuium, et ceciderunt muri Hiericho. Et exterminauit a facie filiorum Israhel Chananeum et Chetteum et Eu[g]eum et Ferezeum et Amorreum et Gergeseum et Hiebuseum, et fecit in terram quam inuasit annos XXXI sic: pugnando fecit annos sex et possidens alios uiginti quinque annos terram illam, fiunt simul anni treginta unum. Fiunt simul ab Adam anni trea milia octingenti octuaginta septem.

3. Et post obitum Hiesu filii Naue praefuit populo Finees sacerdos annos XXIII, fiunt anni LIIII. Fiunt simul ab Adam usque ad obitum Hiesu filii Naue et Finees sacerdotis omnes anni trea milia noningenti decem.

3,5. 42 LX *em.* Frick: XL E'   **3,9.** 54 Froneus E' ‖ post Inachum *scripsi*: cum Inachum E' ‖ 55 Belochus *rest.* Scaliger: Hilochus E' ‖ 56 Petissonius *emendaui; cf. supra* I, 50: Petessonsius E'   **4,2.** 64 Eueum *correxi*

4. Et ab obito Hiesu et Finees usque ad initium Heli sacerdotis, finis autem iudicum filiorum Israhel, anni sunt quadragenti XLV sic.   7⁣

5. Post obitum Hiesu et Finees peccauit populus filiorum Israhel ad deum, et tradidit illos deus Chusateri regi Mesopotamiae et seruierunt illi annos nouem. Fiunt simul anni trea milia noningenti XVIIII. Et clamauerunt ad dominum, et suscitauit illis dominus deus principem Gothonial, fratrem Chaleb iuuenem, de tribu Iuda. Iste pugnauit cum Chusather in bello et interfecit eum. Et iudicauit Gothonial populum annos XXXIIII. Fiunt simul anni trea milia noningenti LIII.   8⁣

6. Et iterum peccauit populus ad deum et traditi sunt a domino Eglom regi Moab, et seruierunt illi filii Israhel annos XVIII. Fiunt simul anni trea milia noningenti LXXI. Conuertentes autem iterum ad deum suscitauit illis principem Naoth, uirum de tribu Efraim, et interfecit Eglom. Et praefuit populo annos LV. Fiunt simul anni quattuor milia XXVI.   8⁣

7. Post Naoth autem iudicauit populum filiorum Israhel Semegas filius eius, et ipse iudicauit Israhel annos uiginti V. Fiunt simul anni quattuor milia LI.   9⁣

8. In diebus Naoth et Semega filium eius iudicum in ipsis scribuntur fuisse Promitheus et Epimitheus et Atlas et prouidens Algus, item Deucalios, et post eos diluuius sub Graecorum. Memoratur Promitheus plasmare homines sicut phittonissae, non autem sic, sed quia sapiens fuit ualde inperitos homines quasi paruulos plasmabat. Atlas autem, Promitheus frater, amabilis astrologus fulgebat: per disciplinam eius et caelum illi fertur deponi. Euripidus autem poeta super nubes dixit Atlatum esse. Epimitheus autem dicitur inuentor lyrae et omne organa musica.   10⁣

9. Et post obitum Naoth et Semega iudicum iterum peccauit populus coram domino deo, et tradidit illos dominus deus Iabi regi Assyriorum, et seruierunt ei annos XX. Fiunt simul anni quattuor milia LXXI.   10⁣

10. Sub isto prophetauit Deborra, uxor Lafiu, et per ipsam tenuit principatum filiorum Israhel Barach, ille de Aminoem, de tribu Neptalim. Iste pugnauit contra Sisara principe Iabis et superauit eum.

4,8. 99–100 Euripides, TrGF 1116 Nauck-Snell

4,4. 74 usque ad initium: *perperam vertit Barbarus* μέχρι ἀρχῆς ‖ 75 XLV *corr.* Gelzer: XXX E' ‖ 95 post eos: *perperam vertit Barbarus* κατ' αὐτούς ‖ Graecorum *scripsi*: Gregorum E' Frick ‖ 96 phittonissae *em.* Frick: phit tonissae E' ‖ 98 amabilis: *legisse Barbarum* ἀρεστός *pro* ἄριστος *recte vidit* Scaliger

Et regnauit super filios Israhel iudicans eos Deborra cum Barach annos XL. Fiunt simul anni quattuor milia CXI.　110

11. In diebus autem Deborra et Barach omnes de Dena scribuntur esse, Athineorum autem tunc regnauit Cecrops qui uocabatur Dipsyis annos L: Dipsyis autem uocabatur, quia statura procerus erat.

12. Post mortem autem Deborra et Barach iterum peccauit populus coram deo, et tradidit illos dominus deus Oreb <et Zeb> Madianitis,　115 et seruierunt eis annos VII. Fiunt simul anni quattuor milia CXVIII.

13. Post haec suscitauit deus Gedeon habentem tricentos uiros, et interfecit Oreb et Zeb et duodecim milia Allofylorum. Et iudicauit Gedeon Israhel annos XL. Fiunt simul anni quattuor milia CLVIII.

14. In diebus autem Gedeoni principis Zethus et Afius filii Zini scri-　120 buntur, et illa Ganymidis et Persea et Dionysu. Amfius autem Cadmu nepus Thibeis regnauit et condidit mura Thibeae.

15. Et post Gedeon praefuit filios Israhel filius Abimelech, et ipse iudicauit Israhel annos III. Fiunt simul anni quattuor milia CLXI.

16. Et post istum iterum rexit filios Israhel Thola filius Fila filio　125 Charram quem de tribu Efraim, et ipse iudicauit Israhel annos XXIII. Fiunt simul anni quattuor milia CLXXXIIII.

17. In diebus autem his illas de Lycurgum et Acteum et Pelopum scribuntur.

18. Et post mortem Tholae filio Fila surrexit Iaher ille Galadita de　130 tribu Manasse. Et ipse iudicauit Israhel annos XXII. Fiunt simul anni quattuor milia CCVI.

19. Et post mortem Iaher principis iterum peccauerunt filii Israhel coram deo, et traditi sunt Amanitis, et seruierunt illis annos XVIII. Fiunt simul anni quattuor milia CCXXIIII. Et clamauerunt iterum　135 ad deum et suscitauit eis principem Iefthe illum Galaditam de tribu Manasse, et liberauit eos, et praefuit populo annos sex. Fiunt simul anni quattuor milia CCXXX.

20. Et post iudicauit Eglom ille Zabulonita annos X. Fiunt simul anni quattuor milia CCXL.　140

21. Et post istum iudicauit Esbal ille Bethlemita de tribu Iuda, et ipse iudicauit Israhel annos VII. Fiunt simul anni quattuor milia CCXLVII.

22. Et post istum praefuit populo Abdon filius Ella ille Farathonita de tribu Efraim, et ipse iudicauit Israhel annos VIII. Fiunt simul anni quattuor milia CCLV.　145

23. Et post istum iterum peccauit populus coram domino, et tradidit illos deus Fylisteis et alienigenis, et seruierunt illis annos XL. Fiunt simul anni quattuor milia ducenti XCV.

4,12. 115 Orib E' || et Zeb *inserui*　**4,18.** 132 CCVI *corr.* Gelzer: CCII E'　**4,23.** 147 illis: *in cod. ex* illos *corr. manus satis antiqua sec.* Schoene

24. In diebus autem illis Ilios aedificata est, et mura Dardani scribuntur esse aedificata, in quo regnauit Dardanus et post istum   15(
Laomedus et Sarpidus et Priamus scolasticus rex.

25. Postquam autem reuersi sunt filii Israhel ad dominum suscitauit illis deus Sampson filium Manoe de tribu Dan. Iste expugnauit Allofylos et iudicauit Israhel annos XX. Fiunt simul anni quattuor milia CCCXV.   15!

26. In diebus autem Sampson iudicis illa qui Dedela et Atrea et Thyesten scribuntur, item autem Orfeus et Museus cognoscebantur et qui ad Eraclem pertinent et Argonautas, de quo Apollonius historiografus scripsit.

27. Et post obitum Sampson sine principem et pacem per annos XL.   16(
Fiunt simul anni quattuor milia CCCLV.

28. Et post haec Heli sacerdos iudicauit Israhel: quo tempore [ille] Ilios capta est ab Acheis et Dardana mura confracta sunt.

29. Huc usque iudices Israhel constauerunt. Iudices enim Israhel secundum proprias eorum generationes finierunt, de illos autem qui   16!
sine genealogia manifestatio haec est.

IV

1,1. Temporibus uero iudicum recensuimus dicendo: In ipsis fuerunt qui ec Diu depinguntur. Unde Picus ille Cronu pronepus partibus occasu ipsis temporibus imperauit.

2. Cronus quidem propater eius in diuisione terrae fuit occidentales partes tenens, sicut sine urbes et sine reges essent: de quo multus   5
est sermo et sine interpraetatione sunt.

2,1. Post Cronis autem perditionem secundum successiones annorum Picus pronepus eius per tempora regnauit in Italia primus, quem et Serapin quidam interpraetauerunt, alii autem Dia Olympium, ceteri autem Plutea Aidonium, et alii Chthonium Posidona. Istorum   1(

4,26. 158–159 Apollonii Rhodii Argonautica

4,24. 149 Ilios aedificata *scripsi*: solis aedificatus E' || 150 Dardanus *correxi*: Darius E' || 151 Priamus *scripsi*: Siamus E'   **4,26.** 156 et Atrea *em.* Scaliger: erat rea E' || 158 Argonautas *emendaui*: opus illorum *Barbarus vertit legens* ἔργον αὐτῶν *pro* Ἀργοναυτῶν || Apollonius: *scil.* Rhodius   **4,28.** 162 ille *expunxi* || 163 Ilios capta *scripsi*: solis confixus E'; *Barbarum permiscuisse* ἥλω *et* ἡλώθη Scaliger *recte notauit*

2,1. 7 successiones *corr.* Frick: successiores E' || 9 Serapin *scripsi*: Serafin E'

autem nominum ei pertinuit pro eo quod ille multa potuisset super omnes.

2. Iste autem in Assyrios in iuuentute regnans Ninus ibi uocabatur et condidit Niniuem ciuitatem Assyriorum. Uxor autem eius Semiramis mulier fuit maligna et praesumens et inpudica, quem Ream uocauerunt, alii autem Iram Zygiam, et alii Nemesim multiformem, ceteri autem Ecatin Chtonicam propter innumeram eius atrocitatem.

3. Iste quidem relinquens uxori imperium occidentis partibus ueniens imperauit. Erant enim omnes partes illas sine urbes et sine regem secundum quod narrat historia.

4. In illis uero temporibus Picus Croni pronepus inueniens terram illam spaciosam [manentem] imperauit in illam annos LXXX patrias possidens.

5. Et illas nobilissimas feminas per magicas et ingenia maligna conuertens et auortiuos faciebat, et sic mulieres, quae ab ipso deludebantur, domos et sedes praeparabant ei et sculptilia multa multa illi configebant sicut placebat eis, et quasi deo eas conmiscuisset et in deum eum esse gloriabantur.

3,1. Post istius autem perditionem Faunus filius eius regnauit in Italiam annos XXXV. Hic factus est uir impius et strenuus ualde.

2. Tunc descendit in Egyptum et ibidem demoratus est inperialem uestem indutus. Et sapiens uidebatur ab Egyptios, per magicas et maleficia eos decipiebat, et suspitiones et diuinationes illos dicebat, auium narrationes et opupas adnuntiationes et equorum hinnitus discebat et mortuorum diuinationes et alia plura mala.

3. Et dum conputatorem illum cernerent et ualde loquacem sapientes Aegyptiorum, Hermem terbeatissimum illum glorificabant pro eo quod linguas eorum bene nouisset ubique, simul autem et polyolbum et multoditatum et deorum illum ministrum suspicabant.

4. Regnauit autem ibi annos XXXV. Fiunt autem ab Adam usque ad initium regni Picu qui interpraetatur Serapidus pronepus Croni anni quattuor milia C.

4,1. Tunc Eraclius ab Spanorum partibus rediens arma sua posuit in Roma, in Boarium forum, in templo clausit. Dicunt enim Eraclium in Latothibis fuisse ec Dius et Alminius.

2. Et fugiens Erysthea, regem Thibeorum, cum omnia sua nauigauit

---

2,2. 14 Semiramis *emendaui*: Semimaris E'   **2,4.** 22 manentem *expunxi*: μένουσαν *pro* μὲν οὖσαν *legisse Barbarum coni.* Scaliger   **2,5.** 24 auortiuos faciebat: stupro uiolabat *vel aliquid simile Barbarus pro* διέφθειρε *debuit*   **3,1.** 29 strenuus valde: *potius* malignus *pro* πανοῦργος   **3,2.** 32 dicebat *corr.* Frick: decipiebat E' || 33 hinnitus *scripsi*: hinnos E'   **3,3.** 36 Hermem terbeatissimum: *cf.* Diod. VI,5,1–3 *et* Iul. Afric., Chron., fr. 12, p. 264 Routh **4,1.** 44 ec Dius *em.* Frick: ecdius E'

et regnauit occidentis partibus: unde immagines auro uestitos sibi conposuit in nouissimis occidentales partibus, qui et usque hodie stant: pro quo et Eurypidus ille poeta memorauit.

3. Fecit autem et filium ex Auge neocorum Aleu filia Telefum quem et Latinum [eum] uocauit. Regnauit autem Eraclius annos XXXVIII.   5(

4. Post mortem autem Eraclii Telefus filius eius qui et Latinus uocatus est regnauit in ipsa prouintia annos XVIII, et de eius nomine Romeos qui et Cittei uocantur Latinos nominauit, qui et usque hodiernum diem Latini uocantur.

5,1. Temporibus illis Frygius Eneas, Anchisso et Afroditis filius, uenit   5⁵
de Lybia et cum Latino se coniunxit et fecit pugna cum illos Rutullos. Et in ipsa pugna Latinus occisus est, et imperium eius sumpsit Eneas et condidit Libyniam ciuitatem in nomine Dido illa Libyssa. Regnauit autem Eneas post Ilii desolationem, anno XVIIII ab Ilii uastatione, et uixit in regno annos XXXVIII.   6(

2. Post autem Eneae mortem Ascanius filius eius regnauit ibi annos XXXV et condidit Albaniam et regnum Albanis inposuit.

3. Post autem Ascanii mortem regnauit Albas Postumius ille Eneae nepus annos XXXVI, et condidit Siluem. Ab isto qui postea reges Siluani uocati sunt.   65

4. Reges autem qui regnauerunt ab Alba in occiduum sunt isti.

Albas Siluius	Eneae nepus	annos XXXVI
Tittus Siluius	regnauit	annos XXXVIII
Francus Siluius	regnauit	annos LIII
Latinus Siluius	regnauit	annos LVI 7(
Procnax Siluius	regnauit	annos XLVI
Tarcyinius Siluius	regnauit	annos XVIII
Cidenus Siluius	regnauit	annos XXXII
Abintinus Siluius	regnauit	annos XXI
Rimus Siluius	regnauit	annos XXVIIII. 75

6,1. Post istos regnauit Romulus in Roma, et condidit Romam et leges Romanis inposuit et causas edocuit. Fiunt uero simul ab Adam usque ad initium regni Romuli qui et Romam condidit omnes anni IIII milia octingenti XX. I. Primus quidem regnauit in Roma Romulus,

---

4,2. 48 Euripidis fr. novum

4,3. 49 ex Auge *scripsi*: ex ipsa *vertit Barbarus qui* ἐξ αὐτῆς *pro* ἐξ Αὔγης *legit* || 49–50 Telefum quem et Latinum uocauit *emendavi*: Telefonum et Latinum eum uocauit E'   **5,1.** 59 Ilii *correxi*: solis E' || anno *emendavi*: annos E' || Ilii *iterum correxi*: solis E'   **5,4.** 73 XXXII *em.* Frick: XXXV E'

a quo Romani dicti sunt, qui et Romam condidit. Et regnauit olympius   80
annos VIIII et dimidium: fiunt anni XXXVIII. Fiunt simul anni IIII
milia octingenti LVIII.

2. II. Post istum regnauit Nummas Pompius ann. XLI: fiunt anni
IIII milia octingenti XCVIIII. Iste primum nummum adinuenit, pro
quo usque hodie nummus dicitur ille dinarius.   85

3. III. Post istum regnauit in Roma Tullius Seruilius annos XXXII:
fiunt simul anni IIII milia noningenti XXXI.

4. IIII. Post istum regnauit in Roma Lucius Tarcynius annos XXIII:
fiunt simul anni IIII milia noningenti LIIII.

5. V. Post istum regnauit in Roma Titus Superbus annos XXXVIII: 90
fiunt anni IIII milia noningenti XCII.

6. VI. Post hunc regnauit in Roma Tulius Seru[g]ius annos XLIIII:
fiunt anni V milia XXXVI.

7. VII. Post hunc regnauit in Roma Cyintus Tarcyniu annos XXXV:
fiunt anni V milia LXXI.   95

8. Simul reges Romanorum a Romulo VII permanserunt annos
CCLI, et ab initio Latini qui fuit filius Eraclii anni DCLXXI. Isti
reges, qui regnauerunt in Romam et in omnem occidentalis parte
terram.

9. Post haec tradidit dominus deus regnum terrae Romanorum in   100
manus Assyriorum, Chaldeorum, et Persarum, et Midorum. Et tributaria facta est terra illa Assyriis, et mansit Roma sine regnum, usque
dum suscitauit deus Alexandrum Macedonem et conditorem.

10. Iste quidem pugnauit contra regem Persarum et superauit eum.
Et tradidit dominus in manum eius regnum Assyriorum, et introiuit   105
in potestate regnum eorum, et concussit ciuitates Persarum et
Medorum, et liberauit omnem terram Romanorum et Grecorum et
Egyptiorum de seruitute Chaldeorum, et leges posuit mundo.

11. Fiunt simul ab Adam usque ad initium Romuli qui et Romam
condidit anni IIII milia octingenti XX, et ab initio Romuli usque   110
Cyinto Tarcinio anni CCLI.

V

1,1. Ecce nunc manifestauimus quidem aedificationes Romanorum
et quomodo quot annos regnauerunt. Necesse enim est ad historiam

---

6,6. 92 Tulius Seruius *emendaui*: Iulius Serugius E'   **6,8.** 97 CCLI *em.*
Frick: CCLV E' || DCLXXI *em.* Frick: DCLXXX E'   **6,11.** 111 CCLI
em. Frick: CCL E'

1,1. 2 quot *scripsi*: quod E'

currere chronografum annos per Ebreorum regna, quibus et clarior
manifestat tempora singillatim et annos secundum ordinem.

2. Sicut prius manifestauimus, ab Adam usque ad finem iudicum   5
Israhel ab initio Heli sacerdotis fiunt anni IIII milia CCCLV. Ecce
nunc regnum primum.

2,1. Post iudices Israhel iudicauit filios Israhel Heli sacerdos, et
ipse iudicauit Israhel annos XX: fiunt simul ab Adam anni IIII
milia CCCLXXV, et tradidit dominus deus arcam in manus alie-   10
nigenorum.

2. In diebus autem Heli sacerdotis Ilii exterminatio facta est ab
Acheis, in quibus memorantur Agamomnus et Menelaus et Achilleus
et quanti alii Danei, de quo historiam posuit Omirus litterator et
scriba.   15

3. Post mortem autem Heli sacerdotis iudicauit Samuhel propheta
filios Israhel. Et reduxit ab alienigenis arcam domini et introduxit
eam in domo Aminadab. Et mansit ibi annos XX. Fiunt simul anni
IIII milia CCCXCV.

4. Post haec unxit Samuhel Sahulem filium Cis regem super Israhel.   20
Iste primus regnauit in Iud<e>a annos XX. Fiunt simul anni ab
Adam IIII milia CCCCXV.

5. Post mortem autem Sahul regis regnauit Dauid filius Iesse de tribu
Iuda annos XL et menses sex, sic: in Chebron annos septem et
dimidium, et in Hierusalem annos XXXIII: fiunt anni XL et dimi-   25
dium. Simul anni IIII milia quadringenti LV et menses sex.

6. Iste reduxit arcam domini a domo Aminadab, et dum duceret
eam declinauit uitulus et <***> obpressit Ozam, et mortuus est. Et
timuit Dauid et introduxit eam in domo Abdede Chettei, et fecit ibi
menses III.   30

7. Prophetauerunt autem sub Dauid Caath et Nathan. Fuit autem
archistratigus Dauid Ioab filius Saruae sorori Dauid. Iste dinumerauit tribus Israhel et inuenit milia DCCC: Leui autem et Beniamin
non dinumerauit. Numerum autem de his qui ceciderunt in Israhel
milia LXX, pro eo quod dinumerati sunt et probare uoluerunt   35
dominum.

8. Post Dauid autem regem regnauit Solomon filius eius annos XL:
fiunt simul anni IIII milia quadringenti XCV et dimidium.

9. Iste aedificauit in Hierusolymis templum duodecimo anno regni

---

3 quibus *scripsi*: quis E'   **2,2.** 12 Ilii *scripsi*: solis E'   **2,4.** 21 Iudea
emendaui: Iuda E'   **2,6.** 28 *ante* obpressit *lac. recte stat.* Frick || 30 menses
V E'   **2,7.** 32 Ioab *scripsi*: Moab E' || 33 DCCC *requiritur*; cf. II Regn.
24,9: CLXX E'   **2,8.** 38 XCV et dimidium *emendaui*: XLV E'

sui. Et prophetauerunt sub Salomon Nathan et Achias ille Silonita   40
et Sameus et Abdeus. Princeps autem sacerdotum fuit super eos
Sadoc.

3,1. Post Salomon autem regnauit Roboam filius eius annos <X>VII
[et dimidium]: fiunt simul anni IIII milia quingenti XII <et dimidium>.
2. Sub isto diuisum est regnum. Et regnauit Hieroboam seruus   45
Salomonis de tribu Efraim in Samaria. Iste fecit scandalum in Israhel,
duas dammulas aureas. Prophetauit autem et <sub> Hieroboam et
Achias ille Silonita et Sammeus filius Ellamei.
3. Post istum regnauit Abiu filius eius annos III: fiunt simul anni IIII
milia quingenti XV et dimidium. Prophetauerunt autem ipsi prophetas.   50
4. Post hunc regnauit Asa filius Abiu annos XLI: fiunt simul anni
IIII milia quingenti LVI et dimidium. Iste in senectute sua podal-
giuus factus est. Prophetauit autem sub ipso Annanias.
5. Post hunc regnauit Iosafat filius eius annos XXV: fiunt simul anni
IIII milia quingenti LXXXI et dimidium. Sub isto prophetauit Helias   55
ille Thesbita et Micheas filius Embla et Abdeus filius Ananei. Sub
Michea autem fuit pseudopropheta Sedecias ille de Chanaan.
6. Post istum regnauit filius eius Ioram annos VIII: fiunt simul anni
IIII milia quingenti LXXXVIIII et dimidium. Et sub ipso prophetauit
Helias, post hunc Heliseus.   60
7. Sub istum autem et filium eius Ochoziam populus in Samaria
stercora columborum comederunt, quando orauit Helias ut non
plueret super terram, et non pluit caelum per annos tres et menses sex.
8. Post istum regnauit filius eius Ochozias annum unum et dimidium: fiunt simul anni IIII milia quingenti XCI. Et sub isto prophetauit   65
Heliseus et Abdoneus.
9. Post hunc regnauit Godolia, mater Ochoziae, uxor Ioram, annos
VII: fiunt simul anni IIII milia quingenti XCVIII. Haec surgens
interfecit filios filii sui, quia erat de genere Achab regis Samariae
uxor Ochozie filii eius. Soror autem Ochoziae filii Iosabe dum esset   70
uxor Iodae principis sacerdotum rapuit Ioham filium Ochoziae, et
hunc inposuit Iodae in regnum. Prophetauit enim et sub Godolia
Elisseus et Abdias et Hiiu.
10. Post haec autem regnauit Iohas filius Ochoziae annos XL: fiunt
simul anni IIII milia sexcenti XXXVIII. Iste occidit Zachariam filium   75
Iodae sacerdotis inter templum et altare.

3,1. 43 XVII *correxi*: septem et dimidium E' || 44 XII *em.* Frick: XVIII
E' || et dimidium *recte transp.* Frick   **3,2.** 47 sub *inserui*: *om.* E'   **3,9.** 67
regnauit *em.* Frick: prophetauit E' || 69 filii sui *correxi*: filiorum suorum E'

11. Post Iohas autem regnauit filius eius Amasias annos XXVIII: fiunt simul anni IIII milia sexcenti LXVI.

12. Post Amasiam autem regnauit filius eius Ozias annos LII: fiunt simul anni IIII milia septingenti XVIII. Hic fuit leprosus usque dum   80 mortuus est. Iudicabat pro eo Ioatham filius eius, quem non sinebat sedere in solium regni. Prophetizauerunt autem sub Ozia Amos et Esaias filius eius et Osee Beeri et Ionas Amathei de Gomor.

13. Post Oziam autem regnauit Ioatham filius eius annos XVI: fiunt simul anni IIII milia septingenti XXXIIII. Et sub isto similiter   85 prophetauerunt Esaias et Osee et Micheas ille Morathita et Iohel Bathueli.

14. Et post istum regnauit Achas filius eius annos XVI: fiunt simul anni IIII milia septingenti L. Et sub isto similiter prophetauerunt Esaias et Micheas, fuit autem princeps sacerdotum super eos Hurias.   90

15. Sub istius regno anno undecimo illa prima olympiada uenit ad Grecis. Fiunt uero simul ab Adam usque initium olympiadae omnes anni IIII milia septingenti XLV. Est autem olympiada anni IIII.

16. Sub istius regno anno VI surrexit Salbanasar rex Assyriorum et uenit in Iudeam et transmigrauit qui in Samaria erant in Midia et   95 in Babylonia. Duo solummodo tribus remanserunt in Hierusalem qui fuerunt ex genere Dauid regnaturi.

4,1. Post Achas autem regnauit Ezechias filius eius annos XXV: fiunt simul anni IIII milia septingenti LXXV. Et sub istum iterum prophetauerunt Esaias et Oseae et Micheas.   100

2. Sub istius regno Romulus qui Romam condidit regnauit olympiadas VIIII et dimidiam. Fiunt anni XXXVIII.

3. Post istum Ezechiam regnauit Manasses filius eius annos LV: fiunt anni IIII milia octingenti XXX [sic]. Iste interfecit Esaiam prophetam: serrans eum diuisit in duas partes, eo quod arguebat eum propter   105 sacrificia idolorum.

4. Post regnum autem Manasse regnauit filius eius Amos annos II: fiunt simul anni IIII milia octingenti XXXII.

5. Post Amos autem regnauit Iosias filius eius annos XXXI: fiunt simul anni IIII milia octingent<i> LXIII. Iste est Iosias, qui super-   110

3,12. 83 Beeri *emendavi*: Ebrei E'   **3,15.** 91 uenit: *perperam vertit* ἦλθε *pro* ἤχθη   **3,16.** 94 anno VI *fortasse rectius quam* anno XVI *cod.* E' *si ad Ezechiam referas: cf.* IV Regn. 18,10   **4,1.** 98 annos XXV *em.* Frick: XXVIIII E' **4,3.** 104 octingenti XXX *em.* Frick: octingenti XXXI E' || sic *exp.* Frick **4,4.** 108 XXXII *em.* Frick: XXXIII E'   **4,5.** 110 octingenti *em.* Frick: octingent E' || 110–111 superposuit membra hominum membris idolorum *scripsi iuxta* IV Regn. 23,16–20: subposuit membra hominum sub membra idolorum E' posuit membra hominum membris idolorum sicut scriptum est (d). Sub isto et pascha inuenta est in Israhel anno XVIII regni Iosiae. A quo enim obiit Hiesu Naue, non seruata est pascha sic nisi tunc.

6. Chelcheus sacerdos inuenit in templo illum librum legis absconditum octauo decimo anno Iosiae.   115

7. Prophetauerunt autem et sub Iosia Oldad mulier Selim, qui fuit uesterarius sacerdotum, et Sofonias et Hieremias [et Oldad] et Baruch. Fuit autem pseudopropheta Annanias Lurdus.

8. Post Iosiam autem regnauit Ioacham filius eius annos IIII et menses III: fiunt anni IIII milia octingenti LXVII. Istum ligauit [Sen]   120
Nachaoch rex Aegyptiorum ferreis uinculis et duxit in Aegyptum, fratrem autem eius Eliachim ordinauit pro eo. Et sub istum iterum prophetauerunt Hieremias et Buzzi et Baruch et Hurias filius Samiae de Cariathiarim.

9. [Sub isto] Regnauit Eleachim pro Ioacham fratrem suum annos   125
XI: fiunt simul anni IIII milia octingenti LXXVIII.

10. Sub istius regno surrexit Nabuchodonosor rex Assyriorum et translatauit qui in Samaria erant in Midia et in Babylonia, et Eleachim regem ligans aereis ligaminis duxit in Babyllonia. Prophetauerunt autem Hieremias et Baruch et Hurias.   130

11. Post hunc regnauit pro Eliachim patre suo Ioachim filius eius annos III: fiunt simul anni IIII milia octingenti LXXXI.

12. Et hunc iterum adduxit Nabugodonosor rex Babyllonis ad se ligatum catenis et multitudinem populi filiorum Israhel, in quibus et Danihelem et qui cum eo erant Ananiam, Misaelem et Azariam cap-   135
tiuos duxit in Babylonia.

13. Et ordinauit Nabuchodonosor in loco Ioachim Sedechiam quem et Iechoniam, fratrem Ioachim iuuenem. Regnauit autem Sedechias qui et Iechonias in Israhel annos XI: fiunt simul omnes anni IIII milia octingenti XCII.   140

14. In duodecimo autem anno duxit et istum in Babylonia Nabuchodonosor et cecauit eum et multitudinem populi filiorum Israhel duxit in Babylonia nisi pauci qui et in Aegyptum discenderunt. Tunc

---

d) IV Regn. 23,16–20

---

112 inuenta est: *fortasse vertit Barbarus* εὑρέθη *pro* ἐτηρήθη   **4,7.** 116 Oldad mulier Selim *scripsi iuxta* IV Regn. 22,14: Elibasillim E' || 117 et Oldad *expunxi*   **4,8.** 121 Nachaoch *scripsi*: Sennachaoch E'; *legisse Barbarum* ἔδησεν σεννεχαω *et alterum* σεν *dittographia ortum esse bene vidit* Frick   **4,9.** 125 Sub isto *expunxi planitatis causa*   **4,12.** 135 Ananiam, Misaelem et Azariam *scripsi iuxta* Dan. 1,6: Annaniam et Hiezechielem E'

et templum in Hierusolimis incendio deletum est permanens per
annos quadringentos XXV.

15. Prophetabant autem in ipsa depredatione Hiezechiel et Naum
et Danihel et Hieremias in Aegypto et Abacum in Hostracina. In
quinto autem anno regni Nabuchodonosor in Babylonia initiauerunt
prophetare Hiezechiel et Naum et Malachias iuuenis et tunc Aggeus
et Zacharias.

16. Usque Sedechiam <quem> et Iechoniam tenuit regnum Iudeorum,
et ultra rex in Israhel non est factus usque in hodiernum diem. Fiunt
uero anni IIII milia octingenti XCII.

VI

1,1. Illi uero reges qui in Israhel et in Iudea et in Samaria finierunt,
et tunc tradedit dominus deus regnum terrae in manus Assyriorum
et Chaldeorum et Persarum et Midorum, et tributaria facta est eis
omnis terra.

2. Vixit uero Nabuchodonosor iudicans omnem terram a Caspianas
portas usque in Eracliae finibus et Aegyptum et omnem Iudeam,
subiectos sibi faciens Pontum et totam Asiam et omnem terram
Romanorum annos XVIIII. Fiunt simul ab Adam anni IIII milia
noningenti XI.

3. Post istum autem regnauit Baltasar filius eius menses VIIII et
dimidium: fiunt simul anni IIII milia noningenti XII. Prophetabant
autem in his diebus Hiezechiel et Danihel et Baruch in Babyllonia.

4. Post hunc autem regnauit in Babyllonia Darius ille primus annos
VIIII: fiunt simul anni IIII milia noningenti XXI.

5. In quinto autem anno Darii regis uidit Danihel uisionem de illas
ebdomadas et prophetauit dicens: 'Aedificabitur Hierusalem lata et
magna' (e).

6. Sexto autem anno Dario filio Asueri, quo regnauit in regno
Chaldeorum, Zorobabel Ebreorum primus ascendit in Hierusolima
et coepit aedificare Hierusalem.

145

150

5

10

15

20

---

e) Dan. 9,25

4,14. 144 incendio deletum est *scripsi*: uenundatum est E'; *Barbarum transtulisse*
ἐπράθη *pro* ἐπρήσθη, ἐνεπρήσθη *susp.* Scaliger   **4,15.** 146 depredatione
corr. Frick: deprecatione E'   **4,16.** 151 quem *inserui*: *om.* E'

1,2. 9 noningenti XI *em.* Frick: noningenti XII E'

2,1. Post istum autem regnauit Cyrus Persus annos XXX: fiunt simul anni IIII milia noningenti LI.

2. In secundo autem anno Cyrus regnans iussit populo filiorum Israhel ut ascenderet in Hierusolima. Tunc templum aedificatur sub quinquagesima quinta olympiada Cyro rege regnante. 25

3. Simul Zorobabel Ebrei ascendentes de Babilonia in Iudea edificare coeperunt templum. Prophetauerunt autem sub Cyro rege Hiezechiel et Danihel et Aggeus et Abacum et Zacharias Baruchei.

4. In ipsis autem temporibus Pythagoras et Anaxagoras famosi filosofi cognoscebantur. 30

5. In ipsis autem temporibus Cyrus interfecit Cryssum regem Lydiae, et Lydiorum regnum dissipatum est sub quinquagesima octava olympiada.

6. Post Cyrum autem regnauit filius eius Cambysus annos VIII: fiunt simul anni IIII milia noningenti LVIIII. Et <sub> istum iterum 35 prophetauerunt Danihel et Aggeus et Zacharias et Abacum.

7. Post Cambysum autem regnauit Darius Nothus frater Cyri annos XXXIII: fiunt anni IIII milia noningenti XCII. Et sub istum iterum prophetauerunt Danihel et Aggeus et Zacharias et Abacum. Sub istum autem missus est Danihel in lacum leonum. 40

8. Post Darium autem Nothum regnauit Xerxes Persus annos XI: fiunt simul anni V milia III. Iste est Xerxes qui expugnauit uniuersa. Et in Athinas ueniens conbusit eas et suspiriosus factus in Babylonia reuersus est.

9. Post Xerxem autem regnauit Artarxerxes filius eius annos XXXIII: 45 fiunt simul anni V milia XXXVI.

10. Sub istum Neemias filius Achillei de genere Dauid qui factus est et pincerna Artarxerxis regis uicesimo quarto anno regni eius petiit regi Artarxerxi, et iussus ab eo edificauit Hierusalem. Et ascendens in Iudea edificabat Hierusalem et finem dedit edificationis templi. 50

11. Mura autem ciuitatis erexit et plateas in ipsa conposuit secundum Danihelis prophetiam qui dicit sic: 'Et edificabitur Hierusalem et circummurabitur' (f). Sub istum et illa aduersus Mardocheum et Hesther: Aman autem suspensus est.

12. Eo temporae Hesdras ascendens in Hierusalem legem docebat. 55 Princeps autem sacerdotum erat Hiesus filius Iosedec.

---

f) Dan. 9,25

2,4. 29 Anaxagoras *correxi*: princeps agoras E'; *legit Barbarus* ἄναξ ἀγορᾶς
2,5. 32 octava *emendaui*: quinta E'   **2,6.** 35 sub *ins.* Frick: *om.* E'   **2,7.**
37 Nothus *scripsi ex Graeco* Νόθος: Stultus E'; *legisse Barbarum* νωθής *vidit*
Scaliger   **2,8.** 41 Nothum *sicut supra* 2,7   **2,11.** 53 aduersus: *perperam vertit* τὰ κατὰ κτλ.

13. Post haec et Africanus dinumerans ipsam prophetiam septuaginta ebdomadarum et septuagesimum numerum extendens ad Christi aduentum.

14. Post Artarxerxem autem regnauit Xerxes filius eius menses II, 60
et occisus est. Et post hunc regnauit <S>ogdianus menses VII: fiunt simul anni V milia XXXVII.

15. Post istos regnauit Darius iuuenis qui uocatur Memoratus annos XVIIII: fiunt anni V milia LVI.

16. Fuit autem sub istos in Hierusalem princeps sacerdotum Ioachim, 65
filosofi autem cognoscebantur illi circa <Di>agoram.

17. Post Darium autem regnauit filius eius Artarxerxis secundus qui uocatur Memoratus annos XLII: fiunt simul anni V milia XCVIII. Fuit autem sub istum princeps sacerdotum in Hierusalem Heliasibus.

18. Filosofi autem cognoscebantur temporibus Artarxerxis Sofoclus, 70
et Heraclitus, et Anaxagorus, et Hirodotus, et Melissus, et Euripidus cantoconpositor, et Protagorus, et Isocrates ritor, et Fideas statuasconpositor, et Theetitus artifex, et Dimocritus Abderitus, et Ippocratis medicus, et Thucudidus ritor, et Empedoclus, et Gorgias, et Zinon, et Parmenidus, et Socratus Athineus, et Periclus, et Eupolus, et 75
Aristofanus comicus. Hii omnes cognoscebantur: unde et Africanus sub Artarxerxe rege dinumerat filosofos.

19. Post Artarxerxem autem Memoratum regnauit filius eius Ochus in Babylonia annos XXI: fiunt simul anni V milia CXVIIII. Fuit autem in Hierusalem princeps sacerdotum Iodae, in Macedonia autem 80
regnauit Filippus ille Alexandri.

20. In his temporibus Ochus rex Persarum et Midorum proeliauit in Egyptum. <***> nouissimus Farao regni Egypti, et cognoscens quia cessauit fortitudo Egyptiorum, caput suum radens et mutans uestimenta sua alio specie fugiit per Piluseum, et relinquens proprium 85
regnum in Macedonia moratus ibidem astrologica arte didicebatur.

2,13. 57–59 Iulius Africanus, Chron. V, fr. 50, pp. 297–306 Routh   **2,18.**
76–77 Iulius Africanus, Chron. fr. novum

57–58 septuaginta *emendavi*: septem E' Frick   **2,14.** 60 menses II *correxi*:
menses V E' ‖ 61 Ogdianus E'   **2,16.** 66 Diagoram *restituendum duce
Scaligero existimavi*: illi circa agoram E'   **2,18.** 71 Heraclitus *emendavi*:
Traclitus E' ‖ 72 Isocrates *scripsi*: Socrator E' ‖ 76 comicus *scripsi*: architector E'; οἰκοδόμος *pro* ὁ κωμῳδός *legisse Barbarum susp*. Wachsmuth   **2,19.**
80 Macedonia *correxi*: Asia E'   **2,20.** 82 *ante* in his: de nectabo nouissimo rege aegypti E' mg. sup. ‖ 83 *ante* nouissimus *lac. stat*. Frick ‖ 84
caput *scripsi*: capud E'

21. Filosofi autem in Athinas Fideas statuasconpositor, et Theetitus magister ludum, et Euripidus poeta, et Di<mo>critus Abderitus, et Ippocratis medicus, et Dimosthenus ritor cognoscebantur, ceteri autem mortui sunt. 90

22. Post hunc autem regnauit in Babyloniam Alsus Ochi filius annos IIII: fiunt anni V milia CXXIII. Fuit autem in Hierusalem princeps sacerdotum Iodae.

23. Post hunc autem regnauit in Babyloniam Darius Midus ille Arsami annos VI: fiunt simul anni V milia CXXVIIII. Istum deposuit 95 Alexander Macedo et conditor. Fuit autem princeps sacerdotum Iaddus.

3,1. Tunc Alexander Macedo et conditor, postquam legem poneret in Ellada et omnem Romanorum terram Syriam quoque et Egyptum et partes Lybiae, tunc uenit in partes orientales et expugnans omnes 100 ciuitates et oppida gentium obsedit regem Persarum Darium. Et tradidit dominus deus in manus eius Darium et omnem fortitudinem eius disperdit et omnem domum eius scrutauit.

2. Et dominauit Alexander Macedo et conditor omnem terram Chaldeorum et introiuit in omnem fortitudinem Darii et legem posuit 105 in omnes ciuitates eius, et tributarii facti sunt ei sicut proprio regi.

3. Ut enim condidit Alexander Alexandriam contra Egyptum, ueniens in Hierusolima domino deo adorauit dicens: 'Gloria tibi, deus solus omnia tenens, qui uiuis in saecula.' Fuit autem tunc in Hierusalem princeps sacerdotum Iaddus. 110

4. Filosofi autem in Athinas sub Alexandro conditore Dimosthenus ritor, et Aristotelis, et Eschinus, et Dimas, et Plato, et Lysias, et Dimocritus alius cognoscebantur.

5. Regnauit autem Alexander Macedo et conditor post Darium Mid[or]um Arsami filium annos VIII: fiunt simul ab Adam usque 115 ad finem Alexandri conditori<s> anni V milia CXXXVII, et tunc Ptolemei.

6. In diebus uero quibus regnauit Alexander Macedo et conditor, postquam superauit Darium regem Persarum, et Porum regem Indorum et omnes gentes subiugauit a Caspiacas portas quae sunt in ortu solis 120 usque in exteriores terminos Eraclii qui iacent in exteriores occidentis partibus contra Garirum.

2,21. 88 Dimocritus Abderitus *legendum sicut supra* 2,18: Dicritus Abdirus E'
2,23. 94 Arsami *emendaui*: Alsami E' **3,3.** 107 contra Egyptum: *perperam vertit* τὴν κατ' Αἴγυπτον **3,5.** 115 Midum *restituendum; legit Barbarus* Μήδων *pro* Μῆδον || Arsami *restitui sicut supra* 2,23 || 116 conditori E'

4,1. Veniens ad mortem Alexander testamentum scripsit, ut unusquisque principum Alexandri regnarent singuli in proprias eorum prouintias, sicut imperauit eis Alexander, sic. Macedonia quidem Arideum quem et Filippum praecepit regnare.

2. Ponton autem Leona dixit regnare.

3. Paflagonia autem et Cappadocia Eumenium scriba memoratum praeordinauit regnare.

4. Insulanos autem dimisit liberos, et procuratores ac dispensatores eorum esse Rodios.

5. Pamphilia et Lucya Antigonum ordinauit regnare.

6. Frigiam autem [et] illam magnam <et> C[aes]ariam [De] Asandro tradidit.

7. Cilicia autem et Isauria et omnia circuita eius Filone ordinauit.

8. Syriam autem usque Mesopotamiam dedit [Ta]Pithone ut regnaret.

9. Syriam uero Cylem uocatam, Fynicem autem interpraetatam, Meleagrom ordinauit dominare.

10. Babylonia autem Seleucum praecepit regnare.

11. Egyptum autem et quae circa eum usque superiore Lybia Filippo qui uocabatur Ptolomeus donauit.

12. Quae autem de superiore Babylone usque Caspiacas portas, principes quidem in ea et satrapes, archistratigum autem eorum Perdicum ordinauit.

13. India autem qui extendit circa Ydaspem fluuium Taxio dedit regnare.

14. India autem qui dicitur sub Indo et usque Ydaspem fluuium extendens Pythonae dominare praecepit.

15. Super Parapannisodum autem Oxydarcum ordinauit regnare.

16. Arachusia autem et Cedrusia Sybartum ordinauit regnare.

17. Arabiam autem totam Stasanoro donauit.

18. Et <S>ogdianiam Filippo minori dedit dominare.

19. Illam autem qui circuit contra aquilonis partes et illam qui habet Yrcaniam Antigono donauit regnare.

20. Carmaniam autem totam Tlipolemo donauit.

21. Persidam autem totam Peucestae donauit.

125
130
135
140
145
150
155

4,3. 128 scriba memoratum: *interpretatio barbarica verbi Graeci* ὑπομνη-ματογ-ράφος **4,6.** 133 Frigiam autem illam magnam et Cariam Asandro *legendum puto*: Frigiam autem et illam magnam Caesariam Deasandro E'; Deasandro *ex τῷ* Ἀσάνδρῳ *ortum censebat* Frick **4,8.** 136 Pithone: Tapithone *cod.* E' *ex τῷ* Πίθωνι *ortum putabat* Frick **4,13.** 146 Ydaspem: Ydastem E' **4,14.** 148 Ydaspem *ut supra* 4,13 **4,18.** 153 Sogdian-iam: Ogdianiam E' **4,20.** 156 Carmaniam *scripsi*: Germaniam E' || Tlipolemo: Tripolemo E' **4,21.** 157 Peucestae *scripsi*: Perco E'

22. Spaniam autem usque Alyo fluuio et Eracleoticum terminum Antipalum ordinauit regnare.

23. Sic uero statuit et donauit Alexander suis principibus, et unus- 160
quisque eorum sic regnauerunt, sicut ipse disposuerat.

5,1. Vixit autem Alexander annos XXXVI. Regnauit quidem annos XVII sic: pugnauit enim annos VIIII usque dum factus est anno-rum XXVIII, illos autem alios octo annos uixit in pace et securi-tate. Subiugauit autem gentes barbaras XXII et Grecorum tribus 165
XIII.

2. Condidit autem Alexander ciuitates XII, qui usque nunc inhabi-tantur: Alexandriam qui in Pentapolim, Alexandriam qui in Aegyptum, Alexandriam qui ad Arpam, Alexandriam apud Issum, Alexandriam Scythiam in Egeis, Alexandriam qui in Poro, Alexandriam qui super 170
Cypridum fluuium, Alexandriam qui in Troada, Alexandriam qui in Babylonia, Alexandriam qui in Mesasgyges, Alexandriam qui in Persida, Alexandriam Fortissimam, et mortuus est.

3. Fiunt uero ab Adam usque ad finem Alexandri conditoris simul anni V milia CXXXVII, et ab obito Alexandri usque ad Cleopatram 175
illam Egyptiam anni ducenti XCIIII sic.

6,1. Post autem mortem Alexandri, ut dictum est, regnauit in Egypto Philippus Ptolomeus, qui fuit consiliarius Alexandri, annos VII. Fiunt simul anni V milia CXLIIII. Fuit autem princeps sacerdotum Ianneus.

2. In his temporibus Menander comicus uidebatur.   180

3. Post Philippum autem regnauit Alexander Ptolemeus quem et ipse consiliarius Alexandri annos XII. Fiunt simul anni V milia CLVI. Princeps sacerdotum autem fuit in Hierusalem ipse Ianneus.

4. Isdem temporibus illi septuaginta Ebrei sapientes illam legem inter-praetauerunt Greco sermone.   185

5. Post hunc regnauit in Egypto Lagaus Ptolomeus annos XX. Fiunt simul anni V milia CLXXVI. Fuit autem in Hierusalem princeps sacerdotum Iaddus.

6. Temporibus istis Hiesus filius Sirach cognoscebatur, qui illam a deo spiratam sapientiam Aebreis edocuit.   190

7. Post hunc autem regnauit in Aegypto Filadelphus Ptolemeus annos XXXVIII. Fiunt simul anni V milia CCXIIII. Fuit autem princeps sacerdotum Onias.

5,2. 169 apud Issum *conieci*: qui Cabiosum E' ‖ 170 Scythiam in Egeis E': *puto* τὴν ἐν Σκυθίᾳ τῇ γῇ ‖ 172 Mesasgyges *em.* Frick: mesas gyges E'   **6,2.** 180 comicus *scripsi ut supra* (2,18): aedificator E'   **6,3.** 181 quem: *legit Barbarus* ὄν *pro* ὧν

8. Post Filadelphum autem regnauit in Aegypto Eu[g]ergetus Ptolemeus annos XXV. Fiunt simul anni V milia CCXXXVIIII. Fuit autem in Hierusalem princeps sacerdotum Simon et post hunc Onias alius.

9. Post Eu[g]ergetum autem regnauit in Aegypto filius eius Filopator Ptolemeus annos XVII. Fiunt simul anni V milia CCLVI. Fuit autem in Hierusalem princeps sacerdotum Eleazarus.

10. Post Filopatorem autem regnauit filius eius Epifanius Ptolemeus annos XXIIII. Fiunt simul anni V milia CCLXXX. Fuit autem in Hierusalem princeps sacerdotum Manasses.

11. Post Epifanium autem Ptolemeum regnauit filius eius in Aegypto Filomitor Ptolomeus annos XXXV. Fiunt simul anni V milia CCCXV. Fuit autem in Hierusalem princeps sacerdotum Simon.

12. Hisdem temporibus illa in Maccabeis finiebantur in Hierusalem sub Antiocho regem Syriae.

13. Post Filomitorem autem Ptolemeum regnauit filius eius Eu[g]ergetus alius in Egypto annos XXVIIII. Fiunt simul anni V milia CCCXLIIII. Fuit autem in Hierusalem princeps sacerdotum Onias alius.

14. Post hunc autem regnauit in Aegypto Soter uocatus Ptolemeus annos XXXVI. Fiunt simul anni V milia CCCLXXX. Princeps autem sacerdotum fuit in Hierusalem Hiesus annos VI et Onias alius annos VII et Ianneus annos XV.

15. Post hunc autem regnauit in Aegypto nouus Dionisus annos XXVIIII. Fiunt simul anni V milia CCCCVIIII. Fuit autem in Hierusalem princeps sacerdotum Simon annos VIII et Iohannis annos XX.

16. Hisdem temporibus Sosates cognoscebatur ille Ebraicus Omirus in Alexandria.

17. Post autem nouum Dionisum [nouissimum] illum et <nouissimum> nouissimorum Ptolomeorum regnauit in Aegypto Beronice Cleopatra annos XXII. Fiunt simul anni V milia quadringenti XXXI.

18. Quod sunt omnes anni Ptolemeorum regna a morte Alexandri usque ad mortem Cleopatre, qui et in Alexandriam Farum condidit, simul anni ducenti XCIIII.

19. Fiunt simul ab Adam usque ad mortem Cleopatrae anni V milia quadringenti XXXI. Et deinceps tradidit dominus deus regnum Aegyptiorum in manus Romanorum usque hodie. Et ultra rex non est in Aegypto factus usque in hodiernum diem.

195
200
205
210
215
220
225

6,8. 194 Euergetus *restitui sicut infra* 6,9 *et* 6,13: Eugergetus E' **6,16.** 218 Sosates: *poeta Iudaicus aliunde ignotus; vide* Cohen *in HThR* 74 (1981), pp. 391 sqq. **6,17.** 220–221 illum et nouissimum *duce* Frick *scripsi:* nouissimum illum et E'

VII

1,1. Et quia minus sunt in Christianorum et Ebraeorum libris istos qui foris sunt gentium scripta temporum, necessitate conpulsus praeuidi exquaerere et coniungere, qui apud nos sunt et quos in chronica deos et iroes uocatos reges, et quae ab eis historialiter acta sunt tradere his in diuino uerbo, incipiens a diebus protopatoris Abraham et Isaac et Iacob patriarcharum et Moyse, et qui post eos iudices facti sunt in Israhel et prophetarum singillatim regna recensare cunctatim, ut nobis per omnium scripturarum eorum unitum sit regnum.

2,1. Assiriorum regna et tempora. Assiriorum primum regem scribunt Bilum, quem et ab Assyriis et Fynices et Persi deum uocauerunt. Hunc Dium Greco nomine interpraetauerunt. Bilus uero primus in Assyrios regnauit et partem Asiae annos LXII.
2. Post haec regnauit Ninus annos LII. Iste condidit Nineuem ciuitatem Assyriorum, et ueniens in Italia uocatus est Picus.
3. Post quem Semiramis uxor eius annos XLII. Hanc Ream uocauerunt propter eius multam atrocitatem.
4. Post hanc Zamis regnauit annos XXXVIII.
> V. Post hunc Arius ann. XXX.
> VI. Post hunc Aralius ann. XL.
> VII. Post hunc Xerses qui et Balleus ann. XXX.
> VIII. Post hunc Armamithrus ann. XXXVIII.
> VIIII. Post hunc Bilochus ann. XXXV.
> X. Post hunc Balleus ann. LII.
> XI. Post hunc Aldatas ann. XXXV.
> XII. Post hunc Mamithus ann. XXX.
> XIII. Post hunc Bagchaleus ann. XXX.
> XIIII. Ita Sferus ann. XX.
> XV. Mamilus ann. XXXV.
> XVI. Spareus ann. XL.
> XVII. Ascatagus ann. XL.
> XVIII. Amintus ann. L.
> XVIIII. Atossa \<quae\> et Semiramis femina ann. XXIII.
> XX. Bilochus ann. XXV.

5

10

15

20

25

30

1,1. 1 *ante* Et quia: singillatim antiquorum regum qui regnauerunt eorundem temporum de primo et secundo tomo manethone E' mg. sup. ‖ 8 scripturarum *emendavi*: scribturarum E'   **2,2.** 14 Italia *correxi*: Asia E'   **2,4.** 17 Zamis *scripsi*: Zinas E' ‖ 19 Aralius: Aranus E' ‖ 24 Aldatas: Altallus E' ‖ 26 Bagchaleus: Magchaleus E' ‖ 27 Ita Sferus: Itas Ferus E' ‖ 28 Mamilus: Mamithus E' ‖ 32 Atossa quae: Attosai E' ‖

XXI. Belleroparus ann. XXXIIII.

XXII. Lampridus ann. XXXII.

XXIII. Sosarus ann. XX.

XXIIII. Lamparus ann. XXX.

XXV. Pannius \<qui\> et Zeus ann. XLV.

XXVI. Sosarmus ann. XX.

XXVII. Mithreus ann. XXXV.

XXVIII. Tautalus ann. XXXII.

XXVIIII. \<T\>euteus ann. XL. Anno isto tricensimo secundo capta est Ilios ab Acheis.

XXX. Thineus ann. XXX.

XXXI. Dercillus ann. XL.

XXXII. Eupalus ann. XXXVIII.

XXXIII. Laustenus ann. XLV.

XXXIIII. Peritiadus ann. XXX.

XXXV. Ofrateus ann. XX.

XXXVI. Ofratanus ann. L.

XXXVII. Acrapazus ann. XL.

XXXVIII. Thonos Concelerus qui uocatur Grece Sardanapallus ann. XXX.

XXXVIIII. Ninus ann. XVIIII.

5. Simul reges XXXVIIII antiqui Assyriorum perseuerantes annos mille quadringentos XXX. Ab istis autem in prima olimpiada anni LXVII. [Assyriorum regnum].

3,1. Egyptiorum regnum inuenimus uetustissimum omnium regnorum. Cuius initium sub Manethono dicitur memoramus scribere.

2. Primum Deorum qui ab ipsis scribuntur faciam regna sic.

I. Ifestum dicunt quidam deum regnare in Aegypto annos sexcentos LXXX.

II. Post hunc Solem Ifesti ann. LXXVII.

III. Post istum Sosin \<***\> Osirim ann. CCCXX.

IIII. Post hunc Oron ptoliarchum ann. XXVIII.

V. Post hunc Tyfona ann. XLV.

35

40

45

50

55

60

65

3,1–6. 58–97 Manetho, Aegyptiaca, fr. 4, pp. 16–23 Waddell

---

38 qui *requiritur*. *om.* E' || 42 Teuteus: Euteus E' || 43 capta est Ilios *scripsi*: confixus est sol E' ; *vide supra* III.4.28 || 45 Dercillus: Cercillus E' || 52 Thonos Concelerus *em.* Frick: Thonosconcelerus E' **2,5.** 57 Assyriorum regnum *exp.* Frick **3,1.** 59 sub Manethono: *perperam vertit* ὑπὸ Μανέθωνος **3,2.** 60 ab ipsis: *perperam vertit* παρ' αὐτοῖς || 64 *inter* Sosin *et* Osirim *lac. statui*

Colliguntur Deorum regna anni mille DL.

3. Deinceps <I>mitheorum regna sic.

I. Prota Anubes ann. LXXXIII.

II. Post hunc Amusim Apiona grammaticus, qui etiam Aegyptiorum   70
scripturas conposuit, secundum Inachum interpraetatur, qui sub Argios
initio regnauit, ann. LXVII.

4. [I.] Post hec Necyorum reges interpraetauit Imitheus uocans et
ipsos <***>

5.]fortissimos uocans annos duo milia C.   75

I. Mineus et pronepotes ipsius VII regnauerunt ann. CCLIII.

II. Bochus et aliorum octo ann. CCCII.

III. Necherocheus et aliorum VII ann. CCXIIII.

IIII. Similiter aliorum XVII ann. CCLXXVII.

V. Similiter aliorum XXI ann. CCLVIII.   80

VI. Othoi et aliorum VII ann. CCIII.

VII. <***>

VIII. Similiter et aliorum XIIII ann. CXL.

VIIII. Similiter et aliorum XX ann. CCCCVIIII.

X. Similiter et aliorum VII ann. CCIIII.   85

Hec finis de primo tomo Manethoni habens tempora annorum duo
milia C.

6.   XI. Potestas Dio<s>politanorum ann. LX.

XII. Potestas Bubastanorum ann. CLIII.

XIII. Potestas Tanitorum ann. CLXXXIIII.   90

XIIII. Potestas Sebennitorum ann. CCXXIIII.

XV. Potestas Memfitorum ann. CCCXVIII.

XVI. Potestas Iliopolitorum ann. CCXXI.

XVII. Potestas Ermupolitorum ann. CCLX.

Usque ad septimam decimam potestatem secundum scribitur tomum,   95
ut docet numerum, habentem annos mille quingentos XX. Haec sunt
potestates Aegyptiorum.

4,1. De regna autem, que in ceteris gentibus facta sunt et paulatim
creuerunt, proferamus temporibus regni Argiuorum.

3,3. 70–72 Apion, Aegyptiaca IV ap. Eus., P.E. X, 10, 16

3,3. 68 Imitheorum *scripsi*: Mitheorum E' || 69–72 Prota Anubes—ann.
LXVII *restitui, textum valde corruptum et inordinatum codex praebet*: Prota Anube
samusim qui etiam Aegyptiorum scripturas conposuit ann. LXXXIII. Post
hunc Apiona grammaticus qui secundum Inachum interpraetatur quem sub
Argios initio regnauerunt ann. LXVII.   **3,4.** 73 *numerum ante* Post hec
seclusi || Necyorum *scripsi*: Ecyniorum E' || 74 *post* ipsos *lac. recte sign.* Frick
3,5. 82 *dynastiam septimam excidisse bene vidit* Frick, *quapropter factum est ut numeri
ante primas sex dynastias positi loco moverentur*   **3,6.** 88 Diopolitanorum E' ||
95 tomum *em.* Frick: totum E'

2.   I.   Primus is Argus Inachus regnauit ann. L. Quo tempore   100
                    Moyses natus est.
             II.   Post hunc Foroneus regnauit ann. LX. Quo anno quin-
                    quagesimo quinto ex Aegypto egressio Iudeorum per
                    Moysen facta est.
            III.   Post hunc Apius regnauit ann. XXXV.   105
            IIII.   Post hunc Argius regnauit ann. LXX.
              V.   Post hunc Criassus regnauit ann. LVI.
             VI.   Post hunc Forbas regnauit ann. XXXV.
            VII.   Post hunc Triopas regnauit ann. LXVI.
           VIII.   Post hunc Crotopus regnauit ann. XXI.   110
           VIIII.   Post hunc Sthenelus regnauit ann. XI.
              X.   Post hunc Danaus regnauit, qui illas filias L, ann. <L>.
             XI.   Post hunc Lyggeus Aegypti <ann.> XLI.
Sub quo Cadamus Aginorus ascendit Biotia Europissa ad exquirendum.
            XII.   Post hunc Abas regnauit ann. XXIII.   115
        <XIII.>   Post hunc Prytus regnauit ann. XXVII.
        <XIV.>   Post hunc Acrisius regnauit ann. XXXI.
         <XV.>   Post hunc Pelops regnauit post <Oi>nomaum ann.
                    XXXVIII. A quo Peloponissus uocatur.
        <XVI.>   Post hunc Atreus et Thyestus ann. XLV.   120
        <XVII.>   Post hos Agamemnus Atreus ann. XXXIII.
3. Colliguntur igitur ab Inacho rege usque ad desolationem Ilii, quod
est octauodecimo Agamemnonis, anni septingenti XVIII.
4. Ab Ilii deuastatione usque ad primam olympiadam anni CCCCVII:
et Porfyrius autem in historia philosofiae sic dixit. Post autem Ilii   125
deuastationem Agamemnonus reliquos annos XV.
5.   <XVIII.>   Post hunc Egesthus regnauit ann. VII.
         <XVIIII.>   Post hunc Oresthus regnauit ann. XXVIII.
            <XX.>   Post hunc Penthilus regnauit ann. XXII.

6. Et Argiorum regnum dissipatum est. Colliguntur uero Argiorum   130
regna simul anni septingenti XC.

4,4. 124–125 Porph., Hist. phil., fr. 200, pp. 223–224 Smith

4,2. 100 is Argus *scripsi ex Graeco sermone* εἰς Ἄργος: isargus E' || 112 L
addidi: om. E' || 113 Aegypti (*scil.* filius) *emendaui:* Aegyptius E' || ann. *inserui:*
om. E' || 114 Sub quo *scripsi:* a quo E' || 116–121 *numeros* XIII–XVII
inserui: om. E' || 118 post Oinomaum *correxi:* cum Nomaum E' || 120 et
Thyestus *scripsi:* ethyestus E'   **4,3.** 122 igitur: nunc E'; *confudit* νῦν *et*
τοίνυν || Inacho: Ichano E' || Ilii: solis E' || 124 Ab Ilii: a solis E' || 125
Ilii: solis E'   **4,5.** 127–129 *numeros* XVIII–XX *inserui: om.* E'

5,1. Siciniorum qui nunc Elladicorum uocantur reges et tempora. Proferamus iterum et Syciniorum qui nunc Elladici uocantur. Disponamus regna a quibus initiata sunt temporibus, et in quibus diffinierunt manifestemus.   135

2. Africanus quidem dixit sic tenere eis omnes annos mille VII: a minuetate autem eorum in primam olympiadam anni CCCXXVIIII, sicut numera<n>tur ab initio Sicyoniorum regni in primam olympiadam omnes anni mille CCCXXXVI.

3. Vicesimo nono autem anno patriarchae Iacob illum Syciniorum   140
initiauit regnum sic:

I. Egialeus	ann. LII.	anni autem Iacob
II. Europs	ann. XLV.	XXVIIII,
III. Telchus	ann. XX.	anni Isaac LXXXVIIII,
IIII. Amfus	ann. XXV.	anni Abraham CXIIII 145
V. Thelxius	ann. LII.	Ellada initiauerunt
VI. Egydrus	ann. XXXIIII.	regna.
VII. Turimachus	ann. XLV	Anno quadragesimo
VIII. Leucippus	ann. LIII.	tertio Leucippi
VIIII. Mesapfus	ann. XLVII.	egressio Iudeorum 150
X. Eratus	ann. XLVI.	ex Aegypto.
XI. Plammeus ann. XLVIIII.		
XII. Ortopolus ann. LXV.		
XIII. Marathus ann. XXX.		
XIIII. Maratheus ann. XX.		155
XV. Echyrus ann. LV.		
XVI. Corax ann. XX.		
XVII. Epopeus ann. XXXV.		
XVIII. Laomedus ann. XLIII.		
XVIIII. Polybus annos XLV.		160
XX. Inachus annos XLV.		
XXI. Festus annos L.		
XXII. Adrastus annos IIII.		
XXIII. Polifidus annos XXXI.		
XXIIII. Pelasgus annos XX.		165
XXV. Zeuxippus annos XXXV.		

4. Usque Zeuxippum tenuit Sicyoniorum regnum permanens annos

5,2–5. 136–180 Iulius Africanus, Chron. III, fr. 29, pp. 282–283 Routh

---

138 numerantur: numeratur E' Frick || regni: regna E' Frick   **5,3.** 160 Polybus *post* Laomedus *posui: in codice inuenitur post* Zeuxippus || 165 Pelasgus *scripsi*: Pelastus E'

noningentos LXXIX. Post Zeuxippum autem reges quidem non
fuerunt, sed praeibant eis sacerdotes <Apollinis> Carnii annos XXVIII.
5. Quorum primus sacerdos Archelaus annum I.   170

Post hunc Automidus annum I.
Post hunc Theoclytus annum I.
Post hunc Euneus annos IIII.
Post hunc Theonomus annum I.
Post hunc Amficyus annos <X>VIIII.   175
Post hunc Charidus annum I.

Qui non sustinens cibaria fugiit. A quo in prima olimpiada ut
fertur scriptura anni CCCXXVIIII.

Fiunt uero omnes Sicioniorum regna ab Egialeo usque in prima
olympiada anni mille CCCXXXVI.   180

6,1. Athineorum reges. Nondum multo transacto tempore Aethineorum
regnum ab Aegypto populi egressio. Anno enim ducentesimo octauo
egressionis primus in Athinas regnauit Cecrops procerus et qui post
eum, sicut manifestantur, sic.
2.   I. Cecrops procerus ann. L.   185
Anno trecesimo quinto Cecropus Promitheus et Epimitheus et Atlas
scribuntur, qui et Diu scribuntur.
        <II. Cranaus ann. VIIII.>
        III. Amfictryus ann. XL.
        IIII. Ericthonius ann. X.   190
        V. Pandius ann. L.
        VI. Erectheus ann. XL.
        VII. Cecrops Erectheus ann. LIII.
        VIII. Pandius Cecropus ann. XLIII.
    [VIII.] Temporibus Pandii Cecropi Cadmus Aginori litterarum   195
        elementa primus duxit ad Grecos.
    VIIII. Egeus Pandionus annos XLVIII.
        X. Thiseus Egei ann. XXXI.
        XI. Menestheus ann. XVIIII.
        XII. Dimofus ann. XXXV.   200
        XIII. Oxyntus ann. XIIII.
        XIIII. Afydus ann. I.

5,4. 168 noningentos LXXIX *requiritur*: quingentos LXXXI E' ‖ 169
Apollinis *inserui planitatis causa*   **5,5.** 170 Quorum *correxi*: quem E' ‖ 172
Theoclytus: Methudutus E' ‖ 175 annos XVIIII *correxi*: VIIII E' ‖ 176
Charidemus: Charidus E' ‖ 177 Qui non *emendavi*: Osuch E'; *perperam vertit Barbarus* Ὃς οὐχ   **6,2.** 188 II. Cranaus ann. VIIII *inserui*: *om.* E' ‖
189–195 *numeros* III–VIII *correxi* ‖ 196 elementa: *uersos* E'; *vertit* στοίχους
pro στοιχεῖα

XV. Thymytus ann. VIIII.

XVI. Melanthus ann. XXXVII.

XVII. Codrus ann. XXI.   205

3. A Cecropo procero usque Codrum anni quadringenti XCII. Post Codrum autem fuerunt dum uixerunt principes. Difyis autem uoca-tus est Cecrops, quoniam procer staturae fuit prae omnibus.

4. Principes perpetui. Post Codrum autem primus filius eius per-petuus factus est princeps Athineorum.   210

    I. Medrus Codri ann. XX.

    II. Acastus ann. XXXVIIII.

    III. Archippus ann. XL.

    IIII. Forbus ann. XXXIII.

    V. Megaclus ann. XXVIII.   215

    VI. Diognitus ann. XXVIII.

    VII. Fereclus ann. XV.

    VIII. Arifrus ann. XXX.

    VIIII. Thispeus ann. XL.

    X. Agamistor ann. XXVI.   220

    XI. Thersippus ann. XXIII.

    XII. Eschylus ann. <XXIII>.

Eschylo anno secundo prima olympiada a[ddu]cta est a Grecis.

5. Colliguntur uero ab initio regni Cecropi in prima olympiada anni octingenti XIIII. Post Eschylum autem illi [XIII]:   225

    XIII. Almeus ann. II.

    XIIII. Corops ann. X.

    XV. Esimidus ann. X.

    XVI. Celdicus ann. X.

    XVII. Ippomenus ann. X.   230

    XVIII. Leocratis ann. X.

    XVIIII. Apsandrus ann. X.

    XX. Erygius ann. X.

6. Et cessauit regnum Athineorum in olympiada uicesima quarta. Fiunt uero omnem Athineorum fortitudinem a Cecropo usque Erygium   235 ann. noningenti septem.

7,1. Latinorum qui et Romanorum reges. Latinorum autem qui et Romanorum regnum fortiorem Assyriorum et Aegyptiorum et Argiorum

---

6,3. 207 dum: sicut E'; *legit ὡς pro* ἕως   **6,4.** 209 perpetui: diabii E' || 209–210 perpetuus: diabius E' || 222 XXIII: *numerus deest in codice* || 223 adducta: acta *seu* celebrata *vertere debuit*   **6,5.** 225 XIII *dittographia ortum recte exp.* Frick || 226 ann. II *requiritur.* X E'   **6,6.** 235 Erygium: Oxyrium E'

seu et Sicyoniorum quem et Grecorum et Athineorum in historia
inuenimus memorantem. Et nos quidem sequi pedes Romanorum   24(
quem et Latinorum tempora disponimus.

2. Latinorum autem regnum ab Eraclio quidem et Telefo, qui et
Latinus uocatur, conamur in quibus prescripsimus dicendo, post quos
regnauit Eneas ille Frygius, Agchissi et Afroditis filius, nono et decimo post uastationem Ilii, in diebus Heli sacerdotis et Samuhelis   24⸓
prophetae secundum Ebraicam historiam.

3. Optinuit autem Romanorum imperium usque annos sexcentos
LIII sic.

        I. Eneas Siluius annos XXXVIII.
       II. Ascanius Siluius annos XXXV.   25(
      III. Albas Siluius annos XXXVI.
     IIII. Tittus Siluius annos XXXVIII.
        V. Francus Siluius annos LIII.
       VI. Latinus Siluius annos LVI.
      VII. Procnax Siluius annos XLVI.   25⸓
     VIII. Tarcinius Siluius annos XVIII.
    VIIII. Cidensus Siluius annos XXXII.
        X. Abintinus Siluius annos XXI.
       XI. Rimus Siluius annos XXVIIII.

Usque Rimum Syluium Latinorum regnum diffamabatur, permanens   26(
usque ad annos CCCCII.

4. Post hunc autem regnauit Romulus qui et condidit Romam, a
quo Romani uocati sunt.

    Romulus regnauit ann. XXXVIII.
    Nummus Pompiius ann. XLI.   26⸓
    Tullius Seruilius ann. XXXII.
    Lucius Tarcinius ann. XXIII.
    Tittus Superbus ann. XXXVIII.
    Tulius Seruius ann. XLI<III>.
    Cyintus Tarcinius ann. XXXV.   27(

5. Colliguntur autem et a Romulo anni ducenti LI. Fiunt uero simul
Latinorum qui et Romanorum anni sexcenti LIII. Defexit autem regnum in olympiada sexagesima sexta. Et tunc princepes ordinati sunt,
usque dum regnaret Gaius Iulius Caesar.

7,1. 239 *et* 241 quem: *bis legit* τὸν *pro* τῶν ‖ 240 sequi pedes: *fortasse vertit*
παρὰ πόδας   **7,2.** 243 post quos *scripsi*: cum quibus E’ ‖ 245 Ilii: solis
E’   **7,3.** 247 usque: *perperam vertit* ἐπὶ ‖ 261 usque ad: ἐπὶ ‖ CCCCII
em. Frick: CCCII E’   **7,4.** 269 XLIIII *em.* Frick: XLI E’

8,1. Tempora regni Lacedemoniorum. Regnauerunt et Lacedemonii 275
per annos CCCL et defecerunt in prima olympiada quae facta est
sub Achaz regem Iudae in diebus Esaiae prophetae, sicut scirent
eorum initium ab Erystheum initiatum.

2. Anno uicesimo Sahul initiauerunt Lacedemoniorum reges, et defecerunt in anno primo Achaz regi Iude, in quo tempore prima olym- 280
piada a Grecis a[ddu]cta est.

3. [I.] Illa autem singillatim regnorum haec.

    I. Erystheus ann. XLII.

    II. Egeus ann. II.

  III. Echestratus ann. XXXIIII. 285

  <IV.> Labotus ann. XXXVII.

    V. Dorystheus ann. XXVIIII.

   VI. Agisilaus ann. XXX.

  VII. Et Menelaus ann. XLIIII.

 VIII. Archelaus ann. LX. 290

 VIIII. Teleclus ann. XL.

    X. Alcamanus ann. XXXII.

  [XI. Automedus ann. XXV.]

4. Simul reges Lacedem[i]oniorum permanserunt in regno annos
CCCL. Et Lacedemoniorum regnum dissipatum est. 295

9,1. Corinthinorum reges et tempora. Corinthinorum regnum stabi-
litum est secundo anno Erysthei regi Lacedemoniorum. Permansit
autem per annos CCCXXIII. Eodem uero tempor[a]e Lacedemonii
congregantes conmutauerunt illos tricentos XXIII annos, quos obtinuerunt Corinthinorum reges. Erystheo regnante Lacedemoniorum 300
anno secundo regnauit autem Corinthinorum primus Alitus, et qui
sequuntur post haec sic regnauerunt.

2.   I. Alitus ann. XXXV.

    II. Exius ann. XXXVII.

   III. Agelaus ann. XXXIII. 305

  IIII. Prymnus ann. XXXV.

    V. Bacchus ann. XXXV.

   VI. Agelas ann. XXXIIII.

  VII. Eudimus ann. XXV.

8,1. 276 CCCL *correxi*: CCCXXV E'   **8,2.** 279 uicesimo: uisesimo
E' || 281 adducta *sicut supra* 6.4.   **8,3.** 282–286 *numeros* I–IV *correxi* ||
289 Et Menelaus *dubitanter duce Scaligero scripsi*: Cemenelaus E' || 291 Teleclus
emendavi: Celeclus E' || 292 XXXII: XXVII E' || 293 XI. Automedus
ann. XXV *expunxi*   **8,4.** 294 Lacedemoniorum *pr.*: Lacedemionorum
E'   **9,1.** 298 tempore: temporae E'   **9,2.** 309 Eudimus: Eumidus E'

VIII. Aristomidus ann. XXXV.

VIIII. Igemonius ann. XVI.

X. Alexander ann. XXV.

XI. Telestus ann. VIIII.

XII. Automenus ann. IIII.

3. Hii Corinthinorum reges sub anno uicesimo primo Sahulis regi Iudae initiauerunt, et defecerunt anno sexto decimo regni Ioatham fili Oziae, patri<s> autem Achaz regis Iudae.

10,1. Macedoniorum reges et tempora. Macedoniorum autem regnum non silendum est. Et enim Romeis obtinentibus fortitudinem nondum longinquo tempore sub Ozia regem Iudeorum anno tricensimo tertio nouimus eam sustentare. Et regnauit per annos DCXLVII, cessauit autem [annos unusquisque] in <centesima> quinquagesima tertia olympiada. Regnauit autem Ozias in Hierusalem et in Iuda annos LII.

2. Sub tricensimo tertio autem anno Oziae Macedonorum regnum ordinatum est, Cranaus primus in Macedonia regnans, sicut numerus manifestat, sic.

3.   I. Cranaus ann. XXVIII.

II. Cynus ann. XII.

III. Tyrimmus ann. XXXVIII.

IIII. Perdicus ann. LI.

V. Argeus ann. XXXVIII.

VI. Filippus ann. XXVI.

VII. Aeropus ann. XXXVIII.

VIII. Alcetus ann. XXVIIII.

VIIII. Amyntus ann. L.

X. Alexander ann. XLIII.

XI. Perdicus ann. XXVIII.

XII. Arcelaus ann. XXIIII.

XIII. Orestus ann. III.

XIIII. Arcelaus alius ann. unum et dimidium.

XV. Amyntus ann. III.

XVI. Pausanius ann. I et dimidium.

XVII. Argeus ann. II.

XVIII. Amyntus alius ann. XVIII.

XVIIII. Alexander alius ann. II.

9,3. 315 uicesimo *requiritur*: tricesimo E' || 316 anno sexto decimo: quinto decimo E' || 317 patris *scripsi*: patri E'   **10,1.** 322 annos unusquisque *seclusi: videtur* ἔτη ἕκαστος *pro* ἐν τῇ ἑκατοστῇ *Barbarum legisse; ergo* centesima *inserui*   **10,3.** 341 Arcelaus: Arceclaus E' || 344 Argeus ann. II: III E'

XX. Ptolemeus ann. III.

XXI. Perdicus alius ann. VI.

XXII. Filippus ann. XXVI.

XXIII. Amyntus alius ann. VI.   350

XXIIII. Alexander alius ann. XII.

Alexander omnia regna tenens Macedonorum regno coniunxit.

4. Post Alexandrum autem conditorem in principes eius rebus uenerunt.

5. Et Macedonorum principatu successit Filippus frater Alexandri, et

sic secundum ordinem.   355

XXV. Filippus frater ann. VII.

XXVI. Casandrus ann. XVIIII.

XXVII. Filii Casandri ann. IIII.

XXVIII. Dimitrius ann. V.

XXVIIII. Pyrrus mens. XI.   360

XXX. Lysimachus ann. V.

XXXI. Ptolomeus Ceraunus ann. II.

XXXII. Meleagrus mens. VII.

XXXIII. Antipatrus mens. II.

XXXIIII. Sosthenus ann. II.   365

XXXV. Antigonus Gonata ann. XXXV.

XXXVI. Dimitrius ann. X.

XXXVII. Antigonus alius ann. XV.

XXXVIII. Filippus alius ann. XLII.

XXXVIIII. Perseus ann. X.   370

6. Haec Macedonorum regna regnantes ab anno Oziae regis Iudae

tricensimo tertio obtinuerunt per annos DCXLVII et cessauerunt in

olympiada centesima LIII.

11,1. Lydiorum regna et tempora. Et Lydiorum regnum tenuit per

annos CCXXXII. Incipiens ab Ardi<s>o primum regem Lydiorum   375

sub Cryssum illum a Cyro Persarum dissipatum finiit in olympiada

quinquagensima octava.

2. Initium uero primae olympiadae inuenitur exordium regni Lydiorum

in anno primo Achaz. Regnauit quidem et Lydiorum principatus per

annos CCXXXII sic.   380

3.   I. Ardisus ann. XXXVI.

II. Alyatus ann. XIIII.

III. Midus ann. XII.

349 XXII: XII E' || 351 ann. XII: XIII E'   **10,5.** 354 princi-
patu *emendavi*: principato E' || 358 Filii Casandri *scripsi*: Pedes Casandrus
E' || 369 ann. XLII: XLV E'   **11,1.** 375 Ardiso *emendavi*: Ardio
E'   **11,3.** 381 Ardisus *scripsi*: Ardirus E'

    IIII. Caudalus ann. XVII.

     V. Gygus ann. XXXVI.   38⸱

     VI. Ardyssus ann. XXXVIII.

    VII. Sadyatus ann. XV.

   VIII. Aliatus alius ann. XLVIIII.

  VIIII. Cryssus ann. XV.

4. Haec Lydiorum regnum, incipiens a principio primae olympiadae   39(
in primo anno Achaz, regis Iudae. Et cessauit in olympiada quinquagensima octaua. Fiunt anni CCXXXII.

12,1. Midorum regna et tempora. Midorum autem regnum obtinuit
per annos CCLXVIIII. Et hos Cyrus Persus destruens regnum eorum
in Persida duxit in principio quinquagensimae quintae olympiadae.   39⸱
In ipsa igitur quinquagensima quarta olympiada fiunt CCXVI, sicut
pridem <quinquaginta> trium annorum primae olympiade Midorum
initium inuenimus esse regnum, quod est quinto decimo anno Oziae
regis Iudae.

2. Quod uero CCLXVIIII annorum Midorum obtinuerunt tempora   40(
sic a principio Arbaci, qui primus regnauit in Midia, usque Astyagum,
quem Cirus exterminans in Persida regnum migrauit.

3.   I. Arbacus ann. XXVIII.

      II. Sosarmus ann. XXX.

    III. Mamythus ann. XL.   50⸱

   IIII. Cardyceus ann. XXIII.

     V. Diycus ann. LIIII.

    VI. Fraortus ann. XXIIII.

   VII. Cyaxarus ann. XXXII.

  VIII. Astyagus ann. XXXVIII.   41(

4. Haec Midorum regna permanserunt per annos CCLXVIIII, a
quinto decimo anno Oziae regis Iuda, hoc est LIII annorum <ante>
primam olympiadam. Finiit autem quinquagensima quarta olympiada,
anno tricensimo octauo regnante Astuago, quem exterminauit Cyrus
Persus in quinquagensima quarta olympiada. Et Lydorum et Midorum   415
regna dissipata sunt sub Cyro Persarum.

13,1. Tempora regni Persarum. Cyrus Persarum rex dissipans regna
Lydorum et Midorum regnauit olympiadas VII et dimidiam. In anno

---

387 Sadyatus: Salyatus E'   **12,1.** 394 hos *correxi*: haec E' || 396 igitur
correxi: nunc E' || 397 pridem: *perperam vertit* πρὸ || quinquaginta *excidisse
censebat* Gelzer   **12,2.** 401 Arbaci *correxi*: Abbaci E' || Astyagum *correxi*:
Artyagum E'   **12,3.** 404 ann. XXX *emendavi*: ann. IIII E'   **12,4.**
412–413 ante primam olympiadam *emendavi*: primae olympiadae E'; *legit
Barbarus* πρώτης *pro* πρὸ τῆς α'

autem primo regni ipsius, in quo contigit consumari septuaginta annos depred[ic]ationi<s> genti Iudeorum, relaxauit multitudinem filiorum Israhel remeare ad propriam habitationem. In quo anno fuit initium quinquagensimae quintae olympiade. Tenuit autem Persarum regnum usque Darium, quem occidit Alexander Macedo et conditor, annos CCXXX sic.

420

2. I.   Cirus Persus ann. XXX.

425

II.   Cambysus ann. VIIII.

III.   S<m>erdius <mens.> VII.

IIII.   Darius iuuenis ann. <XXX>VI.

V.   Xerxes maior ann. XX.

VI.   Artabanus <mens.> VII.

430

VII.   Artaxerxes minor ann. XL.

VIII.   Xerxes iunior mens. II.

<VIIII.> Sogdianus mens. VII.

X.   Darius Nothus ann. <X>VIIII.

XI.   Artaxerxes Memoratus ann. XLII.

435

XII.   Ochus filius Artaxerxi ann. XXII.

XIII.   Alsus filius Ochi ann. IIII.

<XIIII.   Darius filius Arsami ann. VI.>

3. Alexander Macedo et conditor exterminans Persarum regnum traduxit in Macedonia regnum permanentem annos CCXXX, sub olympiada centesima duodecima.

440

14,1. Macedonorum regna et Syrie et tempora ab Alexandro conditore. Alexander Filippi coepit regnare Macedonorum in olympiada centesima undecima, omnia simul regna conprehendens et sub Macedonorum iure redi<g>ens, per annos duodecim et dimidium. Obiit in anno <decimo tertio> relinquens post se principes IIII.

445

2. Filippum fratrem suum Macedoniae regnum, Antigonum autem Asiae reliquid regnare, Filippum uocatum Ptolomeum omnem Aegyptum precepit regnare, Seleucum autem quem et Nicanorem Syriam omnem iussit regnare.

450

3. Qui autem regnauerunt in Syria per tempora sunt ita.

I.   Seleucus qui et Nicanor ann. XXXII.

II.   Antiochus Soter ann. XVIIII.

13,1. 420 depredationis *correxi*: depredicationi E'   **13,2.** 427 Smerdius mens. VII *legendum opinor*: Serdius VII E' || 428 Darius iuuenis ann. XXXVI *emendavi*: VI E' || 430 Artabanus mens. VII *scribendum puto*: Artabanus VII E' || 433–438 VIIII *inserui*: om. E'; *ergo numeros* X–XIIII *correxi* || 434 Darius Nothus ann. XVIIII: Darius Stultus ann. VIIII E' || 438 XIIII. Darius filius Arsami ann. VI *addidi*: om. E'   **14,1.** 445 redigens *correxi*: rediens E' || 446 *verbis* decimo tertio *lac. supplevi*

III. Antiochus Theoidus ann. XV.
IIII. Seleucus Callinicus ann. XXI. 455
V. Seleucus Ceraunus ann. III.
VI. Antiochus Megaclus ann. XXXVI.
VII. Antiochus Filomitor ann. XII.
<VIII.> Antiochus Epifanius ann. XI. Iste est, qui in Iudeis iniquitatem inposuit, cuius historia in Maccabeis. 460
VIIII. Antiochus Eupator ann. II.
X. Dimitrius Soter ann. XII.
XI. Alexander Grypus ann. X.
XII. Dimitrius Grypus ann. III.
XIII. Antiochus Situs ann. VIIII. 465
XIIII. Dimitrius iuuenis ann. IIII.
XV. Antiochus ille Grypi ann. XII.
XVI. Antiochus Cizicinus ann. XVIII.
XVII. Filippus II.

4. Sub Filippo nouissimo Syriorum regnum dissipatum est. Macedo- 470
norum principatum uenit in Romanos, Gaio Iulio Romanorum
Caesare migrans eam. Et permanens per annos CCXXI et Siriorum
principatum dissipatum est.

15,1. Egyptiorum regna et tempora. Egypti autem reges, qui et
Ptolemei nuncupati sunt, regnauerunt post Alexandri discessum annos 475
CCXCIIII sic.

2. I. Filippus Ptolemeus ann. VII.
II. Filadelfus Alexander ann. XII.
III. Lagous Ptolemeus ann. XX.
IIII. Eu[g]ergetus Ptolemeus ann. XXXVIII. 480
V. Filopator Ptolemeus ann. XVII.
VI. Epifanius Ptolemeus ann. XXIIII.
VII. Filomitor Ptolemeus ann. XXXV.
VIII. Eu[g]ergetus Fauscus Ptol. ann. XXVIIII.
VIIII. Soter Ptolemeus ann. XXXVI. 485
X. Filadelfus Soter Ptol. ann. XXV.
XI. Nouus Dionysus Ptol. ann. XXVIIII.
XII. Cleopatra ann. XXII.

3. Dissipatum est Ptolemeorum principatum sub Octauiano A<u>gusto
Romanorum imperatorem, sub imperium eius anno XIIII, perma- 490
nens annos CCXCIIII.

14,3. 459 VIII *inserui: om.* E' **15,2.** 480 Euergetus *correxi ut supra*
VI,6,8.9.13: Eugergetus E' ‖ 482 ann. XXIIII *em.* Frick: XIXIIII E' ‖
484 Euergetus *iterum emendavi*: Eugergetus E' ‖ 488 ann. XXII *em.* Frick:
XII E' **15,3.** 489 Augusto: Agusto E'

16,1.   I. Primus factus est princeps sacerdotum Hiesus filius Iosedec simul Zorobabel.

 II. Post hunc Iacimus filius Hiesu.

 III. Post hunc Eliasibus filius Iacimi.   495

 IIII. Post hunc Iodae filius Eliasibi.

 V. Post hunc Ionathes filius Iodae.

2.   VI. Post hunc Iaddus filius Ionathes. Quo tempore Alexander Macedo et conditor Alexandriam condidit. Et ueniens in Hierusalem domino deo adorauit dicens: 'Gloria tibi, deus, qui uiuis in secula, 500 solus princeps'.

 VII. Post hunc Onias filius Iaddi.

3.   VIII. Post hunc Eleazarus filius Oniae. Quo tempore illi septuaginta Ebreorum sapientes in Alexandria legem interpretauerunt Greco eloquio.   505

 VIIII. Post hunc Onias filius Simoni frater Eleazari.

4.   X. Post hunc Simon filius Iaddi. Quo tempore Hiesus filius Sirach, qui et magnam Ebreis scripsit sapientiam, agnoscebatur.

5.   XI. Post hunc Onias filius Simoni. Quo tempore Antiochus Syrorum rex Iudeos expugnans Greca loquutione coegebat. 510

 XII. Post hunc Iudas Maccabeus filius Oniae.

 XIII. Post hunc Ionathas frater Iudae.

 XIIII. Post hunc Simon frater Ionathae.

 XV. Post hunc Iohannis filius Ionathae, qui dicebatur Yrcanus.

6.   XVI. Post hunc Aristobolus filius Iohannis. Qui primus inposuit 515 deadema regni principatum sacerdotii.

 XVII. Post hunc Ianneus qui et Alexander, rex simul et princeps sacerdotum.

7. Usque ad istum illi qui a Cyro uncti praefuerunt permanentes per annos quadrin\<gen\>tos LXXXIII, quae sunt ebdomadas annorum 520 LXVIIII, quae et a Danihele quemadmodum diffinierunt (g).

8. Usque ad Ianneum autem quem et Alexandrum principem sacerdotum et regem, in quo finierunt, qui secundum ritum principes sacerdotum uncti nominabantur.

9. XVIII. Post hos regnauit Salina[i] \<quae\> et Alexandra uxor eius. 525

10. XVIIII. Post hanc tumultum inter se eius pueri facientes Pompiius Romanorum archistratigus expugnauit Hierusalem tenens usque ad

---

16,1–6. 492–518 Eus., D. E. VIII, 2,62–79

g) Dan. 9,24–26

16,1. 497 Ionathes *scripsi*: Iohannes E' **16,2.** 498 Ionathes *scripsi*: Iohanni E' **16,7.** 520 quadringentos *correxi*: quadrintis E' **16,8.** 522 Usque ad Ianneum *scripsi*: post Ianneum E' **16,9.** 525 Salina quae et Alexandra: Salinai et Alexandra E' **16,10.** 526 hanc *scripsi*: hunc E'

progressionem templi apertionis. Tunc gens illa Iudeorum tributaria
facta est Romanis. Principatum quidem sacerdotii Yrcano tradidit,
Antipatrum autem Ascalona Palestine procuratorem faciens.   530
11. Quo tempore Romanorum primus monarchus Gaius Iulius Caesar.
Regnauit autem annos XVIII. Post hunc Augustus regnauit annos
LVI et qui post eos sequentens.

17,1. Tempora regni Romanorum. Romanorum autem regnauit monarchus primus Gaius Iulius Caesar in olympiada centesima octuage-   535
sima tertia. Iste est Gaius Iulius Caesar, qui bissextum et solis cursum
adinuenit.
2. Post istum regnauit Octauianus qui et Augustus et qui sequuntur
sic.   Consules.

    I. Augustus regnauit ann. LVI. Dedit consulatus XIII.   540
    II. Tiberius regnauit ann. XXIII. Consules V.
    III. Gaius regnauit ann. IIII. Consules IIII.
    IIII. Claudius regnauit ann. XV. Consulus V.
    V. Nero regnauit ann. XIIII. Consules IIII.
    Galbas, Otho, Bitellio ann. I et dimidium.   545
    VI. Titus regnauit ann. III. Consules VIII.
    VII. Dometianus regnauit ann. XVI. Consules VII.
    VIII. Nerua regnauit ann. II. Consules IIII.
    VIIII. Traianus regnauit ann. XX. Consules VI.
    X. Hadrianus regnauit ann. XII. Consules III.   550
    XI. Antoninus regnauit ann. XIII. Consules IIII.
    XII. Marcus Byrrus regnauit ann. XX. Consules XXIIII.
    XIII. Commodus regnauit an. XIII. Consules VII.
    XIIII. Vespasianus regnauit ann. VIIII. Consules X.
    XV. Pertinax, Didius ann. <***>. Consules IIII.   555
    XVI. Seuerus regnauit menses III. Consules <***>.
    XVII. Gitas, Caracallus regnauit ann. <***>. Consules XXV.
    XVIII. Macrinus, Iliogabalus regnauit ann. V. Consulem I.
    XVIIII. Alexander Mameas regnauit ann. XIII. Consules III.
    Maximus regnauit ann. III. Consules II.   560
    XX. Balbinus et Publianus et Cordus annum I.
    XXI. Gordianus regnauit ann. VI. Consules II.
    XXII. Filippus regnauit ann. VI. Consules III.
    XXIII. Decius regnauit annos II. Consulem I.
    XXIIII. Gallus et Volusianus, hii duo regnauerunt ann. III.   565
    Dederunt consulatos VII.

17,2. 542 Gaius regnauit ann. IIII *emendavi*: X E' || 545 Otho: Stultus
E' || 555–557 *numeri desunt in codice* || 563 XXII *em.* Frick: XXI E' ||

VIII

1,1. Ecce quidem manifestauimus ueraciter omnium potestatem regum.
Volumus praecurrere quod ad Romanorum pertinet imperium.
2. Usque Cleopatra enim facta est omnis Egyptiorum Ptolemeorum

---

572 XXVIII *em.* Frick: XVIII E' ‖ 590 Valentinianus: Valentinus E' ‖
595–596 *Zenonis et Anastasii annorum numeri in codice desunt*

1,1. 2 quod *em.* Frick: qud E'

potestas permanens annos CCXCIIII, et post Cleopatra ultra non regnauerunt in Egypto usque in hodiernum diem. 5

3. In diebus, quibus regnauerunt Ptolomei in Egypto, et fecerunt Romani proelium cum Spanis, et superauerunt Romani Spanos et leuauerunt imperatorem Iulium quem et Cesarem uocauerunt. Iste est Gaius Iulius Cesar, qui et bissextum et solis cursum adinuenit. Hic et consolatum unumquemque annum fieri constituit. 10

2,1. Regnauit autem Gaius Iulius Caesar annos XVIII, et post hunc Octauianus qui et Augustus.

2. I. Gaio Iulio Caesare primo, Marco clarissimo.

II. Gratiano et Antonino clarissimorum.

III. Gaio Iulio Caesare secundo et Flauio Marco clarissimo. 15

Irtio et Pansa uirorum inlustrium.

Bruto et Collatino clarissimorum.

Gaio Iulio Caesare tertio et Lepido inlustrium.

Munatio [et] Planco <et ***> inlustrium.

Aemilio et Caesare inlustrium. 20

Antonio et Seruilio clarissimorum.

Isaurico et Crispo clarissimorum.

Octauiano et Pollione clarissimorum.

Censorino et Sabino clarissimorum.

Pulchro et Norbano clarissimorum. 25

Gallo et Agrippa clarissimorum.

Octauiano et <Cocceio> Neru<a> [filio] clarissimorum.

Pompeio et Cornificio clarissimorum.

Libone et Antonio clarissimorum.

Cicerone et Publicola inlustrium. 30

3. Hisdem consulibus Iulius Caesar occisus est. Et sumpsit imperium Octauianus qui et Augustus ann. LVI, et dedit consulatos XIII. Fiunt uero ab Adam usque initium imperii Augusti anni V milia CCCCLXVII.

1,3. 9 Gaius *em.* Frick: cuius E'; *nomina consulum et imperatorum saepe in codice parisino depravata quantum potui emendavi* **2,2.** 13 primo: secundo E' || 15 Marco clarissimo *ex primo consulatu iteratum perperam exp.* Frick *in editione, sed postea* (p. 634) *restituit* || 16 Irtio et Pansa: Iurto et Paneo || 17 Bruto et Collatino: Burto et Cortilano || 19 Munatio Planco et *scripsi et lac. ante* inlustrium *signavi*: Munatio et Plachano E'; *unum eundemque consulem Barbarus perperam reduplicavit* || 20 Aemilio et Caesare: Emelio et Caesario || 21 Antonio et Seruilio: Antonino et Seruiliano || 22 Isaurico: Chryssaorico || 23 Octauiano et Pollione: Octauio et Polione || 24 Censorino et Sabino: Consorio et Sauino || 25 Pulchro et Norbano: Pulco et Enobaudo || 26 Agrippa: Agrippino || 27 Cocceio Nerua *scripsi*: Neru filio E'; *Barbarum legisse* υἱοῦ *pro* κοκίου *recte susp.* Frick || 28 Pompeio et Cornificio: Pompiio et Cornilio || 29 Libone et Antonio: Libono et Antonino || 30 Publicola: Publicollatonem

3,1.   I. Augusto primo et Tollio.

       II. Augusto secundo et Sosio.

      III. Augusto tertio et Crasso.

     IIII. Augusto quarto et Messala.

       V. Aenobarbo quinto et Scipione.

      VI. Augusto sexto et Apuleio.

2.   VII. Augusto septimo et Agrippa.

Hisdem consulibus Chartagina renouata est idos Iulias, Epifi XVIII.

     VIII. Augusto octauo et Silano.

   VIIII. Augusto nono et Tauro.

       X. Augusto decimo et Silano.

3.   XI. Augusto undecimo et Pisone.

In his temporibus, sub consulato Lentuli et Siluani, uidit Zacharias uisionem angeli in templo domini.

      XII. Aruntio et Marcellio.

    XIII. Celso et Tiberio.

    XIIII. Lollio et Aemilio.

     XV. Apuleio et Silio.

    XVI. Saturnino et Cinno.

4. <XVII.> Lentulo et Siluano.

In his temporibus adnuntiauit Elisabeth angelus de Iohanne, in eodem consulatum Lentuli et Siluani, VIII kl. Aprilis.

    XVIII. Sabino et Antonio.

  XVIIII. Lentulo secundo et Lepido.

     XX. Furnio ·et Pisone.

    XXI. Messala et Quirino.

   XXII. Maximo et Tuberone.

  XXIII. Africano et Maximo.

   XXV. Aruntio et Crispino.

  XXVI. Censorino et Gallo.

 XXVII. Nerone et Placido.

5. XXVIII. Balbo et Vetere.

Eodem tempor[a]e missus est angelus Gabrihel ad Mariam uirginem, sub Augusto tertio decimo, octauarum kalendarum Aprilium.

3,1. 35 Sosio: Socio || 37 Messala: Messalo || 38 Aenobarbo: Thenebaudo || 39 Apuleio: Apulia

3,2. 40 Agrippa *em.* Frick: Agrppa E' || 42 Silano: Siluano || 44 Silano: Sullio   **3,3.** 50 Lollio et Aemilio: Tullio etemellio E' Tullio et Emellio *prop.* Frick || 51 Apuleio et Silio: Asperio et Seuerio   **3,4.** 53 XVII *inserui*: *om.* E' || 56 Sabino et Antonio: Sauino et Antonino || 58 Furnio: Rufino || 59 Messala et Quirino: Mesallo et Seriniano || 62 XXIV *om.* E' || Crispino: Prisco || 63 Gallo: Gallione || 64 Nerone: Neronte   **3,5.** 65 Balbo et Vetere: Balbino et Bereto || 66 tempore *emendavi*: temporae E'

XXVIIII. Felecio et Silla.

    XXX. Lentulo et Augure.

    XXXI. Caesare et Austorino.   70

6.   XXXII. Siluano et Paulo.

In sexto autem mense Μαρία ἀπῄει πρὸς τὴν συγγενίδα αὐτῆς Ἐλισάβεδ καὶ ἔκρουσεν πρὸς τὴν θύραν. Καὶ ἀκούσασα ἡ Ἐλισάβεδ ἔρριψεν τὸ
κόκκινον καὶ ἔδραμεν πρὸς τὴν θύραν καὶ ἤνοιξεν αὐτῇ καὶ εὐλόγησεν
αὐτὴν καὶ εἶπεν· Ἐπόθεν μοι τοῦτο ἵνα ἡ μήτηρ τοῦ Κυρίου μου ἔλθῃ πρὸς   75
ἐμέ; Ἰδοὺ γὰρ τὸ ἐν ἐμοὶ ἐσκίρτησεν καὶ εὐλόγησέν σε.᾽

    XXXIII. Prisco et Romano.

    XXXIIII. Iuctore et Protarcho.

    XXXV. Senecione et Bardone.

    XXXVI. Timageno et Nigriano.   80

    XXXVII. Syriano et Peregrino.

7. XXXVIII. Xifidio et Marcello.

In his temporibus, sub Augusto, natus est Iohannis praecursor,
Zachariae filius, VIII kl. Iulias.

    XXXVIIII. Fruro et Autorino.   85

    XL. Augusto et Sacerdo.

    XLI. Pompiiano et Plutone.

    XLII. Augusto et Siluano.

    XLIII. Antulo et Iulio.

8.   XLIIII. Augusto et Silano.   90

Hisdem consulibus dominus noster Iesus Christus natus est, sub
Augusto, VIII kl. Ianuar.: in deserto natus est <in spelunca> cuius-
dam nomine Fuusdu, quod est Eusebii. In ipsa enim die, in qua
natus est, pastores uiderunt stellam, Chuac XXVIII<I>.

Fiunt uero ab Adam usque ad natiuitatem domini nostri Iesu   95
Christi anni V milia quingenti.

9.   XLV. Vinicio et Vero.

    XLVI. Caesare et Seruilio.

    XLVII. Macrino et Saturnino.

    XLVIII. Sacerdo et Voleso.   100

3,6. 72–76 Protev. Iac. 12,2, p. 118 de Strycker   **3,8.** 92 verba ἔρημος
et σπήλαιον leguntur in Protev. Iac. 17,3–18,1, p. 146 de Strycker

---

|| 68 Silla: Suilio || 69 Augure: Auxonio || 70 Caesare: Caesario || 71
Paulo: Paulino   **3,6.** 73–74 *verba* καὶ ἔκρουσεν—καὶ ἤνοιξεν αὐτῇ *om.* E᾽
|| 76 *post* ἐσκίρτησεν *add.* infans E᾽   **3,8** 90 Silano: Siluano || 91 Iesus
Christus *scripsit* Frick: ihs XPS E᾽ || 92 in spelunca *conieci* || 93 Fuusdu *in*
Protev. Iac. *non legitur* || 94 XXVIIII *restitui*: XXVIII E᾽ || 95–96 Iesu
Christi *scripsit* Frick: ihu XPI E᾽   **3,9.** 97 Vinicio et Vero: Bincio et
Birro || 98 Caesare et Seruilio: Caesario et Serbilio || 100 Voleso: Bolenso

10.   XLVIIII. Lepido et Arruntio.

In his diebus, sub Augusto, kalendas Ianuarias, Magi obtulerunt ei munera et adorauerunt eum. Magi autem uocabantur Balthasar, Melchior, Gathaspa.

11.   Καὶ ἀκούσας ὁ Ἡρώδης a Magis, quoniam rex natus esset, ἐταράχθη,   105
et omnes Hierusolima cum eo. Τότε Ἡρώδης ἰδὼν ὅτι ἐνεπαίχθη ὑπὸ τῶν μάγων ὀργισθεὶς ἔπεμψεν αὐτοῦ τοὺς φονευτὰς λέγων αὐτοῖς ἀνελεῖν πάντα τὰ βρέφη ἀπὸ διετίας καὶ κάτω.

12.   Ὁ δὲ Ἡρώδης ἐζήτει τὸν Ἰωάννην, καὶ ἀπέστειλεν ὑπηρέτας ἐν τῷ θυσιαστηρίῳ πρὸς Ζαχαρίαν λέγων αὐτῷ· 'Ποῦ ἀπέκρυψας τὸν υἱόν σου;   110
Οἶδας ὅτι τὸ αἷμά σου ὑπὸ τὴν χεῖράν μού ἐστιν;' Καὶ ἀποκριθεὶς εἶπεν· 'Μάρτυς εἰμὶ τοῦ Θεοῦ. Ἔχε μου τὸ αἷμα. Τὸ δὲ πνεῦμά μου ὁ Δεσπότης δέξεται.' Καὶ περὶ τὸ διάφαυμα ἐφονεύθη Ζαχαρίας.

13.   L. Critico et Nerua.

    LI. Camerino et Birillo.   115

    LII. Dolabella et Silano.

14.   LIII. Cyntilliano et Barbilio.

Ἡ δὲ Ἐλισάβεδ ἀκούσασα ὅτι Ἰωάννης ζητεῖται, λαβομένη αὐτὸν ἀνέβη ἐν τῇ ὀρεινῇ· καὶ περιεβλέπετο ποῦ αὐτὸν ἀποκρύψῃ, καὶ οὐκ ἔνι τόπος ἀπόκρυφος. Τότε στενάξασα Ἐλισάβεδ λέγει· ''Ορος Θεοῦ, δέξαι με μητέρα   120
μετὰ τέκνου.' Οὐ γὰρ ἐδύνατο ἡ Ἐλισάβεδ ἀναβῆναι διὰ τὴν δειλίαν. Καὶ παραχρῆμα ἐδιχάσθη τὸ ὄρος καὶ ἐδέξατο αὐτήν.

    LIIII. Germanico et Capitone.

    LV. Austorio et Silano.

    LVI. Planco et Apuleio.   125

15.   LVII. Pompeio et Flacco.

His consulibus Augustus obiit. Et regnauit Tiberius ann. XXII. Dedit consulatus VII.

3,11. 105 Protev. Iac. 21,2, p. 168 de Strycker: Καὶ ἀκούσας ὁ Ἡρώδης ἐταράχθη; 106–108 Protev. Iac. 22,1, p. 174 de Strycker: Τότε Ἡρώδης ἰδὼν—καὶ κάτω.   **3,12.** 109–110 Protev. Iac. 23,1, pp. 176–178 de Strycker: Ὁ δὲ Ἡρώδης—τὸν υἱόν σου; 111 Protev. Iac. 23,2, p. 180 de Strycker: Οἶδας ὅτι τὸ αἷμά σου ὑπὸ τὴν χεῖράν μού ἐστιν; 111–113 Protev. Iac. 23,3, p. 180 de Strycker: Καὶ ἀποκριθεὶς εἶπεν (Zaxarias E')· Μάρτυς εἰμὶ τοῦ Θεοῦ (uiuentis E'). Ἔχε μου τὸ αἷμα. Τὸ δὲ πνεῦμά μου ὁ Δεσπότης δέξεται; 113 Protev. Iac. 23,3, p. 182 de Strycker: Καὶ περὶ τὸ διάφαυμα ἐφονεύθη Ζαχαρίας   **3,14.** 118–122 Protev. Iac. 22,3, pp. 174–176 de Strycker

3,10. 103 Balthasar: Bithisarea ‖ 104 Melchior: Melichior ‖ *Magorum nomina om* Protev. Iac. ‖ 107 ὀργισθεὶς *om.* E'   **3,13.** 116 Dolabella et Silano: Dolomallo et Sofiano ‖ 121 *verba* Οὐ γὰρ ἐδύνατο ἡ Ἐλισάβεδ ἀναβῆναι διὰ τὴν δειλίαν *om.* E' ‖ 122 αὐτήν: eos E' ‖ 123 Capitone: Carpo ‖ 124 Silano: Siluano ‖ 125 Planco et Apuleio: Plachno et Auito   **3,15.** 126 Pompeio: Pompiiano

LVIII. Tiberio Augusto et Germanico.

LVIIII. Flacco et Rufo.   130

16. LX. Druso et Norbano.

In his diebus ἐπένθησαν Ζαχαρίαν καὶ ἐκόψαντο αὐτὸν τρεῖς ἡμέρας καὶ τρεῖς νύκτας. Et suscitauit eis dominus deus in loco Zachariae Symeonem.

17. Οὗτος γὰρ ἦν ὁ χρηματισθεὶς ὑπὸ τοῦ ἁγίου Πνεύματος μὴ ἰδεῖν θάνα-   135 τον ἕως ἂν τὸν Χριστὸν ἐν σαρκὶ ἴδῃ. Et uidens eum dixit: 'Nunc dimittis seruum tuum, domine, in pace, quia uiderunt oculi mei salutare[m] tuum, quod parasti ante faciem omnium populorum, lumen ad reuelationem gentium et gloria plebis tuae Israhel' (h).

LXI. Tauro et Libone.   140

LXII. Silano et Gerontio.

LXIII. Messala et Balbo.

LXIV. Tiberio Aug. secundo et Cotta.

18. LXV. Agrippa et Druso.

Tunc responsum accepit Ioseph, et accipiens Iesum et Mariam fugiit   145 in Egyptum et fuit ibi menses XII, de quo nunc sileam.

LXVI. Nerone et Lentulo.

LXVII. Cethego et Pisone.

LXVIII. Getulico et Varrone.

19. Et ueniens Iesus faciebat mirabilia sub consulato Asiatici et Silani,   150 in quibus et aqua uinum fecit VI kl. Nou.

Crasso Tiberio.

Seriniano Secundo.

20. Baptizatus est autem ab Iohanne sub consolato Meura, VIII kl. Ianuarias.   155

LXVIIII. Tiberio quarto et Antonino.

21. Transfiguratus est autem in monte sub consolato Rubellionis,

---

3,16. 132–133 Protev. Iac. 24,3.4, pp. 186–188 de Strycker   **3,17.** 135–136 Protev. Iac. 24,4, p. 188 de Strycker

---

h) Lc. 2,29–32

---

129 Germanico: Germano ‖ 130 Flacco et Rufo: Flaubio et Rufino   **3,16.** 131 Druso et Norbano: Drusollo et Sorano ‖ 132 Ζαχαρίαν *ego*: Zachariam E' αὐτὸν de Strycker **3,17.** 135 ὑπὸ τοῦ ἁγίου Πνεύματος: ab angelo E' ‖ 137 salutare *legendum*: salutarem E' ‖ 141 Silano: Siluano ‖ 142 Messala et Balbo: Mesaulico et Balbino ‖ 143 Cotta: Colta   **3,18.** 147 LXVI *em.* Frick: LVI E' ‖ 148 LXVII *em.* Frick: LVII E' ‖ Cethego: Celetho ‖ 149 LXVIII *em.* Frick: LVIII E' ‖ Getulico et Varrone: Getulo et Barro **3,19.** 150 Silani: Siluani

XIIII kalendas Aprelis. Quando autem mysterium agebat cum dis-
cipulis suis, sub consolato Rubellionis, VIIII kal. Aprilis.

LXX. Tiberio quinto et Prisco.   160

22. LXXI. Vinicio et Arruntio.

Eodem tempore natalicium factum est Herodis. Saltauit filia Herodiadis
in medio et petiit capud Iohannis. Et adductum est capud Iohannis
in disco VI kl. Iunias, Pauni II.

23. Traditus est autem dominus noster Iesus Christus a Iuda sub   165
consolato Rubellionis, VIII kl. Aprilis.

24. Videns autem hostiaria Petrum agnouit eum et ait illi: Vere et
tu ex illis es, nam et loquilla tua manifestum te fecit. Et ille negauit
dicens: Non sum. Et confestim gallus cantauit. Nomen autem hos-
tiariae Ballia dicebatur, quod interpraetatur querens.   170

25. LXXII. Tiberio Augusto sexto et Silio.

Eodem anno dominus noster Iesus Christus crucifixus est sub consolato Rubellionis, VIII kl. Aprilis, quod est Famenoth XXVIIII.
Miles autem <crucem custodiens> uocabatur Hieremias, id est Adlas
[crucem custodiens]. Centurio uocabatur Apronianus [alius].   175

26. Illi autem duo angeli qui in sepulchro uocabantur unus Azahel,
quod est iustus deo, alius autem Caldu, quod est fortis. Iudas autem
abiens suspendit se in arbore nomine tramarice.

27. Surrexit autem dominus noster Iesus Christus sub consolato
Rubellionis, VI kl. Aprilis. Ascendit autem dominus noster III no.   180
Maias. Missus est autem Spiritus Sanctus idos Maias. Paulus autem
apostolus post ascensionem domini et post passionem Stephani dierum
in apostulatum ordinatur VI<III> idos Ianuarias, sub consolato Rubellionis, post ascensionem Saluatoris nostri menses VIII, post dies
XI passionis Stephani, pridie Epiphaniae.   185

LXXII. Sulpicio et Sulla.

LXXIII. Persico et Vitellio.

28. LXXIIII. Tiberio A<u>gusto et Druso.

Hisdem consulibus Tiberius obiit. Et regnauit pro eo Gaius ille Gallus
annos IIII. Dedit consulatos IIII.   190

LXXV. Gaio Gallo A<u>gusto tertio et Sulla.

LXXVI. Gaio A<u>gusto quarto et Asprenate.

LXXVII. Venusto et Saturnino.

3,22. 161 Vinicio: Bicino   **3,25.** 171 LXXII *em.* Frick: XXII E' || 174
Miles *scripsi*: Milex E' || crucem custodiens *post* autem *transposui* || 175 alius
dissographia antecedentis -anus *ortum recte secl.* Frick   **3,27.** 183 VIIII *requiri-*
tur. VI E' || 186 LXXII: *sic legitur* || Sulpicio et Sulla: Sipio et Sulano ||
187 Vitellio: Bitellio   **3,28.** 188–192 Augusto *ter emendaui*: Agusto E' ||
192 Asprenate: Apollione

29. Scurdo et Clemente.

His consulibus Gaius Gallus obiit. Et regnauit pro eo Claudius ann.   195
<X>IIII. Dedit consulatos V.

  LXXVIII. Claudio et Tauro.

  LXXVIIII. Crispo et Coruino.

   LXXX. Asiatico et Sil[u]ano.

  LXXXI. Vinicio et Vitellio.   200

  LXXXII. Claudio secundo et Publicola.

  LXXXIII. Vitellio et Gallo.

  LXXXIIII. Cla<u>dio tertio et Antonino.

  LXXXV. Vetere et Suilio.

  LXXXVI. Cla<u>dio quarto et Orfito.   205

  LXXXVII. Sil[u]ano et Crispo.

  LXXXVIII. Marcello et Aviola.

  LXXXVIIII. Nerone filio Claudii et Vetere.

   XC. Claudio Augusto quinto et Vetere.

30. XCI. Saturnino et Scipione.   210

Hisdem consulibus Claudius obiit. Et imperium sumpsit filius eius
Nero annos <X>IIII. Dedit consulatos XIIII.

  XCII. Nerone Augusto secundo et Rufo.

  XCIII. Saturnino et Publio.

31. XCIIII. Nerone Aug<us>to tertio et Pisone.   215

Hisdem consulibus passus est beatus Petrus apostolus, crucifixus in
Roma capite deorsum, sub Nerone, similiter et Sanctus Paulus apostolus capite truncatus. Martyrizauerunt III kl. Iulias, quod est Epifi V.

  XCV. Mario et Gallo.

  XCVI. Nerone et Cornelio.   220

  XCVII. Rigolo et Basso.

  XCVIII. Silano et Crispo.

  XCVIIII. Telesino et Salustio.

   C. Capitone et Flauio.

3,29. 194 *numerum ante consules* Scurdo et Clemente *om.* E' || 196 XIIII
requiritur. IIII E' || 198 Crispo et Coruino: Crispino et Cornilio || 199
Silano: Siluano || 200 Vinicio et Vitellio: Bincomallo et Bereto || 201
Publicola: Publio || 202 Vitellio et Gallo: Bitellio et Gallione || 203 Claudio:
Cladio || 204 Vetere et Suilio: Bereto et Siluio || 205 Claudio: Cladio ||
206 Silano et Crispo: Siluano et Crispino || 207 Marcello et Aviola:
Marcellino et Agiolao || 208 Nerone filio Claudii et Vetere: Nerone filio
Claudio et Bereto || 209 XC *em.* Frick: CX E' || Vetere: Nerua   **3,30.**
210 XCI *em.* Frick: CXI E' || 212 Nero annos XIIII *requiritur.* IIII E' ||
213 XCII *em.* Frick: CXII E' || 214 XCIII *em.* Frick: CXIII E' || Publio:
Puplio   **3,31.** 215 Augusto *corr.* Frick: augto E' || Pisone: Posone || 219
Mario et Gallo: Marcellino et Galliano || 220 Cornelio: Cornifilo || 221
Basso: Bassiano || 222 Silano et Crispo: Siluano et Crispino || 223 Telesino:
Celestino

CI. Romillo et Lucio.   225

CII. Secundo et Maronio.

CIII. Longino et Apulio.

32.   CIIII. Iulio et Paulino.

Hisdem consulibus Nero de imperio labefactus est. Et imperium eius
Galba suscepit menses IIII et occisus est. Et regnauit Otho menses   230
VII et occisus est. Et regnauit Bitelleo menses V et occisus est. Et
imperium sumpsit Vespasianus annos X. Dedit consulatos VIIII.

33. Post consulatum Galbe Italico.

CV. Vespasiano Augusto et Tito filio eius Caesare primo.

CVI. Vespasiano Augusto secundo et Tito Caesare.   235

CVII. Vespasiano tertio et Tito Caesare.

34. CVIII. Vespasiano quarto et Tito quinto.

Hisdem consulibus uicti sunt Iudei sub Vespasiano et Tito impe-
ratoribus et Iudea depopulata est.

CVIIII. Vespasiano et Tito sexto.   240

CX. Vespasiano septimo et Nerua.

CXI. Vespasiano octauo et Commodo.

35.   CXII. Vespasiano nono et Tito.

Hisdem consulibus Vespasianus obiit. Et imperium Titus inuasit annos
II. Dedit consulatos II.   245

CXIII. Tito Augusto octauo et Vero.

36. CXIV. Siluano et Commodo.

Hisdem consulibus Titus obiit. Et imperium eius sumpsit Dometianus
annos <XV>. Dedit consulatos VIIII.

CXV. Dometiano Augusto primo et Messalino et Rufo.   250

CXVI. Dometiano secundo et Sabino.

CXVII. Dometiano tertio et Aurelio.

CXVIII. Dometiano quarto et Dolabella.

CXVIIII. Dometiano quinto et Atratino.

CXX. Fuluio et Crispo inlustrium.   255

CXXI. Glabrione et Nerua.

CXXII. Dometiano sexto et Saturnino.

CXXIII. Dometiano septimo et Nigriano.

CXXIV. Asprenate et Papisco.

CXXV. Senatore et Longino.   260

3,33. 236 CVII *em.* Frick: CVIII E'   **3,34.** 237 CVIII *em.* Frick: CVI-
III E' || 242 Commodo: Commoda   **3,35.** 244 Vespasianus *em.* Frick:
Vespasia E' || 246 Vero: Birro   **3,36.** 249 XV *inserui: om.* E' || 251
Sabino: Sabiniano || 252 Aurelio: Cerilao || 253 Dolabella: Dolomallo ||
254 Atratino: Sauino || 255 Fuluio: Flauio || 257 Dometiano sexto et Saturnino
emendaui: Dometione sexto et Rufino E' || 259 Asprenate: Asperiato || 260
Senatore: Sinatore

CXXVI. Modesto et Bustro.
CXXVII. Dometiano et Priscino.
CXXVIII. Senecione et Palma.
CXXVIIII. Crispo et Sorano <***>.

IX

1,1. XII. Dioclitiano Augusto quinto et Maximi<a>no Caesare secundo.
XIII. Maximi<a>no Caesare quinto et Maximi<a>no Caesare quinto.
   Fausto et Titiano clarissimorum.
   Constanti[n]o et Maximiano clarissimorum.
   Dioclitiano et Maximiano clarissimorum.   5
   Titiano et Nepotiano clarissimorum.
2. Constanti[n]o et Maxim<ian>o nouorum Caesarum quarto.
Hisdem consulibus uenit Dioclitianus in Alexandria et ecclesias exter-
minauit. Et multi martyrizauerunt, in quibus et beatus Petrus episcopus
Alexandrinus capite truncatus est. Martyrizauit VII kl. Decem. In   10
eodem anno castrisius in Alexandria donatus est et Dioclitiano bal-
neum edificatum est.
   Dioclitiano et Maxim<ian>o nobilium Augustorum septimo.
3. Dioclitiano et Maxim<ian>o octauo.
Hisdem consulibus persecutio Christianorum facta est in occiduum.   15
Et multi martyrizauerunt, in quibus et Timotheus episcopus in
Chartagine gloriose martyrizauit.
   Dioclitiano nono et Constantio quinto nobilium Augustorum.
   Dioclitiano decimo et Maximiano octauo inuictissimorum.
4. Constanti[n]o Caesare et Maximiano nobili quinto.   20
Hisdem consulibus Dioclitianus a regno recessit, et Constantius abiens
sedit in Bizantio.
   Licinio et Constantino primo, nouorum Augustorum.

2,1. Licinio et Constanti<n>o secundo.
Hisdem consulibus filius Dioclitiani Maxim<ian>us obiit. Et imperium   25
tenuit Constantius cum filios suos.
   Constantino et Constantio clarissimorum.
   Rufino et Sabino clarissimorum.

---

262 Priscino: Prisco || 263 Senecione et Palma: Senetione et Palmato ||
264 *post* Sorano *desiderantur plurima iuxta adnotationem Scaligeri*

1,1. 1–2 Maximiano *ter emendavi*: Maximino E' || 4 Constantio: Constantino ||
1,2. 7 Constantio et Maximiano: Constantino et Maximo || 13 Maximiano:
Maximo   **1,3.** 14 Maximiano: Maximo || 17 Chartaginae gloriosae E'
1,4. 20 Constantio: Constantino   **2,1.** 24 Constantino: Constantio ||
25 Maximianus: Maximus || 28 Rufino et Sabino: Rufo et Sauino ||

Constanti<n>o Augusto quarto et Licinio Caesare tercio.

Volusiano et Anniano clarissimorum. 30

Gallic[i]ano et Basso clarissimorum.

2. Licinio et Crispo Caesaris.

Hisdem consulibus Constantius obiit. Et imperium obtinuit Constantinus cum quinque filios suos, <Constante> Constantio et Licinio et Crispo et Constantino, et condidit Constantinopolim. 35

Constantino Augusto quinto et Constanti<n>o nouo Caesare.

3. Constanti<n>o Augusto sexto et Licinio minimo primo.

Eodem anno manifestatum est honorabile lignum, crux domini et saluatoris nostri Iesu Christi, in Hierusolima per beatam Helenam imperatrissam et matrem Constantini, XVIII kl. Octobris, quod est 40 Thoth XVII.

Crispo et Constanti<n>o nobilissimos Caesares, filios Augusti, secundo.

Seuero et Rufino clarissimorum.

Crispo et Constanti<n>o secundo Caesare.

4. Probi<a>no et Iuliano clarissimorum. 45

Eodem anno congregata est synodus in Nicea tricentorum decem et octo episcoporum sub Alexandro archiepiscopo Alexandriae, in qua et symbolum sanctae trinitatis manifestatum est et Arrii ferrocitas atque haeresis diminuta est.

Constantino Augusto quarto et Constante Augusto tercio. 50

Constantino Augusto quinto et Constante secundo, inuictissimorum Augustorum.

5. Licinio et Crispo nouorum Caesarum.

Eodem anno in Alexandria episcopus Alexander obiit Farmuthi XXII, et successit ei in sacerdotio Athanasius annos XLVI. 55

Constanti<n>o Augusto sexto et Constantio sexto.

Crispo et Licinio secundo.

Constantino septimo et Constante tercio Augustorum.

Lolliano et Iusto clarissimorum.

Constantino magno octauo et Constantino quarto Augustorum. 60

Gallicano et Simmacho clarissimorum.

Basso et Ablabio clarissimorum.

Pacatiano et Hilariano clarissimorum.

---

29 Constantino: Constantio || 30 Anniano: Annania || 31 Gallicano: Galliciano **2,2.** 34 Constante *inserui* || 36 Constantino: Constantio **2,3.** 37 Constantino *emendavi*: Constantio || 40 XVIII kl. Octobris: VIII kl. Decembris E' || 42 *et* 44 Constantino: Constantio **2,4.** 45 Probiano: Probino **2,5.** 53 Crispo: Crispino || 56 Constantino: Constantio || sexto *pr.*: septimo || 57 Crispo: Crispinio || 60 Constantino quarto Augustorum *correxi et transposui*: Constante Augustorum quarto || 61 Gallicano: Galliano || 62 Ablabio: Albino

Dalmatio et Zenofilo clarissimorum.

Optato et Paulino clarissimorum.   65

Constanti[n]o nouo Augusto primo et Albino.

6. Nepotiano et Facundo clarissimorum.

Hisdem consulibus translati sunt in Constantinopolim Sanctus Andreas
apostolus et Lucas euangelista X<II> kl. Iulias.

Feliciano et Titiano clarissimorum.   70

Urso et Polemio clarissimorum.

Constantio Augusto secundo et Constante nouo Caesare primo.

Acindyno et Proclo clarissimorum.

Constantio tertio et Costante secundo Augustorum nobilium.

Marcellino et Probino clarissimorum.   75

Placido et Romulo clarissimorum.

Leontio et Salustio clarissimorum.

3,1. Amantio et Albino clarissimorum.

Eodem anno Constantinus maior imperator obiit, VI kl. Decembris.
Et susceperunt imperium V filii eius.   80

Constanti[n]o quarto et Constante tercio.

Constanti[n]o quinto et Constante quarto, inuictissimorum Augustorum.

Rufino et Eusebio clarissimorum.

Limenio et Catullino clarissimorum.   85

Sergio et Nigri<ni>ano clarissimorum.

2.   Constantio sexto et Constanti[n]o, nouorum Augustorum.

Hisdem consulibus Arriani inuaserunt ecclesias, et expulsus est beatus episcopus Alexandriae Athanasius.

Constantio septimo et Constanti[n]o nouo secundo Augustorum.   90

Arbitione et Iuliano clarissimorum.

Constantio octauo et Constanti[n]o tercio Augustorum.

Constantio nono et Lolliano.

Datiano et Cereale clarissimorum.

Constanti[n]o Augusto decimo et Iuliano Caesare secundo.   95

Eusebio et Ypatio clarissimorum.

3.   Constantio Augusto undecimo et Iuliano Caesare tercio.

Hisdem consulibus Constanti[n]us imperator obiit. Et regnauit pro eo
Iulianus annos V et dimidium. Eodem anno conpleti sunt X<I>

---

64 Dalmatio et Zenofilo: Dermatio et Zinofilo || 66 Constantio: Constantino
|| Albino: Sauino   **2,6.** 69 XII *emendaui* || 70 Titiano: Taciano || 76
Placido: Placidiano   **3,1.** 78 Albino: Sauiniano || 81–82 Constantio *bis
emendaui*: Constantino || 85 Catullino: Tolino || 86 Nigriniano: Nigriano
3,2. 87 *et* 90 Constantio: Constantino || 91 Arbitione: Arbethione || 92
Constantio: Constantino || 94 Cereale: Cerilao || 95 Constantio: Constantino
3,3. 98 Constantius: Constantinus || 99 anno: anni E' || XI *emendaui*: X
E' Frick

cycli saeculares, ab anno quingentesimo trecensimo secundo. Fiunt   100
uero ab Adam usque ad consulatum huius anni omnes anni V milia
octingenti LII[II].
4.   Iuliano Augusto quarto et Sallustio clarissimo.
Eo anno maris ascendit et iterum recessit, X kl. Augustas, Epifi
XXVII.   105

4,1. Varroniano et Iuliano et Iouiano clarissimorum.
Eodem anno Iulianus imperator obiit, VI kl. Maias. Et regnauit Iouia-
nus menses VII et occisus est. Et regnauerunt pro eo duo fratres Valen-
tinianus annos XI et dimidium, similiter et Valens frater eius annos XIII.
Dedit autem Valentinianus consulatos IIII et Valens consulatos VI.   110
    Valentiniano et Valente Augustorum.
    Tauro et Florentio clarissimorum.
    Valentiniano et Valente Augustorum.
    Gratiano filio Valentiniani Caesare et <Da>galaifo.
2.   Lupicino et Iouino clarissimorum.   115
Eo anno introiuit Tatianus in Alexandria primus Augustalius, VI kl.
Februarias.
    Valentiniano et Valente Augustorum tercio, sub Tatiano Augustalio.
    Valentiniano et Valente Augustorum quarto, sub eodem Tatiano
Augustalio.   120
3.   Gratiano secundo clarissimo, sub eodem Tatiano Augustalio.
Eo anno martyrizauit Macarius Dorotheus in Alexandria, VII idos
Octobris, quod est Faofi duodecimo. Ferarum esca traditus est sub
Tatiano praeside, pro quo tunc erant heretici.
    Modesto et Arintheo clarissimorum, sub Publio Augustalio.   125
4.   Valentiniano et Valente quinto, sub eodem Publio Augustalio.
Hisdem consulibus <S>armati omnem Pannoniam desolauerunt, et
eo anno Valentinianus in bello mortuus est, VII idos Octobris.
    Gratiano Augusto tertio et Equitio clarissimo, sub Tatiano praeside.
5.   Gratiano Augusto quarto et Merobaudo, sub eodem Tatiano   130
Augustalio secundo.
    Hic condidit in Alexandria fluuium, qui uocatur Tatianus, et
portas fecit auro perfusas, quae nunc dicuntur Petrinas.

---

101 huius *em.* Frick: hius E' || 102 LII *requiritur*: LIIII E'   **4,1.** 106
Varroniano: Barroniano || Iouiano: Iobiniano || 107–08 Iouianus: Iobinianus
|| 112 Tauro et Florentio: Paulo et Frorentio || 114 Dagalaifo *emendavi*:
Galaifo E'   **4,2.** 115 Lupicino et Iouino: Luppiciano et Iobino   **4,3.**
122 Macarius *conieci; cf. P.Lips.* I 100, col. IV 3, p. 296 Mitteis: beatus E'
4,4. 127 Sarmati *corr.* Kaufmann: armati E' || Pannoniam *corr.* Kaufmann:
Campaniam E'

6. Valentiniano Augusto quinto et Valente patruo eius Augustorum, sub eodem Tatiano Augustalio.

Eo anno Athanasius episcopus obiit in Alexandri<a>, Pachon VII, et sedit pro eo Petrus archipresbiter annos VII. 13.

Valentiniano nouo Augusto quinto et Merobaudo clarissimo, sub Palladio Augustalio.

7. Valente sexto et Valentiniano Augustorum, sub Tatiano Augustalio praesidae. 140

Hisdem consulibus Valens obiit. Et imperium obtinuerunt Gratianus et Valentinianus nouus.

Ausonio et Olybrio clarissimorum, sub Hadriano Augustalio.

Eusebio et Olybrio clarissimorum, sub Hadriano Augustalio.

Gratiano quarto et Dagalaifo clarissimorum. 14.

Lupicino et Eutropio clarissimorum.

8. Antonio et Eutropio clarissimorum, sub Paulino Augustalio.

Eo anno Petrus episcopus Alexandrinus obiit in Alexandria, <Mechir uicensimo,> et sedit pro eo Timotheus frater eius annos V [Mechir uicensimo]. 15.

9. Ausonio et Olybrio secundo clarissimorum, sub Bassiano praeside.

Eo anno Theodosius eleuatus est in imperio sub Gratiano imperatore, in Sirmio, XIIII kl. Februar.

Et regnauit annos XVI. Dedit consulatos III.

Gratiano quinto et Theodosio primo nobilium Augustorum, sub Ypatio Augustalio. 15.

10. Suagrio et Eucerio clarissimorum, sub Antonino Augustalio.

Eo anno occisus est Gratianus imperator sub Maximo tyranno in Leuduna, VIII kl. Septembris, et eodem anno coronatus est in imperio Arcadius in Constantinopolim, V idus Septembris. 16.

11. Richomero et Chlearco clarissimorum, sub eodem Antonino.

Eo anno Timotheus episcopus Alexandrinus obiit, Epifi XXVI, et sedit pro eo Theofilus archidiaconus annos XXVIII et illos sacrilegos exterminauit.

12. Arcadio Augusto filio Theodosii et Baudone clarissimo, sub Frorentio Augustalio. 16.

Eo anno natus est Honorius in Constantinopolim, V idus Sep.

Valentiniano Augusto III et Eutropio clarissimo.

4,6. 134 patruo *ego*: filio E' Frick ‖ 136 Alexandria *em.* Frick: Alexandri E'
4,7. 147 Lupicino: Luppiciano   **4,8.** 148 Antonio: Antonino ‖ 149–150
Mechir uicensimo *transp.* Frick   **4,11.** 162 Richomero: Richomedo

INDICES

(Numeri ad paginam et versum spectant)

INDEX LOCORUM SACRAE SCRIPTURAE

Vetus Testamentum

Novum Testamentum

INDEX FONTIUM IN TEXTU LAUDATORUM

SUPPLEMENTS TO VIGILIAE CHRISTIANAE

1. Tertullianus. *De idololatria*. Critical Text, Translation and Commentary by J.H. Waszink and J.C.M. van Winden. Partly based on a Manuscript left behind by P.G. van der Nat. 1987. ISBN 90 04 08105 4

2. Springer, C.P.E. *The Gospel as Epic in Late Antiquity*. The *Paschale Carmen* of Sedulius. 1988. ISBN 90 04 08691 9

3. Hoek, A. van den. *Clement of Alexandria and His Use of Philo in the* Stromateis. An Early Christian Reshaping of a Jewish Model. 1988. ISBN 90 04 08756 7

4. Neymeyr, U. *Die christlichen Lehrer im zweiten Jahrhundert*. Ihre Lehrtätigkeit, ihr Selbstverständnis und ihre Geschichte. 1989. ISBN 90 04 08773 7

5. Hellemo, G. *Adventus Domini*. Eschatological Thought in 4th-century Apses and Catecheses. 1989. ISBN 90 04 08836 9

6. Rufin von Aquileia. *De ieiunio* I, II. Zwei Predigten über das Fasten nach Basileios von Kaisareia. Ausgabe mit Einleitung, Übersetzung und Anmerkungen von H. Marti. 1989. ISBN 90 04 08897 0

7. Rouwhorst, G.A.M. *Les hymnes pascales d'Éphrem de Nisibe*. Analyse théologique et recherche sur l'évolution de la fête pascale chrétienne à Nisibe et à Édesse et dans quelques Églises voisines au quatrième siècle. 2 vols: I. Étude; II. Textes. 1989. ISBN 90 04 08839 3

8. Radice, R. and D.T. Runia. *Philo of Alexandria*. An Annotated Bibliography 1937–1986. In Collaboration with R.A. Bitter, N.G. Cohen, M. Mach, A.P. Runia, D. Satran and D.R. Schwartz. 1988. repr. 1992. ISBN 90 04 08986 1

9. Gordon, B. *The Economic Problem in Biblical and Patristic Thought*. 1989. ISBN 90 04 09048 7

10. Prosper of Aquitaine. *De Providentia Dei*. Text, Translation and Commentary by M. Marcovich. 1989. ISBN 90 04 09090 8

11. Jefford, C.N. *The Sayings of Jesus in the Teaching of the Twelve Apostles*. 1989. ISBN 90 04 09127 0

12. Drobner, H.R. and Klock, Ch. *Studien zu Gregor von Nyssa und der christlichen Spätantike*. 1990. ISBN 90 04 09222 6

13. Norris, F.W. *Faith Gives Fullness to Reasoning*. The Five Theological Orations of Gregory Nazianzen. Introduction and Commentary by F.W. Norris and Translation by Lionel Wickham and Frederick Williams. 1990. ISBN 90 04 09253 6

14. Oort, J. van. *Jerusalem and Babylon*. A Study into Augustine's *City of God* and the Sources of his Doctrine of the Two Cities. 1991. ISBN 90 04 09323 0

15. Lardet, P. *L'Apologie de Jérôme contre Rufin*. Un Commentaire. 1993. ISBN 90 04 09457 1

16. Risch, F.X. *Pseudo-Basilius: Adversus Eunomium IV-V*. Einleitung, Übersetzung und Kommentar. 1992. ISBN 90 04 09558 6

17. Klijn, A.F.J. *Jewish-Christian Gospel Tradition*. 1992. ISBN 90 04 09453 9
18. Elanskaya, A.I. *The Literary Coptic Manuscri pts in the A.S. Pushkin State Fine Arts Museum in Moscow*. ISBN 90 04 09528 4
19. Wickham, L.R. and Bammel, C.P. (eds.). *Christian Faith and Greek Philosophy in Late Antiquity*. Essays in Tribute to George Christopher Stead. 1993. ISBN 90 04 09605 1
20. Asterius von Kappadokien. *Die theologischen Fragmente*. Einleitung, kritischer Text, Übersetzung und Kommentar von Markus Vinzent. 1993. ISBN 90 04 09841 0
21. Hennings, R. *Der Briefwechsel zwischen Augustinus und Hieronymus und ihr Streit um den Kanon des Alten Testaments und die Auslegung von Gal. 2,11-14*. 1994. ISBN 90 04 09840 2
22. Boeft, J. den & Hilhorst, A. (eds.). *Early Christian Poetry*. A Collection of Essays. 1993. ISBN 90 04 09939 5
23. McGuckin, J.A. *St. Cyril of Alexandria: The Christological Controversy*. Its History, Theology, and Texts. 1994. ISBN 90 04 09990 5
24. Reynolds, Ph.L. *Marriage in the Western Church*. The Christianization of Marriage during the Patristic and Early Medieval Periods. 1994. ISBN 90 04 10022 9
25. Petersen, W.L. *Tatian's Diatessaron*. Its Creation, Dissemination, Significance, and History in Scholarship. 1994. ISBN 90 04 09469 5
26. Grünbeck, E. *Christologische Schriftargumentation und Bildersprache*. Zum Konflikt zwischen Metaphreninterpretation und dogmatischen Schriftbeweistraditionen in der patristischen Auslegung des 44. (45.) Psalms. 1994. ISBN 90 04 10021 0
27. Haykin, M.A.G. *The Spirit of God*. The Exegesis of 1 and 2 Corinthians in the Pneumatomachian Controversy of the Fourth Century. 1994. ISBN 90 04 09947 6
28. Benjamins, H.S. *Eingeordnete Freiheit*. Freiheit und Vorsehung bei Origenes. 1994. ISBN 90 04 10117 9
29. Smulders s.j., P. (tr. & comm.). *Hilary of Poitiers' Preface to his* Opus historicum. 1995. ISBN 90 04 10191 8
30. Kees, R.J. *Die Lehre von der* Oikonomia *Gottes in der* Oratio catechetica *Gregors von Nyssa*. 1995. ISBN 90 04 10200 0
31. Brent, A. *Hippolytus and the Roman Church in the Third Century*. Communities in Tension before the Emergence of a Monarch-Bishop. 1995. ISBN 90 04 10245 0
32. Runia, D.T. *Philo and the Church Fathers*. A Collection of Papers. 1995. ISBN 90 04 10355 4
33. De Coninck, A.D. *Seek to See Him*. Ascent and Vision Mysticism in the Gospel of Thomas. 1996. ISBN 90 04 10401 1
34. Clemens Alexandrinus. *Protrepticus*. Edidit M. Marcovich. 1995. ISBN 90 04 10449 6
35. Böhm, T. *Theoria – Unendlichkeit – Aufstieg*. Philosophische Implikationen zu *De vita Moysis* von Gregor von Nyssa. 1996. ISBN 90 04 10560 3

36. Vinzent, M. *Pseudo-Athanasius, Contra Arianos IV.* Eine Schrift gegen Asterius von Kappadokien, Eusebius von Cäsarea, Markell von Ankyra und Photin von Sirmium. 1996. ISBN 90 04 10686 3

37. Knipp, P.D.E. *'Christus Medicus' in der frühchristlichen Sarkophagskulptur.* Ikonographische Studien zur Sepulkralkunst des späten vierten Jahrhunderts. 1998. ISBN 90 04 10862 9

38. Lössl, J. *Intellectus gratiae.* Die erkenntnistheoretische und hermeneutische Dimension der Gnadenlehre Augustins von Hippo. 1997. ISBN 90 04 10849 1

39. Markell von Ankyra. *Die Fragmente. Der Brief an Julius von Rom.* Herausgegeben, eingeleitet und übersetzt von Markus Vinzent. 1997. ISBN 90 04 10907 2

40. Merkt, A. *Maximus I. von Turin.* Die Verkündigung eines Bischofs der frühen Reichskirche im zeitgeschichtlichen, gesellschaftlichen und liturgischen Kontext. 1997. ISBN 90 04 10864 5

41. Winden, J.C.M. van. *Archè.* A Collection of Patristic Studies by J.C.M. van Winden. Edited by J. den Boeft and D.T. Runia. 1997. ISBN 90 04 10834 3

42. Stewart-Sykes, A. *The Lamb's High Feast.* Melito, *Peri Pascha* and the Quartodeciman Paschal Liturgy at Sardis. 1998. ISBN 90 04 11236 7

43. Karavites, P. *Evil, Freedom and the Road to Perfection in Clement of Alexandria.* 1999. ISBN 90 04 11238 3

44. Boeft, J. den and M.L. van Poll-van de Lisdonk (eds.). *The Impact of Scripture in Early Christianity.* 1999. ISBN 90 04 11143 3

45. Brent, A. *The Imperial Cult and the Development of Church Order.* Concepts and Images of Authority in Paganism and Early Christianity before the Age of Cyprian. 1999. ISBN 90 04 11420 3

46. Zachhuber, J. *Human Nature in Gregory of Nyssa.* Philosophical Background and Theological Significance. 1999. ISBN 90 04 11530 7

47. Lechner, Th. *Ignatius adversus Valentinianos?* Chronologische und theologiegeschichtliche Studien zu den Briefen des Ignatius von Antiochien. 1999. ISBN 90 04 11505 6

48. Greschat, K. *Apelles und Hermogenes.* Zwei theologische Lehrer des zweiten Jahrhunderts. 1999. ISBN 90 04 11549 8

49. Drobner, H.R. *Augustinus von Hippo:* Sermones ad populum. Überlieferung und Bestand - Bibliographie - Indices. 1999. ISBN 90 04 11451 3

50. Hübner, R.M. *Der paradox Eine.* Antignostischer Monarchianismus im zweiten Jahrhundert. Mit einen Beitrag von Markus Vinzent. 1999. ISBN 90 04 11576 5

51. Gerber, S. *Theodor von Mopsuestia und das Nicänum.* Studien zu den katechetischen Homilien. 2000. ISBN 90 04 11521 8

52. Drobner, H.R. and A. Viciano (eds.). *Gregory of Nyssa: Homilies on the Beatitudes.* An English Version with Commentary and Supporting Studies. Proceedings of the Eighth International Colloquium on Gregory of Nyssa (Paderborn, 14-18 September 1998) 2000 ISBN 90 04 11621 4

53. Marcovich, M. (ed.). *Athenagorae qui fertur. De resurrectione mortuorum.* 2000. ISBN 90 04 11896 9
54. Marcovich, M. *Origines: Contra Celsum Libri VII.* ISBN 90 04 11976 0 *In preparation.*
55. McKinion, S. *Words, Imagery, and the Mystery of Christ.* A Reconstruction of Cyril of Alexandria's Christology. 2001. ISBN 90 04 11987 6
56. Beatrice, P.F. *Anonymi Monophysitae Theosophia, An Attempt at Reconstruction.* 2001. ISBN 90 04 11798 9
57. Runia, D.T. *Philo of Alexandria:* An Annotated Bibliography 1987-1996. 2001. ISBN 90 04 11682 6
58. Merkt, A. *Das Patristische Prinzip.* Eine Studie zur Theologischen Bedeutung der Kirchenväter. 2001. ISBN 90 04 12221 4
59. Stewart-Sykes, A. *From Prophecy to Preaching.* A Search for the Origins of the Christian Homily. 2001. ISBN 90 04 11689 3
60. Lössl, J. *Julian von Aeclanum.* Studien zu seinem Leben, seinem Werk, seiner Lehre und ihrer Überlieferung. 2001. ISBN 90 04 12180 3